Spatializing Politics

Delia Duong Ba Wendel, Fallon Samuels Aidoo (eds.)

Essays on Power and Place

HARVARD DESIGN STUDIES

Spatializing Politics

Delia Duong Ba Wendel,
Fallon Samuels Aidoo (eds.)

Essays on Power and Place

FOREWORD

Susan S. Fainstein vi

ACKNOWLEDGMENTS x

INTRODUCTION

Toward a Spatial Epistemology of Politics
Delia Duong Ba Wendel 2

CONTENTIOUS POLITICS 14

"There Were Streets": Urban Renewal and the Early Troubles in
London/Derry, Northern Ireland
Margo Shea 19

Slum as Infrastructure: How the Politics of Informality Shapes
South Africa's World-Class Cities
Kerry Ryan Chance 51

Political Ground and Spatial Stakes in Ho Chi Minh City, Vietnam
Anh-Thu Ngo 85

POLITICS OF CONSENSUS 114

Imagining Spaces of Peace and Conflict in the Rwandan Radio
Drama Musekeweya
Delia Duong Ba Wendel 119

The Right-of-Way: Critical Infrastructure for the Right to Work in
Postwar Philadelphia
Fallon Samuels Aidoo 153

The Volcanic Heart of Nicaragua: Tiscapa and the Spatiality
of Political Culture, 1936–1990
Ryne Clos 185

BIOPOLITICS 212

*The Permeable Institution: Community Mental Health Centers
as Governmental Technology, 1963–1974*
    Joy Knoblauch 217

Imprisoned Bodies: North Korea and its Kwan-li-so
    Melany Sun-Min Park. 243

*The Right to Live in the World: Architecture, Inclusion, and the
Americans with Disabilities Act*
    Wanda Katja Liebermann 273

POLITICS OF EXPERTISE. 302

Epistemologies of Public and Private Urban Design Expertise
    Orly Linovski 307

From the Street: Civic Epistemologies of Urban Climate Change
    Michael Mendez 337

Immigrant Spatial Politics in Metropolitan Miami, 1957–2005
    H. Fernando Burga 367

AFTERWORD

A Conversation with Toni L. Griffin
    Fallon Samuels Aidoo 400

CONTRIBUTOR BIOGRAPHIES 404

INDEX 412

Foreword

Class, race, ethnicity, gender, religion, and value commitments are underlying forces that play out in political conflict and domination. As abstractions, they are invisible: we see and understand them only through a process of analysis. On the ground, however, they manifest themselves in physical space. In turn, spatial practices reinforce or undermine the potential of these forces to peacefully interact.

Insight into the relationship between social forces and space has developed from transformations in our understanding of space provided by geographer David Harvey and sociologists Henri Lefebvre and Manuel Castells. These scholars caused space—previously defined as territory, source of natural resources, or container of activity—to become redefined as the location of social relations. Locations gained or lost value as a consequence of who occupied and exploited them. Usage, rather than inherent characteristics, determined whether built structures in a particular area produced use or exchange value.

Within the design professions the reciprocity between space and social life has long been recognized. Proposals for the City Beautiful, the Garden City, the Radiant City, slum clearance, public housing, and policies to formalize housing and marketplaces in developing countries reflect this realization. Advocates of these design approaches justified them not simply because they would make places more attractive but because they would allegedly change people's behavior. Such physical determinism, however, failed to take into account the economic and social causes that linked space to behavior. Despite the efforts of well-meaning experts, design solutions to end poverty and discrimination often resulted in major injustices. Slum clearance removed dilapidated structures but failed to remedy the situation of the people living within them and ended up simply displacing them. Efforts to upgrade informal housing often caused the dwellings of the poor to become too expensive for the occupants to remain in them.

Politics conducted through both informal and formal institutions is inevitably spatialized. Urban politics typically involves activities surrounding the demarcation of turf: ghettoization of the poor, gating communities of the rich, "accumulation by dispossession" (i.e., the taking of land from the defenseless in order to amass property wealth or develop infrastructure), and imposition of norms mandating religious observance—all involve spatial relations. Ironically, the discrimination that produces concentrations of deprivation also can stimulate the largest threats to unjust practices. Urban social movements—embodied in the various Occupy movements, the call for the right to the city, and demands for the rights of shack dwellers—depend on the existence of areas where disadvantaged groups in similar situations can mobilize. In democracies that have district-based representation, the sorting of voters in space constitutes a crucial element affecting chances for victory.

Recognition of the relationship between spatial politics and just/unjust outcomes runs through this volume, which identifies both conflict (sometimes violent) and consensus as they work themselves out in space. The essays here approach the subject from a number of disciplinary and area perspectives and do not lead to easy conclusions. Sometimes interaction produces understanding; at other times it reinforces prejudice. Governance of space goes beyond simply affecting people's expectations and life chances. As the essays in the section titled Biopolitics show, spatial forms even limit the freedom of the human body. The investigations chronicled in this volume point to the divergences that result from different vantage points: experts who impose their ideas of rationality are counterposed to ordinary people with subjectivities arising from their personal histories and group affiliations. Moreover, the essays explore how these different types of understanding favor different kinds of actions and enlighten us regarding the relationship between group consciousness and spatial politics.

As our awareness of the importance of spatial relations in mediating social divisions grows, we can better design urban policies that take difference into account and avoid imposition of approaches that favor the already most advantaged.[1] In her book *Justice and the Politics of Difference*, Iris Marion Young critiques decision makers

---

1   In my book *The Just City* (Ithaca, NY: Cornell University Press, 2010), I specify the types of spatial policies that can enhance justice.

who regard societies as composed simply of the aggregate of individuals rather than recognizing the importance of group affiliations.[2] Although these affiliations may transcend particular places, the politics of space nevertheless intervenes, either because groups are clustered or because they are dispersed, because they dominate an area or are consigned to an inferior status within it. Thus, when we are seeking to understand the politics of justice, we must necessarily examine the politics of space. This volume provides a welcome contribution to such an analysis.

Susan S. Fainstein
August 2015

2   Iris Marion Young, *Justice and the Politics of Difference* (1990; Princeton, NJ: Princeton University Press, 2011).

Acknowledgments

This book is the product of dedication and generosity—from its earliest supporters to its final set of contributors. The idea of publishing a book on both the politics of space and spaces of politics emerged from a symposium we organized at the Harvard University Graduate School of Design (GSD) in 2010. The fourth in a series of conferences partly sponsored by Harvard's PhD Program in Architecture, Landscape Architecture, and Urban Planning, "Cambridge Talks IV: Design Politics" brought together anthropologists, historians, and sociologists of spatial production, as well as architectural historians, theorists, and practitioners. In both depth and breadth, the symposium presentations reflected on the diversity and collectivity of political actors that have thought spatially about their actions and activism. We are thankful for this interdisciplinary experience, for it has guided our collaboration and curation of this essay collection.

We are grateful to the Publications Department of the GSD, led by Jennifer Sigler, for the opportunity to contribute to a new series of books on emergent research agendas. Special thanks go to Benjamin Prosky, Assistant Dean for Communications, for enabling this project, and to Melissa Vaughn and Leah Whitman-Salkin, whose editorial advice played a formative role in the book's development. We greatly appreciate the expertise that Nancy Later, the project editor, and Sam de Groot, the graphic designer, brought to the book project. Their keen eye for textual and visual clarity complements the commitment made by book contributors to draw academics and activists into conversation.

The essays in this collection benefited from peer review, both blind and open. Anonymous reviewers offered critical feedback on each authors' political analyses, while known experts in the history, theory, and criticism of architecture and urbanism reflected on our collective contribution to contemporary discourse on space and politics. We especially thank K. Michael Hays, Neil Brenner, and Diane E. Davis for their editorial advice at critical junctures in the book's development. Emerging scholars Sunyoung Park, Nick R. Smith, Hiba Bou Akar, Lowell Brower, and Kyle Shelton also facilitated the curation of the essay collection and reflection on our own contributions. The book thus exemplifies the collaborative yet critical modes of interdisciplinary inquiry that is endemic to spatial scholarship.

Above all, we are indebted to the Graham Foundation for Advanced Studies in the Fine Arts and Harvard University for sponsoring this book. The generosity of the Graham Foundation enabled us to produce a rich collection of essays; Dean Mohsen Mostafavi of the GSD and Allan Brandt, former Dean of the Graduate School of Arts and Sciences, provided institutional support for the anthology's interdisciplinary development; and Harvard University Press is overseeing its distribution to an academic and general audience. Thanks to each of these commitments, *Spatializing Politics* stakes out common ground for collective action on critical questions within academia and beyond.

Delia Duong Ba Wendel
Fallon Samuels Aidoo

Introduction: Toward a Spatial Epistemology of Politics

Delia Duong Ba Wendel

Politics is contingent. It develops from spaces of encounter, where individuals make demands of each other, compare shortage and surplus, create a sense of self, community, and alterity, gain influence, and exert control. In each of these encounters, spaces locate, represent, or form political subjectivity, engagement, and power. The question of how this transpires is the subject of this anthology.[1]

In 12 cross-disciplinary essays, emerging scholars examine a range of geographical and historical contexts to demonstrate how politics develops from and through spaces. In doing so, we identify the political strategies of the powerful and the weak, practices of influence and control both routine and exceptional, and intersections between political realities and imagined alternatives. The essays illustrate the various ways in which spaces are political and politics are spatial. In addition, they collectively define a "spatial epistemology of politics" to articulate both what is specific to a spatial way of knowing and how that way of knowing conceptualizes and activates political thought and action.[2]

A spatial epistemology of politics is particularly attuned to identifying the contingent, place-specific, and contextual aspects of political strategies and processes. It is an approach to knowing that does not seek truth or objectivity,[3] but rather centers on spaces of

1   These political encounters exemplify the "contingent" nature of politics. The bias inherent in this opening statement derives in part from a case study approach, which is foundational to a spatial way of knowing. Such a view does not insist that all spaces are the same everywhere (as will become clear shortly). Nor is the nature of this contingency that of a relativism that is stripped of critical judgment in the interest of examining particularities at work. Rather, in this anthology, micropolitics and larger political processes (structural, hegemonic, global, or otherwise) are revealed in encounters between people in particular places and times.

2   The relationship between spatial knowledge and spatial practices is critical to defining a spatial epistemology of politics. This concept bears the significant influence of Henri Lefebvre; see his *The Production of Space*, trans. Donald Nicholson-Smith (1974; Oxford: Blackwell, 1991). Also influential is the notion of "cognitive mapping" developed by the urbanist Kevin Lynch in *The Image of the City* (Cambridge, MA: MIT Press, 1960). For a political treatment of Lynch's theory, see Fredric Jameson, *Postmodernism; or,*

the Cultural Logic of Late Capitalism (Durham, NC: Duke University Press, 1991), 1–54. German philosophies of spatial understanding from the late 19th century are also relevant here; see, for example, August Schmarsow, "The Essence of Architectural Creation" (1893) and other essays in Henry Mallgrave and Eleftherios Ikonomou, eds., *Empathy, Form and Space: Problems in German Aesthetics, 1973-1893* (Chicago: University of Chicago Press, 1994).

3   Engaging with debates on knowledge and truth, the subjective nature of scientific inquiry and history writing, and the influence of ideological frames for seeing the world, this pithy statement connects to a rich lineage of writers and works, including Roland Barthes, *Mythologies*, trans. Annette Lavers (1957; New York: Hill and Wang, 1972); Michel de Certeau, *The Writing of History*, trans. Tom Conley (New York: Columbia University Press, 1988); Michel Foucault, *The Archaeology of Knowledge and the Discourse on Language*, trans. A.M. Sheridan Smith (New York: Pantheon Books, 1972); Donna Haraway, *Simians, Cyborgs, and Women: The Reinvention of Nature* (New York:

political encounter to explore dynamics of claim making, power, and identity. A spatial epistemology does not provide an exclusive or comprehensive knowledge of politics; it is a situated knowledge of forms, relationships, and geographies that are subjectively perceived by different individuals in distinct historical times. As a kind of situated inquiry, it draws from both conceptual spaces (such as home, street, school, city) and actual spaces (my home, your street, our school, their city) to make deductive, transpositional, scalar, experiential, and imaginative sense of political worlds.

A deductive spatial epistemology works to reveal, uncover, and fill in gaps in ways that may also be described as archaeological or forensic. This mode of inquiry analyzes built forms to discern the types of political ideas or processes that shaped them and the conditions they create for political encounters.[4] A transpositional mode of understanding allows us to make comparative connections—to see oneself in the place of another. A scalar view works to recognize boundaries of knowledge (differences between local and national politics, for example) that are constituted by particular scales of political and social organization. An experiential understanding of political worlds draws from phenomenological data and from one's own sensory and lived experience of political processes and values. Often working projectively, an imaginative mode conjures alternative or future conditions (a utopia, penal colony, or just city) to conceive and realize political ideas. Although preliminary, this index of spatial epistemologies begins to describe how spaces locate, represent, and form politics.[5]

These synopses could bear further grounding, and one needn't look far to do so. A place in mind, amalgamated from various

Routledge, 1991); Claude Lefort, *The Political Forms of Modern Society: Bureaucracy, Democracy, Totalitarianism*, ed. John B. Thompson (Cambridge, MA: MIT Press, 1986); and Michel-Rolph Trouillot, *Silencing the Past: Power and the Production of History* (Boston: Beacon Press, 1995).

4   The term "built forms" refers to a range of spaces, including site-specific art, buildings, civic spaces, landscapes, cities, and infrastructure.

5   With this preliminary formulation we do not intend to suggest that all relationships between spatial knowledge and political knowledge should be instrumentalized. Writing about architecture and the ways in which buildings gain significance, philosopher Nelson Goodman writes, "like other works of art—and like scientific theories, too—it can give new insight, advance understanding, [and] participate in our continual remaking of a world." We might suggest the same is true of spaces more generally. Nelson Goodman, "How Buildings Mean," *Critical Inquiry* 11, no. 4 (June 1985): 652.

experiences and memories, may provide a familiar setting from which to start. There, one may recognize spatial epistemologies of politics in everyday life:

On one end of a street, families have lived together for generations. Here, kids play hide-and-seek, dodging from lot to lot through openings in fences and running down the alleyways between tenements. The children also know where not to go; to avoid the best hiding places that the boarded up buildings and overgrown backyards present to them. Within this urban landscape, modernist row houses from the 1930s stand proud, despite their states of disrepair. They mark a previous era of concern for and experimentation in low-cost workers' housing. But during the last three decades, city officials have reduced the funding needed to maintain infrastructure and police the streets. A great number of houses stand vacant, creating a patchwork of safe and unsafe micro-zones within the neighborhood.

The reasons for abandoning this end of the street vary. Some families left voluntarily to seek out better schools and safer environs. Landlords passively evicted tenants by failing to maintain their deteriorating apartments. City officials moved other residents to subsidized housing outside the neighborhood. With the number of jobs in decline, life is barely sustainable here. Working outside the neighborhood requires long travel times, often on several different city buses. Wages are typically low and barely cover living expenses, let alone provide opportunities for savings. Long hours of menial work leave little time for additional job training or leisure activities. Despite these conditions, this area endures as a home for many who remain in the neighborhood.

Some residents can imagine what their street could be like if they had sources of financial investment and social support. They would renovate properties for affordable housing, develop small-business opportunities and cultural activities on vacant lots, build better schools and health clinics, and install working street lights. They aspire to restore the experience of safety to their street and the appearance of value in their homes.

A few residents have organized in a neighborhood association to envision such change. They gather on the first Saturday of every month in a park that separates their end of the street from the other. Their children rarely play on these grounds, long overrun by the unruly grass that hides broken bottles and other urban detritus, where illicit activities dominate use of the swings and sand pits. By meeting here, these residents carve out a political space in an inhospitable zone to take back control of the park's use (if only temporarily), to debate how they'd like to live differently, and to represent their collective desires to governing authorities beyond. Despite their efforts, the park exists as a de facto barrier to improvements in their area.

Whereas one end of the street has experienced years of disinvestment and progressive decline, the other has flourished from real estate development and inclusion in the city's growth strategy. New homeowners were attracted to the neighborhood's revitalization, its close proximity to professional work, and its plans for future investment. Their arrival changed the district's voting demographics, which dislodged the incumbent representative in a recent state election. Residents here enjoy smooth concrete sidewalks with granite curbs, new row houses with projecting balconies, and a tree-lined street that opens onto the central business district. Most have never crossed the park, and are unaware that their revivalist house styles are inspired by the neglected modernist experiments on the other side.

The two communities are not completely homogeneous. Nor are they fully segregated: overlaps occur in where their children go to school, what crime they are exposed to, and above all, how they aspire to improve their lives and their communities. A few couples have connected with organizers of the monthly gatherings to discuss ways to improve the park and leverage their own influence with the district representative to address wider community concerns. Within the city at large, however, a scarce number care about the future of the other side. In all likelihood, the neglected area will remain excluded from urban transformations, at least until local groups connect to external sources of mobilization and funding.

Introduction

The state and futures of both ends of the street are shaped by individual entrepreneurialism (both licit and illicit) and processes of city planning, investment, and governance. Within such ordinary contexts, spaces become political the very moment they are used as forms of control or influence, or sites from which and about which claims are made. The scene described above presents generalized instances of intersections between spaces and politics, with a primary focus on a politics of class difference. One could assume additional forces are at work there, including internal antagonisms within each community, conflicts involving race and gender, and regional, national, and international influences. On this street, people with power led processes of exclusion, targeted (dis)investment, and demographic shifts for electoral influence. But spatial politics such as these are not just for the powerful. Affluent and marginalized residents alike employ these practices to represent communities and rights, produce sites of activism or interest, and retrieve control of land use and management. Spatial epistemologies situate, reveal, and materialize the politics at work on, in, and through the street.

In this case a deductive spatial epistemology reveals a neglected place within the larger city by visually accounting for what the disenfranchised community lacks and tracking a materialist history of disinvestment in buildings and infrastructure. This disrupts a stable representation of the city as inclusive and equal, and exposes market forces, socioeconomic disparities, and power negotiations. Formal analysis is a critical tool in this praxis: it can trace the representation of political ideas in architectural designs (a socialist sensibility toward workers' housing) and unpack how urban forms produce political effects (how the park's location and design shape political strategy and action). A deductive spatial epistemology allows us to recognize difference and encourages us to ask what factors led to the selective empowerment and suppression of the two communities on this street.[6]

6   A deductive spatial epistemology contributes to a critical politics where counter-claims are advanced—for example, to identify the existence of segregation when it is under-recognized by a popular majority or by those in power. This mode has also formed the basis for research that seeks to fill gaps in historiography, where a written historical record is

A transpositional mode of understanding locates the conditions of blight and affluence on both sides of the park to investigate how these situations coexist so close to each other. It allows neighbors to compare and connect their lives and demands with those of others. Identification, exemplification, and translation represent some of the ways in which one relates to positions that develop as a matter of location and outlook and that are not one's own.[7] Physical proximity is not necessary for the transpositional mode. Rather, the recognition of sameness and difference can develop across the larger urban region and between cities, countries, and continents. It is, in part, what allows us to read our own political experiences in this street.

A scalar spatial epistemology identifies the nested levels from which social, economic, and political forces operate.[8] Through this mode, we understand how politics develops from local and urban scales of knowledge and organization. We also observe how the urban or national scale emphasizes different priorities in future plans and fails to recognize the desires of particular localities. "Scaling up" is a critical characteristic of the politics at work here, and it speaks to the means by which local interests become endorsed by larger, external bodies. A city's engagement with a global market economy to initiate investments constitutes one example, as does a neighborhood activist group's relationship to outside sources of political mobilization and funding.

The diverse experiences of blight and affluence on this street provide particular knowledge of how these communities are valued

limited or not the primary means of knowledge transmission. Formal analysis is key to both recognizing what exclusion looks like in the built environment and privileging alternative forms of knowledge: as a result, it is broadly indicative of scholarship in archaeology, architectural, and urban studies and is frequently employed by scholars investigating cultures not readily treated in the Western canon.

7   The transpositional mode relates in part to the symbolic interactionism, but with a particular emphasis on the settings of these interactions, the influence of places on attitudes and values, and exchanges between these positions. For general reference, see Erving Goffman, *The Presentation of Self in Everyday Life* (New York: Anchor Books, 1959).

8   Within a broad literature in urban and architectural studies that engages with scale, the following writings make salient points as regards relationships between scale and politics: Neil Brenner, "The Limits to Scale? Methodological Reflections on Scalar Structuration," *Progress in Human Geography* 25, no. 4 (2001): 591–614; and Neil Smith, *Uneven Development: Nature, Capital and the Production of Space* (1984; London: Verso, 2010). Two additional books demonstrate relationships between different scales of cultural production within political and institutional organizations: Arindam Dutta, *The Bureaucracy of Beauty: Design in the Age of Its Global Reproducibility* (New York: Routledge, 2007); and Reinhold Martin, *The Organizational Complex: Architecture, Media, and Corporate Space* (Cambridge, MA: MIT Press, 2003).

by others, the political processes that shaped their development, and the oppositional politics that have arisen as a result. Experiential knowledge is thus subjective and empirical: it is a sense of political belonging and reference for political engagement. This mode of understanding is in part visceral and felt, and helps to communicate why militarized zones, cosmopolitan cities, or dense urban slums might be considered desirable and undesirable.[9] Experiential knowledge is also historical, in the sense that memories of past injustices or conviviality persist in the construction of identity: they affect the possibilities of the present and influence the nature of political encounters.[10] In the case of the neglected end of the street, the everyday experience of exclusion motivated some residents to organize and to articulate their demands.

An imaginative spatial epistemology forms and represents the aspirations of residents, city planners, real estate developers, and criminals in this area.[11] Through the imaginative mode, these individuals make and remake the city in their own image of power, control, justice, and profit. Shaping spaces in this way allowed the children to deftly navigate their neighborhood; knowledge of dangerous sites produced their geography of safety. In a similar way, city officials and developers design geographies of control and investment returns across certain parts of the city, leaving out other, unwanted areas. This kind of imagination could not be articulated

9   Phenomenological understanding serves as a key influence in this mode, as is a focus on everyday life and knowledge. See, for general reference, Ash Amin and Nigel Thrift, eds. *Cities: Reimagining the Urban* (Oxford: Polity Press, 2002); Michel de Certeau, *The Practice of Everyday Life*, trans. Steven Rendall (Berkeley: University of California Press, 1984); Henri Lefebvre, *The Critique of Everyday Life: The One Volume Edition* (1947; New York: Verso, 2014); Maurice Merleau-Ponty, *The Phenomenology of Perception*, trans. Colin Smith (1945; New York: Routledge, 2003); and Nigel Thrift, *Non-Representational Theory: Space, Politics, Affect* (New York: Routledge, 2008).

10   The importance of time and history to establishing the political nature of spaces is parsed in Doreen Massey, "Politics and Space/Time," *New Left Review* 1, no. 196 (November–December 1992): 65–84. A theory of relationships between the speed of capital accumulation and the depoliticization of space (or its "deterritorialization") can be found

in David Harvey, *The Condition of Postmodernity: An Enquiry into the Origins of Cultural Change* (Malden, MA: Blackwell, 1990). Compelling examples of the profoundly layered history of everyday experience appear in Veena Das, *Life and Words: Violence and the Descent into the Ordinary* (Berkeley: University of California Press, 2006).

11   Representative of this wide-ranging literature are writings that see the spatial imagination as critical to shaping social relations and not just a preoccupation of leisure (Arjun Appadurai, *Modernity at Large: Cultural Dimensions of Globalization* [Minneapolis: University of Minnesota Press: 1996]); central to projects of cultural identity and nation-building (Benedict Anderson, *Imagined Communities* [New York: Verso, 2006]); and inspired by historically situated values that over time develop cities as palimpsests (M. Christine Boyer, *The City of Collective Memory: Its Historical Imagery and Architectural Entertainments* [Cambridge, MA: MIT Press, 1996]).

without space as reference or source. In these cases, spatial imagination is tethered to experience, but in others (Jeremy Bentham's Panopticon, or Charlotte Perkins Gilman's Herland, for instance) it functions through radical alterity to dream of difference.

Within each of these modes, spatial ways of knowing serve analyses of political encounters and produce political effects. This thin line between understanding and acting is central to a definition of the political in which conceptualization reflexively shapes action.[12] It also suggests that spaces have a more active role in political life than has been generally conceded. In academic and popular discourse, spaces tend to serve as passive containers, symbols, or geographical coordinates for political theories, ideologies, and histories. The essays in this volume challenge this minimalist characterization, and contribute three additional considerations. First, a spatial way of knowing adds a situated knowledge of politics that is contingent upon specific places and people. It is also partial in the sense that spatial epistemologies are subjective and incomplete. As a result of this partiality, spaces are also discursively formed by antagonism and accord in the public sphere.[13] Second, spaces do not merely contain political activity but play operative roles in locating, representing, and forming political subjectivity, engagement, and power. In other words, through their design and transformation, spaces site, articulate, and produce a sense of self in the world, relationships with others, and forms of control and influence. The political effects exemplified in locating, representing, and forming develop from spatial knowledge. Each tracks through the preceding example and the case studies to follow. Lastly, spatial

12   Here again a broad literature, from the history of science to philosophy to innovation studies, emphasizes the influence that framing or defining a "problem" has on its "solution." In the case of politics, Hannah Arendt famously interpreted Aristotle's definition of political life as dually constituted by contemplation articulated in speech and action (praxis) further specified in type by place (in Aristotle's case, the city-state). See Hannah Arendt, *The Human Condition* (Chicago: University of Chicago Press, 1958).

13   Regarding the political nature of the public sphere (as social and physical space), see Arendt, *The Human*

Condition; Seyla Benhabib, "The Embattled Public Sphere: Hannah Arendt, Jürgen Habermas and Beyond," *Theoria* 90 (December 1997): 1–24; Jürgen Habermas, "Further Reflections on the Public Sphere," in *Habermas and the Public Sphere*, ed. Craig Calhoun, trans. Thomas Burger (Cambridge, MA: MIT Press, 1992): 421–61; Chantal Mouffe, "Some Reflections on an Agonistic Approach to the Public," in *Making Things Public*, eds. Bruno Latour and Peter Weibel (Cambridge, MA: MIT Press, 2005): 804–7; and Iris Marion Young, *Justice and the Politics of Difference* (1990; Princeton, NJ: Princeton University Press, 2011).

epistemologies and spatio-political effects are intimately and dialectically related in the thoughts and actions of individuals who make sense of and engage with political worlds. This relationship captures the manner in which spatial conceptualizations reflexively shape political action—and vice versa—such that spaces have political effects, and politics have spatial effects.

In both content and analysis, the essays presented here center on how spaces reveal and form political effects. The authors employ deductive, transpositional, scalar, experiential, and imaginative spatial epistemologies as analytic approaches to their case studies. In each, and as was evident in the street vignette above, spatial modes of inquiry and praxis are both quotidian and analytic. They are therefore also employed by everyday people. Noting this commonality asserts an inclusive view toward the roles of lived experience, ideology, and philosophy in shaping power and political praxis in everyday life. It furthermore underscores one of this book's central claims, which is that spatial epistemologies of politics are intrinsic to both social relations and their analysis.

The 12 case studies explore political encounters in diverse geographical contexts. Authors chart a broad spectrum of political spaces, including public housing, shantytowns, urban streets, rural hills, train stations, monuments, mental health centers, concentration camps, public restrooms, parks, polluted neighborhoods, and city districts. Articulating such an expansive definition of "space" suggests a unitary theory for how site-specific art, architecture, infrastructure, and landscapes offer knowledge of politics, even as each of these distinct typologies further specify the nature of political subjectivity, engagement, and power. The authors also write with cross-disciplinary ambitions, to bridge anthropology, architectural history, conflict studies, environmental design, geography, planning history, political theory, and science, technology, and society studies. With such a view, we treat these various disciplines as both distinct and singularly unprivileged in the knowledge they produce about people and place. *Spatializing Politics* aims to exemplify that spaces are not rigid sites that can only be understood in one way (by those in power, for example) but rather provide a medium for conceptual and political exchanges. These exchanges produce our lived and imagined worlds. From them, we derive criteria for ethical political encounters.

To aid in the navigation of this material, essays are organized in sections that explore the roles of spaces in sustaining four of the most enduring political practices: contentious politics, the politics of consensus, biopolitics, and the politics of expertise. Brief introductions to each section highlight key discourses related to the spatio-political practice under discussion. The first section grapples with ways in which spatial production sustains conflict and difference in society. It highlights the manner in which spaces activate the divergent political claims that develop in both routine contestation and violent confrontation. Portraying consensus as an evolving process and objective of political actors, the second section considers space as a means of activating and materializing agreement (or disagreement) on ethics and power. The third section draws from the writings of Michel Foucault to illustrate how attention to individuals within systems of governance reveals complex relationships between spaces, subjectivity, and power. The final section explores questions related to who has political expertise in making and re-making the built environment. It focuses on the experiences, skills, and views of various stakeholders and professionals who negotiate their often conflicting interests in complex development processes. We see these as organizing frames that inform how particular spatial epistemologies locate, represent, and produce the types of political knowledge and practices under which they are categorized.

The primary aim of *Spatializing Politics* is to situate politics in spaces and in the types of actions and relationships that draw from spatial understanding. Spaces produce enduring conditions that change over time, but they would be devoid of politics without the many individuals, governing bodies, and groups that shape our built environments. As collaborators with and analysts of rich political worlds, we are grateful to the political actors, past and present, who have provided us with insights into political praxis: it is to them that we dedicate this volume.

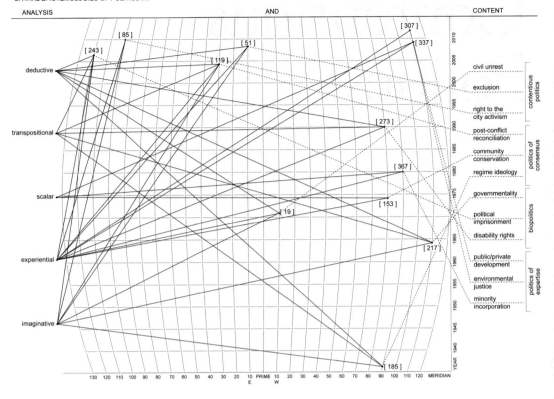

Figure 1   This diagram indexes the spatial epistemologies explored in the twelve case studies of this volume. Each essay is plotted along x- and y-axes representing the historical period and geographic meridian it considers. Page numbers (in brackets) locate the start of each essay. Solid lines that radiate from the essay to the left locate the principal spatial epistemologies both the author and the political actors (the subjects of analysis) engage. Dotted lines that trace to the right indicate the types of political effects that spatial knowledge produces within each case study. Within the conceptual space of the diagram, then, a set of relationships between author and subject, analysis and content, can be observed, which comparatively situate political encounters activated by spatial ways of knowing. Diagram by Delia Duong Ba Wendel.

Contentious
Politics

"Contentious politics" develops from political encounters that are oppositional in nature. Taking various forms, these political practices are intrinsic to community mobilization and protest, and standard to the resistance that forms of rule provoke. They arise from inequality and identity difference. When framed aspirationally, agonistic practices undergird the ideal of a pluralistic society that privileges distributed power. This section engages the diverse perspectives represented in this literature by specifying how urban development creates conflict and sustains difference.

Margo Shea (p. 19) offers a view from Northern Ireland, exploring mid-20th-century civil unrest and urban renewal as interrelated, disruptive forces on security and communities.

Attending to exclusionary practices that are still occurring in South African shanty towns today, Kerry Ryan Chance (p. 51) follows the disenfranchised, who occupy spaces and build alternative housing as forms of contestation.

Anh-Thu Ngo (p. 85) focuses on the uneven development of Vietnam's largest city, where artist activists challenge the profit-driven transformation of urban spaces by staging creative performances for sociopolitical engagement.

These instances of contentious politics develop both from routine, ordinary processes of city making and from exceptional, often violent, confrontations in and about urban spaces. Framed within this category of political thought and action, spaces emerge in these essays as the content of political claims and generators of political organization, representations of injustice and inequity, and places where contention materializes.

REPRESENTATIVE WRITINGS

ON SOCIOPOLITICAL MOBILIZATION

Castells, Manuel. *The City and the Grassroots*. Berkeley: University of California Press, 1983.

Leitner, Helga, Eric Sheppard, and Kristin M. Sziarto. "The Spatialities of Contentious Politics." *Transactions of the Institute of British Geographers* 33, no. 2 (April 2008): 157–72.

McAdam, Douglas. *Political Process and the Development of Black Insurgency, 1930–1970*. 2nd ed. Chicago: University of Chicago Press, 1999.

Tilly, Charles, and Sidney Tarrow. *Contentious Politics*. Boulder, CO: Paradigm, 2007.

ON FORMS OF RULE AND ROUTINE CONTESTATION

Body-Gendrot, Sophie. *The Social Control of Cities? A Comparative Perspective*. Oxford: Blackwell, 2000.

Scott, James C. *Seeing Like a State: How Certain Schemes to Improve the Human Condition Have Failed*. New Haven, CT: Yale University Press, 1998.

Smith, Neil. *The New Urban Frontier: Gentrification and the Revanchist City*. New York: Routledge, 2005.

Tilly, Charles. *Coercion, Capital, and European States, AD 990–1990*. Oxford: Blackwell, 1992.

ON THE POLITICS OF DIFFERENCE

Chakrabarty, Dipesh. *Provincializing Europe: Postcolonial Thought and Historical Difference*. Princeton, NJ: Princeton University Press, 2000.

Colomina, Beatriz, ed. *Sexuality & Space*. New York: Princeton Architectural Press, 1992.

Sandercock, Leonie, ed. *Making the Invisible Visible: A Multicultural Planning History*. Berkeley: University of California Press, 1998.

Sugrue, Thomas J. *The Origins of the Urban Crisis: Race and Inequality in Postwar Detroit*. Princeton, NJ: Princeton University Press, 1996.

Young, Iris Marion. *Justice and the Politics of Difference*. Princeton, NJ: Princeton University Press, 2011 (1990).

ON AGONISTIC AND CRITICAL POLITICS

Keith, Michael. *After the Cosmopolitan? Multicultural Cities and the Future of Racism*. New York: Routledge, 2005.

Lahiji, Nadir. *Architecture Against the Post-Political: Essays in Reclaiming the Critical Project*. New York: Routledge, 2014.

Lefebvre, Henri. "The Right to the City" (1968). In *Writings on Cities*, edited by Eleonore Kofman and Elizabeth Lebas, 147–59. Cambridge: Wiley-Blackwell, 1996.

Mouffe, Chantal. *The Return of the Political*. New York: Verso, 1993.

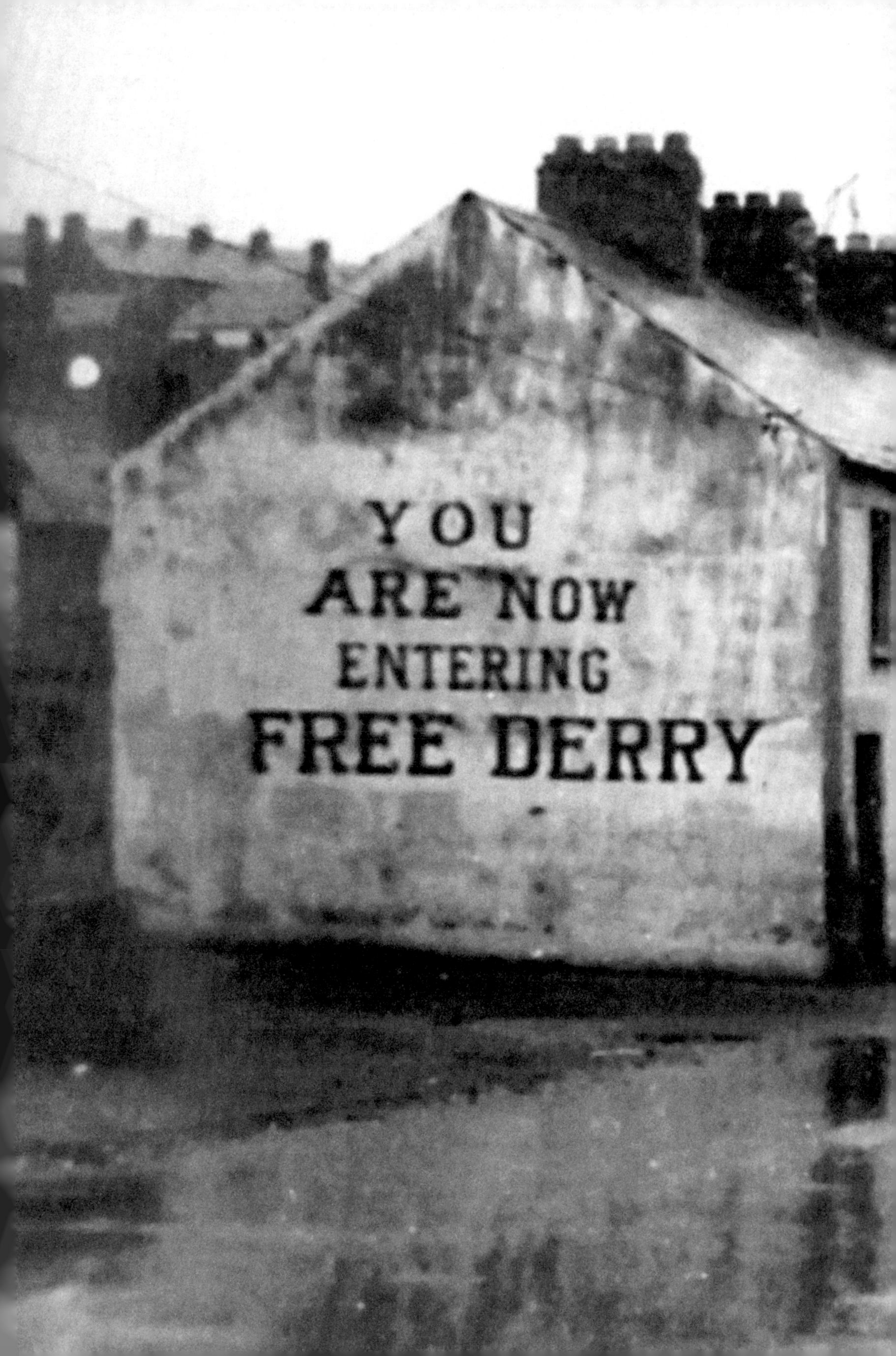
YOU
ARE NOW
ENTERING
FREE DERRY

"There Were Streets": Urban Renewal and the Early Troubles in London/Derry, Northern Ireland

Margo Shea

On July 19, 1969, more than 15,000 people crowded into the church and onto the sidewalks and grounds surrounding St. Eugene's Cathedral. They came to pay their final respects to Samuel Devenny, a 43-year-old father of nine who had died as a result of the violence that engulfed the city of London/Derry, Northern Ireland, that spring.[1] The first casualty of the Troubles in London/Derry, he had been severely beaten by police officers, who entered his home on the evening of April 19 in pursuit of street rioters, and died as a result of his injuries.[2] The outpouring of public grief reflected both Devenny's stature within the community and the shock and sense of injustice that accompanied his death. It was a foreboding sign of the violence and turmoil that would affect many in Northern Ireland in the decades to come.

1   The adult Catholic population of London/Derry was 20,102 in 1966. According to these figures, close to 85 percent of that population attended Devenny's funeral. In this essay, I refer to Londonderry when referencing documents and statutory bodies related to the city; London/Derry to refer to the municipality, acknowledging its divided history and lack of consensus around naming; and Derry to refer to the city as Catholic nationalists experienced and observed it.

2   While the original coroner's report declared that Devenny died of natural causes and denied any link between the assault by police officers and his death, a 2001 report by an attorney hired as part of the Northern Ireland peace process to investigate police actions concluded that the police beating had killed Devenny. "Samuel Devenny Enquiry," the Pat Finucane Centre, http://www.patfinucanecentre.org/cases/devenny/deven3_101001.html; and "Northern Ireland Police are Faulted 32 Years After a Fatal Beating," *New York Times*, October 5, 2001.

Figure 1   London/Derry during the Troubles. The Free Derry Wall was a site of frequent confrontations with the British Army. Source: Photographed by David Barzilay; Jim Collins and Adrian Kerr, *Free Derry Wall* (Derry: Guildhall Press, 2009).

Devenny had been standing at his front door at 69 William Street, watching the riot with his son Harry while talking with two family friends. Clashes between the Royal Ulster Constabulary and young people were commonplace after January 1969. Watching the riots had become customary. They were hard to miss: the Devenny house stood at the east end of William Street close to "Aggro Corner," an intersection that had become a flash point between area youth and the police they delighted in aggravating.

As the police moved down William Street and tensions heightened, Devenny and the others retreated into his home; they were about to shut the door when eight young rioters barreled into the house. Some ran straight out the back door. Others headed upstairs. Devenny locked the door behind the rioters. A moment later police kicked it down. They beat him and several members of his family. The Devennys were not known to be especially political and had not been involved in recent standoffs. The primary evidence against them was their open door.

An open door on William Street in 1969 was not necessarily an affirmation of support for the civil rights movement or of participation in the grassroots rebellion being waged by members of the Catholic and nationalist community. The Derry in which Devenny lived, especially the small streets in and around the Bogside, was a city of open doors. Leaving one's door ajar was a tradition with a long history. With cramped quarters within and friends and relatives without, little divided street and home. Devenny and the others gathered may have been witnessing a novel phenomenon in the rioting before them, but their behavior was anything but new.

When civil unrest began in the streets, rioters utilized their knowledge of backyards and alleyways to escape police. Access was through Catholic Derry's open doors: young rioters found they could count on this geography of neighborliness, entering through a front door, exiting out the back, and disappearing into the meandering alleys that linked the community.[3] Whether doors were left open as an endorsement of the struggle in the streets or simply as a continuation of custom is difficult to know.

3   August 9, 1971, Belfast: PRONI Public Records HA/32/2/45.

For many, the death of Samuel Devenny signaled the start of the Troubles in Derry. By 1969 the quietly understood and politely enforced divides in Northern Irish culture became public, actualized, and animated in the streets, as Catholics, nationalists, and civil rights activists openly challenged divisions. This elicited vociferous reactions from the largely unionist police force and hardline loyalists. Less than one month after Devenny's funeral, the annual Apprentice Boys' Relief of Derry parade on August 12 erupted into a pitched battle between Bogside youth, loyalist agitators, police officers, and the local Catholic community. The "Battle of the Bogside" drew the British Army onto the streets of Northern Ireland on August 14, where they would remain for more than 30 years. "The genie [had] come out of the bottle."[4] During those three decades, Derry experienced both direct and oblique effects of civil war. Violence

4   Eamon Melaugh, quoted in *Battle of the Bogside*, film, directed by Vinny Cunningham (Derry: Perfect Cousin Productions, 2004).

Figure 2 Civil rights meeting at Free Derry Wall. Source: Photographed by George Sweeney; Jim Collins and Adrian Kerr, *Free Derry Wall* (Derry: Guildhall Press, 2009).

5 Paramilitary groups initially included both the official and provisional branches of the Irish Republican Army (IRA), Irish National Liberation Army (INLA), Ulster Volunteer Force, Ulster Freedom Fighters, and Ulster Defense Army. After the Official IRA disbanded in 1972, some members joined the Provisional IRA and others founded the INLA.

perpetuated by the police, security forces, and paramilitary organizations on both sides of the sectarian divide, as well as by citizens themselves, shredded much of the physical, economic, and social fabric of the city.[5] Community life changed dramatically. Familiar ways of understanding the present, past, and future were refigured. The Troubles constituted a deep rupture. The effects of the unprecedented violence it inaugurated were experienced in virtually all aspects of life in Northern Ireland, for decades. More than 3,700 people were killed and as many as 50,000 were injured. Damages to property and expenses associated with security ran in the hundreds of millions of pounds. In retrospect, the figures are staggering. In the midst of the Troubles, the unrelenting violence, the chronic disruption it caused, and the high price it exacted were experienced as simultaneously catastrophic and quotidian.

By the late 1960s, a second rupture was underway. Even as street violence, paramilitary operations, and a pervasive military presence assailed Catholic Derry, a systematic program of urban renewal started to erode the community's physical coordinates. Along with drastic social and political disruptions, redevelopment rocked Catholic and nationalist neighborhoods. The effects of urban renewal reverberated in myriad ways, both within the city's core and on its outskirts. As the Troubles evolved into a protracted civil conflict, renewal progressed to the point where the Bogside and other parts of the South Ward that had been home to Catholics since the 19th century ceased to function as the nationalist population's physical center. In the face of this radical transformation, and in an attempt to redeem a loss they had not yet fully grasped, Catholics and nationalists set out to recast the area as the imagined, if not physical, center of their community.

URBAN RENEWAL, ENVIRONMENTAL DESIGN, AND THE SECURITY AGENDA

By the time civil disturbances broke out in Derry, the Bogside had already become a perpetual building site. Dilapidated, boarded-up houses sat tooth-by-jowl alongside new high-rise flats and tidy maisonettes built between 1966 and 1968, during a first round of development.[6] Civil unrest accompanied urban redevelopment, as bricks, stones, and cement used for building or left behind after demolition projects became convenient fodder for those intent on aggravating the police and, later, the British Army.[7] Indeed, the two processes often

6   John McCourt, quoted in *Battle of the Bogside.*

7   Ibid.

collided. Many local residents remember the booming voice of civil rights steward Vinnie Coyle as he shouted through his megaphone, tongue in cheek, "Dispose! Dispose! Don't Corrugate Here!"—a timely play on words frequently shouted by police, "Disperse! Disperse! Don't Congregate Here!"[8]

8   Myra Canning, interview with the author, August 24, 2008.

Initially, Derry's Catholics cheered the bulldozers and wrecking balls. Tearing down the damp, decrepit houses of the South Ward was tantamount to smashing the physical remnants of a built environment they believed had curtailed political and economic opportunities and threatened well-being. As the homes that lined Wellington Street, Friel's Terrace, Walker's Square, and other micro-neighborhoods fell to the ground and plans for new housing got underway, relief far outweighed regret.

During the civil rights movement, advocates had framed the housing crisis as a concrete byproduct of an entire set of social, political, and economic relations. Subsidized housing for nationalists was restricted to the South Ward to maintain electoral advantages for unionists in a city that was overwhelmingly nationalist and Catholic; thus, the issue held both tangible and symbolic meaning. In 1973, political agitator and civil rights leader Eamonn McCann explained that attacking the housing issue was an assault on unionist power. Most Catholics in the city associated sectarian divisions and polarized politics with day-to-day problems they faced with housing:

The gerrymandered Corporation [city council]

"There Were Streets"

was the living symbol in Derry of the anti-democratic exclusion of Catholics from power. The stated reason for our activities ... was to highlight the housing situation, but they were generally regarded by Catholics as an attack on the whole political set-up; which, of course, they were. There were many in the Bogside who did not approve of our "extremism" and were nervous of our "communistic ideas"—but there were none who would defend the Corporation.[9]

The city's Catholic population largely perceived that forestalled development kept Derry from thriving. Housing went unbuilt in order to retain electoral majorities in unionist wards. Though housing was the most pressing concern, politics and urban planning went hand and hand throughout the 1960s. The campaign to locate the University of Ulster's new campus in Derry failed, leading even liberal unionists from the city to predict that the northwest of Ulster would be left to wither because of its extensive border and its nationalist majorities. Under the Matthew Plan for province-wide development, train lines were cut and public transportation to the city did not keep pace with infrastructure in the rest of the province. Thus, when the local city council was suspended and replaced, under New Town legislation, with appointed commissioners to the Londonderry Development Commission in 1969, Catholic Derry applauded the process and welcomed development, including a "crash" housing program.[10]

9   Eamon McCann, *War and an Irish Town* (London: Pluto Press, 1973), 84–85.

10   In this case, "crash" housing refers to rushed public housing development. See Gerald McSheffry, *Planning Derry: Planning and Politics in Northern Ireland* (Liverpool: Liverpool University Press, 2000).

By 1974 the Bogside's population density had decreased by nearly one half: more than 15,000 former residents had been relocated to housing estates on the outskirts of the city, where 4,000 new units of housing had been built since 1969. As the Troubles evolved from a series of civil disturbances into what the British military referred to as "a classic insurgency" and ultimately a "terrorist insurgency," the "redevelopment" increasingly incorporated architectural and planning elements that facilitated security forces' surveillance efforts and increased their control over movements into, out of, and within Catholic neighborhoods of the old South Ward and the new housing estates.[11] Urban planning was part of a larger governmental framework for counterinsurgency and containment.[12]

The British Army did not make its security concerns and needs explicit to the public. The relationship that existed among the army, police services, Home Affairs, the Department of the Environment, and the Northern Ireland Housing Executive remains shrouded in secrecy. However, by 1971 a Home Affairs briefing document on public attitudes toward security operations called for a "closer interrelationship between civil, military and planning at the level between broad policies on the one hand and the conduct of tactical operations on the other."[13] Indeed, applying a socio-spatial approach—analyzing urban semiotics and physical changes to the cityscape—reveals that security concerns became increasingly relevant to planning considerations.[14]

11   General Sir Mike Jackson, "Operation Banner: An Analysis of Military Operations in Northern Ireland" (London: Ministry of Defense, 2006).

12   For more on the evolution of British policy in Northern Ireland and the constraints under which such policies could be maintained, see Peter Neumann, "The Government's Response," in *Combating Terrorism in Northern Ireland*, ed. James Dingley (New York: Routledge, 2009), 127–56.

13   "Security Operations: Public Attitudes," paper presented to meeting of the Joint Security Committee, June 25, 1971. Public Records Office of Northern Ireland, Belfast Public Records HA/32/5/6, http://cain.ulst.ac.uk/proni/1971/PRONI_HA-32-5-6_1971-06-25.pdf.

14   The methodologies I employ in this section derive from scholarship in urban sociology and geography. For an explanation of the socio-spatial perspective, see Mark Gottdiener and Ray Hutchison, *The New Urban Sociology*, 4th ed. (Boulder, CO: Westview, 2011). See also

Peirce Lewis, "Axioms for Reading the Cultural Landscape," in *The Interpretation of Ordinary Landscapes*, ed. D. W. Meining and J. B. Jackson (New York: Oxford University Press, 1979), 1–12.

Planners who crafted the Derry area redevelopment plan stressed positivist, rational planning sensibilities and sought to apply popular European models to Derry. The team that created the 1968 Londonderry Area Plan, deeply influenced by Patrick Geddes and Lewis Mumford, were self-described utopianists. They aimed to "provide better living conditions and better choices for the people of the area."[15] They intended to redress housing shortages, plan for the obliteration of old, unsafe housing stock, and stress the need for open space provision in residential areas.[16] Drafters of the plan could not predict and did not take into account the civil conflict to come, nor did they foresee the ways increased urban polarization might shape the cityscape.[17] Theirs was a general plan stressing modernist design, lowered residential density, large open spaces, and fluid vehicular movement. Under the leadership of the Development Commission, which after 1971 contained no Catholic or nationalist representation, the area plan was subsequently reconfigured to address the problems associated with the new political situation.[18]

Design initiatives and architectural elements implemented in Derry and other towns and cities in Northern Ireland adhered to "defensible space" strategies popular in the United States, the United Kingdom, and throughout Western Europe in the 1970s. The design concepts were not developed for war zones or areas of civil conflict, yet crime reduction through environmental design proved useful in Northern Ireland. Proposed by Oscar

15 McSheffry, *Planning Derry*, 1

16 *Londonderry Area Plan*, "Problems," sect. 1.3.

17 For more on urban polarization, see Scott Bollens, *On Narrow Ground: Urban Policy and Ethnic Conflict in Jerusalem and Belfast* (Albany, NY: SUNY Press, 2000).

18 In the summer of 1971, all nationalists left the commission as a protest against internment policies and in response to the British Army's alleged "manhandling" of civil rights figures John Hume and Ivan Cooper.

19   Another influential text of this period was written by C. Ray Jeffrey and make the case that the built environment can deter crime; see his *Crime Prevention through Environmental Design* (London: Sage, 1971).

20   Henry Cisneros, *Defensible Space: Deterring Crime and Building Community* (Darby, PA: Diane Publishing, 1995), 7.

21   Jon Coaffee, *Terrorism, Risk and the City: The Making of a Contemporary Urban Landscape* (Farnham: Ashgate, 2003), ix.

22   Ibid.

Newman in the late 1960s and influenced by both the architect's reflections on the Pruitt-Igoe public housing project in St. Louis and emerging studies in environmental criminology, theories of defensible space held that planners could prevent crime by lowering the density of housing and designing deterrents to deviant and criminal behavior.[19] The reduction of visual barriers and design of street patterns that intentionally slowed vehicular traffic and limited options for both pedestrian and vehicular egress counted among the most significant planning strategies.[20] Directed toward reducing crime by instilling accountability and a sense of stewardship in residents of public housing, defensible space concepts relied heavily on proprietary engagement by residents.

As Jon Coaffee observes in his 2003 book on terrorism and city planning, defensible landscapes gave way to defensive ones in Northern Ireland as conflict heightened. "It did not take long for defensible space principles to be adopted and radically applied to urban areas in Northern Ireland such as Belfast and Londonderry in attempts to deter terrorism."[21] Strategies for maintaining public order, "reducing hostile initiative," deterring "terrorist" activity, and enabling "rapid and effective response to attack" became increasingly visible in the emergent environmental design that accompanied urban renewal.[22] Planning increasingly factored into a "colonial war model," aimed at quelling dissent through "the militarization of the administrative and legal systems and their integration into an interlocking strategy of strangling support for insurgents."[23] Over the course of the 1970s, this created "an ever more militarized landscape."[24]

In Derry redevelopment worked to maintain order and create fast, easy access for military vehicles to previously dense and erratically organized urban neighborhoods. The lowered population densities, large open spaces, increased visibility, strategically positioned public buildings, construction of roadways and flyovers, deployment of cul-de-sacs, and eradication of alleys all increased possibilities for surveillance, decreased opportunities for civil disturbances, and limited escape routes out of housing estates. Combined with various edicts of the Public Order Acts prohibiting processions and demonstrations, these adjustments altered the social, political, and physical geographies of Catholic and nationalist Derry.

Decreased population density in what had been the South Ward was the first significant consequence of urban renewal from a security perspective. New estates, built several miles away from the Bogside, Brandywell, Lecky Road, Aberfoyle, and Bishop/Anne Street neighborhoods were designed for police legibility. Thus the Bogside, for centuries the epicenter of Catholic Derry, was effectively decentralized. This made small-scale riots less likely to mushroom into mass disturbances. Curfews, checkpoints, and house-to-house patrols alone quelled demonstrations and protests simply by blocking or limiting access to the Bogside. Since residents of the newly

23   Graham Ellison and Jim Smyth, *The Crowned Harp: Policing Northern Ireland* (London: Sterling, 2000), 73–74.

24   Neil Jarman, "Intersecting in Belfast," in *Landscape, Politics and Perspectives*, ed. Barbara Bender (Oxford: Bloomsbury Academic Press, 1993), 107.

built estates on the outskirts of the city were virtually all Catholics, the erection of army checkpoints at major gateways into the city center and the old South Ward area provided a simple means of policing the nationalist population. Gatekeeping opportunities aided the collection of intelligence information, as anyone coming or going could be stopped, questioned, and searched as a matter of course.[25]

25 Coaffee, *Terrorism, Risk and the City*, 20.

In Ballyarnett, Shantallow, and Galliagh, newly built estates two miles from the urban core, design initiatives also took security into account. Back doors always led to cul-de-sacs: if a knock came at the front door, an escape out the back would be virtually impossible. The Galliagh estate, for example, was comprised of 20 "parks." Within each, single rows of housing were surrounded by open space. Devoid of trees and poorly drained, these spaces proved unsuccessful for sports or play but offered clear sightlines throughout the area.

Residents experienced the effects of renewal and of lowered population density in a variety of ways. For many, these developments introduced an alien element of distance into the family dynamic. Catholic Derry no longer possessed a dedicated, physical center. Since housing was allocated according to a lottery system, extended families were rarely relocated to new estates near one another. Few residents had telephones or cars that could help bridge the distance between home and places of worship, schools, or other gathering places in the South Ward. According to the drafters of the

Londonderry Area Plan, the introduction of this two-to-three-mile distance was negligible, as public transportation would be made available. In practice, however, this distance proved disruptive. Navigating the area via public transportation required significant planning. Even if one's parents or siblings lived in an adjacent housing estate, it might take two hours to reach them on a city bus, which typically went first to the city center and then came back out to the outskirts.

Within the climate of the Troubles, bonds of trust built through proximity, family connections, and long-standing neighborly ties served as insufficient models for establishing relationships in the new estates. Geographies of neighborliness had, after all, been built on place-bounded social and familial networks. The pervasiveness of surveillance and the real threat of internment led many residents to distrust unfamiliar others. For some, a family member or friend's involvement with paramilitary organizations led them to be vigilant when chatting with acquaintances, lest they let some small bit of information slip into the wrong hands. Fear of police informants shaped social dynamics, as did anxiety that one's children might say something revealing to others. As it was impossible to know whether acquaintances had even tangential connections to the paramilitaries, some exercised prudence by not getting to know new neighbors. Being targeted as a terrorist or suspected collaborator was too high a price to pay for a congenial conversation over the clothesline or a cup of tea with a neighbor. Proximity to strangers undermined former Bogside residents' long-standing tactics of social orientation.

Within the urban core, the landscape underwent major shifts. Houses that had once lined the hillside that led from the city walls down into the heart of the neighborhood were torn down. Most had been built in the 19th century and had not stood the test of time well. However, instead of building new homes or parks in these now-open spaces, redevelopment authorities left the land vacant.[26] This design decision created unadulterated views of the streets, houses, and apartment buildings in the Bogside from the city walls above, where soldiers were stationed at British Army surveillance and patrol bases. Decreased density made areas more visible for surveillance, limited the possibilities for blockades and barricades, and increased the speed and ease with which military vehicles and security personnel could enter the area, while it simultaneously restricted the possibility for residents to leave covertly.

Other land use changes also discouraged public unrest. The original plan for Rossville Street, once cleared of row houses, called for additional housing. Instead of building the proposed low-rise flats or erecting popular maisonettes on the site, which would have allowed more residents to stay in the Bogside, a four-lane road was designed to run north-south through the neighborhood. The new road passed directly through the symbolic center of Catholic Derry, known as Free Derry Corner. Barricades that had blocked the area from police and the

26 W. F. Mitchell, *Londonderry Area Plan Public Inquiry–Report on the Public Inquiry by the Chief Professional Commissioner and Recommendations by the Planning Appeals Commission to the Department of Housing, Local Government and Planning* (Belfast: HMSO, 1974).

army in 1969 and 1972 could no longer be erected. Although urban design failed to disable protest, the width of the roadway (nearly 82 feet) facilitated the use of armored vehicles to disperse protestors.[27]

Additionally, a flyover was designed and built by the new Roads Service in 1974 to reconfigure the physical coordinates of "Old Derry." Ostensibly the new infrastructure allowed cars to bypass the city center en route to other towns or residential areas on the other side of the city. Few Derry residents, however, owned their own cars, and most considered traffic congestion a fairly minor problem at the time. Instead, the flyover enabled seamless movement for the military from staging areas on the bridge or close to the city center into the neighborhood. Its erection, together with the destruction of houses along Rossville Street, Pilot's Row, and Lecky Road, ultimately rendered the spaces of protest of the late 1960s and early 1970s invisible.

A drawing created by Bogside artist Kevin Hasson depicts the community "before" and "after" urban renewal, hinting at the alienation it inflicted on the neighborhood. The skeleton of a two-up two-down house stands in the background, with the flyover cascading through it. The Free Derry wall is shown isolated and strangled by the roadway, looking more like a gravestone than a symbol of protest.[28] In many ways the image echoes longtime area businessman Sean Quinn's thoughts. Quinn and his partner Barney Ferris ran a chemist's shop on Lecky Road until the premises were

27   This point was made by Irish Northern Aid Political Action Committee in its booklet *Architecture of Imperialism: The British Army Plan for Belfast and Derry* (New York: self-published, 1990).

28   Kevin Hasson, *Community Mirror* 57 (September 1980).

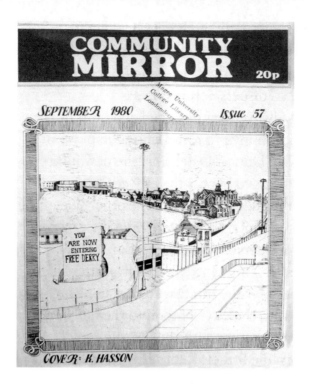

29   Quoted in Laurence
McClenaghan, "Sunday
Interview: The Lecky Road's
Moorecambe and Wise,"
Derry Journal, July 12, 2009.

demolished to make room for the flyover. Quinn recalled, "that was the worst thing to ever happen to the Bogside; it effectively killed a lovely wee community." Barney agreed, "That flyover broke my heart."[29]

As the Troubles continued, the Department of the Environment and the Department of Social Services continued to seize sites of civil unrest in the Bogside as opportunities for redesign and redevelopment. In the late 1970s, a large piece of land on Rossville Street adjacent to the area where many protests and much of the violence associated with the events of Bloody Sunday took place was allocated for use as a community center. In 1980 the

Pilot's Row Community Centre opened its doors. At the same time, the William Street Residential Care Home for Older People was built on vacant land between William and Abbey streets near the intersection with Rossville Street. In a 1985 film made by grassroots political arts activists, architect Peter Maloney was interviewed about planning and the militarization of space in the area. He suggested that the decision to place the center and home there were made to curb violence by investing the space with alternative community value. "No surprise they put senior housing and a community center in the areas where there had been the most public protest, rioting, etc." It stood to reason "people would be very upset" if riotous behavior occurred where elderly people were living, children were playing, etc.[30] Contested spaces were converted to uses that deterred protest and encouraged decorum.

Urban renewal in Derry resembled what was going on in the rest of the United Kingdom, as well as in the United States and Western Europe. The landscape became increasingly legible and uniform as rationality-driven planning reshaped the city. The proliferation of green space, the creation of small residential communities built around cul-de-sacs, and the accommodation of a burgeoning automobile culture through the creation of wide roadways and bypasses allowing for speedier traffic flow were all familiar features of contemporary redevelopment projects. In Derry planning also bolstered anti-terrorism operations, surveillance activities, and security

30   Peter Maloney, in *Planning*, directed by Tom Collins (Derry: Derry Video and Film Collective, 1985), accessed via the North West Digital Film Archives, Nerve Centre, Derry.

tactics aimed at containing civil unrest. It replaced a locally legible landscape with a universally legible one. The transformation of the urban environment through militarization destroyed the physical and social coordinates of Catholic Derry. Geographies of neighborliness became artifacts of an earlier era. The loss of the cityscape during the Troubles signaled the deeper loss of cultural continuity, which occurred at a time when it was needed most.

RESPONDING TO URBAN REDEVELOPMENT

Public responses to the 1973 Planning Inquiry, organized to address community reactions to the newly proposed Londonderry Area Plan, brought to light the ways early enthusiasm for redevelopment turned to ambivalence. Residents voiced fundamental concerns about citizen engagement in the planning process and raised broader issues associated with the process of urban renewal. The battle over Free Derry in the mid-1970s, on the other hand, encapsulated the issues of landscape change in highly contested and symbolically sacred space.

In 1973 a public inquiry was held into the Londonderry Area Plan and its implementation. Consultants assessing the work of the Londonderry Development Commission set up shop in a small bunker in the Guildhall Square to hear public comment about the effects of planning on the city. The gathering place was a poignant reminder of the turmoil confronting

London/Derry: the Guildhall was closed at the time, as city workers attempted to repair what two IRA bombs had destroyed of the facade in 1972.

Representatives of the Bogside Community Association (BCA) raised concerns on behalf of the approximately 14,000 residents of the Bogside area for whom they claimed to speak. While they acknowledged the "outstanding achievement of the Londonderry Development Commission in carrying out an extensive program of housing building which resulted in a greatly reduced waiting list and lower occupation rates,"[31] in the next breath, they leveled criticism at the group, stating that "in the well-intentioned rush to build, the Commission made mistakes."[32] They cited specific problems: the poor quality of materials and workmanship used in some of the new units; the danger, disruption, and invasion of privacy attendant to the construction of the flyover; the infrastructure's effect of isolating the Long Tower neighborhood; the destruction of crucial community spaces; and the separation of elderly people from the rest of the community through the location of homes for the aged, among other issues. Association representatives also expressed concern about the attitudes implicit in development planning. They argued that the problems that were raised were "glossed over" by the Commission "as if they were unfortunate, but after all, understandable in the circumstances."[33] No one seemed interested in or concerned about the fact that the cellars and street corners that had formed such a central part of community

31 *Londonderry Area Plan Public Inquiry.*

32 Ibid.

33 Ibid., 97.

life had been destroyed. Not only had those community spaces become victims of the bulldozer but no one had thought to propose parks or recreational spaces in their place. This lack of opportunity for citizens to engage in the planning process was most clearly criticized when representatives insisted that the plan's theme be changed from "Planning *for* People" to "Planning *with* People."[34]

Dislocation remained the chief complaint. Mr. P. Canny and Mr. J. O'Kane, representatives of the Anne Street, Bishop Street, Hamilton Street, Brandywell, and Foyle Road Tenants' Association, spoke forthrightly about their relatives', friends', and neighbors' disinclination to leave the area. They expressed dismay and frustration that the Development Commission was "not prepared to accept that the land required for accommodation of people with strong personal attachments to the area should be appropriated in order to correct deficiencies resulting from earlier development schemes."[35] As part of a back-and-forth between the tenant's representatives and the consultants, Canny and O'Kane had to answer for the fact that in a survey as many as 16 percent of area residents had expressed a willingness to leave the community in exchange for new and better housing. Canny responded that the survey had been conducted before residents had begun to move into the new housing estates on the edges of the city. He countered the statistics and argued that the barriers to fluid movement between the new estates and the area around the Bogside discouraged residents from leaving.[36]

34   Ibid., 95.

35   Ibid., 97.

36   Ibid., 109.

"There Were Streets"

Residents and spokespeople criticized the new estates as well. Community leader and Catholic priest Father Seamus Bradley took issue with how and where the Development Commission placed families in the outlying housing estates. He queried why—if the Shantallow/Ballyarnett estates already housed 15,000 residents and anticipated adding 4,000 within the next seven years, bringing the total to 19,000, equivalent to 20 percent of the city's overall population—had the planning not included community spaces or activity centers. The amenities, "a small set of swings and slides, a small library not open on evenings or weekends," and a temporary football pitch with "a sea of mud and water on it," were hardly sufficient. Furthermore, Father Bradley continued, "there were no cinemas, dance halls, activity centers or coffee bars." He concluded by arguing that recreation should be planned "at the same time as housing and not years or even generations later."[37] Implicit in his argument was an accusation that the new residential spaces had been designed not with residents in mind but rather according to other exigencies.

37 Ibid.

By the mid-1970s, people had come to realize that the spatial coordinates of their community life had been decimated. In talks, interviews, and community newspaper pieces, former residents reflected on the redevelopment with deep ambivalence. If memory is understood as a process that always serves "the human effort to exist, in both the individual and collective senses," it follows that remembrance about life "before"—before urban renewal,

38 Michael Johnson, "Review Article: Memory, History, Forgetting," *Anglican Theological Review* 89, no. 1 (Winter 2007): 106.

before civil rights, before the Troubles—can be seen as deeply purposeful within the context of the conflict, changes in the cityscape, and the emergent dislocations.[38] One woman, interviewed anonymously, summarized succinctly a widely shared perspective when she described her place of birth and compared it implicitly to the new estates:

> Where I was born and where I lived was Wellington Street, in the heart of the Bogside … a community in itself; it had its people, its shops, but you never had to go to the city center to do any shopping, you could have done everything you wanted to, including bury your dead, because we had an undertaker in that street. Most of Derry was made up of streets like that, communities within communities. When redevelopment took place the city was split up and the people from the streets were moved to housing estates outside the city center. The move was fair enough; they acquired houses, but that was about all they acquired.[39]

39 "The People Talk: Taped Interviews by Tom Lovett and Eddie McGlaughlin," *Community Forum* 2, 1974. In some ways this is the same narrative of loss that emerges out of the urban renewal of Bethnal Green in East London in the 1950s, Eliot Liebow's Tally's Corner in Chicago, Chavez Ravine in Los Angeles, Boston's North End, and the Bronx.

Bishop Daly, in his memoirs about the Troubles, writes that, "the new homes were welcome and long overdue." At the same time, he acknowledges the loss. Bonds developed over many generations, which had cemented these communities together, were beginning to loosen and disappear. "The new communities never acquired the solidarity or cohesion of the communities they replaced."[40]

40 Edward Daly, *Mister, Are You a Priest? Jottings by Bishop Edward Daly* (Dublin: Four Courts Press, 2000), 167.

Mrs. Rooney of Nelson Street, interviewed for a community documentation project that began in 1985, reminded people that cul-de-sacs and housing estates constituted a departure and a rupture in the lives of those who came of age before redevelopment. "Ye know, I think the houses would all be huddled together. There were, you know, there were streets."[41] She insisted that she had wonderful neighbors in the housing estate where she lived at the time of the interview, in 1987. Nelson Street, however, "was long and when ye went down it all the neighbors were at the door and they always had a chat te ye, when ye were passing up and down, d'ye know. That's gone now, no more a that."[42]

41 Mrs. Rooney, interview with Tony Morrow, February 20, 1987. Ulster Folk and Transport Museum, Oral History Interview, tape number 030a, tape reference number 941.62.

42 Ibid.

FREE DERRY CORNER

In response to the area plan, the future of Free Derry Corner became a volatile issue for the community. As part of the Lecky Road Improvement Scheme, houses along that road were to be demolished in preparation for construction of the four-lane roadway that would direct the flow of traffic off the flyover, through the basin of the Bogside, and then up to the Creggan neighborhood or toward the Northland Road and the western outskirts of the city. The houses were the property of the Housing Executive and had been unoccupied for several years. Although they had stood vacant and were known to be in the line of the new road scheme, it came as a surprise to some that the houses at Free Derry Corner were going to be demolished.

43   *Londonderry Area Plan Public Inquiry*, 57.

44   Ibid.

45   Ibid.

46   Although the slogan's appearance has long been attributed to John "Caker" Casey, there is some evidence to suggest that Liam Hillen was the first to scrawl the slogan on what became known as the "Free Derry" Wall. *Derry Journal*, November 16, 2009, http://www. derryjournal.com/ news/a-silent-and-powerful-witness-to-troubled-times-1-2142120.

47   Ibid.

Mrs. P. Murphy, representing the Meenan Park Tenants' Association Committee, declared that area residents were "very concerned and perturbed" when they learned of the planned demolition of Free Derry.[43] She stated, "It was the expressed desire of the majority of the people in the area that it should be preserved as a historical monument and a committee had been formed for the purpose of preserving and protecting it."[44] Divisional Planning Executive James Watson was onsite for the hearings and responded to Murphy, saying that the improvement scheme was "pretty well fixed": the houses at Free Derry would stand only eight feet from the proposed road, representing too great a danger to the public. At the same time, Watson indirectly admitted that Free Derry was a site of significance. He argued that if it was preserved, it would attract attention and pedestrians gathering around the houses and that such activity "would be prejudicial to road safety."[45]

W. F. Mitchell, charged with compiling the results of the public inquiry process, endeavored to address the conflict over Free Derry Corner, specifically, the issue of the house at #33 Lecky Road. At the height of a standoff between B-Special police reserves and student activists on January 5, 1969 (and periodically thereafter), a local resident had scrawled, "You Are Now Entering Free Derry" on the house's gable end.[46] Mitchell began by saying that, "if viewed simply in terms of land use and road planning, there would be no question of retaining a pair of old houses in the median strip of a through-road."[47]

The issue under consideration was whether or not community feelings on the matter trumped planning logic, or "whether or not this conclusion would be outweighed by the fact of their identification with recent political events in the area." While acknowledging that local sentiment mattered, Mitchell questioned residents' attachments to Free Derry:

> Considered in general terms it might be taken that the sensitivities of people to the retention or removal of elements in town structure is relevant, but in the present case there is not much evidence as to how their removal or retention would be viewed in the locality. Mrs. Murphy's written objection does not provide any measure of the support for retention in terms of territory or population, and although the BCA's representatives engaged the attention of the Inquiry for periods totaling two and a half days they did not mention the matter.[48]

Mitchell proposed that all of the remaining houses at Lecky Road, including #33, be torn down and that Free Derry be commemorated with an inscribed stone or plaque, "preferably at the back of one of the footways rather than the center of the road."[49]

Mitchell misread Mrs. Murphy's statement when he asserted that it reflected the opinions of only a small number of people in the Bogside area. Although the members of the BCA had backed away from an initial proposal to create a museum at Free Derry Corner, they had concurred that the gable wall should stay.[50] It would be a

48   Ibid.

49   Ibid.

50   "Derry Journal Reports from June 1975," *Derry Journal*, June 12, 2007, http://www.derryjournal.com/news/community/nostalgia/quot-derry-journal-quot-reports-from-june-1975-1-2111599.

mistake to think that the reconstruction of the landscape around Free Derry would not upset residents; Free Derry became significant because the intersection had long been a gathering place for meeting and sharing news, gossip, and *craic*.[51] Known at the time as Fox's Corner, it was accessible from all ends of the South Ward—from Bishop Street and the Long Tower area, the Brandywell, and Creggan—as well as from the central core of the Bogside, and it grew in significance during the early Troubles. The site did not become significant because "You Are Now Entering Free Derry" was scrawled on the gable wall: the slogan went up because the site was already significant.

A plaque or inscribed stone would not be able to replace or commemorate the lived social and political history that contextualized and made sense of the corner, the slogan, or the wall of a house that had until recently stood in the center of a cramped, struggling, but close-knit community. In 1971 Seamus Deane penned an article in *Honest Ulsterman* entitled, "Why Bogside?" In it he drummed, "Bogside used to be a street. Now it is a condition."[52] The street called the Bogside was gone, along with many others much like it. The tattered old house with its inscribed gable wall standing in the way of the new four-lane roadway shouldered the histories of both the street and the condition.

By the following spring, all but four of the houses at Free Derry Corner had been bulldozed. On May 22, 1975, the BCA invited area residents to a public meeting

51   *Craic*, a Gaelic word used often in Hiberno-English, is best translated as an enjoyable time had with others, often involving music, joking, storytelling, or the sharing of news or gossip.

52   Seamus Dean, "Why Bogside?," *Honest Ulsterman* 27 (January–March, 1971).

"There Were Streets"

to discuss the fate of these remaining houses, located at the intersection of Fahan and Lecky, which remained in question. Association organizer Eamonn Deane stated in the invitation:

> The four remaining vacant houses have become dumping grounds and the place is now both an unsightly mess and a health hazard. The statutory authority whose responsibility the ground is (i.e. The Roads Executive) is undecided what to do and if consensus amongst the various interested groups can be arrived at then pressure can be put on them to do what the people want. I trust that you and your association are interested and look forward to your attendance at the meeting.[53]

The meeting yielded a diversity of opinion. Some residents worried the site was infested with rats and used for illegal dumping. They wanted Free Derry to be torn down and a monument erected on the site.[54] A couple weeks later, the house at Free Derry was gone, with the exception of the wall on which the now infamous slogan had been inscribed. Members of the IRA had done the demolition themselves. They claimed that staff from the Housing Executive and the Road Service refused to do it unless they also knocked down the Free Derry Wall.[55]

53 Bogside Community Association, memorandum, May 22, 1975. Derry City Council Archives, Bridget Bond Collection, Community Associations folder, London/Derry, Northern Ireland.

54 *Irish Times*, May 29, 1975.

55 *Belfast Telegraph*, June 13, 1975.

Figure 4 Free Derry Wall in the 1970s. Source: photographer unknown; Jim Collins and Adrian Kerr, *Free Derry Wall* (Derry: Guildhall Press, 2009).

The Free Derry controversy encapsulates the imaginative geographies of the broader area. As it ceased to be the physical center of community and protest, it took on a deeply spatialized significance, as memory work filled in the gaps of lived experience. In turn, the Bogside became a sacralized memorial landscape even as it was stripped of its day-to-day relevance. As the neighborhoods that had bolstered both Old Derry and even Free Derry disappeared, extended families dispersed, and long-held associations, customs, and values lost resonance, the area was recast as a symbolic site. Physical redevelopment of Derry, coupled with the other ruptures and dislocations of the Troubles, augured emotional and psychic as well as physical dislocations. Life lived according to a communal ethos had a geography. Its foundations lay in the physical spaces of Derry's nationalist neighborhoods and the relationships they sustained. Troubles-era Derry was indeed a ruptured city; its new physical design was directly related to civil unrest.

As Derry's Catholics confronted the drawbacks of urban renewal and reflected on the things they missed about life before the bulldozers, remembrances of the past during this period often couched the difficulties of life amidst civil violence in discussions of the ruptures wrought by redevelopment. Likewise, residents implied broader critiques of the police and army through discussions of contemporary anxieties brought about by dwelling in and navigating spaces of perpetual surveillance and managing the realities of dispersed residential arrangements. Local people experienced the violence of the Troubles through the lens of multiplied loss. Nostalgia for the neighborliness that had accompanied the physical geographies of pre-Troubles Catholic Derry merged with a larger sense of loss wrought by the conflict itself. Derry Catholics utilized reminiscences of vanished neighborhoods and the lives that those neighborhoods had sustained as an opportunity to give voice to what had been lost both because of urban renewal and because of the Troubles. Just as the housing shortage had represented disenfranchisement before and during the struggle for civil rights, redevelopment came to represent the geographical, social, and political dislocations of the Troubles both from within and outside their communities. The lack of trust the state projected onto the community was reflected by elements of broken trust within.

In London/Derry, contemporary Western European and North American urban design strategies were adapted to address the unique challenges of a specific historical moment. This city's redevelopment model differed from those employed throughout the United Kingdom, in that it shaped the design, implementation, and lived experience of the city through civil conflict.[56] The redevelopment of London/Derry facilitated British Army movement in order to support army and police surveillance tactics and to reduce opportunities for unrest

56 Belfast provided one possible exception to this assertion.

within heavily nationalist and republican areas. However unique this case may be, this analysis provides a useful lens for considering not only how myriad political and social factors shape design decisions but also for understanding the ways residents' reactions may engage memory as a form of social commentary and remembered geographies, as imaginative place making amid dislocation.

Slum as Infrastructure: How the Politics of Informality Shapes South Africa's World-Class Cities

Kerry Ryan Chance

I met Monique two weeks after the eviction. At dawn, a team of heavily armed police and private security moved into Delft, a sandy sun-blighted township on the out-skirts of the South African city of Cape Town. Delft is the site of a national flagship project in urban land and housing, called the N2 Gateway. With armored vehicles and sniffer dogs in tow, the eviction team removed about 1,600 residents from the unfinished houses they had occupied two months earlier at the alleged authorization of their local councilor. Many families had moved from wood and corrugated tin shacks located in the backyards of nearby homeowners, in historically "Coloured" (mixed-race) and "African" townships. The concrete-block structures the residents occupied were known as

Figure 1 Activist looking at a transit camp under construction at the N2 Gateway Project. Source: Kerry Ryan Chance, Delft, South Africa, 2008.

BNG houses after a popular 2004 national policy called Breaking New Ground. The policy aimed at making the delivery of state infrastructure more efficient by expanding the role of the private sector in housing programs.

The eviction, broadcast on national nightly news, was violent. Without warning, police fired rubber bullets at crowds gathered in the streets, shooting residents and trampling them as they ran for cover. At least 20 injured people were rushed to the hospital. With nowhere else to go, Monique and about a thousand others remained on the pavement. The municipal government, together with the Democratic Alliance (DA), the largest opposition party to the ruling African National Congress (ANC), responded by providing about 500 of the evicted families with large communal tents; some of a dark green military make, others brightly striped or white with frilly awnings. Latecomers were given "black sails," or plastic sheeting, which they used to build tiny, makeshift shacks behind the tents, unseen from the surrounding highways. The camp, referred to by residents as "Section 1," was eventually encircled with barbed wire and supplied with water taps and portable toilets.

Monique and approximately 500 other residents, however, refused to work with the DA or sign the forms required to acquire space in Section 1. Under the banner of the Anti-Eviction Campaign (AEC), then a leading poor peoples' movement, they instead constructed shacks out of a motley assortment of collected materials at the scene of their eviction. They founded the settlement of Symphony Way, named after the highway that ran through the center of it and was henceforth blockaded in a protest and land occupation that would last for more than two years. In time, their collective grievances would center upon not only their eviction but also "transit camps," which occupants referred to as *amathini* (tin cans, in isiZulu), *blikkies* (little tins, in Afrikaans), or government shacks (in English).[1]

Transit camps are government emergency shelters located in controlled sites. The camps house those displaced by routine environmental disasters, such as floods or fires, in shack settlements. However, the majority of camp occupants are those displaced by processes of urban development, such as the construction of roadways, bridges, and housing projects like the N2 Gateway. Transit camps typically take the form of tent villages like Section 1, or settlements built from corrugated tin and other "temporary" materials. Tens of thousands reside in transit camps, and many more shack dwellers are slated for relocation. Transit camps are rapidly reshaping the urban periphery of Cape Town and other cities across the country.[2] The largest camp in South Africa is located in Delft. State proponents of transit camps posit them as a "formalized" stopgap toward the delivery of permanent houses. For residents refusing relocation, like those on Symphony Way, living conditions in the camps are inadequate, even by the standards of "informal" dwelling and even if temporary.

1 "Transit camps" are also officially referred to as "decant camps" or "temporary relocation areas" (TRAs).

2 Transit camps to house the urban poor are an increasingly international phenomenon—camps have been established in Brazil, Angola, and Kenya. See Marie Huchzermeyer, *Unlawful Occupation* (Johannesburg: Africa World Press, 2011).

In the changing geographies of contemporary urban South Africa, residents like Monique and her neighbors are innovating informal spatial practices used by previous generations, and especially by liberation movements, to construct, gain access to, and transform housing infrastructure. These practices include building shacks and occupying land, as well as mobilizing street-based activities such as mass gatherings and road blockades. I base my findings upon ethnographic and historical research in the cities of Cape Town, Durban, and Johannesburg between 2008 and 2012. Along with participant observation in day-to-day activities in shack settlements and transit camps, I gathered interviews and life histories with activists and ordinary residents about their lives during and after the liberation struggle, and analyzed relevant archival materials, such as national policy documents, postapartheid legislation, mainstream news media and texts produced by movement members.

Following Monique's movements through the streets, the courts, and much of the housing under construction in Delft reveals a resurgent discursive use of the term "slum" in postapartheid South Africa along with evictions from so-called informal settlements to formalized transit camps. These evictions intensified as Cape Town and other urban enclaves were constructed as so-called "World-Class Cities" in preparation to host the 2010 World Cup. The management of "slum" populations in transit camps, while aimed at curbing informality by filling a gap in housing stock, spatially reproduced race-based inequalities and peri-urban precarity in Cape Town. Evictions have given rise to mobilizations among residents, premised upon informal dwelling and informal politics that cut across historically "Coloured" and "African" communities, notably through newly enshrined citizenship rights and the South African courts.

SLUM AS INFRASTRUCTURE

Theories of urban space, studies of informal dwelling, and research on post-colonial politics provide a useful lens through which to examine these contentious spatial practices.[3] Across these literatures, scholars—particularly those working on political authority on the African continent—have emphasized three interlocking theoretical assertions: sovereignty, governmentality, and biopolitics.[4] One of the few, and rarely noted, examples offered by Michel Foucault is the 19th-century housing project. Transit camps share some features with Foucault's example and illustrate ways in which these large-scale institutional processes work intimately together at the level of infrastructure.

For Foucault the layout of a housing project, which in theory localizes poor families (one to a home) and their spatial location within the city (on the periphery), is aimed at controlling bodies, making individuals and their behavior more visible and policing more effective. In addition to these disciplinary measures aimed at bodies, there are regulatory mechanisms that apply to the

3 These sources include Arjun Appadurai, *Fear of Small Numbers* (Durham, NC: Duke University Press, 2006); Bjørn Bertelsen et al., "Engaging, Transcending and Subverting Dichotomies: Discursive Dynamics of Maputo's Urban Space," *Urban Studies*, 2013, 1–18; Neil Brenner et al., *Cities for People, Not Profit* (New York: Routledge, 2011); Ben Cousins et al., *Socio-Economic Rights in South Africa* (Cambridge: Cambridge University Press, 2013); Catherine Fennel, "Project Heat and Sensory Politics in Redeveloping Chicago's Housing Projects," *Ethnography* 12, no. 1 (2011): 40–64; Akhil Gupta, *Red Tape* (Durham, NC: Duke University Press, 2012); Eric Harms, "Eviction Time in the New Saigon: Temporalities of Displacement in the Rubble of Development," *Cultural Anthropology* 28, no. 2 (2013): 344–68; James Holston, *Insurgent Citizenship* (Princeton, NJ: Princeton University Press, 2008); Huchzermeyer, *Unlawful Occupation*; Edgar Pieterse, *City Futures* (London: Zed Books, 2008); Richard Pithouse, "Our Struggle is Thought, On the Ground Running," 2006, Abahlali baseMjondolo, http://www.abahlali.org/files/RREPORT_VOL106_PITHOUSE.pdf; Vyjayanthi Rao, "Risk and the City: Bombay, Mumbai, and Other Theoretical Departures," *India Review* 5, no. 2 (2006): 220–32; Fiona Ross, *Raw Hope, New Life* (Cape Town: University of Cape Town Press, 2010); Ananya Roy, "Slumdog Cities: Rethinking Subaltern Urbanism," *International Journal of Urban and Regional Research* 35, no. 2 (2011): 223–38; and Anita von Schnitzler, "Traveling Technologies," *Cultural Anthropology* 28, no. 4 (2013): 670–93.

4 Keith Breckinridge, *Biometric State: The Global Politics of Identification and Surveillance in South Africa* (Cambridge: Cambridge University Press, 2014); Sharad Chari, "State Racism and Biopolitical Struggle," *Radical History Review* 108 (2010): 73–90; Partha Chatterjee, *The Politics of the Governed* (New York: Columbia University Press, 2004); James Ferguson, *Global Shadows* (Durham, NC: Duke University Press, 2006); Achille Mbembe, "Necropolitics," *Public Culture* 15, no. 1 (2003): 11–40; T. B. Hansen et al., *Sovereign Bodies* (Princeton, NJ: Princeton University Press, 2005); and Charles Piot, *Nostalgia for the Future* (Chicago: Chicago University Press, 2010).

population—in this case, housing project residents—that encourage patterns of saving related to housing… and, in some cases, their purchase. Health-insurance systems, old-age pensions, rules on hygiene that guarantee optimal longevity of the population; the pressures that the very organization of the city brings to bear on sexuality and therefore procreation; child care, [and] education.[5]

Though centered on managing the health and welfare of the population, the housing project was designed above all to remove the urban poor from crowded back alley slums, long regarded as disorderly and criminal.

While transit camps from this perspective might be seen as ever-more efficient sites of control over "slum" populations and urban space, scholars in South Africa suggest that the camps instead have developed conditions for protracted uncertainty, which impacts socio-economic stability and the likelihood of unrest among the urban poor.[6] What Foucault does not address, and what has concerned anthropologists, is how housing infrastructure might be transformed by the spatial practices of the poor, who refuse to be removed, seize access to homes by illicit occupation, manipulate rental agreements, or use carceral spaces like the camps as platforms for collective politics. As Julia Elyachar succinctly puts it, "When practices that violate laws are accepted as the norm, and have legitimacy that is not the state's, they are often called "informal practices."[7] As spatial practices,

5   Michel Foucault, "Governmentality," in *The Foucault Effect*, ed. Graham Burchell et al. (Chicago: Chicago University Press, 1991), 251.

6   Huchzermeyer, *Unlawful Occupation*. My own research is consistent with these findings.

7   Julia Elyachar, "Mappings of Power: The State, NGOs, and International Organizations in the Informal Economy of Cairo," *Comparative Studies in Society and History* 45, no. 3 (2003): 547.

they have an ambiguous—or even outright contentious—relationship to institutions that govern urban areas but nonetheless are so commonly enacted as to have taken on the status of an infrastructural norm. In Monique's story at the N2 Gateway transit camp and Symphony Way shack settlement, informal dwellings doubly function as infrastructure.

Analysis of the problems and possibilities in approaching informal dwellings as infrastructure builds upon AbdouMaliq Simone's analysis of spatial practices in African cities. Focusing on Johannesburg, Simone proposes *people as infrastructure*, which suggests how urban-dwellers, and especially "residents of limited means," collaborate with "regularity and provisionality" in the circulation of goods, knowledge, and power to construct "a platform" that provides for and reproduces "life in the city."[8] Zeroing in on specific spatial practices of informal dwelling, such as the building of shacks at the N2 Gateway site, contributes to efforts by scholars to expand the notion of infrastructure (usually thought to be limited to, or prefigured by, formalized water pipes, roadways, housing units, and electricity cabling) to state-citizen struggles grounded in people's day-to-day activities and material lives.[9] Studying these practices, moreover, at a critical juncture when the foundations of a national flagship housing project are being set, helps illuminate forms of knowledge and expertise that interact with, but are not wholly determined by, formal institutions in the production of urban space. Transit camps, which look and

8 AbdouMaliq Simone, "People as Infrastructure: Intersecting Fragments in Johannesburg," *Public Culture* 16, no. 3 (2004): 407–8.

9 Brenda Chalfin, "Public Things, Excremental Politics, and the Infrastructure of Bare Life in Ghana's City of Tema," *American Ethnologist* 41, no. 1 (2013): 92–109; and Julie Y. Chu, "When Infrastructures Attack: The Workings of Disrepair in China," *American Ethnologist* 41, no. 2 (2014): 351–67.

feel very much like shacks—or worse, are tents, as at Section 1—suggest how informal dwellings become taken up into the technocratic work of states and non-governmental organizations.

Recent studies of infrastructure, some following the work of urban philosopher Henri Lefebvre, have breathed new life into how theories of space and informality might be rethought and recombined in post-Cold War, postcolonial African cities. Indeed, activists too, including the AEC, have made use of Lefebvre's famous phrase "a right to the city" in their placards and press releases, emphasizing that space is not a preexisting or empty container but rather is lived and made.[10] Where governments and corporations have failed to provide available and affordable housing, the urban poor have constructed their own dwellings, complex rental schemes, property agreements, and communal lives. Those without formalized housing, inasmuch as they might desire and await government delivery, do not do so passively; rather, their activities constitute an autonomous capacity for generating not only economic growth, as scholars of the informal economy have argued,[11] but also specific infrastructures for their lives in the city.

While it is important to recognize spatial practices of the poor as generative, scholarship of the last four decades, often critical of how the sector has been operationalized from above,[12] has offered many valuable arguments against bracketing off informality. Three objections are particularly common and salient in the

10   Rosalie de Bruijn, "AbM Launches Right to the City Campaign in Cape Town," May 30, 2005, Abahlali baseMjondolo, http://abahlali.org/node/6750.

11   Keith Hart, "Informal Income Opportunities and Urban Employment in Ghana," *Journal of Modern African Studies* 11, no. 1 (1973): 61–89.

12   See Elaychar, "Mappings of Power."

South African case. First, categorical or ontological distinctions between the formal and informal reinscribe old colonial antinomies of the modern and the traditional, the civilized and the unruly, the cartographic and the *terra incognita*, which have the potential to romanticize or pathologize the urban poor and African cities. The second is that as a hard-and-fast dichotomy it does not hold, for features of the informal sector can be found in the formal sector and vice versa, especially at a time of urbanization and unemployment in a globalized economy. The third is that such a multiplicity of formal and informal sectors exist, and are so varied or contradictory, interconnected, and co-constitutive in their composition, that the categories are too underspecified to be useful. Rather than approaching informality etically, or as an analytic, it may be more useful to examine how both activists like Monique and state agents (particularly, vis-à-vis the social life of policy such as BNG) mobilize local understandings of the informal, and do so tactically to achieve certain political ends. Informality, as both a key discursive category and a set of innovative spatial practices, becomes a staging ground for contested claims over race, class, and citizenship, which map onto and contribute to the production of urban space.

THE EMERGENCE OF POSTAPARTHEID "SLUMS"

Since the presidential election of Nelson Mandela in 1994, the ANC has aimed at dismantling the architecture

13 Anne-Maria Makuhulu, "The Question of Freedom: Post-Emancipation South Africa in a Neoliberal Age," in *Ethnographies of Neoliberalism*, ed. Carol Greenhouse (Philadelphia: University of Pennsylvania Press, 2010).

14 Pieterse, *City Futures*.

15 Patrick Bond, "South Africa's Resurgent Urban Social Movements," Centre for Civil Society Research Report 22 (2004): 1–34, http://ccs.ukzn.ac.za/default.asp?3,45,10,1398; Pithouse, "Our Struggle is Thought"; and Raj Patel, "A Short Course in Politics at the University of Abahlali baseMjondolo," *Journal of Asian and African Studies* 43, no. 1 (2008): 95–112.

of apartheid by extending citizenship rights enshrined in new legislation and national policy. The extension of these rights has included the "eradication" of slums and the provision of formalized housing on a mass scale.[13] Nearly 2.4 million homes have been built, but the post-apartheid state has struggled to keep pace with overwhelming demand: in Cape Town alone, the number of families on official housing waitlists is estimated to rise by 20,000 annually from a half million. In no small measure, these numbers result from wageless urban migration at the fall of apartheid,[14] which the BNG policy document flags as a significant challenge to national housing programs inherited from the previously race-based state. With the lifting of pass laws and other repressive legislation, hundreds of thousands of people moved to urban and peri-urban areas in search of work, education, and other previously unavailable social and economic opportunities, many joining the millions already living in shacks. Since the late 1990s, street protests, often centered on urban land and housing, have been on the rise nationwide.[15]

South Africa's new Constitutional Court, since its first session in 1995, has played a key role in adjudicating these new citizen claims to land and housing. The Constitutional Court is South Africa's highest judicial institution. Section 26 of the South African Constitution obliges the postapartheid state to provide housing, while also safeguarding against arbitrary evictions. The section states:

Everyone has the right to have access to adequate housing. The state must take reasonable legislative and other measures, within its available resources, to achieve the progressive realization of this right. No one may be evicted from their home, or have their home demolished, without an order of court.

Section 26 has been a matter of contention in court cases brought by activists. In 2000 the Constitutional Court— in a landmark case named after Irene Grootboom, a shack dweller in Cape Town—found that the national housing policy fell short of constitutional obligations. The rewritten policy (the previously mentioned "Breaking New Ground" policy) coincided with the construction of the N2 Gateway Project and names it as a "lead pilot project."[16] The document emphasizes that the aim is to "overcome spatial, social and economic exclusion" while advancing the "eradication" of slums through relocations to "a range of ... housing typologies," notably including transit camps.[17] Grootboom ostensibly won her court case and contributed to a new housing vision, celebrated by activists. She died in 2008, however, while still living in a shack in Cape Town, a story often retold in South Africa's shacklands. These retellings usually are framed as a warning about the limitations of legal redress as it touches the ground of lived experience in shack settlements.

The BNG policy also coincided with national efforts to build "World-Class Cities." As scholars elsewhere in the global South have noted, the "World-Class City" is a

16   Marie Huchzermeyer, "The New Instrument for Upgrading Informal Settlements in South Africa: Contributions and Constraints," in *Informal Settlements: A Perpetual Challenge?*, ed. Marie Huchzermeyer and Aly Karam (Cape Town: Juta/UCT Press 2006): 47.

17   Republic of South Africa, "Breaking New Ground: A Comprehensive Plan for the Development of Sustainable Human Settlements," August 2004, http://abahlali.org/files/Breaking%20new%20ground%20New_Housing_Plan_Cabinet_approved_version.pdfz: 12.

18 Asher Ghertner, "Rule by Aesthetics: World-Class City Making in Delhi," in *Worlding Cities: Asian Experiments and the Art of Being Global*, ed. Ananya Roy and Aihwa Ong (Oxford: Wiley-Blackwell, 2011).

future-looking utopian project, whose aims and aesthetics may vary from place to place but is generally characterized by sleek modern design, high levels of governmental efficiency and corporate profitability, and if not the eradication of poverty, at least its orderly management.[18] In 2008, when Monique and her neighbors occupied houses in Delft, the city of Cape Town was preparing to host the 2010 World Cup. Thousands of visitors were expected to drive along the N2 highway corridor that connected the airport to swanky downtown hotels, tourist attractions, and a stadium built for the games. On either side of this corridor are the city's most historic townships and sprawling shack settlements. These areas occupy various national and local registers in contemporary South Africa, including as heroic battlegrounds of the liberation struggle. However, in 2008, the term "slum" reemerged—in new legislation, Parliamentary debates, tabloids, and television news—to describe the city's poorest quarters, earmarked for clearance or development. Shack settlements were matter out of place.

Since the 1930s the term "slum" has been associated in South Africa with efforts to legislate racial rezoning, often under the aegis of effective policing. The 1934 "Slums Act" was a colonial precursor to apartheid-era law. By proclaiming Black communities "slums," land was appropriated by apartheid agents, particularly on the desirable urban city center and immediate periphery. Under apartheid, with the election of the National Party (NP) in 1948, the government soon passed, and later

Slum as Infrastructure

rigorously enforced, legislation that struck out against life in shack settlements. This legislation included the notorious 1950 Group Areas Act, which led to the racial rezoning of Cape Town, and the 1951 Prevention of Illegal Squatting Act, which authorized forced evictions. Empowered by this legislation and in efforts to ruralize Black workers when not on the job, municipalities enacted "slum clearance" initiatives, which residents— especially women—fought, often militantly.

Monique, like her neighbors in Symphony Way, is a longtime resident of Delft and the Cape Flats. The most bitterly recalled removal among residents in Delft is the demolition of the iconic community of District Six, a place known as a thriving arts and cultural center, where 60,000 people were displaced and scattered throughout townships in Cape Town. At other times, apartheid state agents and allied corporations in the mining and textile industries sought to maintain racial segregation and the availability of cheap labor by tolerating or facilitating the growth of shack settlements. Transit camps, then, were used for the screening and repatriation of unwanted Black populations. Progressive lawyers, in the ambiguous late-apartheid years, used transit camp legislation to prevent the removal of people to distant sites and service areas. In the 1970s, a time of intensified unrest, the camps also served to demobilize organized politics by breaking apart long-standing mobilized communities.

While the term "slum" is still pejorative in the post-apartheid period, it has taken on new meanings informed by South Africa's liberal democratic transition. "Slums are bad for our country," said a housing official to Parliament in 2008, speaking in support of expanding clearance programs ongoing since 2000. He continued, "We dream of a tomorrow where all of us can rightfully and proudly proclaim our citizenship.... We dream of a tomorrow that is free of slums."[19] In this and similar statements, evictions—in comparison with apartheid removals—are justified under a liberal logic of citizenship rights, where political belonging is materialized in formalized housing.

19   Lennox Mabaso, "Slums Bill Not a Zimbabwe-style 'Operation Murambats-vina,'" *The Witness*, July 18, 2007, http://abahlali.org/node/1720/.

Yet residents in Cape Town and other cities have resisted—as many did under apartheid—the use of "slum" to refer to their communities, especially because the term so often has been used in the service of forced relocations to less desirable areas, and also because it suggests impermanence to long-standing residency, which in the postapartheid period might provide viable legal standing in tenure claims. Responding to the same 2008 parliamentary debate, Abahlali baseMjondolo, a poor peoples' movement affiliated with the AEC as part of the Poor People's Alliance, said in a press release:

> The word "slum" ... makes it sound like the places where poor people live are a problem ... because there is something wrong with poor people.... But it does not admit that ... places where poor people live often lack infrastructure and toilets because of the failure of ... the government to provide these things. The solution to the fact that we often don't

Slum as Infrastructure

have toilets in our communities is to provide toilets where we live and not to destroy our communities and move us out of the city.[20]

20 "Operation Murambats-vina Comes to KZN," press statement, Abahlali baseM-jondolo, June 21, 2007, http://www.abahlali.org/node/1629.

Figure 2   Anti-Eviction Campaign protest on the steps of the High Court in Cape Town. Source: Kerry Ryan Chance, Cape Town, South Africa, 2008.

The press release presents a rebuttal to Parliamentary debates that echoes sentiments regularly expressed by movement members at community meetings and mass gatherings; namely, that the term "slum" pathologizes settlements while eliding historical struggles with the for-merly race-based state over land and housing. Never-theless, the parliamentary debates and community meet-ings align when both invoke shack settlements with reference to forward-looking housing projects for the urban poor that implicitly tie formalized homes and land tenure to inclusive citizenship.

At the same time, the term "slum" adheres to national panic over crime, perceived as exponentially increasing since the fall of apartheid. A BNG policy document cites "combating crime" and "promoting social cohesion" as an integral part of its "new housing vision."[21] However, crime

21 Republic of South Africa, "Breaking New Ground," 7.

is highly racialized in South Africa. Racialized stereotypes of shack settlements and inner-city dwellings as the
homes of gangsters and prostitutes, marked by potentially
polluting moral and corporal degeneration, appear regularly in mainstream South African news and in popular
media. A housing official quoted in one representative
article characterizes "slums" as "hives of crime" infested
with "raw sewerage," combining fears over public safety
with public health.[22] South African travel websites echo
familiar middle-class warnings against visiting townships:
"[Corrugated tin shacks] are breeding grounds for crime
and violence. The majority of all crime occurs in these
slum areas.[23]"

Residents I spoke with in Cape Town and other cities
suggest that their criminalization is tied in part to spatial
practices, such as the building of shacks and the occupation of land, which are illicit and sometimes illegal. But
they view these practices as necessary to make urban life
viable and secure. "The poor are criminalized for the life
we are living," movement members often told me.[24]
Residents also suggest that their political activities, yet
again, have been cast as a threat to public safety. Since
1994, the ANC has endeavored to demobilize the popular
street politics that characterized the late liberation struggle by cultivating participation in formal democratic
institutions, such as voting, joining local ward committees, and applying for housing subsidies. The Democratic
Alliance, governing the city of Cape Town, has shared
the ruling ANC's official condemnation of rising street

22 "Jo'burg Cleans Out
Inner City Slums," IOL online,
November 4, 2002, http://
www.iol.co.za/news/south-
africa/jo-burg-cleans-out-
inner-city-slums-1.31118#.
UeHAekTNobo.

23 "Safety and Crime in
South Africa," Southafrica-
Travel, http://www.
southafrica-travel.net/
miscellaneous/southafrica_
safety.html.

24 S'bu Zikode, "We Are
the Third Force," Abahlali
baseMjondolo, 2005, http://
www.abahlali.org/node/17.

protests.[25] Officials have referred to these protesters—and Abahlali and AEC members, in particular—as a "criminal"[26] force posing a potential "danger to democracy."[27]

While the term "slum" in South Africa is stamped with its own historically located local and national meanings, its deployment during the build up to the 2010 World Cup reflects its resurgent use in international development. In recent decades, international institutions have launched studies, projects, and programs, including the United Nations Millennium Development Goals, to combat "slum growth" on a global spatial scale.[28] South Africa adopted the Millennium Development Goals with vigor, incorporating them into national policy and law. In 2009 South African officials in the province of KwaZulu-Natal passed a new "Slums Act," which was expected to form a national legislative template. The act centrally featured transit camps. It aimed to "eliminate and prevent the reemergence of slums" by the year 2014. While 2008 marked a ramping up of "slum" clearance initiatives, the fact remained that in South Africa there were more people living in and moving into shacks than there were formalized homes that could be built within the same timeframe. "Slum eradication" would produce a population still awaiting formalized housing, but removed from their homes in existing shack settlements. For this excess population, there were transit camps.

25   Bond, "South Africa's Resurgent Urban Social Movements."

26   "NIA Launches Probe into Riots," Sunday Times, May 29, 2005, http://allafrica.com/stories/200505310947.html.

27   "Mbeki Warns of 'Threat' from Township Rioting in South Africa," Agence France Presse, May 25, 2005.

28   "11 Numbers You Need to Know about the Global Housing Crisis," Amnesty International, October 6, 2011, http://blog.amnestyusa.org/africa/human-right-to-housing-11-numbers-you-need-to-know/.

Figure 3 Transit camp at the N2 Gateway Project after the installation of prepaid electricity meters. Source: Kerry Ryan Chance, Delft, South Africa, 2008.

TRANSIT CAMP DWELLING AT THE N2 GATEWAY

When the N2 Gateway Project broke ground, then Housing Minister Lindiwe Sisulu—the daughter of famed ANC liberation heroes—called it "the largest housing project ever undertaken by any government." The project literature proposes that formalizing informality would result in "integrated," "mixed income" "human settlements"—a gateway from the apartheid city to the "World-Class City." Initially a joint endeavor undertaken by various levels of government, the management of the N2 Gateway soon was outsourced to a private company called Thubelisha and a composite second tier of public-private partnerships, including one involving First National Bank.[29] Along with rental and bonded units that were too costly for shack dwellers, the last and only phase of the N2 Gateway Project consisted of subsidized

29   The original plans for the N2 Gateway were modified over time, partly in response to the rotation and sacking of elected officials and project partners. Of the 25,000 homes under construction, the majority were to accrue value for investors. Rental and bonded units were too costly for shack-dwellers like Monique and her neighbors. The inaugural residents of the "low cost" rentals went on rent boycott for several years, after Thubelisha failed to repair major defects, including huge cracks in the walls, leaking roofs, and faulty keys. The bonded units were

to be built on land occupied by the Joe Slovo shack settlement, home to some 20,000 families.

housing in Delft—the same houses Monique and her neighbors occupied. Seventy percent of the houses would be allocated to shack dwellers and 30 percent to backyard dwellers, populations racially coded, respectively, as "African" and "Coloured." These official designations resulted in some tensions between communities that later would trouble the mobilization at Symphony Way at times. For those who were not allocated these subsidized houses, all that remained were transit camps.[30]

During my visits to the Delft camp in 2008, the surrounding gates were locked at particular hours, with a police trailer and armored military vehicle stationed at the single entrance. As I found in other camps, access inside is often controlled. The shelters in Delft and camps in Durban and Johannesburg usually consist of a one-room, 215- to 280-square-foot box with a corrugated tin roof and sides, which residents point out leaves little room for families to change or grow. Some structures, built in rows, share a wall made of a single piece of metal sheeting.[31] Many camps are without energy infrastructure. Cooking facilities depend upon whether residents have access to prepaid electricity or have an illicit connection (in which case kettles and hot plates are used). On special occasions, where large portions of food are required, women cook over fires outside. For those who do not have electricity, or cannot afford to feed the prepaid meters, the use of fires or paraffin stoves along with candles for light is routine, which result in occasional camp conflagrations.

30 Little scholarly or journalistic attention had been paid to this new generation of transit camps when I began my research. Many camps are invisible from the vantage of middle-class suburbs and city centers. After poor peoples' movements—particularly the Symphony Way AEC—applied public pressure, conditions in the camps increasingly have been covered by the local and international news, notably during the 2010 World Cup.

31 The size of transit camps compares unfavorably to Reconstruction and Development Plan (RDP) houses, the most common concrete-block structures built after 1994, which are about 325 square feet with two rooms. They are also smaller than the notorious "matchbox" houses built in townships under apartheid, which were typically 560 square feet with four rooms and a living area.

Access to water is highly variable. Most camps are fitted with communal taps providing cold running water, but when these are broken, residents frequently rely on neighbors outside the camps, at times causing some inter-community tension. Water, largely gathered by women from the taps, is stored in buckets inside the home. Most camps also are fitted with outdoor communal latrines, but these very often are blocked or broken, sometimes leading residents to "privatize" them—that is, maintain them and charge for their use. When toilets are not functioning, buckets containing lime are typically used, along with other types of containers or methods. Residents use the "fly toilet," for example, which refers to a process of relieving oneself in a bag and throwing it as far as possible into the bushes.

As for work, most residents are unemployed or labor in the informal sector—in construction, domestic labor, gang activities, or hawking, for instance. Some do, however, work in the formal sector. Formal sector jobs depend on where the camp is located, but across cities and regions, security work is common. Residents are most often moved as a "community" rather than as individuals. Frequently they are placed in the same camp with other "communities." In Delft this has caused conflicts between rival gangs. What people do all day, of course, depends heavily on how or if they are employed, as well as on their age, gender, and other factors, but there are many communal activities in camps, including entrepreneurial projects such as *spaza* (shops) and *shabeens* (bars) that draw crowds (despite efforts to police them); active religious groups of various kinds, such as Pentecostal churches and madrasas; volunteer associations; and organized social movements, and political party structures, as well as cultural committees.

Camps are typically built far from where residents have lived for many years. An erosion of social networks means residents, especially women, often fear for their safety after dark. As this suggests, location matters. Many have lost their jobs, where transport costs are higher and shops less accessible. Those on HIV/AIDS medication struggle to get access to treatment at neighborhood clinics, even in short-distance moves. Unable to be accommodated in local classrooms, children in Delft have been placed in "temporary" camp schools; before this development, they were bused some 15 miles back to their previous township schools. Some postapartheid camps have taken on the status of permanent settlements: "Happy Valley" transit camp, for instance, which was built 14 years ago, and "Red City," which acquired its name from the rust that has replaced the shiny gleam of the original tin structures.

From Cape Town to Durban to Johannesburg, whether for reasons of livelihood, location, or autonomy, residents are protesting against transit camps through increasingly cross-regional and trans-local political and legal networks. Residents in the Delft and other camps would hear about a march by word of mouth from neighbors, for instance, at community meetings, at the water taps or taxi ranks, via cell phone text messages, or would literally seeing it unfold on the streets. Like Monique, those protesting have been arrested, shot at by police, and portrayed by officials as thwarting urban development. As an Abahlali press statement put it, the camps project an indefinite and precarious future for shack dwellers:

> We have a situation where people are being removed from a slum, and sent to another slum. Only this time it is a government-approved slum and is called a transit area.... [The state] does not give any guarantees as to where these "transit areas" will be located, what services will be provided there, if communities will be kept together or broken up [or] how long they will have to live in these places. We know that all through history and in many countries, governments have put their political opponents, the very poor, people who were seen as ethnically, cultural and racially different, and people without I.D. books in camps. These camps are always supposed to be temporary—a "transit" between one place and another. But very often these camps have become places of long and terrible suffering.[32]

32 "Eliminate the Slums Act," press release, *Abahlali baseMjondolo*, June 21, 2007, http://www.abahlali.org/node/1629.

Here, movement members posit equivalence between their self-made shack settlements and government transit camps as informal dwellings. However, they reject the N2 Gateway's promotion of transit camps as formalized temporary infrastructure in anticipation of brick-and-mortar homes.

Complicating the spatial futures projected by the N2 Gateway are the many practical ways that residents inhabit housing in Delft. Sitting with Monique on Symphony Way, outside the makeshift AEC office, we talked about how she came to reside there. For her the story of the Symphony Way begins, years earlier, with her days spent cleaning homes in the city's luxurious suburbs. She lived in a backyard shack made of wood and scrap metal, which she rented from a couple—themselves barely making ends meet—who lived in a formal, state subsidized home. When the electricity worked at all, it could be switched off by her landlords, which left her reliant upon candles and paraffin, both hazardous and expensive.

Seeking better conditions, she moved to "The Hague," one of the many sections of Delft with Dutch appellations, into a council house of her own. The owners, who rented it, lived in another area of the Flats. After local officials learned of this (entirely common) "grey market" rental of state housing (an arrangement also common with transit camp structures), the owners, under threat of legal action by the council, arrived at 3:00 in the morning to evict Monique and her daughter, carrying their belongings onto the street. She appealed to the Delft police, explaining that she had lived in the house for more than a year, had no notice of eviction, and had no place to go. The police told her that she could not take the matter to court, given that she was not the rightful owner of the house.

Following this eviction, Monique and her daughter lived on the street in the back of a *bakkie* (pickup truck). When her employers at the cleaning company learned of her situation, they helped her access accommodation in Delft through their connections at the N2 Gateway Project. Along with victims of a massive 2005 shack fire in the Joe Slovo shack settlement, Monique moved into a Delft transit camp called Tsunami. During her time in Tsunami, local experts discovered the walls of the temporary structures had been made with asbestos, a matter of criminal investigation.[33]

33   Pearlie Joubert, "A Lethal Find," *Mail & Guardian*, December 1, 2007, http://www.mg.co.za/article Page. aspx?articleid= 326470&area=/insight/ insight__national/.

After her daughter developed a bronchial and skin condition, which required full-time care, she left her job. By the end of the year with doctor fees mounting, Monique began work for a building contractor hired by Thubelisha, laying the foundations and fitting the plumbing for the N2 Gateway houses. She, along with other temporary workers, eventually went on strike, saying they were never paid for this work. Unable to sustain basic subsistence, Monique moved with her neighbors into the unoccupied N2 Gateway houses, with official but fraudulent allocation letters issued by their DA local councilor, who was later arrested.

Thubelisha and state agents quickly sought and secured their eviction through the courts. Monique was a respondent in the failed appeal. Echoing other officials,

Slum as Infrastructure

Judge Van Zyl, who granted the order, said that residents cannot "take the law into their own hands. There would be anarchy in the country if this were allowed."[34] Monique and other residents inferred that "anarchy," here, played on racialized fears of crime. As the Judge stood to leave the packed courtroom, Delft residents shouted, "Ons gaan nêrens!"[35]

On the day of the eviction, Monique's elderly neighbor recounted that after being shot in the side with a rubber bullet and falling to the ground, a police officer kicked and swore at her. The same day, Housing Minister Sisulu's office issued a statement containing no mention of the injuries or of the police violence captured by news cameras. The official version of events again cited the dangers of "anarchy" at the center of progressively realized rights:

> This morning at dawn, the Sheriff of the Court moved into Delft, supported by police.... The rule of law must prevail.... [The] government has built ... more houses than any other country in the world.... The N2 Gateway ... is a project that should be nurtured and guarded by all South Africans.[36]

While state agents emphasized law and order, the national news framed the scenes of the eviction as harkening back to unrest of the mid-1980s. Moreover, the eviction suggested how responsibility was vacated for housing demands newly legitimated by postapartheid law. When public criticism mounted over the eviction at

34   "We're Not Budging," *IOL online*, February 7, 2008, http://www.iol.co.za/index.php?set_id=1&click_id=15&art_id=vn20080207115012433C374131.

35   "We're not budging!" in Afrikaans.

36   "N2 Gateway Must Be Protected from Anarchy," Department of Housing, February 19, 2008, http://www.info.gov.za/speeches/2008/08022009451002.htm.

37   Housing Minister
Sisulu, quoted in Verashni
Pillay, "Delft Residents
Stranded," 24 News,
February 19, 2008.

38   Ibid.

39   Ibid.

40   Asa Sokopo, Murray
Williams, and Andisiwe
Makinana, "Delft Refuse,
Resist Eviction," The Star,
February 19, 2008.

the N2 Gateway, Sisulu said she instructed Thubelisha
to do "everything in their power to assist the people of
Delft … to move back to their previous places of accommodation" and to provide them with transport for that
purpose.[37] Thubelisha's project manager denied receiving
any such directive and said that the sheriff or the court
was "solely responsible" for the eviction.[38] The sheriff also
denied responsibility, saying, "The order [from the
Court] says I must evict the people and remove their
belongings to a place of safe custody and that is what I
did."[39] Monique and other residents, having given up
their former shacks and backyard dwellings, had nowhere
to go after the eviction. The police spokesperson said this
too was illegal: "The court order instructed the residents
to leave the entire area…. [I]t was illegal for them to
remain on the street." He added that a "[private security]
guard was posted outside each empty house to prevent
people from returning."[40] Here, the sovereign power to
evict is authorized by dispersed governmental modes of
managing slum populations, which may aim at control
but instead occasioned a two-year-long protest that
began and ended in peri-urban precarity.

AN INFRASTRUCTURAL POLITICS OF THE POOR

Upon this terrain, residents have mobilized an infrastructural politics based on collective identification as "the
poor" across historically race-based communities, which
borrow from old practices of the liberation struggle such

as mass gatherings and land occupations, and new practices such as entry into the desegregated courts. Some residents of Symphony Way—especially young people, like Monique—characterize their political activities, their involvement with what they call *umzabalazo* ("the struggle" in isiZulu), as beginning with the fall of apartheid. Others—like Monique's neighbor, Ashraf Cassim, the founding chairperson of the AEC—were involved in various capacities with liberation movements, including the ANC, whether through military operations, local branches, or trade unions.

Cassim told me the origin story of the Anti-Eviction Campaign, which began in 1999 on the Cape Flats. After dabbling in gang activities, Cassim worked for a printing company responsible for typesetting pocket compendiums of the new South African Constitution. There he said he learned of Section 26 and postapartheid protections against arbitrary evictions. From the vantage point of his mother's council home—amid aggressive cost-recovery measures—he watched as removals intensified on the Flats. An elderly man, his mother's neighbor, was among the first to be ejected from his home. In response residents orchestrated a mass gathering, referred to as a "blockade," that overwhelmed security forces and prevented the delivery of an eviction notice, which is required by law.[41] The police returned the next day with military personnel and with state agents who claimed to the press that the AEC was a front for criminal gangs. Cassim, identified as a leader by security forces, was

41 "Blockades" would become the signature of the AEC as it expanded branches to Chicago, Detroit, and Los Angeles during the US foreclosure crisis.

beaten bloody. His front teeth were kicked in by a steel-tipped police boot. The blockade, however, held ground and the elderly man remained in his home.

This emergent infrastructural politics of the poor is not only comprised of street protests but also activities that arise from daily life in townships and shack settlements, such as building without a permit or disabling state electricity meters. In this way Monique and other residents characterize living on the pavement of the N2 Gateway—what would prove a long, hard time for many—as a mode of representing themselves in their appeal for permanent housing. Monique lived on Symphony Way in a two-room shack, which she constructed from collected scrap materials: cloth-advertisements, a plastic sail, wood planks, and a patterned linoleum floor. Inside was kitchen and sitting area, carefully fitted with Styrofoam counter-tops, a *bakki* (pickup truck) seat couch with mauve and green ruffled pillows, and window curtains.

From the early weeks, tire blockades (sometimes burning) were set up on either side the settlement so that police vehicles could not enter. A crèche, community kitchen, vegetable garden, and children's day camp were launched, run by volunteers. A night watch patrolled until the early hours to serve as protection, especially from the hazard of unattended fires or candles. Residents held mass community meetings every night. In addition to marches in the Cape Town city center, residents organized soccer tournaments and informal theater about pavement life. As word of their land occupation spread, they hosted journalists and activists from across South Africa and the globe, and their story was broadcast by a spectrum of print and television news from the *Guardian* to *Al Jazeera*. Through these practices Symphony Way visibly asserted, from the "slums" hidden from view in the city, struggles over urban space between the poor and public-private partners in development. This infrastructural politics suggests how residents appeal to formalized institutions: through constitutional clauses and existing housing policies in the courts, and through informal activities conducive to particular infrastructural norms.

Symphony Way and the Delft transit camp at the N2 Gateway Project, examined in relation to each other, demonstrate that the informal spatial practices of the poor produce infrastructure that have shaped—and continues to shape—urban space in contemporary South Africa. These practices, moreover, have transformed under liberal democratization. Infrastructural politics melds old and new spatial practices that make the poor visible within the city, not toward the end of policing but toward the end of staking a citizenship claim upon space in the city. In the postapartheid period, "slum elimination" in Cape Town and other cities has meant the eviction of shack dwellers close to urban centers and their relocation to undesirable sites on the periphery, which they cannot afford or where they have little incentive to remain. While transit camps are posited as more efficient sites of surveillance and policing (as well as the maintenance of the biological welfare of "slum" populations), the transit camp in Delft suggests how these sites achieve the opposite of what policy intended.

Figure 4 Shacks constructed on Symphony Way in a protest and land occupation at the N2 Gateway Project. Source: Kerry Ryan Chance, Delft, South Africa, 2008.

Since 2012 the government has secured the eviction of 20,000 families from the Joe Slovo shack settlement in Langa for relocation to Delft. At times, including in court cases, Joe Slovo residents have joined forces with the AEC in Delft. Residents (some of whom have lived in Joe Slovo for more than two decades) appealed their removal in the Constitutional Court. The court called for negotiations. These are still in progress, many years and street protests later, which have included renewed violent clashes with police.[42] As for Monique and her neighbors, following another protracted legal battle they were removed from Symphony Way. Some scattered to other townships and shack settlements on the Flats, while others were placed in transit camps. Those who remain are still collectively demanding permanent residence in Delft, though the AEC has largely demobilized.

42 Residents' proposed plans include in situ upgrades and interim basic services where they live, which reaffirms some of the principles set out in BNG policy.

Slum as Infrastructure

Thubelisha has been declared insolvent, after facing corruption charges in the Western Cape and other provinces. However, some officials report that transit camp construction has been scaled back amid the public pressure exerted by residents like Monique and her neighbors.

Whether on the streets, in the courts, or in global media flows, poor residents inhabit visible political roles from the margins of the city. Their production of new spatial forms of citizenship and identity redefine infrastructure at the intersections of race and class. Contrary to utopian or apocalyptic representations of "slums," which cast residents as laying in wait for the developmental state or undermining it, these are places of thriving political and legal life, with complex histories that reveal the contradictions of lived experience when juxtaposed with neat distinctions of formal and informal space. As Monique said the last time I saw her before she disappeared from Symphony Way, "The reason I think I should stay [on the pavement] is because I'm a citizen and have a right to a home. Also, it's about the future of my child.... I never want her to live in a shack or any another such structure again."[43]

43 Personal communication, May 21, 2008.

Political Ground and Spatial Stakes in Ho Chi Minh City, Vietnam

Anh-Thu Ngo

We were a ragtag motorbike gang, cruising in the midday heat amid a land of rubble in Saigon, Vietnam.[1] We were not looking for anything specific, just surveying the state of things in an area of the city's District 2 that had been flattened in the past few years in order for a "New Urban Zone" to be built. We rounded a corner near the entrance to the former Thủ Thiêm ferry that carried passengers to and from the central business area of District 1. On one side of the street, some residents in post-lunch stupor sat on plastic chairs in front of their modest homes, staring at the razed lot across the way. Rocks and debris were strewn everywhere. A boulder read, "Sunrise Café has moved," followed by a phone number. We stopped our bikes. The leader of the group spotted joss

1   Funding for this research came from the Fulbright IIE US Student Program and the Wenner-Gren Foundation Dissertation Fieldwork Grant.

Figure 1   Saigon's synchronous and differential spatial development. Ad hoc shack communities line the city's canals, new apartments rise behind them, and a billboard advertises technology to enhance leisure and enjoyment. Source: Anh-Thu Ngo, 2012.

sticks scattered on the ground, swept them up, and passed them around to each member. We lit them and planted them in the dirt, as Vietnamese people do to honor the dead at a gravesite. To break the silence that followed, someone half-joked, "It's performance art." The act was in the spirit of the group's modus operandi, conducting happenings in makeshift manner as expression apart from institutional art.

The scene played out like a well-staged production. From our vantage point, we had a view of the budding skyscrapers of District 1, with their branded façades, juxtaposed against the wasteland that was Thủ Thiêm in District 2, on our side of the Saigon River. Across the way in the background, the newly erected 68-story Bitexco Financial Tower soared in phallic emblem of Saigon's rise to cosmopolitanism. Farther down the street, where we were, a lone wall stood sentinel. Other parts of what was once a house lay in a pile around it. A Magritte-like window of negative space remained in the wall, its shutters nowhere to be seen. The opening framed the demolition crane that approached. It seemed to wheel toward us in slow motion. "Who has a video camera? Someone should have brought a camera." One of the guys in the group, who was always photographing, whipped out his point-and-shoot. As we stood watching, the truck's lumbering yellow arm swung at the wall, sending plumes of dust into the air, showing no mercy to an opponent who had already surrendered.

Figure 2 Remnants of demolition on the District 2 side of the Saigon River. Meanwhile, high rises such as the symbolic Bitexco Tower soar across the way in District 1. Source: Anh-Thu Ngo, 2012.

I made this outing with a band of artists whom I will call CODE, short for "Call On Demolition Experts." The group's name takes inspiration from the advertisements plastered on walls around the city announcing demolition services. From the time we were introduced, I had become interested in the ideas voiced by Linh, the de facto leader of the group.[2] He was eager for CODE to engage with the changes of the city. CODE was a loose collective of creative people with a stake in opening up possibilities of expression in a country where such articulation was restricted by an authoritarian regime and the relative lack of infrastructural support for contemporary art practices. The challenge was figuring out how and in what ways the group could do so.

The moment with the joss sticks was a spontaneous way to bear witness—a mundane passing gesture that would not register anywhere else. Its significance lay in the context of its enactment: the endeavors of Linh and

2   The names of group members have been changed.

CODE to find a home base from which to create responses to Saigon's developments. Such efforts, in relation to the government's steamroller of spatial reordering, open up the realm of the political and offer glimpses of emergent civic agency. This engagement is distinct from the antagonistic patterns of citizen protests over government-backed land grabs that increasingly make headlines. It sidesteps the locked-horns mode of encounter between state-business alliances and concerned citizens looking for opportunities to assert both financial and political claims. CODE's activities make up a different kind of discourse. Still, the process of seeking expressive and creative space (both abstract and concrete) is a political endeavor. Although it does not advance on the typical spaces of politics, such pursuit broadens our consideration of these realms—an important tactical and epistemological move in relation to the entrenched monopoly on power and space in Vietnam. In this way we might consider, and therefore give analytic legitimation to, everyday citizens' practices that push against the hegemony of state forces.

In broad terms, politics is a contest of power. Conventionally, politics is the reserve of suited officials. It is the stuff of news cycles and ballot boxes. Because entities like media or government or corporations often dictate the terms of political debate, they retain control over depictions of power claims. Seldom does the creativity that artists express garner attention as political acts. But the will to stand one's ground and to have a stake in the spaces of daily life grows apart from familiar headlines in the sphere of politics. To make new meaning of a space, in a way in which such significance is not endorsed widely, is to contest the power to value it in a political manner.

Theorist Henri Lefebvre provides a useful framework for shifting our epistemological orientation to account for a politics where space is not merely a pre-given container in which lives unfold.[3] Actors produce space in multiple configurations through their social activities, values, and perceptions. With this view, we can regard space with eyes alert to the complex arrangements that render everyday environments so seemingly natural. By extension, we pay attention in a different manner to potential subjects of analysis as worthy grist for the academic mill.

In Vietnam, the state has exerted much effort to control spaces as a project of incorporating the citizenry into an independent, unified nation in the 20th century. Citizens' relationships to land emerge from a particular legacy of communist spatial ordering practices. Amid this background, we can understand the potential for liberation or lack of subversion vis-à-vis state agendas by

3 Henri Lefebvre's writings have had widespread influence on researchers' approaches to thinking about space. Drawing on Lefebvre's work, geographers like David Harvey and Edward Soja also take a materialist view of social interactions, emphasizing agents engaged in relations of spatial production. These scholars provide expanded matrices for conceptualizing space. Generally, their models include divisions along perceptual, representational, and experiential categories, or efforts to reconcile physical and psychical divides in spatial epistemologies. These rubrics are helpful in calling attention to the typological multiplicity of spaces. With spatial concepts foregrounded, however, what should be concomitant concern for temporality often remains out of focus. Henri Lefebvre, *The Production of Space*, trans. Donald Nicholson-Smith (1974; Oxford: Blackwell, 1991); David Harvey, *Spaces of Global Capitalism: Towards a Theory of Uneven Geographical Development* (New York: Verso, 2006); and Edward Soja, *Postmodern Geographies: The Reassertion of Space in Critical Social Theory* (New York: Verso, 1989).

Figure 3 Multimedia art event in Ho Chi Minh City. CODE members light candles as political protest against police action. Source: Anh-Thu Ngo, video still, 2011.

examining citizens' mundane activities. For example, looking at a day in the social life of the art group CODE gives us a picture of the spatial negotiations that can gain importance as the realm of politics expands in Vietnam, through citizens' increasing challenges to state power and through analysts' broadened consideration of these nascent acts.

SPATIAL PRACTICES: A HISTORY

Those who look for Saigon on a contemporary map of Vietnam will not find it. The place appears as a prominent dot on the lower curve of the s-shaped country, marked as "Ho Chi Minh City." After their war victory against the American-backed Southern regime of the Republic of Vietnam, officials of the new Socialist Republic of Vietnam merged the existing Sài Gòn and nearby Chinese community of Chợ Lớn with the surrounding Gia Định Province in 1976 under the name of "Thành Phố Hồ Chí Minh" (or TP. HCM, Ho Chi Minh City), in honor of the Communist Party's revolutionary leader.[4] Such an act reveals the Party's eagerness to bring this former capital of the old regime into the communist fold, to remake an enemy region in accordance with the ideological ambition of the new unified state. In unofficial parlance, the city's denizens refer to it by the former name of "Sài Gòn" still, sometimes invoking this same designation to mean the central business area of District 1 as well. The difference between official appellation and

4 Hồ Chí Minh (the most salient of several pseudonyms for the man born as Nguyễn Sinh Cung) was prime minister (1945–1955) and president (1945–1969) of the Democratic Republic of Vietnam (North Vietnam).

everyday reference carries the weight of collective memory. Imaginaries of old hold, laying bare the gap between political design and lived experience.

The political act of renaming was not limited to the city itself. It extended to the streets throughout the country. The names reference designated national heroes of Vietnam's struggles against the oppressive rule of foreign forces throughout its history. As anthropologist Michael Herzfeld has pointed out of such practices in general, "the commemorative naming of streets illustrates the shift from indexical relations to iconic homogenization through the spatialized construction of a collective, heroic ancestry."[5] The task of rebuilding a nation in the worldview of the victors has to do as much with appointing the appropriate repertoire of signifiers available to the public as it has to do with laying pipes and foundations. To have citizens invoke the heroic ancestors in daily speech that refers to spaces of social conduct and exchange is to activate this pantheon as *the* viable (as in living and lived) archive. Bound in such a way through these spirits, the citizenry must remember that this land is made of the ancestors' sacrifice and is lived on in their name. (Of course, the heroes of old will be no more.) This revisionist historiography writ large asserts a lineage that binds together the communist heroes with prehistoric and even some monarchic figures deemed worthy of upholding the narrative of a triumphantly independent Vietnam,[6] able to defend against foreign invaders such as the Chinese, French, and Americans.[7]

5   Michael Herzfeld, "Political Optics and the Occlusion of Intimate Knowledge," *American Anthropologist* 107, no. 3 (2005): 370.

6   The monarchy, particularly the last reigning Nguyễn dynasty, represented feudal forces antithetical to the revolutionary cause. Its hierarchic, tradition-bound structure was part of the oppressive apparatus that the revolutionary ideal sought to obliterate. The revolutionary leaders were ambivalent about the last reigning Nguyễn monarch, Bảo Đại, who was seen as both a puppet of the French colonizers and a potential ally with the clout to win the allegiance of the central provinces for the unification of the country. As for dynasties long gone, select kings made the cut for commemoration, as their names grace street signs to remind posterity of their valiant contributions to Vietnamese history.

7   The practice of erasing pasts through new naming and new building has been part of the long, palimpsestic history of the region. For example, the area that is now Saigon was swampland around a Khmer village called Prey Nokor. The 17th-century Viet (or Kinh, the majority ethnic group in Vietnam) expansion into Khmer areas in the Mekong Delta slowly cut off the latter population from fellow Khmer in present-day Cambodia, thus rendering the Khmer around the Delta a minority group within the borders of what would become Vietnam.

8   The others are China, Cuba, Laos, and North Korea.

9   Many of my peer interlocutors in Saigon did not know the historical significance of the people after whom the streets we traversed were named. A well-read friend raised this issue when he "quizzed" a fellow companion about various referents as we crossed major intersections on motorbike: not knowing the "answers," the fellow traveler received a mini history lecture.

10   Kim Ninh, *A World Transformed: The Politics of Culture in Revolutionary Vietnam, 1945–1965* (Ann Arbor: University of Michigan Press, 2002), 125.

The Communist Party of Vietnam holds power as one of five remaining single-party socialist states worldwide.[8] Its attempts to tightly control the historical narrative that arguably has rendered a generation of young Vietnamese apathetic to the lessons of that biased history.[9] Today, some street signs appear with details including birth and death years and a brief biographical reference to "explain" the figure named. The state's effort to clarify and uphold the relevance of street names for the population indicates that political exertions have to be maintained and adjusted continually, to align intended agendas with the civic experience of those plans. It also highlights the high stakes of political control over the spaces of the citizenry—even spaces as seemingly mundane as the streets of everyday life.

With the August Revolution of 1945, the communist agenda to build a new country rested on upending the old social order and legitimizing claims to authority. Spatial reallocation was an integral part of this process. In their endeavor to remake society and rid it of old hierarchies, the Vietnamese communists prioritized land reform. They seized properties in the name of the common cause and fairer reapportioning by authorities. Plans for the redistribution of land in the early 1950s expanded into policies for collectivized agricultural production by the end of that decade. During this phase, politics infiltrated at the neighborhood and village level, as communist team leaders spearheaded the effort to "catch the roots, string the beads."[10] This expression refers to the work of cadres to convert the broad peasant base in order to undermine and overthrow the bourgeois landholding class. They embedded themselves in villages to "catch the roots," or pinpoint peasants likely to set an example by informing on their purportedly abusive landlords. In practice, the land seizure and attendant targeting of "class enemies" not only alienated many of the wealthy or middle class supporters of the communist cause for national liberation but resulted in brutality and starvation as well. Later, communist officials offered an apology for the errors of land reform.[11] With the 1975 victory over the South, spatial ordering policies focused on de-urbanization by moving city populations to New Economic Zones in the hinterlands and garden zones on the urban fringes, where citizens were to participate in collectivized agricultural production with the aim of creating surplus for other areas.[12] The surplus never materialized, and many families started to repopulate urban areas by the early 1980s in search of jobs.

These radical transitions in land tenure emphasize a history where the twinning of politics and space is purposive. In a context where interpretations of Marxist-Leninist ideology have structured society for decades, the spatial and materialist approach to rule is evident. During their rise to power, the Vietnamese communists recognized that agricultural cooperatives were a way to restructure state-society relations and thus were part and parcel of building legitimacy.[13] In order to realign means of production, the leaders had to make certain spatial

11 Thaveeporn Vasavakul, "Vietnam: The Changing Models of Legitimation," in *Political Legitimacy in Southeast Asia: The Quest for Moral Authority*, ed. Muthiah Alagappa (Palo Alto, CA: Stanford University Press, 1995), 267.

12 Patrick W. Naughton, "Agricultural System Adjustments in Vietnam: 1975–81," *Agricultural Systems* 12 (1983): 113–23; and William Turley, "Urban Transformation in South Vietnam," *Pacific Affairs* 49, no. 4 (1977): 607–24.

13 Vasavakul, "Vietnam," 262.

claims. The vision for a new Vietnam entailed a reimagining of the social order as well as of land. A clearance of physical and psychic space needed to take place. A metaphor used in a 1945 document calling for "A New Culture" signals the interwoven nature of the political, the social, and the spatial: "As in other spheres, the task of construction in the cultural arena has to begin with destruction: for a new culture to develop, it needs a cleared piece of land that contains no vestiges of feudalism or colonialism."[14]

14   Nguyễn Hữu Đang and Nguyễn Đình Thi, "Một nền văn hóa mới" (Hanoi, 1945), quoted in Ninh, *A World Transformed.*

If fundamental spatial claims provide legitimacy to the state, Party leaders recognize that continual adjustment has to be made in these claims. The utopic plans for land reform and the attendant social revolution were lofty goals but in practice, left the nation hungry and scarred. Acknowledging that land reform and collectivization had steeped the population in poverty, the Party turned to market-oriented Renovation, or Đổi Mới, in 1986. In fits and starts, production and capital flows increased, and by the mid-2000s Vietnam was dubbed a new "tiger economy," sustaining the highest growth rates within Southeast Asia until the global downturn of 2008.[15]

15   See Jonathan Pincus and Vu Thanh Tu Anh, "Vietnam: A Tiger in Turmoil," *Far Eastern Economic Review* (May 2008), http://www.moj.gov.vn/vbpq/en/Lists/Vn%20bn%20php%20lut/View_Detail.aspx?ItemID=8269.

CONTEMPORARY SPATIAL POLITICS

As the country's economic system shifted, HCMC/Saigon got a facelift. Benefitting especially from American rapprochement and the return of imports in the mid-1990s, Vietnam's business center is in the process of transforming. Authorities began by clearing out shacks that had sprung up on the edges of the city's canals. In District 1, businesses decked selected streets in the garb of luxury branding. New office spaces, air-conditioned malls, and condominiums proliferate within the urban landscape. Politicans endeavor to create conditions amenable to business interests and in the process, line their own pockets. The capacity to rename or redraw boundaries, update or install infrastructure, and retrofit, raze, or erect buildings comes in exchange for envelopes of kickback money. With government and business in cahoots, authority over spatial configurations remains in certain elite echelons. The hierarchies of old that communist ideology sought to overturn originally have sedimented anew.

Present-day developments entail a whole system premised on vestiges of land allocation bureaucracy. Even as the state relinquishes its hold over sectors of enterprise, legal and nominal claim to owning all land is important for solidifying exclusive control of power. The fundamental underpinning—that all land is used at government discretion—still pervades transactions around property. The state administers land use rights to people and businesses, including leases to foreign entities, for varied durations (sometimes up to 99 years).[16] With transforming development goals, the government wants to stimulate economic activity (especially in the real estate sector) and encourage multinational companies to enter the market. However, the regulations around land and building use

16 See Socialist Republic of Vietnam Ministry of Justice, 2003 Land Law, http://www.moj.gov.vn/vbpq/en/Lists/Vn%20bn%20php%20lut/View_Detail.aspx?ItemID=8269.

are opaque, and enforcement is even more tangled a process. These circumstances at once enable property owners' maneuverability and put them at the mercy of government officials who can demand payment for accommodating services (in deed transfers, for example). Vaguely worded or discrepant laws have not been reconciled enough to ensure transparency or functional legal recourse.

In part due to such circumstances, citizen protests over land seizure have been making the news for the past few years throughout the country and in the international media.[17] Undeniably, such civic acts of assembly are an important resurgence in Vietnam, where the government has to maintain the delicate balance of retaining its exclusive authority while demonstrating to international stakeholders (such as foreign investors) that its citizens possess certain basic freedoms. Still, the pattern of protests is predictable. Citizens gather in demonstration as tensions mount over issues like fair compensation or coercive eviction. The police rein in the protesters and jail some of them to make an example of people who stick their necks out too far. These cycles have not yet radically altered the power gradient of civic engagement. Some researchers are optimistic about the implications of citizen pushback against the government in the context of urban development.[18] The potential of such acts to shift government practices systemically remains to be seen, however.

Whereas studies of Western governmentality attain cogency in laying bare the subtle penetration of state

17 For example, see http://www.rfa.org/english/news/vietnam/protest-10092012173911.html and http://www.bloomberg.com/news/2013-12-08/vietnam-tightens-land-seizure-law-after-protests-southeast-asia.html.

18 Annette Kim, "Talking Back: The Role of Narrative in Vietnam's Recent Land Compensation Changes," *Urban Studies* 48, no. 3 (2011): 493–508; and Andrew Wells-Dang, "Political Space in Vietnam: A View from the 'Rice-Roots,'" *Pacific Review* 23, no. 1 (2010): 93–112.

power in diverse nooks of society,[19] the brick-and-mortar manifestation of bureaucratic socialism in Vietnam is readily apparent. Straight-faced, uniformed officials march through the rooms of ward, district, municipal, and provincial offices with unflinching authority to wield red stamps at their discretion. Developing the idea of governmentality as a spatialized force, Akhil Gupta and James Ferguson point to the images of verticality and encompassment that accompany notions of state-society relations and show how these spatializing metaphors manifest in mundane practice.[20] So explicit is the role of government in all aspects of Vietnamese life, however, that it is personified rather than abstracted as spatial metaphor. In my conversations with Saigonese interlocutors, reference to the government or state took the form of the third-person pronoun (ông = old man; tụi nó = they, informal), where state powers were not imagined as above the populace (as in the verticality paradigm) but rather as an embodied individual or group of individuals. The history of state insinuation into the pores of neighborhood and village existence might account for such difference in Vietnamese imaginaries. The "greedy" landlord, bureaucrat, or developer attains personality and individuality in confrontational discourse, as Annette Kim has shown in analyzing narratives of land disputes in Vietnam.[21] With this kind of personification, the Party apparatus largely remains apart from criticism, as antagonisms play out in tête-à-tête style. This move might be considered strategic, in that it allows actors to gain

19   Graham Burchell, Colin Gordon, and Peter Miller, eds., *The Foucault Effect: Studies in Governmentality* (Chicago: University of Chicago Press, 1991).

20   James Ferguson and Akhil Gupta, "Spatializing States: Toward an Ethnography of Neoliberal Governmentality," *American Ethnologist* 29, no. 4 (2002): 981–1002.

21   Kim, "Talking Back."

ground without being stifled at-large for the grave crime of anti-government propaganda. However, it also confines the terms of debate to case-by-case resolution. It enables the hegemonic structure to remain intact.

SPATIAL CLAIMS AND AGENCY: A RECONSIDERATION

Sidestepping these explicit political spaces for a moment, might we consider the relationship of space and politics in expanded form by taking stock of nascent modes of expressing agency in a setting within which such display is highly regulated and even censored?[22] In HCMC/Saigon, spaces are continually in-the-making. The discursive divide inherent in the invocation of the city itself reflects a parallel, psychic differentiation in which "they" (government officials, developers, the "other" holding power) have control over the spatial and material configuration of HCMC's areas, while Saigon as lived and remembered takes on different (thought not altogether distinct) contours. If the planning and development seem to lead inevitably to generic skyscrapers and gated communities for people of means, then other citizens' claims to the future of the city matter. "These seething forces are still capable of rattling the lid of the cauldron of the state and its space, for differences can never be totally quieted," writes Lefebvre.[23] Of the state's rendering of spaces, he elaborates:

> [I]n addition to being a means of production it is also a means of control, and hence of domination,

22 Wells-Dang's "rice-roots" analysis of political space in Vietnam serves as a model for this approach. See Wells-Dang, "Political Space."

23 Lefebvre, *The Production of Space*, 23.

of power; yet, that, as such, it escapes in part from those who would make use of it. The social and political (state) forces which engendered this space now seek, but fail, to master it completely; the very agency that has forced spatial reality towards a sort of uncontrollable autonomy now strives to run it into the ground, then shackle and enslave it.[24] With an autonomy that stands apart from the state's spatial determination, Saigon's spaces of tomorrow harbor potential, depending on who activates and makes claims over such domains.

Geographer Doreen Massey provides a useful definition for space upon which to build notions of political agency. Massey offers three propositions for considering space: (1) "space as the product of interrelations"; (2) space as "contemporaneous plurality," as "coexisting heterogeneity"; and (3) "space as always under construction, ... as a simultaneity of stories-so-far."[25] In this framework, temporality is part and parcel of a spatial conception. The making of spatial configurations and imaginaries is dependent on overlapping or shifting scales of time. Massey's view allows for coterminous possibilities as well as space-time boundaries that extend variously. This position allows us to complicate the rigidity of fixed spaces and timeframes by considering the multiple time horizons that inhere in various agents' claims to spaces. The protests over eviction and land compensation in Vietnam register as eventful, but what of other timeframes within spatial claims? Ordinarily, the lived

24 Ibid., 26.

25 Doreen Massey, *For Space* (London: Sage Publications, 2005), 9.

experience of daily routines—navigating well-worn paths and socializing in the realm of the personal and familial—is taken for granted and rendered apolitical. By discounting the political stakes of everyday life, we do not call into question or reexamine what might be otherwise. We do not take stake in the routinized conditions that those in power have established to uphold their legitimacy. To expand our regard of the political, we must scrutinize other modes of spatial claims as acts of civic agency. To take seriously the political aspects of daily life is to expand notions of what can be considered worthy of attention, demoting the usual suspects and perhaps democratizing the process by which we think ourselves political agents, making claims to physical and psychic spaces.

Agency, to be clear, is distinct from empowerment. While mention of agency might imply laudable self-determination, the concept should not be conflated with empowerment.[26] "Empowerment" is often part of a discourse that can obscure the differential capacities of actors through an elision of the subject-object divide in favor of the asserted moral inviolability of the term itself.[27] Too often, "empowerment" as a term is taken at surface value, as the moral end of discussion. If we press with questions, "Who is being empowered?," "By whom?," "In what ways?," "For what ends?," we end up with an altogether different sense of achievement of liberating ideals. If we pay analytical attention to shifting engagements, we might form a picture of the structural

26   For a nuanced discussion of the anthropological projects of interpretation about self-determination, see Webb Keane, "Self-Interpretation, Agency, and the Objects of Anthropology: Reflections on a Genealogy," *Comparative Studies in Society and History* 45, no. 2 (2003): 222–48.

27   For a critique of buzzwords such as "empowerment" in development policy, see Karen Brock and Andrea Cornwall, "What Do Buzzwords Do for Development Policy? A Critical Look at 'Participation,' 'Empowerment' and 'Poverty Reduction,'" *Third World Quarterly* 26, no. 7 (2005): 1043–60.

lower limit to civic agency in the face of increasing government control.[28] When does agency matter? As scholars, when we assert that subjects of study express agency, we have to consider to what degree such self-determination means a shifting of the power gradient. Certainly, then, we cannot be glib about agency as empowerment.

In Vietnam, civic agency is structured by a discernible relationship to communist legacies of tight regulation over the appropriation of spaces. Even if agency cannot be conflated with empowerment, the roots of power are embedded in particular assertions of agency. To have agency is to have an important baseline on which to build power, even if it is not a guarantee of it. Certain forms of agency are meaningful alternatively, because they are not overt or recognizable challenges to government exertions.[29] They are not as visible a threat to state power as is, for example, citizen assembly for demonstrations. Beyond the highly visible cases of land protests, other forms of spatial claims have potential to be pathways to empowerment. They might have the capacity to shift the terms of spatial negotiation beyond a certain structural impasse.

CODE AND STAKES IN THE FUTURE OF THE CITY

The land in Thủ Thiêm had been in a limbo state for a few years, with about 85 percent of residents cleared out by early 2010.[30] Hundreds of families remained, however, making their lives amid rubble and debris. Thủ Thiêm is a section in the easternmost part of the city, separated

28 Here, I use "limit" in the mathematical sense, to indicate the persistence of agency even under a concept of infinite government power. People express themselves in everyday ways even if government exerts "totalitarian" control.

29 An example of such a form includes Mandy Thomas' demonstration of the disappearance of the public at formal state events and an increase of the public's use of spaces such as parks and squares in informal fashion. Mandy Thomas, "Out of Control: Emergent Cultural Landscapes and Political Change in Urban Vietnam," *Urban Studies* 39, no. 9 (2002): 1611–624.

30 Erik Harms, "Beauty as Control in the New Saigon: Eviction, New Urban Zones and Atomized Dissent in a Southeast Asian City," *American Ethnologist* 39, no. 4 (2012): 739. For a discussion of the temporality of Thủ Thiêm's development, see Erik Harms, "Eviction Time in the New Saigon: Temporalities of Displacement in the Rubble of Development," *Cultural Anthropology* 28, no. 2 (2013): 344–68.

Figure 4 Empty field transformed for a wedding celebration. CODE members create an arch and lighted pathway for the bride and groom with found materials. Source: Anh-Thu Ngo, 2012.

Figure 5 Performance art. Attendees set ablaze an oversized teapot, traditionally used in wedding tea ceremonies to honor relatives and ancestors, at the end of the night. Source: Anh-Thu Ngo, 2012.

from District 1 by the Saigon River. For years it was mostly swampland. Professionals in the planning and construction industries talked of its spontaneous settlement and the need for more concerted governance. They conveniently glossed over the reality that neighborhoods had long thrived there—enough so for the installation of fixtures such as temples and ward offices. Plans had been in the works for more than a decade for the development of this neglected area, a neighborhood especially appealing to planners given its proximity to District 1. Thủ

Thiêm was slated to be Saigon's new green economic zone, with planners' and developers' visions for profit adorning brochures and billboards, heralding "civilization" to come. With the opening in late 2011 of a tunnel allowing motorbike and car passage from District 1 to Thủ Thiêm, and since other parts of District 2 were flourishing as expatriate enclaves, the transformation seemed underway finally.

When I raised the topic of urban change with Linh, he took the opportunity to air his many grievances about the course of transformations in the city. Immediately he pointed to Thủ Thiêm as a zone that needed to be considered. I had taken rides throughout the area in 2010, but I did not know many Saigonese who traffic it, unless they lived or worked there. Linh's focus on Thủ Thiêm as a space warranting an art intervention grew during the course of my talks with him. In early 2012, Linh and fellow CODE members convened for conversation to call attention to the group's stakes in the development of Saigon, to recognize that they were involved, as city denizens, even if the plans of developers circulated in another realm.

The members of CODE comprise a group of young creative types, mostly in their 20s and 30s. They hold various jobs in media and design and occasionally gather for self-labeled performance art events. Linh told me in our first meeting that the name reflected the group's deconstructive aims. CODE got together to call things into question and to transgress social norms. They were intent on tearing down the creaky structures of old, even without always knowing what would go up in place of them. Linh liked to convene CODE affiliates at a warehouse space in the outer-lying reaches of Thủ Đức District for spontaneous performances. These events often featured Linh scrawling designs on barely-clothed women. Performance art had been practiced in Vietnam to various ends since the late 1990s, but CODE's audience still engaged in the novelty of overt sexuality during live events. Although other sectors of the small art community did not make much of these body-painting sessions, the group did attract a regular crowd of free-spirited followers who made art, played music, and caroused together. I once asked Linh about the membership of CODE; he responded that it was no one and anyone.[31] CODE was for all who wanted to participate. Linh dismissed the idea that he was in charge of the band of artists—even as he relied on the perception of his name as being synonymous with the group, as a means of finding his moorings within art circles.

On a sunny February morning, I accompanied Linh and about ten other group members to a meeting with the director of the Goethe-Institut in Saigon. CODE wanted to raise funds to find a base from which to launch its projects responding to Thủ Thiêm. To think about the future of Thủ Thiêm was to take on the future of Saigon. CODE members were less concerned with protests over compensation rates for eviction than with what might become of this new city zone. What would develop from

31   In a local newspaper write-up about a "performance" event organized by group members, Linh mentioned that CODE had a membership of about one thousand worldwide. Other CODE affiliates with whom I spoke laughed at this hyperbolic figure. While this particular gathering accommodated more than 100 guests, a more typical attendance at CODE events was 30 to 50 people.

the vast stretches of litter-strewn lots where some people had dug in their heels, bracing for the uncertainty of a transition period? In comparison to District 1's central business district, Thủ Thiêm seemed a derelict stepsibling of a space, where lives were put on pause, families sent packing, homes demolished, and memories scattered in the rubble. CODE members wanted to re-appropriate these scenes and offer opportunities for dialogue on the idea of the changing city. Doing so would provide a chance to respond with ordinary citizens' outlooks and hopes for their future spaces. At the same time, CODE was losing its home base in Thủ Đức. Rent was increasing, and the group did not operate with a budget. CODE needed a new space for gathering and was considering incorporating these circumstances into its project to respond to Thủ Thiêm. CODE members used this opportune moment to look at the possibility of shifting focus to a new mode of engagement. By embedding themselves in the environment of Thủ Thiêm, the group members would take on the notions of living in the rubble of the concrete city as the reality facing Saigon.

The Goethe-Institut is a German nonprofit organization with headquarters worldwide that provide support for arts and cultural initiatives. Its building was tucked into an alley in District 3. The mild-mannered director greeted us in a conference room. CODE had brought a slideshow of pictures of its Thủ Đức activities. Members took turns explaining its general intent and spirit and its aims for Thủ Thiêm. The director received the presentation well. He liked the initiative and promised that support would be forthcoming if CODE could identify specific projects to undertake within certain timeframes. Infrastructure for contemporary art practices (and funding especially) was extremely limited in Saigon, and Vietnam in general. Many artists with whom I spoke complained about the lack of resources, so the Goethe-Institut's positive response to CODE was a small but heartening victory. After the meeting, we sat on the terrace to discuss next steps. The artists tossed around some thoughts about overtaking an empty building as a workspace and exhibition hall, creating a forum for dialogue, and producing participatory videos. Throughout months of my chats with Linh, it had become clear that he had absorbed interesting notions and could talk about grand plans for art interventions. However, his capacity to get CODE organized enough to propose substantial ideas or to execute them was not equally apparent. As conversation died down, someone suggested riding to Thủ Thiêm to take in the place as a group. At the outset of this essay, I described CODE's subsequent gesture of witness, an enactment of ritual among rubble.

The attempt at engaging a nongovernmental organization to fund activities related to CODE's spatial claim over the future of Thủ Thiêm and the ordinary act of paying homage that followed on the group's outing can be considered subversions of the tightly controlled arena of political brinkmanship where citizen protest and official authority confront each other. These mundane, in-process gestures can expand the spaces in which stakes in the future of the city are planted. To engage in dialogue and expression—to take the city on as an art practice and mode of living—is to enact an intervention in and attempt at civic life that is almost entirely lacking in the context of the state's bureaucratic engine. Linh relayed to me that CODE operated by a different logic than some galleries and art spaces around Saigon. In cultural institutions and well-established art settings, the Ministry of Culture would have final say on what materials were appropriate for display at public events and gatherings. CODE could not conceive of artistic and civic participation in the same manner as these other organizations because its aim was to push the boundaries of acceptability. While Article 60 of Vietnam's constitution guarantees a right to artistic creation and criticism, Article 253 of the Penal Code allows for prosecution of those "disseminating debauched cultural products," a vague umbrella phrase that enables officials to exercise authority at whim and that can lead artists to censor themselves or their own work.[32]

A GENEALOGY OF THE RADICAL

Here is where the agency that CODE demonstrates is constrained structurally and cannot be extolled as a form of empowerment (yet). In its recognition of the extensive reach of government in controlling creative endeavors, perhaps it has cordoned off certain spaces of exchange

32   Article 60 of the Constitution reads: "The citizen has the right to carry out scientific and technical research, make inventions and discoveries, initiate technical innovations, rationalize production, engage in literary and artistic creation and criticism, and participate in other cultural activities. The State protects copyright and industrial proprietorship." Article 253 of the Penal Code ("Disseminating debauched cultural products") begins: "1. Those who make, duplicate, circulate, transport, sell or purchase, stockpile decadent books, newspapers, pictures, photographs, films, music or other objects for the purpose of dissemination thereof, or commit other acts of disseminating debauched cultural products in one of the following circumstances, shall be sentenced to a fine of between five million dong and fifty million dong, to non-custodial reform for up to three years or to between six months and three years of imprisonment." See http://www.moj.gov.vn/en/Pages/home.aspx.

and possibility. Further, we might critique CODE's move on the spaces of Thủ Thiêm as opportunistic, particularly since none of the CODE members on the outing lived in District 2. Yet, considering a prevailing mentality of each neighborhood-unto-itself in the diverse communities that make up the urban metropolis, CODE's engagement is an extension beyond the usual spatial imaginary of Saigon. Paradoxically, governance of the Marxist-Leninist variety left many alienated from their land. CODE's attention to Thủ Thiêm sets a model for its conception as an open land, one in which diverse agents can take part, even if the billboards branded with developers' names dominate visually and materially.

On another level, the group's refusal of social boundaries and exclusivity proved an admirable model, especially in the context of a society with deep roots in a Confucian order of hierarchy. But Linh's words echoed certain communist ideals for radicalization and liberation in the mid-20th century. His thoughts on the need for deconstruction, on a clearance of space and on maintaining equality among group members harken to the discourse of communist reformers. Unsurprisingly, he is from a family of northern transplants to Saigon and grew up with the language of the victorious revolutionaries. In this context, an assessment of agency becomes more complicated. Furthermore, the radical ideals stemming from interpretations of Marx were also drivers for European avant-garde circles such as the Surrealists and Situationist International. "The leading surrealists sought to decode inner space and illuminate the nature of the transition from this subjective space to the material realm of the body and the outside world, and thence to social life," remarks Lefebvre.[33] It is no coincidence that Lefebvre's contributions in rethinking space as a nexus of power relations in everyday life is an epistemological effort derived from reading Marx. It is an interpretive agenda that takes seriously the mundane and potentially transformative situations of daily living. His *Critique of Everyday Life*, in which he theorizes the idea of moments in relation to the concept of everyday life, influenced the Situationist International.[34] Its members took their cue from other experimental collectives such as the Surrealists and from readings of Marx to create (performative) "situations" that subverted the capitalist modes pervading everyday life.

Even as Linh and members of CODE have limited exposure to schools of thought in Western modern and contemporary art, and even as their weak English and other foreign language skills preclude them from deep engagement with Euro-American theories, they have become savvy Internet browsers. They investigate and share art and political resources online with regularity and are exploring the idea of art as public practice. While they did not frame their affective and aesthetic urban tour through the Situationists' theory of the *dérive*,[35] their engagement is no less embedded in the politicization of everyday spaces. "Performance" art bears (and even bares) these lineages, alerting us to the multiple valences

33 Lefebvre, *The Production of Space*, 18.

34 Henri Lefebvre, *The Critique of Everyday Life*, trans. John Moore (1961; New York: Verso, 2002).

35 Sometimes translated as a "drift," *dérive* is a practice of urban wandering propelled by a subconscious draw from the surrounding architecture, landscape, and aesthetics. It is an experiment and technique at the same time, with the aim of generating new, authentic experiences that subvert the monotony and predictability of capitalist life.

of the political. Of course, questions of relevance and impact and inclusion always pervade such art practices. But that these ideas are fermenting in Vietnam is something to recognize. When the Ministry of Culture seeks to suppress expressions of sexuality, social deviation, or political subversion, such practices are necessary for alternative considerations of the possible.

Marxist social theory can be deployed for political and epistemological revisions, whereby the same premises can lead to authoritarian policies or the possibility of advocating for more equitable claims to spaces. When we consider politics as everyday presence and spaces as constantly in-the-making, we tap into the elemental insight of the Communist Party's founders in order to turn existing conditions on their head. This theoretical move undermines the monopoly of authorized naming and deciding that seems to inhere in governments, in figures cloaked in officialdom, in those with deep pockets and deeper senses of entitlement. Doing thusly destabilizes the reified, and at times rarefied, events and forms on which politicians and developers build their careers. CODE's alternate space-time engagement with Thủ Thiêm unfolds as a process of asserting rights to the city. These rights might not manifest in actual legal or political clout, but they do enable a sense of participation; they exemplify the staking of claims to new spaces of development.

In examining CODE's engagement with Thủ Thiêm, a two-fold epistemological revision emerges: (1) Politics reimagined and broadened would include the everydayness of contestations of power; and (2) Spaces would be recognized as ever in-the-making, even without blueprints. These paradigms are useful because they allow us to move from a conflict-centered focus to a new way of paying attention. Methodologically, such a framework enables us to shed new light on situations, to be attuned to the ordinary acts that are as much about attempts to reimagine and express anew as they are about exerting one's authority.

In considering the usefulness of "the everyday" as a conceptual basis for contextualizing the possibilities of expanded agency, we might look to design professionals' engagement. In urban studies, Margaret Crawford's ideas on everyday urbanism in Los Angeles, California, altered approaches to design practice.[36] The idea of letting local people and processes determine design principles enshrines the tangled aspects of the everyday as the salient force by which decisions over design and planning should be made. Everyday urbanism demotes the "specialist" designer in favor of populist concerns regarding planning choices. It is a model that urges those within positions of expertise to loosen their grip and open up dialogue about certain spatial practices.

But what are the implications for the "everyday" or "local" people entering into this new conversation? Can

36 Margaret Crawford and John Kaliski, eds., *Everyday Urbanism* (New York: Monacelli Press, 1999).

they count on the resources and prolonged engagement of the experts? The shape-shifting approach of everyday urbanism is a positive attitude to have in responding to lived exigencies, but whose motivations should we consider to have primacy? When an "expert" decides it is time to move on to another type of project, what becomes of the design legacy for that community? In an in-process city such as Saigon, the everyday urbanism approach would undermine politicians' and developers' visions for a Singapore-like urban ideal of generic skyscrapers and pruned street medians. Those with the power to make the city regard their posts as vanguards of civilization, where "civilization" is epitomized in the (b)order-enforcement of planned communities and air-conditioned retail promenades. The possibility of deferring to the masses seems like a far-off ideal when plurality of voices might mean dispersing or delaying the economic returns of politicians and financiers.

All to say, political and cultural contexts of creation matter. Our revised understanding of spatial and political production is a way of knowing, still, that subverts facile state-society divisions, that carries the weight of palimpsestic structures and beliefs, and that questions the relationship between acts of self-determination and empowerment. With this consideration of the interplay of spatial claims and political agency, we can attend with greater sensitivity to the plethora of approaches available in building a city, governing a nation, or simply being with one another.

Politics of
Consensus

A "politics of consensus" privileges collective deliberation and agreement as the ideal or normative goal of political encounters. Framing politics in this way decenters conflict to focus on how norms, principles, and forms of rule are negotiated and established as common interest. When considered along with spaces, contemporary literature raises questions regarding the nature of the "public sphere," how the built environment represents the legitimacy of authorities and the erosion of citizen endorsement, the scales of association and governance needed for accord, and relationships between universal and particular rights. The essays in this section enter this discourse to identify how political spaces bring individuals together and activate (dis)agreements on ethics and power.

In Rwanda's rural hills, Delia Duong Ba Wendel (p. 119) locates reconciliation strategies that co-develop from fictional stories of peace and actual experiences of genocide, to envision a shared future that could take place.

Fallon Samuels Aidoo (p. 153) identifies train stations as critical sites for diverse suburban commuters, who collectively mobilized to preserve this common space and the right to work in 1960s Philadelphia.

Writing from a view high above Nicaragua's capital city, Ryne Clos (p. 185) traces a history of monuments that simulate the consent of the governed in authoritarian regimes obsessed with symbols of power.

The varied spaces of these case studies enact a politics of consensus to represent ideology and aspiration, and to establish grounds (both real and imagined) for collective action. Altogether, they reveal that discerning the common good is an imperfect and iterative process.

ON THE NATURE OF THE "PUBLIC SPHERE"

Arendt, Hannah. *The Human Condition*. Chicago: University of Chicago Press, 1958.
Benhabib, Seyla. "The Embattled Public Sphere: Hannah Arendt, Jürgen Habermas and Beyond."
    Theoria 90 (December 1997): 1–24.
Habermas, Jürgen. "Further Reflections on the Public Sphere." In *Habermas and the Public Sphere*,
    421–61. Edited by Craig Calhoun. Translated by Thomas Burger. Cambridge, MA: MIT Press, 1992.
Sennett, Richard. *The Fall of Public Man*. New York: W. W. Norton & Co., 1974.

ON LEGITIMACY AS A PRECONDITION FOR CONSENT TO GOVERN,
AND SPATIAL REPRESENTATIONS OF POWER

Fraser, Nancy, and Axel Honneth. *Redistribution or Recognition? A Political-Philosophical Exchange*.
    London: Verso, 2003.
Habermas, Jürgen. *The Legitimation Crisis*. Translated by Thomas McCarthy. Boston: Beacon Press,
    1973.
Vidler, Anthony. *The Writing of the Walls*. New York: Princeton Architectural Press, 1987.
Von Hoffman, Alexander. *House by House, Block by Block: The Rebirth of America's Urban
    Neighborhoods*. Oxford: Oxford University Press, 2004.

ON THE SCALES OF ASSOCIATION AND GOVERNANCE NEEDED FOR ACCORD

Davis, Diane E. "Whither the Public Sphere: Local, National and International Influences on the
    Planning of Downtown Mexico City, 1910–1950." *Space and Culture* 7, no. 2 (May 2004): 193–222.
Harvey, David. *Justice, Nature and the Geography of Difference*. Oxford: Blackwell, 1996.
Holston, James, and Arjun Appadurai. "Cities and Citizenship." *Public Culture* 8 (1996): 187–204.
Putnam, Robert D. *Bowling Alone: The Collapse and Revival of American Community*. New York:
    Simon & Schuster, 2000.
Stone, Clarence N. *Regime Politics: Governing Atlanta, 1946-1988*. Lawrence: University Press of
    Kansas, 1989.

ON RELATIONSHIPS BETWEEN UNIVERSALISM AND PARTICULARISM

Barton, Craig E., ed. *Sites of Memory: Perspectives on Architecture and Race*. New York: Princeton
    Architectural Press, 2001.
Hayden, Dolores. *The Grand Domestic Revolution*. Cambridge, MA: MIT Press, 1982.
Rajchman, John, ed. *The Identity in Question*. New York: Routledge, 1995.
Taylor, Charles, ed. *Multiculturalism*. Princeton, NJ: Princeton University Press, 1994.
West, Cornel. "The New Cultural Politics of Difference." *October* 53 (1990): 93–109.

Politics of Consensus

Imagining Spaces of Peace and Conflict in the Rwandan Radio Drama *Musekeweya*

Delia Duong Ba Wendel

On May 26, 2004, fictional stories from *Musekeweya* [moo-say-kay-wayuh] first entered the homes of Radio Rwanda listeners. The timing of the broadcast was purposeful, as the radio drama debuted during the 10th anniversary of the genocide to address the recurrent challenges that violence posed for cohabitation in the country. To confront this difficult past in a manifold present, writers created a liminal reality that strategically omitted references to ethnic groups and specific locations in the country. In place of actually existing conditions, *Musekeweya's* fictional narratives conjure an alternative world in Rwanda's rural countryside, where space, subjectivity, peace, and conflict intimately intertwine. The poetics of *Musekeweya* operate transitively at the intersection of the

Figure 1 "Like those people living there, we live together in our homes and districts; sometimes there is peace and other times sorrowful crying." Excerpt from *Musekeweya*, Episode 1, aired May 26, 2004. Source: Delia Duong Ba Wendel, Rwanda, 2013.

imaginary and the actual, shifting between different scales and contexts, individuals and communities, everyday life and national peacebuilding objectives. At each of these junctures, listeners relate to the lives broadcast over the airwaves through exchanges with their own.

Musekeweya's imagined spaces join lived worlds through a "metonymic peacebuilding process."[1] Metonymy is a literary trope that emphasizes exchange or interaction by developing a relation of similarity between *this* and *that*.[2] Metonymy bridges gaps in domains of signification. As a type of analogy, it is close in definition to metaphor. However, metaphor recodifies meaning, substituting *that* for *this*, whereas metonymy co-constitutes both conceptual domains by referring to associated contexts and reciprocal significations. In the case of *Musekeweya*, metonymy forms a bridge between actually existing Rwandan society and an analogous imagined society through conceptual exchanges in the minds of listeners. A world of peaceful coexistence is co-constituted by both imagined and actual semantic worlds—that is, by the radio drama and the diverse lived experiences of Rwandans. At these intersections, peace does not exist a priori. It is instead approximated by metonymic exchanges that require both displacement (transference of the radio drama narratives to reality) and emplacement (seeing oneself in the lives of imagined others).

Spaces structure these exchanges. In the fictional narratives, archetypal characters are associated with specific

1   This is my own conceptualization of *Musekeweya*'s effects. All observations and analyses are not necessarily shared by the show's organizers. A longer version of this essay appears in my PhD dissertation, and includes additional sections on the writers and actors, the educational strategies of the organizers, and other spatial tropes (home, the wild, bridges, the rural domain) featured in the radio drama. My research in Rwanda was supported by a SSRC International Dissertation Research Fellowship and Harvard Sheldon Fellowship, and facilitated by generous access to the radio drama by Radio La Benevolencija.

2   For Roman Jakobson and Jacques Lacan, metonymy referred to one of many processes in which language and psychology coproduce representational systems for making sense of phenomena not fully formed. For Jakobson, metonymy helped to describe the neuropsychological conditions of aphasia and the types of connections the aphasic makes between her own vocabulary and accepted significations. For Lacan, drawing from earlier definitions by Jakobson and Sigmund Freud, metonymy forms part of the linguistic structure of the unconscious, or how one represents and situates oneself in the world. Roman Jakobson, *Fundamentals of Language* (The Hague: Mouton & Co, 1956), 55–82; and Jacques Lacan, *Ecrits: The First Complete Edition in English*, ed. Bruce Fink, trans. Bruce Fink with Héloïse Fink and Russell Grigg (1957; New York: W.W. Norton & Co, 2006), 412–41.

Imagining Spaces of Peace and Conflict in the Rwandan Radio Drama *Musekeweya* hill communities, conflicts develop from land-based relations, and peace is ritualized in spatial practices. Spaces constitute a representational system at once relational, semiotic, individual, and physical. They exist as situations and locations but also conceptually extend to identify historical experiences, present-day political encounters, and future hopes and concerns. Through processes of displacement and emplacement, listeners and characters alike build worlds that constantly shift in their constellation of references to fictive and real contexts. Exploring the spaces of *Musekeweya* through episode recordings and scripts reveals how an imagined geography orders the signifying world of the radio drama to structure narratives, define conflict, and imagine conditions and norms for peace.[3]

Musekeweya is an educational entertainment program for Rwandans that works to legitimate its peacebuilding strategies and achieve consensus on the means to coexist. The program's status as fiction is clearly identified in every broadcast; the series creator (the organization La Benevolencija) and episode's writer are mentioned by

3   All episode (audio and script) translations from Kinyarwanda are my own.

Figure 2   Child performing as a *Musekeweya* listener. Source: Delia Duong Ba Wendel, Rwanda, 2012.

name. *Musekeweya* is written and acted by Rwandans, who bring life to educational messages they codevelop with a consulting team of professional psychologists. New episodes air weekly in the local language, Kinyarwanda, and are highly popular throughout the country: a recent survey estimated 84 percent of residents living in 28 of Rwanda's 30 districts listen to the show regularly.[4] These findings resonate with the content of fan letters and my interviews with more than 600 listeners in 36 villages throughout the country, to illustrate the ways in which listeners engage with and transpose *Musekeweya*'s narratives. The nature of this reception is paramount to fully appreciating the intentions and effects of *Musekeweya*'s metonymic peacebuilding strategy.

Previous studies of *Musekeweya* have underemphasized the effects of the writing, local language, and space—in short, the construction of the fictions as a whole—on listeners.[5] Shifting to a spatial epistemology of the radio drama underscores the critical importance of a spatial imagination, spatial practices, and spatial tropes to the narratives and to how listeners view the organizers' objectives. Reflecting on this spatial knowledge reveals how a grounded imagination helps to build peace.

AN IMAGINED GEOGRAPHY

Musekeweya is set in two hilltop villages that frame a fertile valley that lies below, dividing them. These Rwandan villages are known by the names Muhumuro and

4   Nora Wegner, "*Musekeweya* 2013 Popularity Survey," Radio La Benevolencija Report, June 2013, unpublished.

5   Suzanne Fisher, "Tuning into Different Wavelengths: Listener Clubs for Effective Rwandan Reconciliation Radio Programmes" (paper, Fourth International Conference on Entertainment-Education and Social Change, Cape Town, South Africa, September 26–30, 2004); Bert Ingelaere, Jean-Bosco Havugimana, and Sylvestre Ndushabandi, "La Benevolencija Rwanda Grassroots Project Evaluation" Radio La Benevolencija Report, August 10 2009, unpublished; Elizabeth Levy Paluck, "Reducing Intergroup Prejudice and Conflict with the Mass Media: A Field Experiment in Rwanda" (PhD diss., Yale University, 2007); Ervin Staub and Laurie A. Pearlman, "Reducing Intergroup Prejudice and Conflict: A Commentary," *Journal of Personality and Social Psychology* 96, no. 3 (2009): 588–93.

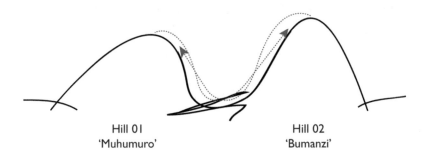

Figure 3   Sectional representation of *Musekeweya's*
imagined geography. Source:
Delia Duong Ba Wendel,
2013.

Hill 01   Hill 02
'Muhumuro'   'Bumanzi'

Bumanzi. Every week, the imagined geography that
separates the two villages is collapsed as the lives of the
village families intertwine in tales of love, friendship,
jealousy, conspiracy, and ultimately, conflict over land.
The two hills have distinct land types: Muhumuro's soils
are less nutrient-rich than Bumanzi's, and the agricultural capabilities of these hills naturalize differences in
their communities' prosperity and morality. The valley is
the most valued space in the serial drama, charged with
potential by the presence of water and consistent agricultural production. In *Musekeweya,* land is the means for
subsistence, the measure of inequality, and that which
was originally shared but presently disputed. At the intersection of the imagined and the actual, *Musekeweya* nar-
rates life worlds so familiar that they might be anywhere
in Rwanda. And yet, ethnicity is noticeably absent from
these conflict narratives.

   Musekeweya's fictions respond to the real challenges
of living together after the 1994 genocide in Rwanda.
Contrary to most news media representations, the

genocide was not the result of some intrinsic ethnic difference. Rather, it was a struggle for power initiated by political elites, who organized mass violence by redeploying a narrative of ethnic disparity. Radio played some role as a popular medium that broadcasted hate propaganda and distributed kill orders before and during the genocide.[6] April 6 to July 14, 1994 was one of many periods of targeted killings that essentialized a Hutu-Tutsi difference through violence, fixing the fluid identities of individuals who commonly identified across ethnic lines through affinities to work, kin, community, region, or class. The estimated 800,000 people that died amounted to more than three-quarters of the Tutsi population in residence and included thousands of Hutu who refused to participate as perpetrators of the genocide.[7] Hundreds of thousands more were raped, wounded, fled their homes in terror, and suffered unspeakable trauma. The killings were local and personal: they occurred in everyday and civic spaces, such as homes, hospitals, government offices, schools, universities, and churches, on a massive scale throughout the country. *Musekeweya* developed in response to these acts. It sought to disassociate conflict from ethnicity and radio from massacres. It operates through the registers of intimacy and large-scale distribution that were characteristics of the genocide and that bring added challenges to peacebuilding strategies which continue in Rwanda today.

Musekeweya's transposition of ethnic conflicts to land disputes is central to its post-genocide peacebuilding

6   The extent to which radio broadcasts caused violence is debated. See Scott Straus, "What Is the Relationship between Hate Radio and Violence? Rethinking Rwanda's 'Radio Machete,'" *Politics & Society* 35, no. 4 (2007): 609–37; Allan Thomson, ed., *The Media and the Rwanda Genocide* (London: Pluto Press, 2007); David Yanagizawa-Drott, "Propaganda and Conflict: Evidence from the Rwandan Genocide," *Quarterly Journal of Economics* 129, no. 4 (2014): 1947–94.

7   Alison Des Forges, *"Leave None to Tell the Story": Genocide in Rwanda* (New York: Human Rights Watch New York, 1999), 6.

strategy. The naturalization of ethnic difference that had so violently divided Rwanda during the genocide is here formed from a different nature: topography. The radio drama registers the specificity of Rwanda's geography even as it subsumes the history of the genocide under an alternative realism of land conflicts. The centrality of land to conflict narratives is highly relevant in Rwanda, the most densely populated country in Africa, where an average of 1,000 people per square mile live together. Topography immediately disturbs the assumed flatness of this abstracted areal unit, providing Rwanda with both a popular reference as the "land of a thousand hills" and a source of critical land scarcity. The common experience of topographic difference—of hills and valleys—lends further credibility to the drama's historical omission. The omission in turn provides some fictive freedom for *Musekeweya*, allowing topography politics to form the basis for an alternative, spatialized, discourse for peace and conflict.

To introduce this alternative discourse, which displaces the preexisting through a foundational metonymic exchange, *Musekeweya* aired its first episode with the following narrator's introduction:

> This evening, I will start to inform you of the story from the hills of Muhumuro and Bumanzi. Like those people living there, we live together in our homes and districts; sometimes there is peace and other times sorrowful crying. It is a long and happy story. Let me start the stories for you all to hear![8]

8 Radio La Benevolencija, *Musekeweya*, Episode 1, introduction, aired May 26, 2004. Trans. from Kinyarwanda by Delia Duong Ba Wendel [D.W.]

Metonymic exchanges rely on contiguity: the semiotic, spatial and/or temporal associations needed to relate concepts. Episode 1 begins with a declaration of psycho-spatial contiguity between the drama's imagined narratives and the lived spaces of Rwandan listeners. The narrator notes the emotional and domestic analogies between these two places (theirs and ours) to establish the stories' relevance to listeners: like those people living there, we [also] live together in our homes with peace and sorrow. The displacement (they are like us) and emplacement (we are like them) evident in the manner in which the hills are introduced is supplemented in subsequent episodes by narratives that focus on the planning and aftermath of attacks from one hill to the other, as well as stories on life and love. Narratives of related emotions and experiences produce the content through which peacebuilding and conflict mediation tools, signs of trauma, and motives for violence are conveyed and understood. Critically, the lack of a visual register in the radio drama requires listeners to fill a significant gap in the construction of the alternative narrative's relevance.

"Spatial figures"—spatial tropes and imagined spaces that signify beyond the literal—bridge these gaps to form powerful metonymic exchanges. The term "spatial figure" here specifies a category of spatial motifs that work as figures of speech in the drama. Spatial figures require narratives for their meaning. Colloquialisms such as "*yari mu Mbyo*" and "*ndi ku gasozi*" exemplify everyday uses of spatial figures in Rwanda. Briefly, *yari mu Mbyo* literally translates as "he was in Mbyo," but here Mbyo is both a specific place in Rwanda and a toponym for wilderness, such that if he were in Mbyo he was nowhere, or in the bush and alone. Similarly, *ndi ku gasozi* translates as "I am on the small hill" but connotes emplacement in unfavorable situations such as poverty, despair, or misfortune. These are widely used idioms that employ spatial figures (*Mbyo*/wild place and *agasozi*/small hill) as spatial referents for subjectivity. Although the former may constitute metonymy and the latter, metaphor (indeed, various spatial figures referenced in the radio drama form from different tropes), the second-order function of these spatial figures is to construct metonymic exchanges between fiction and reality. Spatial figures are constructed from (actual and conceptual) spaces and (vernacular and fictive) narratives to establish relationships between individuals, landscapes, and domains of signification.

In Episode 2, we learn that Muhumuro and Bumanzi were originally one community. Through women's gossip and a father's bedtime story, we are told that ill-informed government representatives intervened to separate them into two administrative areas in 1920. We are not told why the authorities did this, only that the government claimed ownership of the valley and gave exclusive farming rights to Bumanzi residents. Though colonialism is never explicitly named, 1920 effectively associates the event to a period when Belgium consolidated its control over Rwanda and Burundi (1919–1924). At the beginning of the episode, two central female characters try to ascertain who else knows this origin story, which is clearly not common knowledge: the origins of the villages' conflicts have long been eclipsed by entrenched feelings of inequity and anger. The episode concludes with the questions of a petulant child trying to make sense of why his neighbors fight. The boy is lulled to sleep by his patient father, who recalls the history of the communities' conflicts. The scenes' intimacy amplifies the importance of this information with emotion, while conveying the spiraling nature of the hills' conflicts. No longer referential to their origin, fighting between the hills is fueled by an accumulated history of injury and righteous recourse to violence. These scenes allow us to identify distance as a spatial figure. In the sonic spaces of the radio drama, an elastic distance governs intimacy and rumor transmission. Political distance marks government decisions as out-of-place and out-of-touch with rural localities, and a temporal distance sequesters the origins of the communities' conflicts to a particular time and place to relinquish residents of full blame for the drama that arises thereafter. The collapse of emotional distance in the scenes draws listeners in to intensely experience the grief of the characters in the aftermath of the conflicts. The characters' temporal distance from the actions of authoritative others provides listeners with a believable scapegoat for the communities' conflicts. The sources of unequal and unfair conditions are historical *and* external to the communities, and the result of a mismatch between local dynamics and governmental policies.

Figure 4 The valley as resource and source of conflict in Rwanda. Source: M. Ibarra, 1995.

When this distancing strategy is considered in relation to the actual history of conflicts in Rwanda, it raises important questions as to the possibility and efficacy of associating blame to structural conditions alone. For the radio drama organizers, the transposition of ethnicity to land conflicts and the incorporation of historical distance in the conflict narrative is critical to opening up a future space-time, even while it problematically leaves the past behind. Contextualized thus, *Musekeweya* characters cannot be fully blamed for their actions. For listeners, this is a subject position that is both empathetic and transferable. It is a site of transposition that attempts to reconcile perpetrators and survivors. With blame squarely on those outside the community (in both time and place) and therefore out of the control of residents, the radio drama does not dwell on this etiology. Instead, it relies on distance to seal the correlative power of the metonymy between imagined and real. The land conflicts that result continue with a life of their own.

In *Musekeweya*'s imagined geography, the valley between Muhumuro and Bumanzi is a spatial figure that signifies a peaceful past and a present unevenness. Before 1920, the two hill communities had shared and farmed this fertile lowland together. After government intervention, the valley was solely possessed by Bumanzi hill residents. It not only forms the source of the communities' conflicts but also the primary threat to Muhumuro residents' survival. Embedded in this fictive history are a series of anachronisms. Colonial administrators paid little attention to valleys, choosing instead to restructure the chiefly administration of hills. It was only after Rwanda's independence that governments controlled valley farming to counteract famines (1980s), protected valley marshes and wetlands from residential occupation (2004), and designated valley lands as state owned (2004). Beginning with the 2004 Draft Land Law, valley farming rights were distributed in the form of new, long-term leaseholds. Farming leaseholds were sometimes given to residents who self-identified as having farmed valley plots in the past. But oftentimes these leaseholds were unfairly allocated, as they were in *Musekeweya*, or provided to agribusiness conglomerates. The legal disruption of valley farming rights in *Musekeweya* thus had more similarity to the 2004 Draft Land Law than to 1920s Belgian colonial policies. Though this anachronism was not an explicit form of resistance on the part of the radio drama's writers, it effectively creates colonialists as analogs for contemporary authorities. The substantial changes to land tenure, territorial administration, and livelihoods experienced by *Musekeweya* characters were similar to what listeners throughout Rwanda experienced when the episodes first aired in 2004. Through these associations, the radio drama sidesteps direct confrontations with contemporary government policies, while maintaining the relevance of the conflicts for listeners. Represented as legal entities, valleys are introduced as realist, governed spaces of dispute that are metonymically correlated to listeners' own experiences with land conflicts and insecure tenure.

Hills, by contrast, are not represented as legal entities. Hills represent primordial culture: ur-sites of settlement and interaction that are essentially Rwandan. Prior to the genocide, houses were mostly dispersed, and the hill was a primary social and geographical unit with which people identified.[9] In *Musekeweya*, the term *umudugudu* (village) is never mentioned. Muhumuro and Bumanzi are called *imisozi* (hills) rather than *imidugudu* (villages). This omission presents a subtle but strategic provocation in relation

9   Louis de Lacger, *Ruanda* (Kabgayi: A. Perraudin, 1940), 73; Jacques Maquet, *The Premise of Inequality in Rwanda: A Study of Political Relations in a Central African Kingdom* (London: Oxford University Press, 1961), 21; Danielle de Lame, *A Hill among a Thousand: Transformations and Ruptures in Rural Rwanda*, trans. Helen Arnold (Madison: University of Wisconsin Press, [1996] 2005), 13; Pierre Sirven, "La sous-urbanisation et les villes du Rwanda et du Burundi" (PhD diss., Universite de Bordeaux III, 1984), 3.

to contemporary policies. After 1996 living in villages became the only form of legal residence in Rwanda, and after the 2000 decentralization policy was put in place, the village became the smallest governing unit in the country. Thus, *Musekeweya* reorients listeners to an archetypal mode of dwelling in a lived world not associated with contemporary administration and relocation. When the two female neighbors converse in Episode 2, we have the sense that the geographical limits of hills are not coextensive with their social environments: "a long time ago Muhumuro and Bumanzi were one hill." Physically, the two settlements have always occupied two different hill crests, but the radio drama's representation of the hills establishes them as social units of belonging and identity, rather than strictly geographical contexts or even as planned village forms. Representing the communities as hills preserves the possibility of a return to a primordial socio-geographical unity. Therefore the origin story contains a spatial definition for peace, if it could ever be realized again.

When the hills are set in relation, a hill-valley-hill cross section provides a diagram for social, economic, and political divisions. *Musekeweya*'s first seasons rely on the discursive equivalent of a sectional drawing to provide a simple, positional relationship of differences (two hills separated by a lowland). This sine curve supports the *Musekeweya* definition of conflict as relational, not situational; recurring, rather than exceptional. As the narratives in Season 1 unfold, it becomes clear that the residents of Bumanzi are prosperous and content, while many Muhumuro residents are mired in jealousy and poverty. This causes some Muhumuro residents to launch an attack on Bumanzi (Episode 36). In Season 2, the primary instigator of the attack is freed from prison by authorities who ascertain that no concrete evidence identifies him as a perpetrator. Anger in Bumanzi builds and provides cause for a reprisal attack from this hill to the other (Episode 125). The attacks themselves are only minimally narrated: most happen under cover of night, and our primary understanding of what occurs comes from the directionality of the attacks and the victims' grief and anguish as they tell of their experiences afterward. This privileges the space of the aftermath rather than the space of violence, which would have been psychologically jarring to many listeners. A sectional representation of the dynamics between the two hills supplants a more minute description of the violent acts to help soften the psychological effects of their narration.

This architectural representation of space also traces the potential for conflict recurrence, or what the radio drama's academic consultant refers to as the "continuum of destruction," to emphasize the historical, reciprocal progression of violent acts.[10] A planimetric or perspectival representation of these spaces would have emphasized different relationships. The writers could have represented this valley as a lowland that snakes between many hills, forming a foundation—both topographic and agricultural—for the lived worlds situated above. They could

10   Ervin Staub, *The Roots of Evil: The Origins of Genocide and Other Group Violence* (Cambridge: Cambridge University Press, 1989), 79–90.

have narrated daily walks from one crest into the valley, to farm or gather water, and up to the next hill; or to trace experiences on narrow paths that carve into steep slopes to move from one home to another. But the radio drama's scenes are for the most part static: characters conspire, socialize, and help one another process the trauma of the conflicts within domestic enclosures while referencing the conflict-ridden dynamics outside, between hills. In this sectional representation of conflict, a topographic essentialism binds fictional and actual conflict narratives. A spatial schema metonymically forms to reorient Rwanda's conflict and peace narratives.[11]

These spatial figures achieve several objectives: they locate these spaces in Rwanda, they define the basic contours of the conflicts, they seed a return to a space of peace, and they remind listeners that these conditions are transferable—not only between the hills but also between fiction and reality. Thus, the pedogenic differences between the hills are not necessarily fixed: these psychological, social, and economic conditions can be displaced. *Musekeweya*'s narratives extend this notion by deploying the hill-valley-hill spatial figure as a recurring motif. The "continuum" of conflict is represented by the attacks and counterattacks, wherein characters on both hills are seen to be equally prone to violence. A "continuum" of peaceful coexistence is represented by the close friendship of two old men who grew up on separate hills, and two forbidden lovers who come from opposing hills but develop a deep friendship and

11   I first sketched a sectional representation of the hills in an interview with a *Musekeweya* writer to illustrate his description of the drama. Seeing it, he affirmed that the drawing accurately represented their imagined space. All subsequent identifications and analyses of spatial figures are my own and developed from my translations and analyses of episode audio recordings and scripts.

partnership despite their hills and families. Both character pairs appear throughout the drama as prospects of
love, mutual cooperation, generosity, and conviviality.
These topographic relationships provide a schema for an
alternative discourse on conflicts, and the familiarity of
the hills creates a quotidian context for new peacebuilding rituals that can travel with ease to everyday contexts
in other spaces.

Spatial figures develop at these intersections of the
imagined and actual, and transform narrow, simplistic
narratives of conflict into more complex narratives of
peaceful coexistence. This effectively creates a ritualized

Figure 6 Topographic map
of Rwanda with village
research sites. Circles note
the experiential extent of
village life: residents' average
walking distance from house
to farming field. Source:
Delia Duong Ba Wendel,
2013.

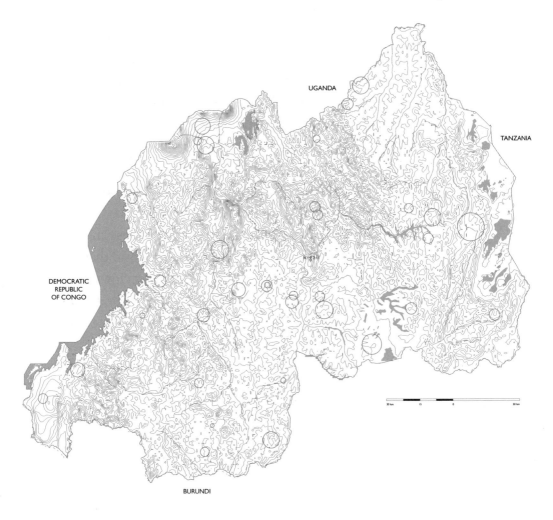

space through which listeners and characters can under-stand why people fight and how they might start to heal and reconcile. And it is to the listeners that we turn to, next.

A CULTURAL GEOGRAPHY

12 Fan letters (2004–2011) and e-mails (2009–2013) to Radio La Benevolencija, Kigali, trans. D.W.

Musekeweya's ritualized space is constructed by spatial figures and activated by individuals at their own liminal thresholds between the imagined and the actual. The radio drama's fans represent this metonymic exchange in their letters to the show creators.[12] They write with poems inspired by the drama, suggestions for issues to emphasize, and praise for the ways the drama has helped them identify and resolve conflicts in their own commu-nities. Some are more specific, requesting visits with characters in their homes to offer advice on the troubles that have befallen them. The announcement of the wed-ding between the forbidden lovers garnered an increase in fan mail: listeners wrote to promise to help raise money for the dowry to ensure the wedding's occurrence and asked where the wedding would take place so that they could attend. All dramatic productions have their most fervent supporters, and the majority of these missives represent the extremes of emplacement and displace-ment. However, in the course of my interviews with rural residents in 2013, in approximately half of the 614 homes I visited in 36 villages throughout Rwanda, interviewees shared their own *Musekeweya* stories. In two of these villages, residents identified themselves as living through the actual conditions of conflict and peace narrated in the radio drama's fictions. To explore these views, I spent several days visiting with individuals living in 34 homesteads on two facing hills that self-identified as "Muhumuro" and "Bumanzi."

In this cultural landscape, a long valley with sorghum fields, ficus trees, and banana and mango groves is framed by two crests. The two opposing hillsides are populated with sloped farming plots and homesteads constructed on leveled clearings. It is the hot, dry harvest season when I visit the communities, and residents on both hills see me from their farming fields and travel up to the clearings outside their homes to exchange greetings. Most individuals in the area are around 40 years of age and were born in these hills; others are newly arrived, younger couples or elderly women whose family members had been killed in 1994 or imprisoned thereafter. On one hill, residents often point to houses around them to note where their brothers, uncles, and fathers had built homes. On the other crest, individuals are less forthcoming with their hill's genealogical map. One woman clarifies why when she points across the valley, telling me that "the houses that were attacked belong to people who are no longer there."[13] In most homes, children are present: dutifully returning from school, from neighbors' houses with embers for the cooking fire, or from the valley where they collect water from a well that the communities share. On one of its short sides, the valley opens up to snake around

13 In order to protect residents' identities, this and other interviews are referenced only by a number and letter code. 130711_BLU_13-37 (trans. B.U. and D.W.).

both peaks; on the other, a third crest physically connects the hills with a road that leads outward from the villages, along which new shops and dwellings were constructed around 2009. Shoulder-width and wider footpaths connect the hills at various heights throughout the valley.

On one of the hills, I visit a man and ask if he listens to *Musekeweya*. He answers:

> Sometimes when I go to listen to *Musekeweya*'s objectives and the things that it points to, I realize that Giheta A and Giheta B are the same. Giheta B across there, before it was exactly the same: people worked together. Actually you see, we studied together there in Cyambwe. Students from across would pass here on the path and we would go together. But it was sad that, we came to see this hill attack that one across there during the fighting in 1994. People died there, killed by people from here. So I really think that it's the same. Now if I compare this and that period, you see that now it's like unity has come back somehow, they reconciled. Giheta was like Muhumuro and Ruseke was like Bumanzi.[14]

14   130712_BER_12-23
(trans. B.U. and D.W.).

As our conversation unfolds, it became clear that we are seated on Giheta hill, which had been shortened from its previous name Giheta A. Before 1994, the opposite hill was called Giheta B. Both hills were located in the same administrative sector. After 1994, Giheta B was renamed Ruseke and redistricted to distinguish it from the community that attacked them. The day before, another man told me that before the genocide, the hills were disproportionately settled by different ethnic groups: Giheta was majority Hutu, with only a few Tutsi families, and Ruseke was majority Tutsi. Both men were clear about the direction of the genocide fighting: once Giheta residents had "finished destroying the houses and eating the cows of those [Tutsi] here, they went across there [to Ruseke]."[15]

The violence that residents endured at the hands of their neighbors is unimaginable. I am not privy to residents' narratives of their genocide experiences. Individuals that mention the attacks summarize them in terms of their contextual effects and rarely narrate the attacks in the first person.[16] The more open statement from the man living downhill on Giheta, who noted that "people died there, killed by people from here," served to mark his own involvement in the attacks while masking full admission of culpability. Earlier in our conversation, he had self-identified as someone who had "confessed his crimes," but here he subsumed his own identity under the group identity of the hill.[17] He was born on this hill, was in his late teens in 1994, and returned to the hill to start a family eight years later. For years after the genocide, residents did not use the paths between the two hills because they were afraid of repeat and reprisal attacks. Other quotidian practices would renew fears during the first years as well: the sight of Giheta residents picking up hoes to farm in the valley would alarm Ruseke residents

15   130711_BER_15–29 (trans. B.U.).

16   130712_BLU_10–23; 130712_BER_15–03; 130712_BER_12–23 (trans. B.U. and D.W.).

17   In Kinyarwanda, *umweye w'icyaha* (confessor of crime) is a term used to refer to those who admitted a role in genocide crimes, and embedded within its use is a sense of readmittance to a community in return for confession or imprisonment.

because the tool had been used in the killings. Here, hills and homes metonymically refer to that which is more painful, and everyday practices such as walking and farming remain overly charged with violent effects and intents.

In place of detailed attack narratives, residents emplace their hills within the radio drama to represent their conflicts in schematic form. For the first man that I spoke with, these conflicts and metonymic associations are in the past: "Giheta *was* like Muhumuro and Ruseke *was* like Bumanzi." For another male living on the hill that was attacked, these relationships are historically continuous: "Ruseke and Giheta *have always been* the same as Bumanzi and Muhumuro."[18] Alternatively, a female resident suggested that Giheta and Ruseke inspired the fictions, noting that "the writers relate Muhumuro and Bumanzi to what happened here; sometimes they are talking about us."[19] In these metonymic exchanges, the dialectical co-constitution of histories and futures is evident, for the fiction is based on reality as much as reality develops from the fiction.

Muhumuro and Bumanzi signify more than hills immersed in the challenges of peaceful coexistence. Residents emphasize that the hills are not merely places for living and farming; they are subjectivities. Accordingly, a female Giheta resident claimed that *Musekeweya* could only be located in Rwanda, elaborating that: "it is alone because of Muhumuro and Bumanzi, and the many things in the play related to the genocide

18   130711_BLU_11–19 (trans. D.W.).

19   130711_BER_14–37 (trans. B.U.).

and how people killed others because of their ethnicity."[20] In one sense these hill identities refer to the ethnic groups that the radio drama omitted. They stand in for official collective identities, such as "perpetrator" and "survivor," that the government employs to reference genocide-related subjectivities. These terms replace ethnicity in public discourse, but they fail to articulate the range of actions and the complexities of the genocide. To illustrate this, one "confessor of crime" ended our interview with a request for clarification as regards official identity labels. He asked me, as an authoritative outsider, whether a person who was hunted during the genocide because he was a Tutsi, but lucky because he was married to a Hutu, yet targeted by the current government as a genocide accomplice, considered a survivor?[21] Muhumuro and Bumanzi open subjectivity beyond official categories such as "perpetrator" and "survivor" by locating instigators of violence and peacemakers on both hills. As one Ruseke resident put it, "Muhumuro and Bumanzi are here, but we are not all alike in these things in the whole village, it's just that not all people are good."[22]

When conflicts are narrated in *Musekeweya*, fictional characters and spatial contexts intertwine as archetypal metonyms for subjectivities. Again, these subjectivities are co-constructed from hills (as social spaces and as distinct places) and characters to construct larger domains of signification. While fictive characters prevail as signifiers of violent and peaceful behaviors, they are also associated with places that form criteria for group

20 130712_BER_10-19 (trans. B.U.).

21 130711_BER_13-35 (trans. B.U. and D.W.).

22 130711_BLK_12-00 (trans. D.W.).

membership. Spaces thus represent the importance of groups to both mass violence and communal living.

One resident introduced this collapse of subjectivity and space when he identified similarities between fiction and reality:

> You see, those characters are like those people in our homes [in Giheta] and those homes in Ruseke. It's like when they talk about Rutaganira—and the way that he used to sow segregation but now he is reformed—others like him confessed their crimes and apologized.... I also see Batamuriza's home. They are there.[23]

23   130712_BER_15-03
(trans. B.U. and D.W.).

In the radio drama, Rutaganira and Batamuriza are characters defined by their relationships. Rutaganira is the instigator of violence from Muhumuro. He is jailed, later released, and eventually redeems himself by confessing his wrongs to help forge peaceful cooperation between the hills. Batamuriza is the young female protagonist in love with a boy from Bumanzi (the forbidden lovers) who is trapped by her mother Zaninka, another prominent character from Muhumuro who hates the other hill. Over the course of several seasons, both characters overcome the restrictions and burdens of their hill and homes, which signify places particularly prone to feelings of inequity and violence. Thus, the characters and their spaces hold transformative potential for residents, and this is referenced in the metonymic exchanges between Muhumuro/Giheta and Bumanzi/Ruseke. In our discussions residents did not call upon the characters as a means to escape their reality or obfuscate their histories: rather, residents displaced the transformative potential of these characters from *Musekeweya* homes to theirs to recuperate possibility—to situate an alternative discourse of peace in their everyday interactions and spaces.

While metonymic exchanges between *Musekeweya* and real life worlds were often referenced by interviewees throughout Rwanda, in Giheta and Ruseke the frequency of this congruence was exceptional.[24] This was due to two community leaders, Claude and Protogene, who transposed *Musekeweya* onto this cultural landscape. A few years after 1994, both men returned to their respective hills to find residents immersed in rampant distrust, anger, and grief. Claude started listening to *Musekeweya* when it first aired in 2004, and as he put it, "first, I followed *Musekeweya* a lot, and I tried to do what they do…teaching people, giving testimonies…things that could make people reconcile and become one."[25] He had the idea that Giheta should reach out to Ruseke to ask for forgiveness, but he knew that their very presence would make the others fearful. So Claude contacted his childhood friend, Protogene. I gathered that their collaboration was not guaranteed when Protogene described the circumstances in which he agreed to work with Claude:

> If Claude's older brother came and killed the parents who brought me into the world, knowing that Claude is Claude, I know that Claude didn't play any role in that. Even that one who did, he has admitted it. That is the humanity that I'm talking

24 Among the 34 residents interviewed on these hills, only three did not listen to *Musekeweya*, and the remaining 31 interviewed residents listened with varying frequency. But all had stories that referenced places, characters, and issues from the radio drama.

25 130712_BER_15-03 (trans. B.U.).

26 130712_BER_15-03
(trans. B.U.). Protogene likely
used "if" as a gentler introduction to his view, because
Claude was next to him in
our group discussion.

about.... It isn't possessed by many people, but
Claude cannot be punished for his older brother's
crimes.[26]

Protogene here disentangles Claude from the culpable
group, even as they both confirm their membership on
each hill. The leaders clarify why they transferred the
Musekeweya hill subjectivities to Giheta and Ruseke: the
fictional hills do not identify guilty parties; they identify
which actually existing hill should make amends and
which hill should forgive. The fictive hill subjectivities are
not condemnations, nor wholly fixed identities. This is
why both men look at each other knowingly and chuckle
in response to my question, "do you know of any villages
that are like the ones in *Musekeweya*?" Claude laughed
and said, "ours is Muhumuro, the other is Bumanzi!"[27]

27 130712_BER_15-03
(trans. B.U.).

Before the *gacaca* community trials took place here in
2007, both men began speaking with their hill communities and ascertained that, in addition to the upcoming
confessions that Ruseke residents expected of their
neighbors, there was a desire for reparations and atone-
ment. The property damage to Ruseke residents' houses,
farming yields, and livestock alone was estimated at 40
million in local currency.[28] Repayment was beyond the
capabilities of all area residents, and so the leaders turned
to *Musekeweya*'s origin story—"one hill, long ago, that
farmed together"—for inspiration.[29]

28 130712_BER_12-23
(trans. B.U.).

29 The hills' origin story
forms the subject of the
drama's theme song, which
repeats at the beginning and
end of every episode.

In 2008 the leaders initiated acts of forgiveness farming in the valley that separates Giheta and Ruseke. One
woman who moved to Giheta that year recalled how the

leaders initiated this displacement: "they said: 'these ones are like Muhumuro, and these are like Bumanzi people'— like that. They looked for something that would bring them together again. As a result, if they named them like this [as Muhumuro] they would need to go there and farm for those they wronged."[30] Because she was a new arrival, the young woman felt disconnected from the hill group with which she was identified, and yet she accepted the relevance of the metonymy to some extent, clarifying: "Giheta was the one that attacked Ruseke, so you understand that some people there were like Muhumuro." In this way, the metonymy is neither perfect nor accurate. Claude and Protogene approximated peacebuilding by transforming the exceptional nature of the genocide into habitual and geographic relationships between hill residents and between imagined and actual life-worlds. In Giheta a man who self-identified as a "rescuer" described the first acts:

> after *gacaca* had left, our village leader took the first step and went to apologize across there…. Hundreds of citizens, around a thousand, went on a sunny day over there to apologize to the whole country. They farmed for them, they sowed crops, farmed cassava, sweet potatoes, they gave a work day—around two thousand scattered in the fields. They asked for forgiveness and [the others] agreed to give us forgiveness.[31]

Although the numbers were likely inflated by the respondent's enthusiasm, another woman added that children,

30   130711_BER_8-52 (trans. B.U.).

31   130711_BER_15-29 (trans. B.U.).

32   130712_BER_10–19
(trans. B.U.).

who had no part in the genocide violence, went with their parents and neighbors "to ask forgiveness there."[32] The children's involvement indicates the extent of the hill subjectivities' associational power, which resulted in unfair and totalizing categorizations. The apologies were both spoken and ritualized in spatial practices like planting, sowing, weeding, and harvesting; and for some, these acts were later recalled as myth.

The distinction between a spatial imagination and spatial practice is not abrupt, particularly in the context of a micropolitics that seeks to overturn intractable conflict. This is a claim derived from Michel de Certeau, who insisted that spatial practices are types of counter narratives—formed against alienation and reification in his case, or against intrinsic difference and historical inevitability in the Rwandan case—that individuals engage in everyday life as a mode of political produc-

33   Michel de Certeau,
"Practices of Space," in *On
Signs*, ed. Marshal Blonsky
(Baltimore, MD: Johns
Hopkins University Press,
1985), 122–45.

tion.[33] For example, through the spatial practice of walking one can choose a route, pace, blockages, and circumventions and thus produce a succession of minute symbolic significations with syntactic structure and meaning. Walking becomes a form of narrative construction. This renders spatial practices as a type of everyday historiography, or a means for dreaming and acting out alternative narratives. And as we've seen, *Musekeweya*'s spatial imagination is not unidirectional: through spatial practices, Giheta and Ruseke residents have also written their own hills into the radio drama's narratives.

Forgiveness farming brought contact between the hills, re-signifying everyday spatial practices as pragmatic coexistence. Today, the paths between the hills have opened back up to foot traffic. Every day, younger residents travel to the valley to stand in line and collect jerry cans of water. Some Giheta residents continue to farm fields for widows on Ruseke. As a result Protogene is certain that 100 percent reconciliation has been achieved. Other residents were decidedly more cautious, suggesting that the level of mutual trust and forgiveness among hill residents was lower. There is some sense that these spatial practices are linked to reconciliation, but they may also represent a return to historical communal living; a practical mode of survival when one has limited means. Although this may be the case, these spatial practices were unlikely without the ritualization of farming as forgiveness.

Protogene elaborated on his and Claude's pragmatist approach to peacebuilding by projecting intense emotions onto daily practices of walking and meeting:

> Never in my life would I have thought that I could pass on the same path with the person who made me an orphan or whatever, and killed my siblings, killed my relatives, killed my parents, who killed my family. I never thought I would talk to him again. But, as days go by, life cannot stop because others' have gone. You cannot achieve anything by yourself, you cannot get anywhere by living by yourself.[34]

34 130712_BER_15-03 (trans. B.U. and D.W.).

It is not entirely clear whether full reconciliation can ever be achieved, or indeed if that is even an expectation among the residents of "Muhumuro" and "Bumanzi." Certainly, Claude's and Protogene's efforts in placing their hills in the radio drama have helped to situate the conflicts between the communities within an other spatial narrative and incorporated the possibility of transformation in the subjectivities of the hills. The spatial figures of Muhumuro and Bumanzi are displaced onto Giheta and Ruseke as essentialist identities for the purpose of peacebuilding, not adjudication. As such, *Musekeweya* is oriented to future relationships, not to the fictive or real past, and this biases a limiting view of the role of history in peacebuilding practice. The effect of the metonymic exchange is a spatiotemporal slippage: because both hills in *Musekeweya's* imagined geography are associated with conflicts and reconciliation, the toponyms achieve the admission of past wrongs and the possibility of future peace in one reference. In this schema the hills cannot exist without the other. They are bound by relations of conflict and peace that are voiced and enacted in familiar, quotidian spaces. In turn, hill residents are emplaced back into the homes of *Musekeweya* characters by the leaders' proclamations of the hills' similitude and organized reenactments of the radio drama's peacebuilding practices.

Figure 7 Topography politics in Rwanda, the "land of a thousand hills." Source: Delia Duong Ba Wendel, 2013.

Imagining Spaces of Peace and Conflict in the Rwandan Radio Drama *Musekeweya*

In Rwanda, peacebuilding takes several forms. It is
the cessation of violence, the attempt to reconcile, the
process of adjudication, and an iterative stability.
Musekeweya stabilizes by imagining new perspectives
on the present and future to form, embody, and recast
relationships between self and community. Foundational
to these processes is a spatial imagination that develops
from significant spatial figures. The spatial imagination
intervenes in sociopolitical processes, negotiates the conditions of these processes at different scales, and both references and transcends particular historical times.
Musekeweya's spaces are thus liminal: they operate at the
threshold of the imagined and the actual, with neither
providing a full understanding of ideology, conflict, or
peace. The imagined is incomplete because it needs the
consensus of actual individuals to legitimize its relevance.
It also needs listeners to fill in gaps between what is and
is not represented. The actual is incomplete because of
the lingering effects of the genocide and the challenges
that exist to peaceful coexistence. This very incomplete-
ness—this mode of approximating and relating—characterizes the metonymic peacebuilding strategy activated
by the radio drama.

In these Rwandan hills, the metonymic exchanges
between fiction and reality coproduce narratives that
remain only hypothetical or organizational until they are
instantiated in space as ritualized, spatial practices.

Peace is an ideal that does not fully exist in either imagined or actual worlds. Though it is powerful as a construct, *Musekeweya*'s spatial imagination ultimately needs both the consensus of listeners and their spatial practices to approximate conditions for peace.

Spatial practices invest everyday, pragmatic activities with peacebuilding purpose. They become ritualized through their repetition and reference to ideals. In this way, everyday acts by individuals in Giheta and Ruseke were revalued by the radio drama. These acts in this place created a ritualized space that propels residents downhill from their homes and into the valley. In imagined and actual "Muhumuro," "Bumanzi," and the valley between, the performative and the spatial intertwine to develop alternative worldviews. These processes are metonymic, not mimetic; associational and based on exchanges, rather than didactic or doctrinal. The ritualized space that develops from the metonymic exchanges challenges predetermined subjectivities and forms a critical foundation for sustained coexistence.

The Right-of-Way: Critical Infrastructure for the Right to Work in Postwar Philadelphia

Fallon Samuels Aidoo

A dead tree near St. Martins Station in northwest Philadelphia fell on a commuter's car in 1960. The owner of the car parked daily at a meter licensed to Auto Parks, Inc. by the Pennsylvania Railroad (PRR), but he sought damages from James T. Nathans, a nearby resident, not the PRR or the City of Philadelphia. Liability remained in question for two years, since the city had not incorporated the street where the parking space was located and the tree was rooted on PRR property outside Auto Parks's leasehold. The PRR ultimately assumed responsibility for damages that occurred within its property lines, but only after litigious debate with its lessee over the physical extent of its rights and responsibilities for land maintenance. In the meantime, the number of dying trees on

Figure 1   An underutilized parking lot and a high-rise condominium, which replaced green space at the Pennsylvania Railroad Co.'s Chestnut Hill Station, 1969. Source: Photographed by Peter Gilchrist; Chestnut Hill Historical Society.

153

1   James F. Nathans to Pennsylvania RR Real Estate Department, April 11, 1962. St. Martins Station Grounds Committee Papers (hereafter SMSGC), Chestnut Hill Historical Society (CHHS), Philadelphia, Pennsylvania.

2   Solicitation, St. Martins Station Grounds Committee, 1962. SMSGC papers, box 1, CHHS; "Commuters Seek to Beautify St. Martins Station," *Evening Bulletin*, April 3, 1962.

3   Suburban railroad station and landscape conservation figured prominently in the preservation movements of the Progressive Era and the Great Depression. See John R. Stilgoe, "The Railroad Beautiful: Landscape Architecture and the Railroad Gardening Movement, 1867–1930," *Landscape Journal* 1, no. 2 (1982): 57–66; and Jeffrey Karl Ochsner, "Architecture for the Boston & Albany Railroad," *Journal of the Society of Architectural Historians* 47 (June 1988): 109–31.

4   "Commuters Ask PUC to Bar Rail Fare Rise," *Philadelphia Inquirer*, July 31, 1951, 20. "Commuter Fare Case for 1949–1951," Reading Company Legal Department Collection (Acc. 1520), box 1139, Folder 19-9, Hagley Museum & Library, Wilmington, DE. On the social capital and cultural cache of Main Line suburbs, see Kenneth Jackson, "The Main Line: Elite Suburbs and Commuter Railroads," in *The Crabgrass Frontier: The Suburbanization of the United States* (New York: Oxford University Press, 1985).

PRR's property line seemed to underscore the fact that the boundary between public and private space had been eroding for some time.[1]

What made the boundary between public, private, and common space so porous, and so contested, in the postwar period? Who benefited from and furthered this boundary's erosion? Who suffered as a result? The Nathans found answers to these questions in a solicitation for contributions to the St. Martins Station Grounds Committee (est. 1962), a "blue-chip band of commuters" intent on reinforcing and, when necessary, restructuring the maintenance work of PRR's station attendants.[2] These white-collar suburbanites were by no means the first to preserve the workplaces of PRR's Maintenance-of-Way Employees—a union of railway superintendents, agents and groundskeepers. They were, however, the first commuter collective to underwrite and undertake the management of railroad stations and surrounding grounds within Philadelphia city limits.[3]

By the time the St. Martins Station Grounds Committee formed in 1962, suburban neighborhood improvement associations and cost-conscious railway executives had already established legal parameters, accounting protocols, design standards, and social norms for preservation of the Pennsylvania Railroad's Main Line. At public utility commission hearings in 1950, the civic leaders of garden cities and industrial suburbs solicited reinvestment in their sprawling station grounds and storied station houses.[4] Such legal tactics proved fruitful in the case of Lower Merion Township, which arranged (outside of court) for PRR to treat its Wynnewood Station as a "community facility," since commuters no longer treated the station as critical infrastructure for their daily back-to-the-city movements.[5] Not coincidentally, reclassification of suburban rail stations as spaces embedded physically and functionally in their surroundings came at a time when PRR president James Symes sought public aid—both financial and political in nature. The postwar boom in car ownership and truck transport wrought fiscal distress that only deregulation or subsidization could remedy, Symes argued before a US Senate committee on transportation in January 1958. A few months later, Philadelphia mayor Richardson Dilworth would similarly testify to the physical deterioration and economic decline of railroad suburbs.[6] Both the company's and the city's appeals to Congress for public financing of facilities management failed to materialize in the comprehensive Community Facilities legislation they proposed, but the Housing Act of 1960 appropriated funds for research and development of sustainable railroad properties throughout the Rust Belt. Within this R&D framework and with regional resilience as the objective, PRR's vice president for special operations authorized PRR's real estate managers to partner with entrepreneurial community-based organizations of Greater Philadelphia and their enterprising counterparts throughout the northeastern and midwestern United States.[7]

5 Lower Merion Civic Council shared its license to care for PRR's Wynnewood Station as it would other "community facilities" with the St. Martin Station Grounds Committee. See SMSGC Papers, box 1, CHHS.

6 "Statement of James M. Symes, President, The Pennsylvania Railroad Company, before the Surface Transportation Subcommittee, Senate Committee on Interstate and Foreign Commerce," Hearings on the Railroad Situation, January 13, 1958; "Summary of Mayor Dilworth's Testimony before the Senate Subcommittee on Housing, May 14, 1958," Records of the Richardson Dilworth Administration, Philadelphia City Archives (hereafter PCA), box 3781, Philadelphia, PA.

7 On the rights-of-way of railroad companies and their right to transfer their privileges to a variety of partners, see José Gómez-Ibáñez, Regulating Infrastructure: Monopoly, Contracts and Discretion (Cambridge, MA: Harvard University Press, 2003). I drew insight into concessionary policies and practices of the PRR postwar from its SEPTA Service Contracts, 1968–1973. PRR Passenger Operations Records, acc. # 1807, box 1662/110.1, Center for the Study of Business, Technology and Society, Hagley Museum and Library, Wilmington, DE (which financially supported part of this research). See also print and digital publications of the Rails-to-Trails Conservancy at http://www.railstotrails.org/resource-library.

Of course, land concessions to community-based organizations came with conditions, namely, the maintenance of cultural, managerial, and physical landscapes that had long protected the place of railroads in the public domain. A license to work on the aging buildings and lush grounds owned by PRR's Real Estate Division enjoined the signatories in a joint venture of regulating and redeveloping the recalcitrant landscapes that trains traversed. The licensing agreements that PRR signed with four of Philadelphia's railway conservancies in the early 1960s reveal that these legal documents left space for both parties to relegate specific spaces and spatial practices within their purview to third parties. The latter could include numerous subcontractors, from landscapers and architects to security and union apprentices; each of these did, in fact, work on behalf of a railway conservancy in Greater Philadelphia during the postwar period.[8] The costs associated with outsourcing (particularly, of liability insurance and contractual fees) persuaded some conservancies to mobilize labor from within their own ranks or join up with block clean-up groups already engaged in the laborious tasks of landscape preservation. As these organizations later became a part of community gardening councils or community development corporations, their political strategies underwent critical evaluation by both activists and academics. Far less is known about the power and politics of those community-based organizations that took up railway conservancy but passed on the political and financial liabilities

8   The railway conservancies examined by the author include the West Mount Airy Neighbors Association (hereafter WMAN) Railroad Improvement Committee; Allen Lane Station Committee, Inc.; St. Martins Station Grounds Committee, Inc.; and the Chestnut Hill Community Association Maintenance Committees. The Volvo Research and Education Foundation provided financial support for this archival research in local historical societies. Members of the Urban History Association, the International Association for the History of Transport, Traffic and Mobility, and Harvard's Transforming Urban Transport Project research team provided critical feedback in October 2014.

to men and women with experience in asset and facilities management.[9]

The concessions retained and contracts granted by one such organization raises important questions about the right to work on a right-of-way—a once and future common space for labor and leisure, union laborers and corporate executives.[10] Drawing primarily (although not exclusively) on governmental, corporate, community, and private records of the St. Martins Station Grounds Committee (SMSGC), this case study of railway conservancy offers a micro-history of white-collar work prescribed and performed on Pennsylvania Railroad property as its ill-fated merger with the New York Central railroad company took shape in the 1960s. Following the lead of historian Carolyn T. Adams to think spatially and critically about collective thought and action among bourgeois communities in suburban Philadelphia, this study sheds light on how railway conservancy—a labor of love for blue-chip professionals past and present—cedes and seeds space for blue-collar brotherhoods.[11]

GROUNDING MOBILIZATION

St. Martins Station Grounds, a residence and workplace of railway attendants, epitomized the intractability of suburban tracts within city limits circa 1960. Most of Philadelphia's gentry no longer used this Pennsylvania Railroad station or any of the four other commuter rail stations located less than a mile from it in Chestnut Hill,

9   See Stephen Graham and Nigel Thrift, "Out of Order: Understanding Repair and Maintenance," *Theory, Culture & Society* 24, no. 3 (2007): 1–25; and Claudia Arandau, "Security that Matters: Critical Infrastructure and Objects of Protection," *Security Dialogue* 41, no. 5 (2010): 491–514. See also Colin McFarlane and Jonathan Rutherford, "Political Infrastructures," *International Journal of Urban and Regional Research* 32, no. 2 (June 2008): 363–74.

10   Labor unions that interacted with early conservationists offer some insight into the interplay between labor, leisure, and residency in rail rights-of-way. See Denver W. Hertel, *History of the Brotherhood of Maintenance of Way Employees: Its Birth and Growth, 1887–1955* (Washington, DC: Ransdell, 1955), 174–75; and H. W. Jacobs, "The Square Deal to the Railroad Employee," *Engineering* 21 (May 1907): 328–52.

11   On suburban Philadelphians in urban governance, see Carolyn T. Adams, *From the Outside In: Suburban Elites, Third-Sector Organizations and the Reshaping of Philadelphia* (Ithaca, NY: Cornell University Press, 2014).

12   Philadelphia's postwar "gentry" here refers to familial estates owning real estate, railways, and banks for multiple generations and also newly moneyed real estate developers, builders, lenders, insurers, realtors, appraisers, regulators, and lawyers. See ibid., introduction.

13   An early thesis on gentrification linked suburban mobilization and city investment using these same Chestnut Hill dwellers as sample subjects; see Neil Smith, "Toward a Theory of Gentrification: A Back-to-the-City Movement by Capital, not People," *Journal of the American Planning Association* 45 (1979): 538–48; and Neil Smith, "Gentrification, the Frontier, and the Restructuring of Urban Space," in *Gentrification of the City*, ed. Neil Smith and Peter Williams (Boston: Allen & Unwin, 1986), 15–20. Geographers and historians that have vigorously debated his concept of "the urban frontier" have yet to revisit Smith's data regarding the physical and social movements of elites living in railroad/streetcar suburbs that make up Philadelphia's "crabgrass frontier."

14   Marketers Research Service, Inc., "The Marketability of the Chestnut Hill Lines of the Pennsylvania Railroad," 1958; and Opinion Research Corporation for Reading Company, "Suburban Shopping Patterns," 1960.Verticle Files, Hagley Museum and Library, Wilmington, DE.

15   Two cases studies illuminate the intractability of Rust Belt real estate transactions for railroad companies: Guian McKee, "Blue Sky Boys, Professional Citizens, and Knights in Shining Money: Philadelphia's Penn Center Project and the Constraints of Private Development," *Journal of Planning History* 6, no. 1 (2007): 48–80, focuses on the "Chinese Wall," and Elihu Rubin, *Insuring the City: The Prudential Center and*

a streetcar suburb bordering the city–county line.[12] Instead they chose to move with Mayor Richardson Dilworth to Society Hill, a collection of renovated colonial townhouses downtown, or to commute by carpool along the newly constructed (yet always congested) Schuylkill Expressway to law offices, hospitals, and courthouses in Center City Philadelphia.[13] Having grown skeptical of its capacity to retain the remaining commuters, whose patronage supported the upkeep of railways, the PRR looked to sell off the land parcel-by-parcel along with all other peripheral properties, before the Interstate Highway Act of 1956 went into effect. Time was not the only factor; the federal legislation, which subsidized 90 percent of the cost of freeway construction, enabled free commuting by car in the Philadelphia tri-state area and similar metropolitan regions.

The PRR targeted real estate developers, insurance companies, state turnpike authorities, and metropolitan transit districts for land sales. A series of marketing studies by the nation's leading management and financial consultants suggested, however, that such transactions would be legally complex and politically contentious.[14] The protracted process of turning over just a few parcels proved instructive, demonstrating that the PRR could not dispose of land—even the maligned "Chinese Wall" of elevated rail yards or desirable unused land at the top of Chestnut Hill—without clearance, assembly, rezoning, and remediation of the land underneath it.[15] Consultants advised that, instead of selling stations-grounds, the PRR

the Postwar Urban Landscape (New Haven, CT: Yale University Press, 2012), explores the problematic properties of PRR's competitor, the Boston & Albany Railroad.

rightsize them. This finance-focused method of identifying liabilities and indemnifying assets required no regulatory approvals or fiduciary accreditations, only authorization from shareholders and debtors to release and/or lease real property to for-profit and nonprofit organizations that could maintain them.[16]

Following consultants' advice, PRR proceeded in 1957 to approve intermediate, itinerant uses of its station-grounds. These low-cost installations and provisional activities, which might be called "tactical urbanism" today, fell under the catchall "lessee operations" in post-war real estate parlance.[17] Initially, PRR's Real Estate Division consented only to the conversion of open space into parking spaces. Plans to turn over nearly every square inch of unused land in Greater Philadelphia to Auto Parks, Inc., a for-profit developer and manager of pay-to-park lots, immediately met with opposition from citizens, community boards, and municipal zoning officials. Each contested PRR's enterprise of land concessions to parking concessionaires on different grounds: the spiraling cost of commuting, traffic congestion on local streets, and misuse of public subsidies.[18] Municipal judges often ruled on the side of budding business improvement districts, which found most cars parked in Auto Parks lots belonged to city customers and not ex-urban commuters, suggesting commercial rather than public use of PRR's right-of-way. Appeals court judges found more merit, however, in PRR-sponsored maps of "transit blight," which depicted the adverse effect of unwanted

16   The concept of rightsizing real estate preoccupied management consultants in the 1950s, including the firm that PRR retained, Peat Marwick Mitchell & Co. See William Thomas, "Operations Research vis-à-vis Management at Arthur D. Little and the Massachusetts Institute of Technology in the 1950s," *Business History Review* 86 (Spring 2012): 99–122.

17   On historical precedents for contemporary "tactical urbanism," see Emily Talen, "Do-It-Yourself Urbanism: A History," *Journal of Planning History* (September 2014): 1–14.

18   The PCA has not preserved postwar transcripts of zoning boards and appeals courts hearings on land use. However, the *Germantown Courier* closely followed cases involving parking concessions and concessionaires in the 1950s and serves as the primary source of this account. Discontinuous issues are held by the Germantown Historical Society, Philadelphia, PA. On suburban property owners attracting city dwellers through railway investments, see David Contosta, *Suburb in the City: Chestnut Hill, Philadelphia, 1850–1990* (Columbus: Ohio State University Press, 1992); and David Contosta and E. Digby Baltzell, *A Philadelphia Family: The Houstons and Woodwards* (Philadelphia: University of Pennsylvania Press, 1998).

19   Peat Marwick Mitchell
& Co. for Pennsylvania RR
Company, "Joint Develop-
ment Potential of Pennsylva-
nia Railroad Rights-of-
Ways," 1960.

20   The PA Public Utility
Commission ruling was
celebrated by the not-for-
profit Chestnut Hill Parking
Company, which assumed
that PRR's authority to lease
land to both for-profit and
nonprofit concessionaires
would yield contracts for
parking design, develop-
ment, maintenance and
management; see "Solution
Sought to A&P Parking
Problem; PRR also Involved,"
Chestnut Hill Local, June 19,
1958, 1.

vegetation, unfettered vandalism and unproductive vagrancy throughout PRR's open spaces on the value of abutting properties and the extent to which lenders, insurers, and realtors would service the entire area.[19] For state Public Utility Commissioners—which possessed the deciding vote—Auto Parks's license to lease, landscape, and regulate railroad property represented PRR's invest-ment in the back-to-the-city movements of Main Line commuters and Main Street customers.[20]

In spite of legal challenges and political controversy, "lessee operations" on PRR property grew in scale and scope in the 1960s, beyond the park-n-ride facilities of Auto Parks, Inc. Under the direction of Philadelphia's own Passenger Service Improvement Corporation (PSIC), station grounds came to include bus stations, trolley turnarounds, and other multi-modal means of ridership recruitment and retention favored by its underwriters—the Southeastern Pennsylvania Transportation Compact, the US Housing and Home Finance Agency, and the Pennsylvania Department of Community Affairs. The artifacts of PSIC "operations" joined the rest of PRR's real estate portfolio, as well as those of a PRR competitor—the Reading Company—on the auction block in 1973. When the Reading Company and the Pennsylvania Railroad Company (Penn Central) went into bankruptcy in the 1970s, receivers of their assets and debt—the federal gov-ernment's Consolidated Rail Corporation (CONRAIL, est. 1973) and American Railroad Corporation (AMTRAK, est. 1970)—released high-maintenance commuter rail stations and other unrecoverable debt-ridden real estate to community-based organizations that registered their conservation committees as nonprofit corporations with the state business bureau. Challenged by the courts to protect back-to-the-city movements from the special interests of nonprofit, community-based organizations, Pennsylvania legislators finally authorized and financed the Southeastern Pennsylvania Transportation Authority (SEPTA) in 1981 to retain regional railways in Greater Philadelphia and reorganize work on their stations and grounds.[21]

21 For a detailed discussion of divestment from commuter rail sites and services throughout Greater Philadelphia, see Fallon Samuels Aidoo, "Groundwork for Gentrification: Critical Infrastructure Protection for Back-to-the-City Movements, 1950–1990" (PhD diss., Harvard University, forthcoming).

THE RIGHT TO WORK, REVISITED

Not by chance, the St. Martins Station Grounds Committee officially formed in February 1962, when public reinvestment in the city's privately held rail rights-of-way gained political and physical traction. The Passenger Service Improvement Corporation (PSIC)—a joint venture of the Pennsylvania Railroad, Reading Company, National Railway Executives Association, and the City of Philadelphia—had formed in December 1960 to replace the meters and meter maids of Auto Parks with other regulatory regimes—namely, railroad personnel. Wherever Reading Company and the Pennsylvania Railroad Company re-appropriated their rights-of-way to the PSIC, railway executives gained the right to police the use of railroad property, even land leased to for-profit concessionaires and nonprofit conservancies.[22]

22 Principles of Agreement for Operation Northwest, August 1960 and December 1960, "PSIC, 1960," box 22, series VIII. Citizens Council on City Planning Files, Urban Archives, Temple University (hereafter TUA), Philadelphia, PA.

Regulatory and physical restructuring of station grounds occurred track-by-track, station-by-station, beginning with the railway that connected Chestnut Hill, Philadelphia's most affluent suburb within city limits, to Center City. Initially city councilmen refused to finance "passenger service improvements" for patrician patrons of the Pennsylvania Railroad, but PSIC's directors convinced them to underwrite the development of parking spaces in open space in the name of research and development.[23] Wherever PSIC subsidized low-fare service, low-cost aluminum boxes capped by corrugated tin roofs would replace high-maintenance historic station houses.

23 "Council Assails PSIC for Seeking Taxpayer Support," *Philadelphia Inquirer*, October 11, 1962.

Figure 2 A low-cost aluminum shelter, which took the place of a high-maintenance station-house at Torresdale Station, northeast Philadelphia, 1959. The installation accompanied an 18-month experiment in ridership recruitment that ended up lasting an additional five years. Source: Records of the Richardson Dilworth Administration, Philadelphia City Archives.

These new passenger shelters would sit on concrete or brick platforms, elevated above blacktop lots "without cyclone fencing or the sturdy and expensive lights the city normally puts on its higher cost lots."[24] If these architectural and managerial changes proved profitable for the Reading and Pennsylvania Railroad companies, PSIC

24 Ibid.

could scale up the operation to include other quadrants of the city and additional partners: the US Housing and Home Finance Agency and county commissioners had already pledged to support operations on a regional scale.[25]

PSIC's claims to rights-of-way through Chestnut Hill stood on shaky ground—that is, the less-than-perfect track record of railway personnel in charge of PRR operations. After decades of community approval, the maintenance-of-way practices and personnel of Sam Hill, superintendent of PRR's Chestnut Hill stations, had come under scrutiny.[26] To govern the grounds around St. Martins Station, the superintendent had mobilized businesses, residents, and political and civic bodies that could insure PRR station grounds at once anchored Chestnut Hill's commercial corridor and remained an "extension of the home atmosphere."[27] In 1960, for example, Hill commissioned wives of business owners who were members of the Chestnut Hill Development Group (CHDG) to dig up weeds, clear debris, and plant seeds around Chestnut Hill stations once a season. This "women's work" occurred frequently enough to aid in the economic development of their husbands' businesses but not so often as to displace or delegitimize the work of Maintenance-of-Way employees under Hill's supervision. Led by "Mrs. G. Homes Perkins," the wife of University of Pennsylvania's city planning director, CHDG's Maintenance Committee first surveyed station grounds and located vacant lots in need of its care. They prescribed

25   John A. Bailey, Passenger Service Improvement Corporation, "Application for Operation Levittown," addressed to Robert Weaver, Secretary of the US Housing and Home Finance Agency, February 1961. Records of the Richardson Dilworth Administration, box A-2222, PCA.

26   For an example of correspondence received by Sam Hill citing specific complaints and recommendations, see Allston Jenkins and J. Albert Fleitas to Sam Hill, Chestnut Hill Station, PRR, April 13, 1962. SMSGC papers, CHHS.

27   Chestnut Hill stations served as parkland for nearby residents. See for example Charles Mulford Robinson, *Suburban Station Grounds* (Boston: Boston & Albany Railroad, 1905), quoted in Stilgoe, "The Railroad Beautiful," 65–66. On community engagement with these sites in the 1950s, see also "Development Group Members Discuss New Improvements," *Chestnut Hill Local*, June 9, 1960, 1; and "Fourth of a Series: Chestnut Hill, Before and After," *Chestnut Hill Local*, September 22, 1960, 1.

28 "What Do You Know? About the Chestnut Hill Development Group? The Chestnut Hill Parking Company?" *Chestnut Hill Local,* January 21, 1960, 4.

"soft control" for plots covered with cars but lacking pavement, shade trees, and curbs. These and other improvements went to protect parked cars from the elements and separate them from pedestrians, patrons, and personnel.[28] In spite of Hill's efforts to reign in overgrown stations with grading machines and gardening tools, seasoned laborers and housewives, business improvement districts and governmental authorities mistook his former home and garden at St. Martins station for a vacant lot—a prime place for commuter parking spaces.[29]

29 "Solution Sought to A&P Parking Problem," 1.

Although only one member of the SMSGC lived close enough to St. Martins Station to have witnessed the managerial work that Hill had undertaken there throughout each day, its five members and hundreds of early supporters joined the *Germantown Courier* and the *Chestnut Hill Local* in colorfully recalling Hill's tenure as a proprietor of petunias, parking, patrons, and personnel.[30] St. Martins Station users interpreted his moving up to PRR's Chestnut Hill terminus (and up the PRR corporate ladder) in 1958 as a regrettable but well-deserved maneuver away

30 See, for example, "Development Group Members Discuss New Improvements," *Chestnut Hill Local,* June 9, 1960.

Figure 3 St. Martins Station and surrounding grounds as a workplace and a stop on the journey to work, 1909. Source: John McArthur Harris slide collection, Chestnut Hill Historical Society.

from the destabilized grounds on which his station house now stood. A farewell party thrown by the Chestnut Hill Community Association and Chestnut Hill Historical Society brought hundreds to the station grounds to celebrate Hill and lament Downtown St. Martins' bygone days of fiscal security and profitable productivity. As Chestnut Hillers celebrated the fact that Hill, a trusted member of their community in spite of his company's divestment from conservation operations, would gain more say over PRR real estate, they lamented that his replacement would lack both the financial and social capital to keep buildings and landscapes at Chestnut Hill's doorstep "in good and attractive order."[31]

Instead of replacing Hill as superintendent, the commuter collective SMSGC decidedly set out to become a partner of PRR's consummate company man.[32] Its founders met at St. Martins Station in the fall of 1961 with intentions of reinforcing Hill's efforts to incorporate citizens and commuters into railway conservation without infringing upon existing organized labor. Allston Jenkins, a St. Martins homeowner who had transformed Philadelphia Conservationists, Inc., into an advocacy arm of National Lands Trust by 1960, recognized the value of philanthropic support to reclaiming neglected grounds from dysfunctional public-private partnerships.[33] He surmised, however, that novice conservationists alone could manage inquiries and mobilize interventions in public and private disinvestment at station-grounds measuring just over an acre. Notably, SMSGC shied away from

31   Jenkins and Fleitas to Hill.

32   The committee expressed its subsidiary position to the PRR in all of its initial solicitations for financial support from community members but later drop explicit references to the "Pennsy." Around the same time, it dropped "Grounds" from its name to indicate it had taken responsibility for the entire station area (house and surrounding grounds). See SMSGC papers, boxes 1 and 2, CHHS.

33   SMSGC's founding members included Philadelphia's premier defender of the disenfranchised, Henry T. Heath, of the law firm Duane Morris; John Todd, an architect that redesigned Chestnut Hill's historic homes and gardens for the modern age; and J. Albert Fleitas, a local business owner. See James Gross, "Philadelphia Award, 1960: Allston Jenkins," in *Philadelphia Award 90th Anniversary*, ed. David Haugaard (Philadelphia: Historical Society of Pennsylvania, 2012), uncirculated manuscript (as of May 2013, according to Gross). Obituary, "Henry Heath, 85, Legal Champion of Poor," *Philly. com*, February 3, 2005; and "Remembering AIA Philadelphia Member, John P. A. Todd, AIA," AIA *Philadelphia Chapter News*, January 7, 2015.

incorporating as a nonprofit within the State of Pennsylvania throughout most of its tenure, even though doing so would have given its donors tax exemptions. Preferring a grassroots form and egalitarian mode of collective action, the organization refused to elect executive leadership or accept limited liability for the actions of those commissioned to act on its behalf. Nevertheless, the process of removing "penciled writing on the walls" and repairing the "revolting tunnel underneath the railroad tracks" enrolled Jenkins and fellow station-grounds stewards in institutionally, politically, and legally complex forms of conservancy.[34]

Maneuvering around epistemic boundaries preoccupied the St. Martins Station Grounds Committee from the start, as members set out to differentiate their stewardship of maintenance-of-way employee workplaces from the work of superintendents. The first of many self-deprecating solicitations by the committee in 1962 called on recipients to "become a charter contributor to the only known organization devoted to grass cutting and weed pulling in Ye Old Greene Countrie Towne" and offered no criticism of railroad property or personnel.[35] To make sure that recipients of flyers and mailings saw the roles they played on station grounds as complementary to the *work* of superintendents and their staff, donation request forms concluded, "Join us. This will be fun!"[36] SMSGC explained to naysayers (only a few of which wrote to the committee) that superintendents determined which operations on station grounds counted as

34 See Jenkins and Fleitas to Hill.

35 SMSGC Solicitations, 1962. SMSGC papers, CHHS.

36 Ibid.

productive and profitable; they discerned which concessions put the railroad companies at risk and which rendered rewards.[37] Stewardship at a critical distance from superintendents, who invited constructive criticism and volunteerism, behooved community members seeking more distributed governance of PRR stations.

As much as the committee supported Superintendent Hill, it also commissioned grounds work by local contractors it knew and trusted to work alongside maintenance crews assigned to St. Martins Station anonymously under union labor contracts. Whereas other block clean-up crews across Philadelphia and in Chestnut Hill routinely performed grounds work themselves, the St. Martins committee initially participated only in clean-up days, which they organized in the interest of civic engagement with the station grounds and fundraising for the maintenance of that landscape. Their sweat equity went toward other endeavors: namely, carrying out protracted, painstaking correspondence with PRR's real estate and operations executives regarding capital improvements in addition to time-consuming observation of landscapers hired to turn over soil, dig up dead trees, clear away railroad debris, create flower beds, pot plants, and cut the grass. These regulatory actions yielded not only prompt repairs and dutiful contract labor but also hundreds of small donations (on the order of $5 to $25) throughout the year from appreciative members of the community. Proceeds went exclusively to contractors' fees (including liability insurance, as well as materials, tools, and labor costs),

37   SMSGC to James F. Nathans, April 24, 1962. SMSGC papers, box 1, CHHS.

38   St. Martins Station Grounds Committee, Ledger of Donations. SMSGC papers, box 1, CHHS.

39   Balance Sheets. SMSGC papers, box 2, CHHS.

40   The recession of the early 1980s imperiled the government corporations in charge of PRR stations (CON-RAIL and AMTRAK), thereby increasing the scope of work that SMSGC could undertake and underwrite, effectively hastening railroad reorganization. See "St. Martins Station Renovation Fund-raising Campaign," brochure, n.d. SMSGC papers, box 2, CHHS. See also, Mark H. Rose, Bruce E. Seely, and Paul F. Barrett, *The Best Transportation System in the World: Railroads, Trucks, Airlines and American Public Policy in the Twentieth Century* (Columbus: Ohio State University Press, 2006), chapter 9.

41   Capitalization original. License Agreement between Pennsylvania Railroad and St. Martins Station Grounds Committee, April 1, 1962. SMSGC papers, box 1, CHHS.

leaving little resources for promotion or publicity.[38] The committee's revenue repeatedly fell short of its expenses, leading Jenkins to ask the Chestnut Hill Community Association and Chestnut Hill Development Group to make up the difference with donations to the Community and Maintenance Funds that each amassed.[39] Even amid the recession of the early 1980s, the committee still held steadfastly to its only inviolable principle—to enable, not embody, the right to work on the right of way.[40]

A license to conserve St. Martins Station Grounds proved critical to the committee's work. As a "licensee" of PRR property, SMSGC acquired the same property rights and responsibilities granted to Auto Parks, Inc. To both, the PRR extended "a mere personal license or privilege" to construct and deconstruct the built environment around St. Martins Station. Whereas Auto Parks agreed to grade, pave, and protect lots, the committee requested and received "permission to landscape, beautify, and/or use for garden purposes ALL THAT CERTAIN AREA situated in the vicinity and adjacent to St. Martins Passenger Station."[41]

The language of this agreement evaded three important questions: What constituted "THAT CERTAIN AREA" for which the SMSGC could claim rights and responsibilities? Who else was allowed to use or occupy, landscape or beautify, these areas? And, what recourse did the committee have to regulate or remediate the actions of third parties, such as the leaseholder Auto Parks, Inc. or the station agent overseeing the entire area? The map originally attached to the St. Martins Station Grounds Committee's license provided no clear answer to these questions, as it only indicated as off-limits the land leased by Auto Parks, a house to be leased to a station agent, and the 10-foot clearance area on either side of the track. After the committee began its operations, it continued to negotiate the limits and liabilities of its right to work on gaps in property management at a distance from contracted labor.[42]

Such an ambiguous license to prescribe work on station-grounds offered both risks and opportunities for an organization that looked to redefine what took place on station-grounds. For-profit Auto Parks, Inc., which paved open spaces, and the nonprofit St. Martins Station Grounds Committee, which preserved open space, occupied different places on the PRR balance sheets but shared space on PRR station grounds. This arrangement incentivized the SMSGC to perform husbandry on hardscapes, and Auto Parks, Inc. to indemnify the SMSGC's operations. A spatial arrangement between Auto Parks and SMSGC, without a legal agreement between the two parties, allowed both to abdicate mutual responsibility toward one another in the course of safeguarding their concessions. Only the ethics of proprietors in St. Martins—that certain area of Chestnut Hill known for its housing cooperatives, tenants associations, and long-term lessees—insured the stewards of Hill's legacy profited from and protected the rent-paying, revenue-generating concessionaire, and the latter returned the favor.[43]

42   Jenkins and Fleitas to Hill.

43   John F. Bauman, *Public Housing, Race and Renewal: Urban Planning in Philadelphia, 1920-1974* (Philadelphia, PA: Temple University Press, 1987), chapters 1 and 2.

Just as the St. Martins Station Grounds Committee broke ground, the City of Philadelphia's passenger service improvement plans uprooted the seeds of cooperative stewardship it had sown. In a letter dated August 30, 1962, Philadelphia's managing director John A. Bailey informed the committee that much of the land surrounding St. Martins Station—both PRR property and adjoining estates—would be added to the city plan in "a legal action [that did] not require physical changes."[44] Bailey's letter did not explain how the city intended to make public ways out of private space without changing the physical properties of land leased by concessionaires (Auto Parks) and conservancies (SMSGC). Instead he offered platitudes to SMSGC for its "willingness to do something" about the condition of station grounds. Bailey's praise for "actions such as [theirs], where a group of citizens decide that they will take an active part in the management of [a station] which they use," [45] proved premature: PSIC's plans to extend public streets and public parking regulations to private ways of access to St. Martins Station incited Allston Jenkin and his peers to produce visual records of their stewardship and distribute them widely.[46]

SMSGC's publicity enticed George and Charles Woodward, trustees of Chestnut Hill's largest real estate trust, to partner with the railway conservancy in its defense of communal property rights. On May 17, 1962, Charles Woodward informed Allston Jenkins of his plans

44   John A. Bailey, PSIC, to Allston Jenkins, April 19, 1962. SMSGC papers, CHHS.

45   Ibid.

46   Photographic documentation by Franklin Williamson and George Harding, published in *Philadelphia Inquirer Magazine*, February 28, 1965, and the *Evening Bulletin*, April 30, 1962, respectively.

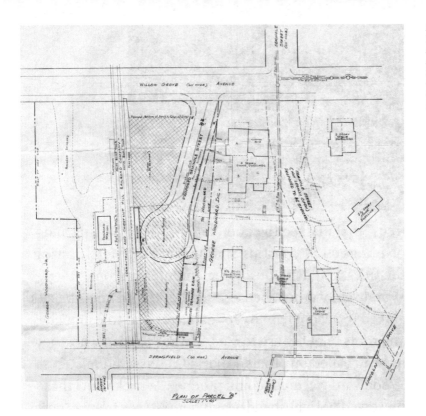

Figure 4 City Plan for St. Martins Station Grounds, as amended by the executor of abutting estates, 1962. Source: St. Martins Station Grounds Committee papers, Chestnut Hill Historical Society.

to contest the city's expropriation of common spaces for tenants of his family's estate.[47] Whereas PSIC envisioned a 60-foot-wide parkway through luxury rental housing would protect commuters' cars from impropriety on the part of tipsy commuters, neighborhood youth, and Auto Parks, Inc., Woodward proposed the city's consulting engineers extend Seminole Street, a public way, into spaces under SCSGC's governorship. Expecting the committee to approve of his endorsement, Woodward admitted "one serious defect in [the] proposed plan": "it would probably destroy the three or four buttonwood

47   George Woodward to Allston Jenkins, May 7, 1962. SMSGC papers, CHHS.

48 Ibid.

49 Ibid.

trees" that marked the boundary between parking and plantings on St. Martins Station grounds. Merely saving the trees would not be a sufficient intervention, Woodward warned, because neither the city nor the PRR agreed to accept liability for damages that tree branches and roots might cause to cars.[48] Surely, a man whose letterhead called on others "to be a CONservationist," Woodward wagered, could produce "a trick plan" that preserved both husbandry and homesteads from a "pernicious" city plan in the name of "passenger service improvements."[49] On this point, Woodward and the SMSGC ultimately disagreed.

The SMSGC lamented the loss of shade trees, but it also took issue with ceding its land grant before exhausting the power of that privilege. If the committee accepted how Woodward redistributed railroad property to the city, concessionaires, conservancies, and citizens, it would forestall and potentially prohibit work as yet unimagined as part and parcel of PRR property stewardship. Renewed annually, SMSGC's and Auto Parks's licenses could outlive the tenure of PSIC operations, which Philadelphia's City Council reassessed every six to twelve months. By contrast, the PRR's partnership with the City was precarious.[50] Although it signed on to "Operation Northwest," PRR colloquially referred to PSIC's efforts to make rail transportation affordable and accessible as "Operation Beaver"—a tongue-in-cheek critique of the marginal returns that they expected from public investments and interventions.

The SMSGC shared the PRR's skepticism of public enterprise, specifically, its promise of public-private partnership in protecting patrons of public transit from disinvestment. Unwilling to consent to a repudiation of their own regulatory regime, SMSGC's Allston Jenkins informed the PSIC and Woodward in September 1962 that it would approve only one change to the land leased to it: return to an estate plan when public, private, *and* philanthropic sectors of governance produced and prevailed on PRR property.[51] The conservancy's appeal to the past appeared regressive to PSIC directors, as it returned land to a family wealthy enough in the 1880s to provide the PRR with the land and the financial resources needed to construct a Main Line branch through its Chestnut Hill land holdings. But the SMSGC had also proved progressive in its task-force organization, impromptu collectivism, and entrepreneurial governance. The conservancy ceded its land concession to the only institution vested in conserving space for superintendents of the right-of-way within railways: the Woodwards. Knowingly, the SMSGC chose

50   See correspondence between PRR division engineer E. E. Zacharias, Jr., PRR board chairman Stuart T. Sanders, and chairmen of the WMAN Railroad Improvement Committee; for example, E. E. Zacharias to James O. Scott, March 20, 1964. WMAN collection, series II, box 4, TUA.

51   Allston Jenkins, SMSGC, to John A. Bailey, PSIC, September 29, 1962. Henry Houston Estate Papers, Estate Ledgers, 1938, 1940, 1951, CHHS.

estate geography, which upheld socio-spatial conditions to which it subscribed, over a new geography of the state that would uproot those foundations for financial and cultural investment.

Through over a half-century-old land covenants and property management principles, the Woodwards not only preserved the cultural landscape of St. Martins but also conserved the place of railway executives within it. Paved private ways on Woodward property provided vehicles and pedestrians access to St. Martins Station where PRR personnel like Hill supervised drop-offs and pick-ups—not just commuters engaged in a kiss before a ride but also homeowners picking up consumer goods from downtown department stores and small business owners ordering raw materials from Pennsylvania's Dutch country.[52] Although public use of private ways denied "complete legal frontages to [a George Woodward, Inc.] triple-house" (a three-family dwelling), blue-chip tenants such as the aforementioned Nathans family shared liability for operations taking place at their doorstep with Hill, whom they were assured kept the grounds free of litter, debris, and hazards.[53] Converting private ways on Woodward property or PRR property into public space would rupture the cooperative form of ownership that both the Woodwards and PRR required their lessees to maintain.

Cooperative ownership of St. Martins Station grounds inspired stewardship far beyond the confines of the SMSGC's leasehold—and the socio-spatial boundaries within which the PRR, state public utility commissioners,

52 James F. Nathans to Pennsylvania RR Real Estate Department, April 11, 1962. SMSGC Papers, 1962, CHHS.

53 Ibid.

and the city's Passenger Service Improvement Corporation expected it to work. Throughout Chestnut Hill and suburbanized neighborhoods of northwest Philadelphia, 40-something, married, white professionals took up residence in station houses and with it, the maintenance of surrounding station grounds on behalf of both the Reading Company and the Pennsylvania Railroad Company. Whereas railroad superintendents like Hill paid rent and received paychecks from a publicly traded corporation, stewards residing in PRR station houses between 1960 and 1985 paid $150 to $500 monthly, plus time and sweat equity, to the station committees of tax-exempt neighborhood associations. These conservancies charged their lessees with participation in a comprehensive set of critical infrastructure protection practices: husbandry, property surveillance, landscape design, safety inspections, crime prevention, building restoration, workforce development, and service quality control. Some orchestrated clean-up days from April to October, while others arranged for youth, recidivists, felons, and racial minorities to perform routine maintenance of the station-grounds under neighborhood watch programs. A few tenants of station houses even met monthly with nearby homeowners to discuss how the Brotherhood of Maintenance-of-Way Employees repaired stations, removed hazards, and reconstructed dilapidated structures, or how PRR superintendents assessed parking lot usage, city plans, and other service improvements promised and/or performed by the present purveyor of public transportation. Defying claims of "bowling alone" before the phrase became commonplace in the 1990s, bourgeois and gentrifying communities of northwest Philadelphia developed local knowledge and color commentary that the Pennsylvania Public Utility Commission adopted as a "public accounting" of which trains should continue to go unmanaged and which buildings should be maintained during the bankruptcy proceedings of PRR and Reading Company in the 1970s.[54]

The PSIC's compromising position vis-à-vis land concessionaries they purported would be partners in urban renewal at once stoked the fury and grounded the fears of a budding body politic preoccupied with just how the city's investments in suburban commutation would make back-to-the-city movements materialize. As early as October 11, 1962, city councilmen refused to appropriate an additional $1 million requested by the city architect to "simply remodel 25 commuter stations" into public transportation sites.[55] "Are we going into the railroad business? First we buy cars and now we're restoring stations?" asked one councilman. Another lamented, "We're now subsidizing the railroads to about $2M a year. How much further must we go?"[56] These men were not known to be fiscal conservatives or even stingy with public funds for private enterprise; they had just appropriated several million dollars for the electrification of the Reading Company's only commuter rail line still operating on steam power within city limits (the Fox Chase Line) and had procured twelve new train cars for the Pennsylvania

54 State acknowledgement not endorsement of these conservancies' claims to critical infrastructure protection first came in a Letter from the Pennsylvania Public Utility Commission to the Railroad Station Committee of the WMAN, June 3, 1969. WMAN collection, series II, box 4, TUA. On the political influence of collectively organized local knowledge and action, see Robert Putnam, *Bowling Alone: The Collapse and Revival of American Community* (New York: Simon and Schuster, 2001); and Richardson Dilworth, ed. *Social Capital in the City: Community and Civic Life in Philadelphia* (Philadelphia, PA: Temple University Press, 2006).

55 "Council Assails PSIC for Seeking Taxpayer Support."

56 Ibid.

Railroad. Restoration work for Reading's existing train cars at the city's expense included repair and repainting of interior surfaces, reupholstered seats and seatbacks, new electrical systems, enhanced interior lighting, safety glass, and exterior repainting.[57] In other words, Philadelphia's elected bodies invested heavily in suburban mobilization throughout the 1960s, without any agreement on which spaces and stewards constituted critical infrastructure for urban revitalization.

Despite publicity in the city's most widely read periodicals in 1962, the spatial politics of railway conservationists remained a mystery to elected officials. On the one hand, the conservancy's estate planning reassured Philadelphians, who flocked to St. Martins to live in historic homes within a quarter-mile of train stations, of the critical infrastructure they needed to earn capital gains through daily commutation to Philadelphia's business district.[58] More than a century after annexation by the City of Philadelphia, arrival at St. Martins Station in 1962 still marked one's entrance into Chestnut Hill—a garden city within the city, where "quasi-governmental" neighborhood improvement associations had extended the city's grid of streets, sewers, electricity, and water infrastructure without municipal aid.[59] While PRR closed and abandoned two of Chestnut Hill's five stations in the 1960s, it released St. Martins Station Grounds to a committee of commuters committed to partnership with other protectionists—be they superintendents, concessionaires, or real estate trusts.

57 "Memorandum with Respect to Negotiations which Will Need to Be Conducted within the Next Few Weeks between Railroads and PSIC"; Appendix to "Application of PSIC for a Loan for Purchase of Twelve Rail Diesel Cars," PSIC Agreement Negotiating Committee Minutes, August 1960. Records of the Richardson Dilworth Administration, box 2222, PCA.

58 Ibid.

59 Contosta, *Suburb in the City*, 260–62.

The SMSGC measured disinvestment in historic stations and their expansive grounds quite differently than would a public accountant of asset management, however. In contrast to the city managers of "Operation Beaver," SMSGC thought spatially about how to house rail riders and railway executives and ways to shelter their cars, conservancies, and concessionaires. In doing so, these men of means favored and trusted men with expertise, experience, and a penchant for experimentation in distributed forms of cultural landscape preservation. Because of such diffuse agency on the land that SMSGC was licensed to landscape, its track record was (and remains) hard to measure.

———

At their first meeting on PRR's inbound train platform in 1961, the St. Martins Station Grounds Committee espoused only to labor leisurely over infrastructure disinvestment they witnessed there—not to become one of dozens of railway conservancies that collectively operated as a fail-safe system for Greater Philadelphia commuters and communities come the mid-1970s. The organization's precarious partnerships with public and private institutions epitomizes, however, the concessions at play in securing the right to work. Simultaneously granting and claiming space, this nonprofit concessionaire took on responsibilities of their guarantor, an employer of building superintendents and landscape attendants, in order to grant these men governorship of labor and leisure in times of fiscal austerity and corporate restructuring. By agreeing to mobilize knowledge and action on the condition of common spaces into the foreseeable future, both station stewards and superintendents, concessionaries and communities, contractors and corporations, came away with something when the possibility of getting nothing proved probable.

Concessionary agreements, forged through private correspondence and public utility contracts, miscommunicated consensus and safeguards against its collapse to the very cities and citizens invested in them. Knowledge of which guarantees, such as the equitable provision of workplaces throughout Pennsylvania Railroad properties, would expire when remained limited to those who executed the contracts: conservancies. Both public and private bodies with a stake in the city's future found themselves at a loss—politically and financially—when each tried in SMSGC's early years to engage critically and constructively with the spatial epistemologies of conservationists at work on rights-of-way. Without experiential and tacit knowledge of the common space that SMSGC strived to preserve, neither the city's Passenger Service Improvement Corporation nor the Woodward Estate could defend or appropriate the conservancy's right to protect and police private property of public utility. In this instance and increasingly, many other cases of cultural landscape preservation, artifices of public-private partnership—leaseholds and land covenants—at once rupture the unitary constitution of "common space" while rendering physical, economic, and political frameworks for its reconstruction and repair.

The SMSGC's stewardship of such fiscally insecure and politically contentious grounds in the 1960s illustrates how a city's white-collar suburbanites can set aside their recourse to white flight for the common good of the city's blue-collar and blue-chip communities. Whereas conservative collectives at the center of "whiteness studies" typically seek out places away from city politics and problems to call their own, this case of railway conservancies shows that they can also chart a "space of their own" to share with diverse populations inside city limits by working outside the protections and privileges of city government. The cost of eschewing rugged individualism proved affordable and worthwhile, in this case. Concession to railroad companies and their regulatory regimes in the form of licenses to work on station grounds and leases for landscaped space enabled St. Martins men to contest both city power and suburban autonomy.[60]

Admittedly, highlighting a single case of critical infrastructure protection, a complex and common mode of conservation, can play a polarizing yet productive role in contemporary debates over who operates, underwrites, and manages services and spaces of public utility—from public education to public transit. In fact, the rights-of-way discussed here have already become a "third rail" in urban discourse—a potentially electrifying line of critical inquiry into concessions with its fair share of dangers.

60 Neither mobility nor transportation figures in the "new suburban history." See Becky M. Nicolaides and Andrew Wiese, eds., *The Suburb Reader* (New York: Routledge, 2006); and Thomas Sugrue and Kevin Kruse, eds., *The New Suburban History* (Chicago: University of Chicago Press, 2006). A few works, however, substantiate spatial epistemologies of suburban mobilization in metropolitan America. See, for example, Eric Avila, *Popular Culture in the Age of White Flight: Fear and Fantasy in Suburban Los Angeles* (Berkeley: University of California Press, 2004); and Kevin Kruse, *White Flight: Atlanta and the Making of Modern Conservatism* (Princeton, NJ: Princeton University Press, 2005).

Investigative journalists working for the *Philadelphia Inquirer* in the 1970s aroused a backlash with their series of feature magazine articles on homesteading as a mode of public space privatization. Those who occupied railroad buildings and tended to the surrounding landscape "know they are on the right side of the track," one article began, slighting those that made station grounds a part of the community development movement by clearly demarcating the boundary between the homesteads of stewards and the homes and gardens of station agents.[61]

What is the place of railway conservancies and stewards when the right to the city belongs to all who claim it? Who is the "right man for the job" of maintaining railways (and other infrastructure)? These questions remain open for investigation by blue-chip and blue-collar communities, especially as nearly every major city and many suburbs underwrite "green-collar" and "no-collar" consortiums to convert abandoned railways into parkways and conserve them for non-motorized travel and leisure, as New York City's Friends of the Highline have done. For the St. Martins Station Grounds Committee, in particular, railway conservancies that took responsibility for the upkeep of station grounds had the right to regulate buildings and landscapes, not the right to reside in or resettle the station houses they restored. When the Brotherhood of Maintenance-of-Way Workers sought authority to restore stations, not just maintain them, the St. Martins Station Committee did not join fellow licensees and lessees of railroad property in contesting

61   "They Know They Are on the Right Side of the Track," *Philadelphia Inquirer,* April 29, 1977.

62 SEPTA Commuter Rail Station Improvement Program Meeting Minutes (attendance list of complainants and constituents), April 1, 1977. WMAN, series II, box 4, TUA.

unionization of all railway maintenance.[62] Instead, Philadelphia's consummate blue-chip conservancy continued to ground maintenance work for blue-collar brotherhoods in its own boundary work. Such a concessionary way of situating itself in urban space may just have laid the groundwork for working-class communities to construct and conserve their own right-of-way.

EL PUEBLO
NICARAGUENSE
AL GENERAL

ANASTASIO
SOMOZA

MANAGUA D.N. 27 MAYO
1937

The Volcanic Heart of Nicaragua: Tiscapa and the Spatiality of Political Culture, 1936–1990

Ryne Clos

On a clear day, Tiscapa's profile is visible from most of Managua. Elevated several hundred feet above the city, the rim of the (now dormant) volcano contains several natural and human-made symbols of Nicaraguan national identity through the ages: the small lagoon formed inside the ancient crater, the ruins of Somoza's most notorious dungeon, a toppled equine statue imported from Italy, a massive wooden monument to national hero Augusto Sandino, and, for a brief electoral campaign in summer 2011, a billboard with a political advertisement. Both literally and symbolically, Tiscapa has served as a center of political epistemology for the city as well as the nation. Its various symbols have assisted the citizens in coming to know the governing logic of the various ruling regimes.

Figure 1 The former placard for the statue of Anastasio Somoza atop Mussolini's horse, now leaned against the dethroned remains of the monument. The National Historic Park of Tiscapa maintains the ruin as a reminder of tyrannies broken. Source: Telemaco.

On Tiscapa, successive national and state administrations have endeavored to foster political consensus.

In most cases, however, such attempts have failed, as Nicaragua's political instability over time attests. The two most important governments in Nicaragua's tumultuous history, especially from a state-building perspective, are the dynastic dictatorial regime of the Somoza family (1936–1979) and the ambitious revolutionary regime of the Sandinistas, which took power once the Somozas were removed (1979–1990). Unsurprisingly, these two governments sought to impose their authority over Nicaraguan society by utilizing opposed logics of governance. Under Somoza, Nicaragua was governed within the matrix of what Jacques Rancière terms the "police." Police functions at the level of society as a whole and is chiefly interested in maintaining an already established order. It is a minimalist statecraft. The Sandinistas, on the other hand, operated under an Althusserian logic of governance, centered upon individual citizens in an effort to achieve interpellation, a maximalist statecraft. Both of these logics were manifest within symbols erected by their respective governments within the metaphorical space of Tiscapa.

"Police" implies a strict surveillance state and a reliance on force to maintain a tenuous order. While it is true that Somocista Nicaragua eventually devolved to such authoritarian depths, this connection should be avoided. What Rancière intended was something much less onerous to Western audiences; in fact, police is the governing logic of the United States and European Union member countries. The primary goal of the police state is not to brutalize citizens into submission; rather, it is to prevent dissensus by simulating consensus. According to Rancière, what underlies this governing style is a "there is nothing to see here" mentality: the police state atomizes society by pretending that all is well and that the population is in agreement, even if this is not the case.[1] It is not a regime that reaches out to each individual as a way of gaining that individual's personal support for the government. It rejects this type of micro-governance for a more "macro" approach.

In a Rancièrean point of view, the state needs submissive cooperation, which he calls circulation. To be a state means that the cooperation of the people has been obtained while deploying as few resources as possible. For such minimalist statecraft, the negation of politics, of free and critical thinking and of open contestation of power, is required. In other words, consensus does not actually exist, but states must work to simulate it; dissensus is stamped out through the erection of artificial

1 Jacques Rancière, *On the Shores of Politics*, trans. Liz Heron (London: Verso, 1995), 177.

consensus. For this, the people need to be assured that "there is nothing to see here," so that they will continue to circulate in their normal routines. If they stop to examine whether or not there is actually something to see (if they, in Rancièrean terms, break their circulation), this may elicit creative thought. The police is a management scheme, taming the social through categorization, which is maintained by circulation.[2] Free thinking arising at an interruption of circulation may result in subjectivization: the citizen becomes a subject with her/his own agency to take action in the world. The consequence of subjectivization is politics, which is negation of the police.[3] Politics is, by its nature, ephemeral, rare, and exceedingly unstable. A political actor (meaning a genuine subject) going beyond the confines of police, threatens to pull down an entire government, because such an actor will reveal that the consensus upon which this government rules is really just simulation.[4]

The Althusserian complement to Rancièrean political theory is the idea of "interpellation."[5] According to Althusser, ideology is able to activate one's inherent subject-ness in such a way as to join citizens to the state apparati that govern their daily lives.[6] In this system, each citizen is "hailed" by the government as a distinct, pre-existing subject and is brought into the fold of national society. Althusser summarizes this logic in the phrase, "hey, you there."[7] Rather than the state attempting to keep people out by means of the police and circulation, the state in Althusser's view brings people in by means of

2   Kristin Ross, *May '68 and Its Afterlives* (Chicago: University of Chicago Press, 2002), 22–24.

3   Jacques Rancière, "Politics, Identification, and Subjectivization," in *The Identity in Question*, ed. John Rajchman (New York: Routledge, 1995), 63–70. For the most focused discussion of subjectivization, see 66–68.

4   Rancière is a very systematic and abstract thinker. He rarely states propositions baldly. To present his thought as I have here requires synthesizing a number of his works into a broader framework. For this reason, citing a single chapter and page of a single work to identify discrete ideas is difficult. Rancière's works consulted in this paragraph include the following: *On the Shores of Politics*; "Politics, Identification, and Subjectivization"; "Ten Theses on Politics," trans. Davide Panagia and Rachel Bowlby, *Theory and Event* 5, no. 3 (2001); *Disagreement: Politics and Philosophy*, trans. Julie Rose (Minneapolis: University of Minnesota Press, 1999); and Ross, *May '68 and Its Afterlives*.

5   It is worth pointing out that Rancière studied under Althusser. He is rightfully considered an Althusserian scholar; however, this does not mean that the political philosophies of the two of them must be in fundamental agreement. At their root, they adopt diametrically opposed theories of what a state is or should be. Whereas Althusser reveals confidence both in the ability
and the desirability of a state to employ micro-level processes like interpellation as a way of forging genuine consensus, Rancière instead posits that states, except in certain extreme circumstances, cannot do this, and, further, it would be a terrible reality if they could do it.

6   For Althusser, subjectivization is a birthright, whereas for Rancière it is something obtained through a process. Althusser explains his ideas of political subjectivization and subjecthood in his 1969 essay "Ideology and Ideological State Apparatuses (Notes towards an Investigation)." Reprinted in

his *Lenin and Philosophy and Other Essays*, trans. Ben Brewster (New York: Monthly Review Press, 1971), 127–86.

7   Althusser, "Ideology and Ideological State Apparatuses," 174.

hailing them, the "hey" recruiting the subject. He calls this process interpellation.

Reaching out to each individual as a distinct member of the population is micro-statecraft. The Althusserian theory of the state opposes the macro-statecraft asseverated by Rancière. In Althusser's view the state is an actor capable of controlling its citizen-subjects through the ideological penetration enabled by interpellation. The people are still manipulated through a state-centered consensus, but it is a radically different type of consensus consisting of individuals being personally convinced by the regime to "buy into" the state-building project. Whereas for Rancière stability is maintained by the state at a societal level, for Althusser stability comes from the agreement of each individual citizen. His is a much more interventionist system of governance. For Rancière, such intervention and ideological convincing at the level of the individual citizen is neither possible nor necessary. This is the primary distinction between these two related theorists: for Rancière, the state does not need to convince its citizenry to cooperate, but rather convince its citizens to not dissent.

The fundamental principles of these opposing political systems adopted by the Somozas and the Sandinistas are represented in the built environment of Tiscapa. The space displayed for the population the way that each regime sought to simulate consensus in order to govern the country. Somocismo's Rancièrean police state is revealed by the structures of the presidential palace, the

Monument to Roosevelt, and the Mazmorras prison, as well as the invitation-only access to Tiscapa.

Sandinismo's reliance upon Althusserian interpellation as its governing methodology is highlighted by the democratization of the space of Tiscapa, the partial destruction and renaming of the Somocista edifices, and the utilization of Tiscapa's metaphorically fertile soil for help in constructing a new national myth founded on defiance and resistance. The Nicaraguan population's knowledge of the political under these state administrations was dictated by a spatial epistemology activated atop Tiscapa, the country's political space par excellence.

TISCAPA AND SOMOCISMO AS RANCIÈREAN POLICE REGIME

Somocismo was initiated following the Nicaraguan civil war of 1926–1933. During that war, the state battled against a number of Liberal warlords. The Nicaraguan government forces were supported both logistically and militarily by an occupation force of US Marines, and the war was characterized by a series of pacts between the battling factions and the US forces. By the end of 1927, only one warlord—Augusto Sandino—remained in the fight. His duel against government and US forces lasted six more years, finally ending after the war-weary US forces grew cash strapped, in light of the Great Depression. Before leaving Nicaragua, the occupation forces brokered a ceasefire and created a government defense force, called the National Guard. The leader of the Guard was Anastasio Somoza Garcia. While Sandino had agreed to the ceasefire, he then entered a political battle for influence over the new president, Juan Sacasa, against Somoza. Both military men vied for the greater voice, culminating in the assassination of Sandino by the National Guard in February 1934. In an auspicious and ironic twist, Sandino was gunned down atop Tiscapa. With the threat of his greatest rival eliminated, Somoza staged a coup and became president of Nicaragua in 1936. He held this position (in various guises) until his assassination by the poet Rigoberto Lopez Perez in 1956. Somoza's eldest son, Luis Somoza Debayle, replaced him. Luis died of a heart attack in 1967 and his younger brother, Anastasio Somoza Debayle, followed him on the throne. The third Somoza would head the Nicaraguan government until the revolutionary overthrow of July 1979.

The original Somoza set about an ambitious state-building project of trying to incorporate the great masses of the Nicaraguan citizenry, heretofore ignored by every government in the country's history, into the national fold. At the same time, he sought to curry the favor of the traditional elites upon whom stable government had always depended. In many ways, Somoza was brilliantly successful, proving that he was an astute politician and skilled coalition builder. He destroyed the legacy of Sandino by banning all books about the former warlord except the one he himself wrote, which discredited Sandino as a bandit, Communist, and one who defied

8 Anastasio Somoza Garcia, *El verdadero Sandino o el calvario de los Segovias* (Managua: Tipografía Robelo, 1936).

the core Nicaraguan values of family and Church.[8] He was able to give workers and peasants a sense of belonging and a claim to a better future (one that they would never receive under any Somoza) through various promises of unionization and agrarian reform. Finally, he bought off the support of the elites by showing how his concessions to the underclass were part of a cold, rational political calculus to ensure broad quiescence and the maintenance of the status quo. A final core tenet of Somocismo was an absolute non-tolerance of violent challenge. Somoza consented to oppositional political parties (including a Moscow-line Communist Party), held periodic elections for these parties to contest, and permitted a free press that often criticized him, but he did not allow dissent that escaped the formulaic nature of his version of rigged democracy. He was ruthless in crushing any armed revolt that arose within Nicaragua under his watch. All of this is consistent with Rancière's notion of the police: he did not reach out ideologically through state apparati to convince Nicaraguans to consent; rather he constructed a simulated consensus that persuaded most Nicaraguans to cooperate with the rules of governance because everyone else was doing so and any rule-breaking resistance would thereby be futile. In other words, in Somoza's Nicaragua, there was nothing to see here.

In the space atop Tiscapa, every pillar of Somoza's state-building process was given imposing physical expression. The presidential palace, in which three generations of Somozas lived, was located at the summit of the volcano. Another symbol of Somocismo situated there was the Monument to Roosevelt (or Monument to Liberalism), built in 1939 as a sign of friendship between two good neighbors, Somoza and Franklin D. Roosevelt. A third structure highlighting the parameters of the Somoza regime was Mazmorras, a notorious dungeon where high profile political prisoners were held and brutally tortured.

Figure 3   Monument to Roosevelt, which cemented the dictatorial Somozas in the history of liberalism in 1939. The Sandinista regime, which ousted Somoza in 1979, renamed it the Monument to Revolutionary Martyrs in honor of citizens' sacrifice for liberation. Source: Telemaco.

The palace symbolized the opulence and separateness of the Somoza family, as well as the watchful eye of the leader. It was built a few years prior to Somoza's coup, but the population of Nicaragua associates it with the family dictatorship. Ernesto Cardenal echoed the general sentiment when he called it the "feudal palace" in his masterful poem "Oracle over Managua."[9] By means of the palace, the rulers lived above the city, not beholden to the grind of daily life in the searing poverty of the urban slums spread out to the north of the volcano. They occupied a panoptic position from which they gazed over

9   Ernesto Cardenal, "Oracle over Managua," in Ernesto Cardenal, *Zero Hour and Other Documentary Poems*, ed. and trans. Donald D. Walsh (New York: New Directions, 1973), 43–68; citation from 53.

Figure 4   The imposing Presidential Palace, as seen by citizens below (prior to the earthquake on December 23, 1972). Source: City of Managua.

their subjects—an ever-watchful presence, ready to trample any sign of out-of-line behavior. The Somozas governed by decree, and their residential perch *above* Managua and its people was the perfect symbolic marker of the distance between the rulers and the ruled in the country: the former were neither involved nor immersed in the struggles of the latter.

In the time of the Somozas, Tiscapa was gated and guarded. Access was limited and by invitation only. This institutionalized, in spatial symbols, the nature of the political in Somoza's Nicaragua. The state existed as a body that came down (or spoke down) to the people, promising hope and change and a better future, but never opened a forum to give them their own voice. Citizens were spoken to, not spoken with. The Somoza regime made no genuine attempt to curry popular favor or convince the people of the good nature of their rule. Instead, they sought to fortify the illusion that there was no alternative to Somocismo by pointing to an implied social consensus.

The mountain, the gates, and the imposing architecture of the massive palace all represented a politics of simulated consensus. Somocismo was simple to understand: "Behave and your children may have a better life, but step out of line and you will be destroyed." This was an uneasy, illusory consensus dependent upon the bayonets of the National Guard, but it was in fact a real consensus at the same time, maintained for more than 40 years. The simulation was realistic enough—the assurances of nothing to see here sufficiently convincing—to prop up the Somoza regime for decades. In the simulated consensus prevailing in Nicaragua at the time, the beautiful, opulent palace and the limited access to the mountaintop embodied the better future of consumerist privilege that anyone in Nicaragua might achieve, even while the panoptic positioning of the palace pointed to the danger of misconduct.

In reality, consistent with a Rancièrean view of the state and society, the political did not exist under Somoza. Politics was reduced to a simple referendum whereby Nicaraguans either agreed to play within the rules or not.[10] The palace on Tiscapa represented this well. "Stay down there, where we can see you, and do as you are told," it seemed to say. The coalition of purchased elites and toiling underclass yearning for a promised future of good things, came to know the regime and its rules for society through this space of simulated political consensus.[11] The separateness of the presidential palace, set above the city in its restricted

10   In their book *The Politics of Antipolitics: The Military in Latin America* (Lincoln: University of Nebraska Press, 1978), Brian Loveman and Thomas M. Davies, Jr., introduce the concept of "antipolitics" into Latin American historiography. "Antipolitics" represents the collapse of the state into the military; Latin American militaries, in the name of modernization and progress, took over governments and eliminated genuine political challenge. It is in this sense that I refer to the abolition of politics under Somoza.

11   The blatant corruption and greed of Anastasio Somoza Debayle in the wake of the Christmas 1972 earthquake would shatter this consensus. The people saw that the promises made from Tiscapa were hollow. The elites saw the people no longer bought into the concessionary scheme of Somocismo. Both groups then moved away from the regime and established various movements to replace Somoza.

environment, symbolized this simulation of consensus.

Similarly, the Monument to Roosevelt speaks to simulated consensus on Tiscapa. A processional staircase, pearly white and flanked by low walls, leads to an elevated plinth where, between two giant stone pillars, is displayed a commemorative bust of the US president mounted on a pedestal. The stairs rise in a series of four discrete sets of approximately 12 steps each. On the first two landings, cannons stand sentinel. On the third and fourth landings, a manicured hedge grows, extending around the statuary. Two pillars, approximately 25 feet tall, tightly frame the pedestal, which also contains a plaque describing the monument. There is a single vanishing point structuring this composition: the pedestal containing the bust of Roosevelt, the symbol of Somoza's liberal order of obedient cooperation. The citizens had one path and one acceptable goal.

The monument encapsulates additional aspects of Somocismo: the close relationship with the United States and the martial nature of the established order. Somoza was nominally the head of the old Liberal Party and his liberal order was aptly symbolized by cannons, statuary, and manicured shrubs. To the people, this space clearly denoted the strict law-and-order nature of Somocista police through its appearance of shiny newness, maintained with great care and protected by irresistible force. Its well-tended hedges delineate circulation, like Somocismo's creating a cooperative circulation of citizens internally and portraying Nicaragua as stable, dependable, and well-maintained internationally. The landscaping was a clear spatial metaphor about Somocista consensus: on a surface level, everything is tidy. The sparkling surface and right-angled edges suggest, "Everything is in order, as always." The cannons, however, warn against stopping to question this. They belie the superficial image of political consensus by promising a fiery fate to those who dared to attempt to mount the stairs in the wrong fashion.

The monument produced other spatial metaphors as well. By adding the appellation of "to Roosevelt," Somoza performed two simultaneous symbolic tasks. First, he reached out to his Good Neighbor to the north, a man respected throughout Latin America because of his promise to fight fascism throughout the world. By adding Roosevelt's name, Somoza pointed to his own anti-fascist nature, the promise of democracy, and a good future. He was co-opting Roosevelt's Four Freedoms as a fundamental aspect of his own liberal rule. It gave Somocista governance a veneer of striving toward Roosevelt, intended to teach the citizenry that his simulated consensus was functioning as intended. By commemorating the Good Neighbor policy, Somoza also illustrated how powerful his police order was, as his relationship with Roosevelt promised destruction to anyone who dared to examine whether there was, in fact, something to see here.

The second task accomplished by the "to Roosevelt" in the monument's name was the subversion of the

12   Theodore Roosevelt drew the ire of Latin Americans with his aggressive foreign policy to the region. His presidency in the first decade of the 20th century was characterized by the Platt Amendment toward Cuba; the reassertion of the Monroe Doctrine with the addition of the "Roosevelt Corollary"; the Canal controversy between the United States, Panama, and Nicaragua; and the invasion and occupation of the Dominican Republic. Shortly after Roosevelt left office, the United States invaded and occupied Nicaragua, an occupation ended only by Sandino's years of violent resistance. It is no surprise that Roosevelt had so rankled Darío.

beloved poem of Ruben Darío, titled "To Roosevelt," penned in 1905 and addressed to Theodore Roosevelt rather than Franklin.[12] One of the most accomplished modernist poets in the world, Darío was celebrated by Nicaraguans as their greatest historical figure, a hero who brought glory and fame to the nation. "To Roosevelt" was among Darío's most widely appreciated works within Nicaragua, because of its political nature and its tone of defiance. In the poem, he points to the contradictions of US foreign policy to Latin America. He warns the US president, who he calls Hunter, that God and history are on the side of the Latin Americans and that US hegemony depends on force of arms alone, a force of arms that will surely one day cease to be so dominant. By building a monument and dedicating it "to Roosevelt," Somoza was attempting to co-opt this legacy.

Somoza wanted to be the greatest Nicaraguan, beloved and celebrated by his countrymen as the hero who put the country on the map. He also wanted to show that Nicaragua was a Good Neighbor to the United States rather than a defiant nuisance. Darío metaphorically challenged Somocismo's police by indicating that, in fact, there was something to see here: a nefarious and parasitic imperialist relationship, with the United States draining Nicaragua of its riches by force of arms. Such a view had to be foreclosed to maintain the simulation of consensus and the cooperation of the citizenry. Somoza wanted to un-do the antagonistic name-calling of Darío and show that for the new Nicaragua he was building, the

United States was an obdurate ally, not a threatening hunter. Even US dominance based on a surplus of weaponry was mimicked in his Nicaragua (in the cannons guarding the monument). In this manner, the politics of consensus-building and the spatial epistemology of Tiscapa inflect even the naming of Somoza's monument to Liberalism.

The third spatial representation of Somocista consensus atop Tiscapa was the most diabolical: the Mazmorras prison. Into the dungeons of this pitiless structure were cast the most dangerous political prisoners in Nicaragua. Throughout the reign of the three Somozas, hundreds of armed challenger groups rose up against the dictatorship, some (as mentioned earlier) quite effectively. The most successful of these armed rebellions was the FSLN-led insurrection which ultimately eclipsed the third Somoza. When dissidents were captured by the regime, however, they were often placed in captivity in Mazmorras. This was an ironic inversion of the dynamic of the ruling regime, as the only "ordinary" Nicaraguans invited to come to the gated top of Managua's volcano were those challenging the government's existence. Somoza brought his enemies up with him, onto his own level above the city. Once imprisoned, rebels would be mercilessly tortured, in ways both creative and conventional. One particularly famous torture involved caging prisoners with the dictator's exotic cats, a lion and panther. The cats became their own symbolic institution, mentioned in numerous dissident poems in the 1970s, and came to be spatial representations of Somocismo in their own right. The knowing conveyed by the cats dismantled the simulated consensus of Somoza: the former police order had reached its limit. A lion's den in the middle of the capital city disrupted Somocista circulation and led to an increasing amount of subjectivization, the death knell for any Rancièrean police order.

Mazmorras helped to complete the spatialization of Somocista state building by highlighting its essential ambiguity. It demonstrated that while Tiscapa was the space of consensus building in Somoza's Nicaragua, this consensus was always a simulation. The three most important architectural representations were the palace, surveilling and separate; the monument to Roosevelt, subverting Darío's fame and highlighting Nicaragua's good neighborliness; and the dungeon of Mazmorras, pointing to Somoza's ruthless persecution of those who tried to broaden the definition of the political in "his" Nicaragua. His ownership of the country was unquestioned atop Tiscapa, where only Somozas and their invited guests were welcome. When the Sandinista insurrection achieved its final victory and entered Managua triumphantly in July 1979, Tiscapa remained a space teaching the people of the nature of the government, but for a radically different regime.

Figure 5   Silhouette of Augustino Cesar Sandino, a national symbol of revolution. The wooden statue towers over the space that once housed the Somoza regime which Sandinista forces and followers deposed. Source: Telemaco.

The remodeling of Tiscapa-as-political-space began on
the very day of the revolutionary triumph, July 19, 1979,
when an angry mob of Managuans ran up the hill that
they had never before been allowed to access to begin
dismantling the old presidential palace, hated symbol of
a spurned dictator. There are two approaches to Tiscapa,
one via automobile and road, which leads to the volcanic
crater and the monuments very easily but leaves the traveler a fair distance from the other sites, and one via foot
and paved staircase. Most of the mob rushed up the staircase, which more directly accessed the vacated residence
and the Mazmorras prison. The staircase passes through
a garden in which stood the Statue of Justice (according
to legend, its likeness depicted Salvadora Debayle, wife
of the original Somoza and mother of his two sons). In
the rush up the staircase, an anonymous member of the
mob beheaded the statue. There was a new political consensus, of democratization and people power to be perpetuated in public space. A new Nicaragua had begun,
symbolized by some "refashioning" on Tiscapa.

The Sandinista revolutionary junta initiated a new
state-building project from scratch, seeking both to erase
the remaining vestiges of Somoza's collapsed rule and
replace Somocismo with Sandinismo, a Nicaragua of lit-
eracy, full stomachs, and vaccinations, of art, popular
Catholicism, and a mixed economy. The FSLN was much

more ambitious than any of the Somozas and they displayed their audacity in their treatment of Tiscapa. They democratized this space, making the former private playground of the megalomaniacal dictator into a public park, the Parque Histórico Nacional Loma de Tiscapa. The palace was destroyed. The prison was mostly ruined as well, but part of its dungeon was left there deliberately, with twisted stubs of rebar dangling from the cracked foundation. The architectural erasure was a symbol of the excision of Somoza from Nicaragua's political culture and popular imagination, but by leaving that process incomplete the Sandinistas left behind a scar, so that the people would never forget. This purification ritual of near-complete, intentionally partial dismantling of Somocismo's edifices and their replacement by new Sandinista monuments and buildings was repeated all over the country, but most ardently and symbolically on Tiscapa, due to its personal connection to Somoza. Across Nicaragua, the old National Guard barracks became cultural centers, the former National Palace (where the faux-parliament made laws under Somoza) became a national history museum, and several sites destroyed by indiscriminate government bombing or corruption were left intentionally in ruins.[13] Sandinista governmentality was decidedly spatial and Tiscapa emphasized that basic logic of the revolutionary regime nearly to hyperbole.

13 Most famously, when the Sandinistas oversaw the rebuilding of Managua, they refused to name the streets as a permanent symbol of Somoza's corruption and greed.

In addition to erasing old symbols, the Sandinistas renamed some of the old structures left intact and brought in new symbols of the new Nicaragua. Guiding this process was the implementation of an Althusserian model of governance, where the interpellation of individual citizens was accomplished by "hailing" them, replacing the simulated consensus of Somoza with a "real existing" consensus. One of Somoza's more famous qualities, humorous in light of his public dedication to Roosevelt and the Allied cause in World War II, was his obsession with the fascist Benito Mussolini. One notorious manifestation of Somoza's great personal admiration for the Italian leader was his purchase an old bronze statue depicting Mussolini astride a massive horse. Somoza had the rider's head replaced with a bust of his own head, transforming the statue of Mussolini into a statue of Somoza on horseback. In May 1954, Somoza publicly unveiled the statue of himself, which he placed in front of the national baseball stadium (which he had also named after himself). The statue was about twice life-size and was mounted on a pillar approximately 20 feet tall, so that it was both imposing and ostentatious. Ernesto Cardenal sarcastically captured the moment in verse in his 1954 poem "Somoza Unveils Somoza's Statue of Somoza in the Somoza Stadium." Somoza Stadium was not atop Tiscapa, but the horse would make its way there during the early stages of Sandinismo state building.

On July 20, 1979, the day after the storming of Tiscapa and the beheading of the Statue of Justice, another similarly angry mob invaded Somoza Stadium and pulled the statue to the ground. They obliterated the effigy of Somoza, but left most of the actual horse intact where it had toppled. From here, its story is murky, but at some point in the very early stages of postwar reconstruction, a truck moved the remains of the statue to Tiscapa and ignominiously dropped it there. There, at Tiscapa, remained the rear half of the horse, together with the plaque from its unveiling ceremony in May 1954.[14] The Sandinista government built a fence around it and left it in the new park on Tiscapa, to serve as a warning to imperialists and tyrants to stay out of Nicaragua. This was the new popular conception of Somoza, the result of the disruption of circulation and the rise of subjectivization: an egotistical, US-imposed foreign tyrant. Hatred of Somoza was nigh-universal in Nicaragua in 1979, whereas support for the more radical programming being postulated by the Sandinistas was not. In effect, by parlaying anti-Somoza sentiment as a facsimile of Sandinismo, the FSLN junta played to the surest sympathies of the people as it began its (ultimately failed) effort to construct genuine consensus modelled on Althusserian statecraft.[15]

In transporting the toppled horse and leaving the beheaded statue standing in the newly democratized Tiscapa, the FSLN made visible a new politics of consensus in its early stages: so too did their renaming of the monument to Liberalism/Roosevelt. The FSLN decided the site should be rededicated to the martyrs of the revolutionary struggle. Renaming the Monument to Revolutionary Martyrs not only reclaimed the "To Roosevelt" for Darío, taking the national legacy away

14   In case the symbolism is missed by a quick reader, what remained of the statue was the horse's ass.

15   The statue is not the only Mussolini artifact to be found atop Tiscapa. Mussolini knew Somoza personally and once gave him an Italian tank. For most of the 1980s, the tank and a placard explaining it (a direct link between Somoza and fascism) were on display in Managua, but not Tiscapa. It is unknown when the tank was moved from its location in the earthquake ruins to the top of the volcano. Because I do not know which state-building regime is responsible for placing it in the consensus-building space of Tiscapa, I have left it out of my analysis.

from the spurned dictator and returning it to the celebrated poet, but it also enshrined a new pantheon of national heroes. It was not the martial sentinels of the National Guard, defenders of the core values of the country and represented by the stately cannons, who encapsulated the heroic nature of Nicaraguan citizenship; it was the dead insurgents, rebellious youths, romantic poets, the beheaders of statuary in angry mobs who would now serve as the model of the national mythos. The cannons no longer symbolized the threat of a fiery death to challengers of a martial law-and-order, but rather somber, respectful mourning of those who were killed to make the revolution possible. They were no longer an open threat of the police order meant to guarantee unquestioning circulation: their killing ability surrendered, they now represented honor and sacrifice. This was the heart of Sandinista state building. Historian Luciano Baracco has explained the diffusion of a new Sandino narrative as the essential tenet of Sandinismo, which is a component of the broader Sandinista efforts at interpellation and of constructing a mythos of resistance and defiance.[16] Tiscapa played a pivotal role in all of this reconstruction of the Nicaraguan imaginary, as its monuments sought to interpellate the citizenry as Nicaraguan nationals in an historical line of grand resistance fighters.

Another crucial element in the renaming of this monument was that it announced the severing of good neighborliness with the United States. In Sandinismo, Yankee

16   Luciano Baracco, *Nicaragua: The Imagining of a Nation: From Nineteenth-Century Liberals to Twentieth-Century Sandinistas* (New York: Algora Publishing, 2005).

imperialism was averred as the ultimate source of Nicaragua's historical dependency and weakness. Such connections had to be stamped out. In this way, the FSLN also readopted Darío's pivotal "To Roosevelt" for themselves; by reclaiming the monument and the poetic phrasing on behalf of the resistance and away from the old government-US partnership, they were naming themselves as the divine retribution against the Hunter of which Darío foretold in his verse. The destined failure of the preponderant US-American advantage in force of arms to hold back the people of Latin America (who had an equally imposing dominance in regard to spiritual force of arms) that had been prophesied by Darío in 1905, was symbolically claimed by the Sandinista state builders. They represented Latin America's inherent superiority over the materialistic, cultureless United States. Obliterating the reference to Franklin D. Roosevelt in the monument helped the Sandinista government claim the epistemological space of Tiscapa to teach this line of thinking to the park's visitors in the 1980s, hailing them as members of a society defying US geopolitical/imperial machinations.

Tiscapa represented the spatial politics of Sandinismo in a less concrete way as well. This was in the rebuilding of Managua following the twin disasters of the Christmas 1972 earthquake and the 1977–1979 insurrectionary war. Somoza had never reconstructed the capital city after the tremor. Instead he had smuggled the international relief money into his own bank accounts (by 1972, every construction firm in Nicaragua was owned by the Somoza family, so reconstruction aid went directly to the dynasty). In pre-earthquake Managua, Tiscapa was in the geographical heart of the city. In the post-earthquake, post-revolution Managua, however, the city shifted geographically by pivoting away from the traditional center along Lake Managua (to the north of the city) and toward the south and east. As the Sandinista government rebuilt the city, Tiscapa was literally decentered within Managua. It remained symbolically important, of course, but was no longer visible from every point in the city. The new generation of Managuans, the first born into the Sandinistas' new Nicaragua, lived in a city where they likely could not see the symbols atop Tiscapa from their homes. In a less-than-deliberate way, the importance of Tiscapa was diminished by this series of moves.

It is worth noting, as well, that the Sandinista junta members did not live atop Tiscapa. In Sandinista Nicaragua—the new Nicaragua, where "Our Vengeance toward Our Enemies Will Be the Pardon" (a central tenet of the Sandinista self-image)[17]—the need for a watchful gaze over the city was abolished. Order was not imposed from above in a revolutionary society, but rather organically sprouted in the streets, from below. This demonstrates, spatially, the difference between Somoza's Rancièrean style and the new Althusserian methodology of the Sandinistas. In a Rancièrean state, order is imposed by police who circulate society under their watchful gaze, whereas in the Althusserian model, the

17 This is the title of a famous pamphlet written by one of the original Sandinista founders as a way to explicate the revolutionary government's official policy toward the human rights violators of the Somoza regime, including the torturers. Tomás Borge, "Our Vengeance toward Our Enemies Will Be the Pardon," pamphlet, 1981.

people are "won over" by the government, so that their consent is authentic and not maintained through constant surveillance.

A final Sandinista effort to redefine political culture in Nicaragua by using Tiscapa as a space of consensus was the erection of an enormous wooden statue of Sandino, 59 feet tall on the highest point of the volcano. This was done in 1990, in the throes of the hotly contested electoral battle between the Sandinistas and a US-backed opposition coalition. The FSLN lost these elections, but the massive Sandino statue remained. In Sandinista Nicaragua, Sandino became ubiquitous in public spaces all over the country as the essence of government interpellation efforts. This was a direct consequence of two pillars of Sandinismo: the propagation of a Sandino mythology as a national mythology and intense government patronage of the arts. The FSLN sought to restructure Nicaraguan national identity as centered on resistance and defiance against foreign forces holding the homeland back and selected Sandino as the most prominent example of this rebellious spirit of fighting for an independent Nicaragua. In the effort to bring this message to Nicaraguans, the government, via the empowered Ministry of Culture, sponsored thousands of murals and statues of Sandino. The wooden image atop Tiscapa was the largest of such efforts as well as the most visible and high profile. Erected on the location where Sandino had been assassinated, the entire project was so pregnant with meaning, so blatant in its display of political intent, that the metaphorical nature of Tiscapa's space as the space of epistemology teaching about the current manifestation of political consensus was undone. No metaphor was now necessary. Clearly this proclaimed the old duel between Somoza and Sandino, who competed for government favor in the 1930s, had ultimately been won by Sandino, even though Somoza had initially seemed victorious. This was the essence of Sandinismo: the reversal of the previously obvious order of things and the establishment of a radically new common sense. Managuans could now look to Tiscapa and see, not a lion's den or the panoptic device of a hated tyrant, but the resolute and defiant personification of resistance to imperial manipulations.

Tiscapa has served, under various regimes, but especially those of the Somozas and the Sandinistas, as an epistemological space displaying the nature of government to the citizens of the country. In post-revolutionary Nicaragua, Tiscapa's significance has diminished, particularly because of the re-centering of Managua's daily life into the non-earthquake zone. But it has not disappeared entirely. The neoliberal regimes of the 1990s re-envisioned the volcano not as a museum of the political past or harbinger of a ruler's political visions but rather as an ecological attraction for tourists, designed to boost a sagging national economy. Now, in the shadow of the enormous wooden Sandino, foreigners can zipline over the crater lake and enjoy the magnificent view, which includes Lake Nicaragua and several volcanic peaks. The last of the neoliberal presidents, Enrique Bolaños, in a bid to regain his dwindling popularity, commissioned a monument to a 1954 rebellion on the 50th anniversary of that uprising in April 2004. This statue commemorates an event far outside the national memory of most Nicaraguans, as the rebellion was put down by Somoza (one of the chief state builders in national history) and ignored by the Sandinistas (the other major state builder). In addition, the monument is quite unsightly. These two factors help explain why the statue did not save Bolaños, who was replaced by a revamped Sandinista party in the 2006 elections. This iteration of the Sandinistas continues to control the Nicaraguan presidency, partially with the help of a campaign billboard erected on Tiscapa in the months prior to the 2011 elections. This was an ugly advertisement, depicting candidate Daniel Ortega against a pink background.[18] Regardless of the billboard's impact on the electoral outcome, its presence at Tiscapa shows the continued salience of the site in the imaginations of politicians seeking to govern the country.

18   The pink is key: the color softens the Communist/Marxist/Castroist red the Sandinistas had used since their 1960s founding. Here again, Tiscapa teaches the Nicaraguan public about the nature of the political regime.

Biopolitics

Building on the writings of Michel Foucault, a broad scholarly literature in "biopolitics" tracks the techniques and institutions that control, regulate, and oppress citizens. This approach informs studies that examine how power is distributed to manage individuals and populations for sovereign security, conformity, surveillance, and sometimes punishment. A subset of Foucault's analysis centers on mental asylums, cities, penitentiaries, and other environments (both affective and physical) that, within his interpretive framework, limit movement, discipline bodies, control behaviors, and exercise systems of rule. The essays in this section explore additional examples of such governing spaces.

Joy Knoblauch (p. 217) follows a postwar experiment in United States health policy in which the federal government, architects, and psychologists collaborated to treat mental illness through a combination of pharmaceutical intervention and decentralized community clinic design.

Melany Sun-Min Park (p. 243) investigates North Korea's imprisonment of political dissidents and their families, exposing the internment camp as an intensified microcosm of a country-wide system of control and oppression.

Turning to building codes and design standards, Wanda Katja Liebermann (p. 273) demonstrates how institutional norms and legislation in the United States limit not only the design of accessible spaces but also our normative perception of disability.

In each case, spaces produce particular forms of subjugation, revealing complex relationships between subjectivity and governmentality.

ON MICHEL FOUCAULT'S (SOMETIMES DIVERGENT) CONCEPTS OF BIOPOLITICS AND BIOPOWER

Foucault, Michel. *The Birth of Biopolitics: Lectures at the College de France, 1978-1979*. Edited by Michel Senellart. Translated by Graham Burchell. New York: Picador, 2008.

——. *The Birth of the Clinic: An Archaeology of Medical Perception* (1973). New York: Vintage Books, 1994.

——. *The History of Sexuality*, volume 1 (1976). Translated by Robert Hurley. New York: Vintage Books, 1990.

——. *Security, Territory, Population: Lectures at the College de France, 1977-1978*. Edited by Michel Senellart. Translated by Graham Burchell. New York: Picador, 2007.

——. *Society Must Be Defended: Lectures at the College de France, 1975-1976*. Edited by Arnold I. Davidson. Translated by David Macey. New York: Picador, 2003.

USEFUL ELABORATIONS ON THE CONCEPTS BY OTHER AUTHORS

Deleuze, Gilles. "Postscript on the Societies of Control." *October* 59 (Winter 1992): 3-7.

Gandy, Matthew. "Cyborg Urbanization: Complexity and Monstrosity in the Contemporary City." *International Journal of Urban and Regional Research* 29, no. 1 (March 2005): 26-49.

Nilsson, Jakob, and Sven-Olov Wallenstein, eds. *Foucault, Biopolitics and Governmentality*. Stockholm: Sodertorn University, 2013.

Osborne, Thomas. "Security and Vitality: Drains, Liberalism and Power in the Nineteenth Century." In *Foucault and Political Reason: Liberalism, Neo-Liberalism, and Rationalities of Government*, edited by Andrew Barry, Thomas Osborne, and Nikolas Rose. Chicago: University of Chicago Press, 1996.

Rabinow, Paul, and Nikolas Rose. "Biopower Today." Biosocieties 1, no. 2 (June 2006): 195-217.

Teyssot, Georges. "Heterotopias and the History of Spaces" (1977). In *Architecture Theory since 1968*, edited by K. Michael Hays, 298-305. Cambridge, MA: MIT Press, 2000.

Wallenstein, Sven-Olov. *Biopolitics and the Emergence of Modern Architecture*. New York: Princeton Architectural Press, 2009.

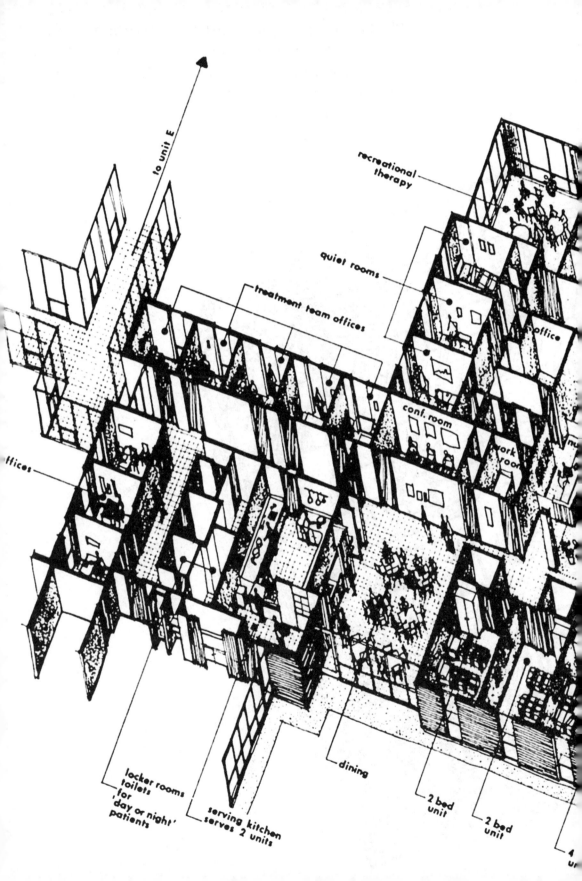

to unit E

recreational therapy

quiet rooms

treatment team offices

office

conf. room

work room

offices

locker rooms toilets for 'day or night' patients

serving kitchen serves 2 units

dining

2 bed unit

2 bed unit

PLAN OF a typical 30-bed treatment cluster shows the arrangement of patient rooms around a nurses' station and treatment areas, and the provision of common rooms and living room to allow varied patient activities.

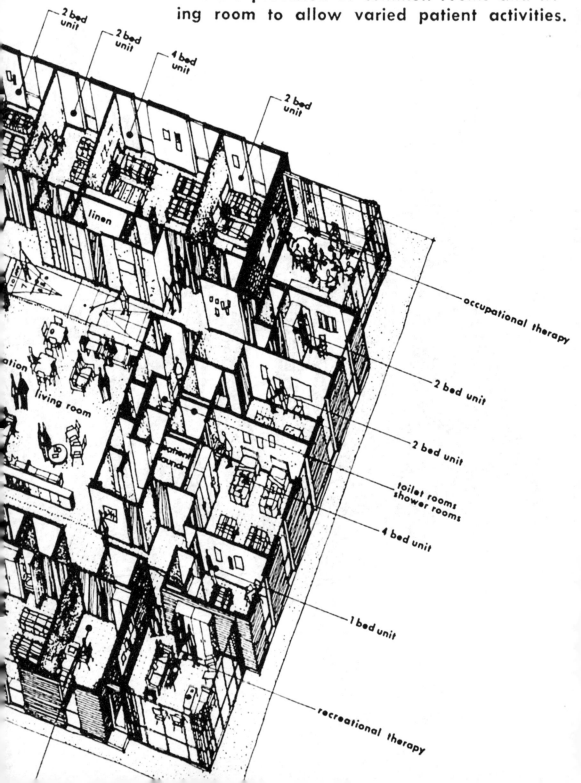

2 bed unit

2 bed unit

4 bed unit

2 bed unit

linen

ation
living room

occupational therapy

2 bed unit

2 bed unit

toilet rooms
shower rooms

4 bed unit

1 bed unit

recreational therapy

The Permeable Institution: Community Mental Health Centers as Governmental Technology, 1963–1974

Joy Knoblauch

In 1963 the director of the National Institute of Mental Health (NIMH) offered architects in the United States the opportunity to design a new type of psychiatric architecture. In an essay published in *Architectural Record*, Dr. Robert Felix invited architects to lend their ingenuity to the search for a new building typology that he hoped would become as much a part of American life as the elementary school and the post office.[1] These new buildings would provide an image for the federal program to transition mental health services from a clinical to a public-health model, from the lab to the city: a transition that constituted nothing less than the extension of federal expertise into the community and the individual psyche. The Community Mental Health Centers Construction

1   Robert H. Felix, "The Community Mental Health Centers, a New Concept," *Architectural Record*, November 1963, 162–64.

Figure 1   E. Todd Wheeler of Perkins and Will, Zone Mental Health Center, 1968. Source: Charles F. Read, "Zone Mental Health Center," *Hospitals* 42 (February 1, 1968): 111.

Act was the culmination of a movement that opposed the institutionalization of the mentally ill, manifest in books such as Erving Goffman's *Asylums* (1961), Thomas Szaz's *The Myth of Mental Illness* (1960), and the report by the Joint Commission on Mental Health and Illness titled "Action for Mental Health" (1961). Proponents of the new community psychiatry argued for the importance of treating the whole city as a patient, in contrast to the models of "intrapsychic supremacy" which had dominated the psychoanalytic era of the previous decade. Community mental health was a new, ambitious approach accompanied by a massive construction program.

The construction act was signed in 1963 by President John F. Kennedy to allocate funding for a national system of 2,000 facilities to meet the mental health needs of all Americans regardless of their ability to pay. The Community Mental Health Centers (CMHCs) were to be new, permeable institutions that would provide psychiatric care on a mostly outpatient basis in facilities located within the patient's community, instead of in remote residential institutions. The new field of community psychiatry was a translation of formerly clinical practices to a public health model. Not coincidentally, many of its proponents (including Dr. Felix) had a background in public health. One sympathetic summary declared that community mental health amounted to a realization that "therapists cannot sit back and passively wait for the sick to request treatment."[2] In the new model, all areas of life would be subject to psychological intervention at the

2   Bruce Denner and Richard H. Price, eds., *Community Mental Health: Social Action and Reaction* (New York: Holt, Rinehart and Winston, 1973), 2.

hands of experts who would locate and treat mental illness in the population.

Following on the settlement house model, community mental health centers treated the mentally ill in their "natural setting," but rather than being run by charitable or philanthropic organizations these would be part of a federally accredited system. Embedded in their communities and tailored to the local population, the centers were intended as a network of field stations, and one of their main tasks was to determine the prevalence of mental disorders in a given urban or rural area. In contrast to urban renewal schemes, the program aimed to solve urban problems through attention rather than the bulldozer. Even so, some centers were coordinated with areas of urban renewal, and community psychologists treated the ailments of those who struggled to adjust to having been relocated.[3] Although part of a single federal construction program, the centers themselves were not well coordinated with each other or with other federal programs; nor were they smoothly integrated with urban renewal initiatives.[4]

As urban field stations, the aesthetic of the community mental health centers was a key political tool. This aesthetic provided an image for the program that would hopefully persuade patients and community members to enter and receive the attention of psychologists. In this way the architecture acted as a kind of three-dimensional, environmental propaganda, spreading the NIMH's message of the value of psychology for all.

3   See also Robert L. Warren, "Mental Health Planning and Model Cities: 'Hamlet' or 'Hellzapoppin,'" in Denner and Price, eds., *Community Mental Health*, 47–58.

4   For example, the Community Mental Health Centers Construction Act was not integrated with the 1965 Medicare Act, which limited coverage for care in psychiatric hospitals to 190 days in a citizen's lifetime but did not limit psychiatric care in a general hospital. Murray Levine, *The History and Politics of Community Mental Health* (New York: Oxford University Press, 1981), 174.

Figure 2 Proposal by architect Wilmont Vickrey and psychiatrist Joseph J. Downing for a new typology known as the community mental health center (CMHC). Source: Clyde H. Dorsett Papers. Avery Drawings & Archives Collections, Columbia University, New York, New York (hereafter, Dorsett Papers).

Declaring the need to avoid the design mistakes of the past, and to create a new image for psychiatric care, the NIMH sponsored design research that brought architects into contact with psychiatrists, who sensitized the architects to the patient population. Similarly, the architects shared their knowledge of design with the psychiatrists and the NIMH, enriched by an articulated form of modern architecture and the young field of architectural programming. The result was a unique refinement of the program-driven architecture of the 1960s, which stands as a reflection of the welfare programs of the Great Society and the growing expertise of social science. These designs for community mental health centers provided an image of welcoming modernity, newly tailored for different types of communities and forming a new architectural strategy suited to an increasingly democratic, increasingly psychologized, biopolitical society.

Dr. Felix's call to architects was answered, and the program was launched with an avant-garde architecture that conveyed a softened modernism. The NIMH

Figure 3 Architects and psychiatrists at work at the 1965 Rice Design Fete, directed by Clyde H. Dorsett of the National Institute of Mental Health shown here, seated, at the center of the photograph. Source: Coryl La Rue Jones, ed., *Architecture for the Community Mental Health Center* (Bethesda, MD: National Institute of Mental Health, 1967), 27.

continued to foster collaboration between architects and psychiatrists on the subject of community mental health center design. In the same year, the NIMH appointed an architect, Clyde Dorsett, to oversee the grant application process, a process that included three stages of drawing submissions: schematic, preliminary, and working drawings. A few years later, Dorsett and the NIMH sponsored a prototype study for a San Francisco facility by architects Ellis Kaplan and Herbert McLaughlin in concert with two psychiatrists, Dr. Joseph J. Downing and Robert A. Kimmich. The San Francisco study was published in a large, award-winning volume that was intended to serve as an early guideline for potential applicants to the CMHC program.[5] Following on the success of the San Francisco study, the NIMH sponsored an intensive, two-week working session at Rice University in Houston, Texas.[6] The Rice Design Fete, as it was called, gathered the top architects and psychiatrists at work on new institutional designs. Six pairs of architects and psychiatrists participated in the Fete, and each pair was responsible for

5   The results of this study were published as Coryl La Rue Jones, ed., *Planning, Programming and Design for the Community Mental Health Center* (Bethesda, MD: National Institute of Mental Health, 1965).

6   The NIMH-sponsored event was held as the third annual Rice Design Fete. Previous Fetes examined schools and industrial fallout shelters.

directing a group of five architecture students and one community mental health trainee as they developed their scheme.

The design charrette was organized around prototypical American communities. Each team was asked to use the demographics, aesthetics, and programmatic needs of one community as the basis for its design. The information was taken from actual locations in the United States, but the locations were used "anonymously" as a way to study the utility of design in solving various mental health challenges in urban and rural communities. The quasi-scientific, data-rich mode of typological analysis used in the charrette has a long history, wherein human populations are analyzed and matched up with the style of architecture deemed to fit them best.[7] The prototypical, anonymous towns allowed for a flattening and standardizing of difference as a means of predicting and controlling variation. The six typologies used were "metro-suburban rural," "research-oriented," "urban slum ghetto," "state and general hospital," "midwestern rural," and "heterogenous urban."[8]

Architect William W. Caudill of the research-based firm of Caudill Rowlett Scott teamed up with Dr. Alfred Paul Bay, Superintendent of the Topeka State Hospital and Consultant in Psychiatry to the us Public Health Service.[9] Caudill, Bay, and their team proposed a long, linear building that would be a literal bridge between the hospital and the community. In a similar attempt to express the connection of treatment and city, David

7   Georges Teyssot, "Norm and Type: Variations on a Theme," in *Architecture and the Sciences: Exchanging Metaphor*, ed. Antoine Picon and Alessandra Ponte (New York: Princeton Architectural Press, 2003), 140–73.

8   Coryl La Rue Jones, ed., *Architecture for the Community Mental Health Center* (Bethesda, MD: National Institute of Mental Health, 1967).

9   Participant biographies, in "Rice Design Fete," pamphlet. Clyde H. Dorsett Papers, Department of Drawings and Archives, Avery Architectural and Fine Arts Library, Columbia University, New York. See also William Caudill and Rice Design Fete, *The Bridge: A Report on Mental Health Facilities from Caudill Rowlett Scott* (Houston, TX: Caudill Rowlett Scott, 1966); and "'People Involvement': Research, Planning Teams, Economy and Regionalism Dictate the Designs of Caudill, Rowlett and Scott," *Architectural Record* 137 (January 1965): 111–26; and Avigail Sachs's assessment of Caudill's expertise as "a project to define the parameters of 'man's comfort,'" in Avigail Sachs, "The Postwar Legacy of Architectural Research," *Journal of Architectural Education* 62, no. 3 (2009): 57.

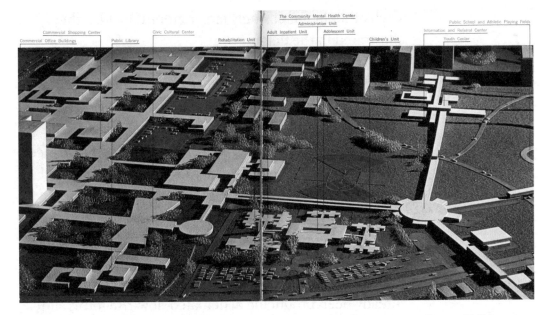

McKinley and Dr. A. R. Foley designed a "continuous form" consisting of smaller elements where programmatic components were articulated as separate volumes. Architect Kiyoshi Izumi continued a longer collaboration with Dr. Humphrey Osmond, but instead of producing a building design Izumi presented a diagrammatic language of nested circles, indicating the various combinations of individual and group spaces in his scheme.[10] Izumi and Osmond's team started with the census data for their catchment area of 150,000 people, somewhere in the southwestern United States. The team identified the area as composed of various ethnic and social groups, ranging from suburban residents to "hillbillies." Their strategy was to create an environment where such diverse persons could be encouraged, slowly, to interact with

Figure 4 McKinley and Foley's mental health center as "continuous form," blending with the megastructure of a prototypical suburban mall and hospital. Source: Jones, ed., *Architecture for the Community Mental Health Center* , 32–33.

10 According to Erika Dyck, in her *Psychedelic Psychiatry: LSD from Clinic to Campus* (Baltimore, MD: Johns Hopkins University Press, 2008), Osmond was the one who introduced Aldous Huxley to mescaline, leading to Huxley's classic book *The Doors to Perception* (New York: Harper & Brothers Publishers, 1954).

each other in increasingly larger groups, an idea they illustrated in the diagrams.

The design research encouraged architects to grow their formal and programming expertise and to focus on the problem of designing in a society wherein everyday life was increasingly psychologized.[11] Caudill and others had been working on an expertise in programming since the 1940s, and studies of form were also underway and available for the architects of CMHCs to borrow from in creating the new, more community-based image. While Alison and Peter Smithsons's "How to Recognize and Read Mat Building" was not published until 1974, the couple, as well as Aldo van Eyck and Louis Kahn, had already been producing articulated, low-rise forms similar to several of the schemes for the anti-monumental CMHCs. Quotes from these architects adorned the margins of the NIMH design manuals. These forms were brought to bear on a newly psychologized public.

After World War II, the social science of psychology increasingly infused American culture, spurred by the US government's new faith in the field and its experts. Prior to the war, the only federal agency devoted to mental health was the Division of Mental Hygiene, an organization responsible for screening new immigrants for mental soundness, treating drug addiction, and providing counseling in federal prisons.[12] In 1949 the NIMH was formed as a cabinet-level agency within the National Institute of Health, which was itself part of the Department of Health, Education, and Welfare. The

11   Professional association membership grew from 3,634 in 1945 to 18,407 by 1970. Ellen Herman, *The Romance of American Psychology: Political Culture in the Age of Experts* (Berkeley: University of California Press, 1995), 259.

12   Even then, the mental health organization was a subset of the public health effort. Levine, *History and Politics of Community Mental Health*, 42.

budget of the NIMH increased rapidly, from $8.7 million in 1950 to $315 million in 1967.[13] As the agency grew, the NIMH's budget and influence led it to conduct extensive research outside the laboratory and the psychiatric hospital in an attempt to justify its role and effectively compete within the also expanding National Institutes of Health around them. By 1964 a majority of the NIMH's research budget was spent on work that was not directly related to psychiatry or biological sciences. Sixty percent of the funding went to psychologists, sociologists, anthropologists, epidemiologists, and others who studied the broader implications of environment on mental health. The rising influence of the NIMH itself reflects the growing status of psychology, but it also reflects the federal government's intimate involvement in the mental health of its citizen population, a hallmark of the shift to an increasingly biopolitical form of governance.

Psychologists argued for a broader definition of mental health, with less clear lines between sick and well and between patient and community. Delinquency, alcoholism, and even family dysfunction were coming under the domain of the psychiatrists' care, making formerly "well" patients "sick." At the other end of the spectrum, pharmacology and a drive for de-institutionalization meant that many who would formerly have been committed to remote facilities were no longer hidden away. Along with the new definition of mental health, the field began to call for a new understanding of the role of the environment in care. Supported by the Great Society agenda to

13 Herman, *Romance of American Psychology*, 248.

14 Alice O'Connor, *Poverty Knowledge: Social Science, Social Policy, and the Poor in Twentieth-Century US History* (Princeton, NJ: Princeton University Press, 2001). Specifically, the NIMH sponsored sociologist Lee Rainwater's study of Pruitt Igoe, Christopher Alexander's Center for Environmental Structure, and Peter Eisenman et al.'s Institute for Urban and Architectural Studies, a subject I describe in my dissertation and forthcoming book.

expand what historian Alice O'Connor calls "poverty knowledge," the NIMH studied the cycle of mental illness and poverty, as well as urban and architectural factors affecting mental health, spawning a Center for the Study of Metropolitan Problems.[14] But whereas these were primarily research programs, the CMHC Act included a large construction program, which in essence constituted a commitment by the federal government to build centers for community-based mental health care for all citizens. Because of the increasingly broad definition of mental

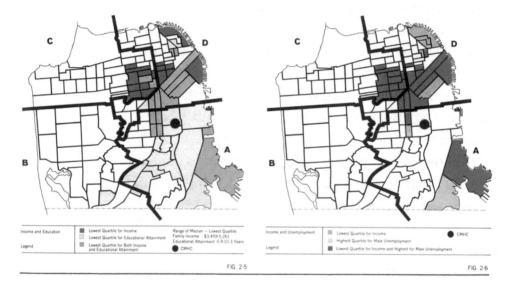

FIG. 2-5

FIG. 2-6

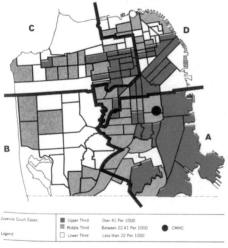

FIG. 2-7

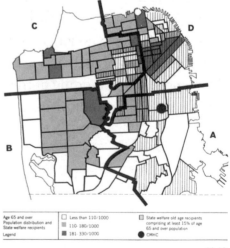

FIG. 2-8

health in the postwar period, the CMHC program included both study and development of urban communities—mapping delinquency, alcoholism, and other socially disruptive conditions in urban neighborhoods and constructing community-based institutions to prevent or correct them.

Despite key professional and political motivations for de-institutionalization—such as the efforts of the Group for the Advancement of Psychiatry (GAP)—the movement out of the hospital was only possible because of a new class of psychoactive drugs. Indeed, the drugs had such an impact on treatment that one could argue that, without them, CMHCs would never have existed. Introduced in 1955, Thorazine is the most commonly known commercial variant of chlorpromazine, which was itself the product of research on the potential for histamines to be used as a sedative for surgery.[15] By the early 1960s, the use of Thorazine and similar drugs had advanced to the point where they made it possible for many patients with mental illness to function somewhat normally outside an institutional setting. The drug produced a state of calm and unconcern in patients, allowing many to wake up and begin to speak again, although it also created the zombie-like patient familiar from films of mental hospitals.

The biological restraint provided by the so-called chemical straitjacket profoundly impacted the amount of physical restraint that the architecture needed to provide, thus rendering the community mental health center viable. Even those who needed inpatient care could be

15 On the history of chlorpromazine, see David Healy, *The Creation of Psychopharmacology* (Cambridge, MA: Harvard University Press, 2002), 97.

Figure 5 NIMH-developed maps of urban demographics, used to guide site selection for community mental health centers. In San Francisco, the ideal location for the new CMHC was represented by a black dot. Source: Coryl La Rue Jones, ed., *Planning Program and Design for the CMHC* (Bethesda, MD: National Institute of Mental Health, 1967, 23.

allowed greater freedom within the walls of the new institution. Psychoactive drugs internalized the architecture of restraint, altering the "internal environment" of the patient's mind and freeing up the external architecture, as would later be noted by architects Hans Hollein and Ron Herron. Indeed, this conception of the CMHC as anti-restraint was presented in a NIMH publication through a graphic juxtaposition of a restraining mechanism known as a Utica Crib to the new architecture of the CMHC. In a sense, the drugs made it possible for the environmental controls to be dissolved into the individual patient's brain chemistry.

Unsurprisingly, the internalization of control was frightening to many; particularly by the late 1960s and early 1970s, as criticisms of psychiatry generally—and the CMHC programs specifically—grew.[16] For example, in 1968 Dr. Kenneth Keniston published the essay "How Community Mental Health Stamped Out the Riots, 1968–1978," chronicling a fictitious "Operation Inner City" that followed a strategy of "total saturation" of psychological experts to stop the riots once and for all.[17] Another psychiatrist, Chaim Shatan, accused the CMHC program of setting up a "government-subsidized conveyor belt" that led psychiatrists to adapt the modern factory model, deploying management techniques rather than seeing many disorders as behavioral adaptations to larger social and class issues.[18]

Given the late 1960s context of racial tensions, urban riots, and the targeting of CMHCs to low-income

16   "The City as Patient," in Herman, *Romance of American Psychology*, 222–26.

17   Kenneth Keniston, "How Community Mental Health Stamped Out the Riots (1968–1978)," in Denner and Price, eds., *Community Mental Health*. There were, of course, earlier critiques of psychiatry, such as *One Flew Over the Cuckoo's Nest* (1962) and *Titicut Follies* (1967), but the critiques mentioned here are targeted particularly at the community mental health program.

18   Chaim Shatan, "Community Psychiatry—Stretcher Bearer of the Social Order?," *International Journal of Psychiatry* 7 (May 1969): 319.

populations, it is understandable that the use of drugs made many people uneasy. In order to quell such concerns, Thorazine and a similar drug, Stelazine, were advertised to psychiatrists as a modern tool for a modern psychiatry, using "primitive" art as a foil against which to make the comparison. Juxtaposing the paraphernalia— smooth blue pills, sleek eyedroppers, and brown glass containers associated with administering the drug—with the organic forms, fuzzy hair, and smiling face of a "primitive" art object, one ad for Stelazine in 1976 emphasized the modernity of the drugs while at the same time naturalizing them. A similar ad for Thorazine called such drugs the "basic tools of Western psychiatry," comparing them to "the basic tools of primitive psychiatry" exemplified by religious art from the Ewe people of Togo, Africa.[19] This attempt to show drugs as simply the more advanced, reliable, modern form of a very old, basic practice was also colored by racial overtones, given the choice of African art as the background against which to present the modern pills. Other advertisements made the connection between drugs and race more clearly, as in the

19 The art in the Thorazine ad comes from a New York gallery, and the caption labels the art as from Tongo (in the South Pacific) as well as from Togo (in Africa). The caption does specify the tribe as the Ewe, who reside in Togo (not Tongo). Both advertisements were produced by Smith Kline and French Laboratories in Philadelphia. Thorazine advertisement and Stelazine advertisement, *Hospital and Community Psychiatry*, August 1976. Clyde H. Dorsett Papers.

Figure 6 Stelazine advertisement, *Hospital and Community Psychiatry*, August 1976. Source: Dorsett Papers.

20   Psychiatrist and historian of psychology Jonathon Metzl has spotlighted this racial message reinforced by advertisements for Haldol, which promote the drug's efficacy in treating symptoms of "aggression" using a drawing of an angry African American man. Jonathan Metzl, *Prozac on the Couch: Prescribing Gender in the Era of Wonder Drugs* (Durham, NC: Duke University Press, 2003), 30.

21   Sven-Olov Wallenstein, *Biopolitics and the Emergence of Modern Architecture* (New York: Princeton Architectural Press, 2009), 10.

22   Foucault describes this as "a set of elements" that are "immersed within the general regime of living beings." Michel Foucault, *Security, Territory, Population: Lectures at the College de France, 1977-1978*, ed. Michel Senellart, trans. Graham Burchell (New York: Palgrave Macmillan, 2009), 75.

Haldol advertisement featuring a burning building and an African American shaking his fist, described by historian Jonathon Metzl. [20]

The politics of psychopharmacology, or of the CMHC program itself, are not easily classified as either liberatory or repressive; rather, they are a bit of both. While the advent of psychopharmacology and de-institutionalization changed the architectural manifestations of psychiatry and the relation of the state to its citizenry, it was only the latest development in a political mode that was considerably older: that of biopolitics. Writing in the mid-1970s—roughly the same time as the CMHC program—about changes in 18th- and 19th-century France, Michel Foucault describes a shift from an era of sovereignty, wherein power was exerted by the sovereign's right to "take life," to a situation characterized by the management of life. In short, and to borrow a more recent formulation from architectural theorist Sven-Olov Wallenstein, "the body politic becomes a living entity that must be attended to, not just a source of disturbances that must be repressed."[21]

The biopolitical model thus centers around the concept of a living population, conceived of in aggregate and as individuals. In order to be considered a population, a group must contain a heterogeneous mix of individuals, a statistically describable plurality that is conceived of as quasi-natural or akin to a population of animals.[22] The second criterion is that the population serves as a political force, a collective entity that can "offer a surface" on which state power is exerted.[23] Foucault argues that the complexity of this demographic surface means that:

> the relation between the population and the sovereign cannot simply be one of obedience or the refusal of obedience, of obedience or revolt.... If one says to a population "do this," there is not only no guarantee that it will do it, but also there is quite simply no guarantee that it can do it.[24]

23 Ibid.

24 Ibid, 71.

Instead of rebellion or obedience, liberation or repression, the biopolitical condition presents the subject with the problematically abstract idea of moving toward a more "humane" exercise of power based in an understanding of the physical and biological capacity of the population. While the exertion of power becomes more intimate, even to the extent of brain chemistry, there is at the same time a new responsibility for the state to attend to the needs of its population so that it remain productive and healthy in order for the state to have the capacity for power. It is this need to attend to a population that characterizes the government programs of welfare that made use of social science and its knowledge of aggregations of

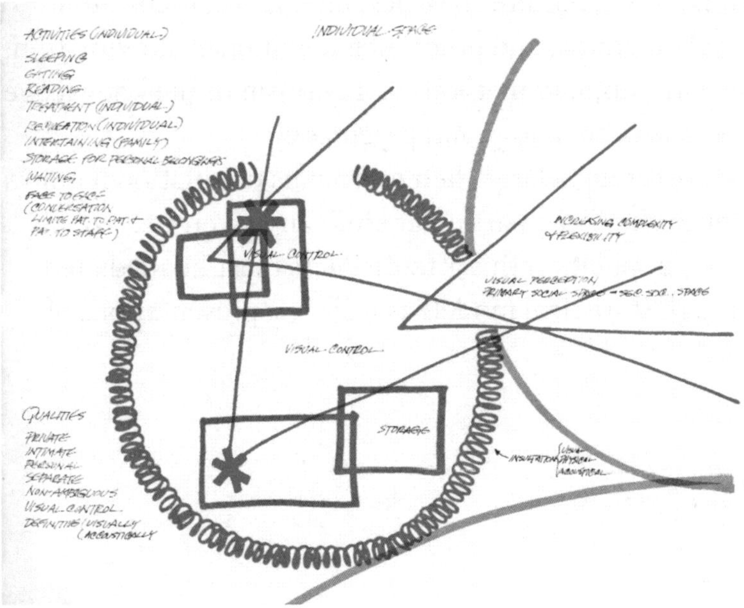

Figure 7 Visual control diagram, collaboratively developed by architect Kiyoshi Izumi, ARIBA [*sic*] and Dr. Humphrey Osmond, MD. Source: Jones, ed., *Architecture for the Community Mental Health Center*, 57.

human subjects. By extension, then, to try to decide whether any given patient was liberated or repressed by the CMHC program is to invoke the mismatched terms of a previous political model. A member of the population would be both more controlled and more free than a single subject in relation to a single sovereign.

Because the controls are diffuse and extend even down to the scale of a Thorazine molecule, they can be said to have permeated the environment and even the bodies of the subjects. The result is a softer form of control, with less clear and less visible boundaries, replacing physical restraints with a complex of urban, architectural, and even chemical systems of attention and management. Because of the uncertainty of the complex capacity of a population, the relation of the state to the population was correctly diagnosed by Shatan as that of a manager or administrator, needing to study the features of the population's heterogeneity in order to assess its ability to sustain the kind of action the state desires: productivity, reproduction, and (by the 20th century) consumption. More concretely, this shift means the government will require statistics, interviews, maps, functional diagrams, and other such techniques, ranging from the early, applied methods of Taylorism to the knowledge products of sociology and psychology.

Governing a large, heterogeneous population requires attentiveness of a particular kind, and given the size of the US population this attentiveness must be mediated through statistical models as well as representations of the population and its attributes. The growth of fields such as human ecology, urban sociology, and information technology assisted the NIMH and other agencies in developing policies for their social programs. At the largest scale, the design and location of CMHCs relied upon the government's knowledge of its population gathered through the census. The program aimed to build one center for every 200,000 persons, measuring the spacing of the institutions by population density rather than travel distance or county government. Each geographically contiguous area was referred to as a "catchment area," borrowing a term from human geography, which suggests that the population acts like a natural resource, flowing to the center as in the way that, for example, rainwater flows to a watershed.[25] At the urban level, the NIMH required applicants to show that they had considered demographic trends, juvenile delinquency rates, surrounding income levels, and the location of other health resources in the area in order to locate the facility to greatest effect.

25 The term "catchment area" appears to be common within the field of human geography, with the *Oxford English Dictionary* including the usage "catchment area" under "catchment" in a sentence from 1970 that refers to the area from which a primary school draws its students.

Clyde Dorsett tracked the progress of the CMHC program through a map of the United States divided into catchment areas. Once a grant was approved and a facility was under construction, the area was colored in yellow and a pink pin was stuck in the map. A blue pin replaced the pink one once the building was completed. The image of the map was used as the cover of an undated NIMH brochure about the program called "A Citizen's Guide to the Community Mental Health

Centers Act," marking the importance of the geographical component of the federal program. Even so, the catchment model had its challenges, as was recognized at the time. Dividing population by census tract created problems because the areas were not organic and thus the lines excluded resources that may have existed just across a boundary line. Moreover, the geographical approach tended to privilege visible problems (such as graffiti or social dysfunction) over chronic ones (such as adjustment disorders faced by returning servicemen and women). In rural areas the territories often became so large that transportation became a major issue.[26] Even so, the census approach established a clear rhetorical goal with a clear map of its progress.

26   Levine, *History and Politics of Community Mental Health*, 554. For the idea that catchment area-based psychology tends to focus on "visible" problems more than others, see Anthony F. Panzetta, "The Concept of Community: The Short Circuit of the Mental Health Movement," in Denner and Price, eds., *Community Mental Health*, 248.

Figure 8   Detail from the nationwide map of CMHCs, January 1976. Blue pins mark constructed facilities, pink pins mark facilities under construction, and yellow shading indicates "catchment areas served." Source: Dorsett Papers.

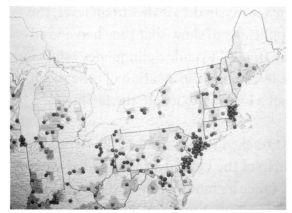

The image of the program was key, and when the map was not used, the other representation featured on brochures was often architectural. While buildings were designed to fit particular areas, as in the Rice Design Fete, the welcoming aesthetic was a key goal of Dorsett and his team. In order to attract patients to return again and again for outpatient treatment, the facilities needed to be designed to appeal to patients and their families. To do so, the architects needed to understand the audience or market they were serving as explored in the design charrette. But Dorsett and the other architects and psychologists knew that the new centers would have to look very different from the restricted, inpatient psychiatric hospitals of the past. The new architecture could not look like the massive hospitals for the insane constructed in the 19th century. But also, and increasingly, the new architecture needed to be different from the midcentury modern hospitals and the psychiatric wards that they housed. Most commonly, these were the so-called block-style modern hospitals that were built in the United States after World War II, under another large, federal construction program known as the Hill-Burton legislation. The Hill-Burton codes practically required a single, wide corridor with doors on both sides (known as a "double-loaded" corridor) due to requirements for modern medical equipment as well as egress for all the non-ambulant patients. The resulting form was typically a single block, a monolithic form often communicating its separation from its context through a plinth or an open first story.

In contrast, the community mental health center architects developed a new institutional typology able to communicate an image of welcoming to the patient. One strategy for communicating openness was to use soft transitions between inside and out, as expressed by Dorsett in a series of patterns he developed in collaboration with Christopher Alexander, patterns which were eventually published in *Pattern Language* with credit given to Dorsett. In contrast to the block-style hospital, this typology also communicated its welcoming by using a formal articulation of programmatic elements, which reduced the monolithic appearance of the building. The articulated forms indexed the scale of the human activities within, from single-patient rooms to gathering spaces. In the 1967 publication of the Rice Design Fete, Dorsett and the other designers expressed their goals in terms of the theories of James Stirling and Louis Kahn regarding the importance of achieving a "direct expression" of programmatic volumes.[27] The ideal was to have the shapes of the program elements legible from the exterior, as well as being legible in plan.

CMHC architecture involved numerous attempts to soften the long, inflexible ward hallway of the block-style hospital, enlarging it into lounges, and twisting it into circular arrangements. Often, the design worked to articulate individual treatment rooms and patient bedrooms, to bring intimacy and territory into the anonymous forms. In some cases, individual pavilions or lobes were created, as in a scheme by E. Todd Wheeler of Perkins and Will. In others, where the hallway was turned into a central lounge space, territories were often marked off with columns and fixed furniture. Additionally, individual elements were articulated with thicker walls and called

27   Jones, ed., *Planning Program and Design for the Community Mental Health Center*, 43. Dorsett et al. also quote from Kevin Lynch, Peter Blake, William W. Caudill, Arthur Drexler, and John E. Buchard.

out on the drawings in heavier line weights. In the case of the scheme by McKinley and Foley, the hierarchical groupings of patient rooms were linked with filleted corners, referring to masonry walls that would spotlight these forms in the final building. The legibility of programmatic units in plan and in the final building performed a crucial function in the CMHC architecture; namely, it allowed the architect to argue that the form responded to the patients within and to psychiatrist's understanding of the use of the facility. Through such tailored forms, the architect communicated to patients— and to the NIMH bureaucracy—that the design was responsive to program and to the patient population.

The question of the community mental health centers' effectiveness should to some extent be easily assessed. How many of the 2,000 facilities were constructed, how much federal funding was disbursed, and what was the resulting reduction in involuntary commitment in remote facilities or psychiatric wards in general hospitals? Such questions would, one would expect, have become part of the public record. Despite the reports of that other great tool of the Great Society–era government, the Presidential Commission, these numbers are rather hard to come by.[28] An assessment by community psychologist Murray Levine in 1981 complained of the biases of government reports that declared their own success and of

28   Jimmy Carter appointed a Presidential Commission on Mental Health, the results of which were hampered by minority reports (two of which literally covered minority populations, women, and African Americans), late releases of the written document, and the usual writing by committee. Levine, *History and Politics of Community Mental Health*, 178.

uncritical social scientists who simply collected numbers without sufficient interpretation. Levine did conclude that in 1967 there were 186 CMHCs with federal support, and in 1970 there were 450. He reported that growth declined after 1970, with only 43 more receiving funding and an unknown number no longer in operation. By 1975, 603 CMHC's had received some funds, but only 507 were operational.[29] Further confusion resulted from demographic splintering, wherein elderly populations were transferred to nursing homes, children received separate coverage, and many others were treated under the Alcohol, Drug Abuse, and Mental Health programs whose budget grew to include approximately half for mental health services.[30] While it does appear that hospitalizations decreased, it is hard to know whether those would-be patients were treated in community mental health centers, trickled down into other programs, or simply went untreated, as many likely did. Further attempts to assess the effectiveness of the centers as pieces of literal, physical infrastructure are complicated by the fact that in the early phases, the program did not include funds for staffing. It is hard to assess the success of a facility that had little or no staff.[31]

So while the buildings that were constructed did function as field stations, to some extent, the more intriguing lesson of the CMHCs may come from the way that design briefly became a tool of government. The imaginative, typology-based investigations of the early 1960s were employed as initial propaganda for the

29   Ibid., 63.

30   Ibid., 174.

31   With Johnson's election in 1964, he had enough clout to push for staffing grants in 1965 with the PL-89-105 act. Ibid., 55.

program, but the architecture slowly dispersed into the network of unremarkable environments where the program persisted, immersed in strip malls and other anonymous office buildings. One can speculate that enough "knowledge" regarding the use of this social technology had been generated to lead proponents of community psychology to declare that the therapeutic or psychological component itself bore too much of a social stigma and needed to be further minimized.[32]

Though again, it is hard to isolate the exact cause of the transition from purpose-built structures to more mundane, existing facilities, amidst all the known factors. Not the least of which was the reduction in funding available at all levels of government as the welfare state waned, throughout the Vietnam War and the Nixon and Ford administrations. From 1970 onward, President Nixon opposed the program—and indeed most expenditures for mental health—as well as research and training in health more generally. He "impounded" funds that Congress had authorized, refusing to spend them.[33] In 1975 Congress overrode President Ford's veto of legislation that would extend and revise the original CMHC Act. Today, the community mental health program stumbles along, despite the oft-cited fact that, on any given day, the Los Angeles County Jail holds more people with mental illness than any state hospital or mental health institution in the United States.[34] While hardly a remote mental hospital, the jail falls well short of the community ideal envisioned by Dr. Felix at the optimistic start of the program.

32   For example, Denner writes as early as 1973 that "it may be against the public interest to create resistance by emphasizing the therapeutic aspect of any community endeavor." Denner and Price, eds., *Community Mental Health*, 9. He mentions Head Start and Job Corps specifically as community programs that function with less resistance when presented as less "therapeutic." Still Denner remains optimistic, and notes that, "The movement has the potential to create whole new caseloads by transforming the status of large numbers of people. If some community therapists had their way, people who seem self-destructive (drug addicts, hippies), people who resist social change (tenants who respond poorly to urban renewal), people who present a threat to the state (Black Panthers, KKK) would all be analyzed, forced into therapy, and transformed according to the socially approved modes and norms of behavior."

33   He lost a major battle in this war with the 1973 case of *National Council of CMHCS vs. Weinberger*. Levine, *History and Politics*, 63.

34   Renee Montagne, "Inside the Nation's Largest Mental Institution," National Public Radio, August 13, 2008; and NPR Staff, "What Is the Role of Jails in Treating the Mentally Ill?," September 15, 2013.

Perhaps the salient feature of this episode in the history of architecture as a political tool is not that design did not succeed—that designers and psychologists working together did not establish a definitive new typology for the community mental heath center. Rather, the enticing aspect of the story is the way that pharmaceuticals and complex, modern democracy came to use the aesthetics of the mental health center for persuasion while preserving an illusion of free choice. In the era of violent student and civil rights protest, a time of deep distrust of government and mass social ideals, the NIMH turned to designers to help smooth the roll out of a new program to manage the intimate mental needs of the population. While preferable to abusive treatment in remote mental hospitals, the brief experiment in permeable institutions for mental health care shows that when the bars disappear, new space is opened for the agency of design. As the 1970s wore on, the federal commitment to positive mental health for every American was abandoned, but the use of statistics, mental models, and avant-garde design as a means of persuasion proliferated in the marketplace and in the design of everyday environments. Whether as hospitals, housing, retail, or urban design, focus groups and big data continue to be used by social scientists and consultants to tailor environments to user needs. The institution has indeed become permeable, moving past the walls of the mental health center and into many more areas of the designed environment, for better and worse.

20만 감금… 하루 15시간씩 노역

강냉이로 연명… 요덕에 재일동포만 5천3백명

북한의 정치범 수용소
※괄호안은 수용인원, 명

온성 (27,000)
회령 (20,000)
희천 (10,000)
동신 (7,000)
영변 (15,000)
경성 (15,000)
용천 (5,000)
덕성 (10,000)
개천 (15,000)
정평 (10,000)
승호리 (6백여명)
요덕 (50,000)
북창 (5,000)

함경북도
양강도
함경남도
평안북도
평안남도
황해북도
황해남도
지강도
평양

수용소시설 배치도

집단농장
처형장
경비초소
집단수용소
관리소
외곽철책선
사상학습소
내부철책선

82년이후 4곳 증설

「核(핵)계획 극비문서」로 본 이중성

【東京=夫炳\煜기자】1일…

日(일), 겉과 속 달랐

强化 키로

오 드라머는 「時代感覺」살려야한다 ……12면

애등 제거

"금지" 움막서 終身노동

日奉·許鳳學도 收容

8 强化 키로

朝鮮漫評   吳龍

北傀

감옥 共和國

아시아監査院長회의 개막

會員國간 交流논의

議長에 李溪基院長

北傀 만행 중지하라
反共연맹 성명발표

萬物相

Imprisoned Bodies: North Korea and its *Kwan-li-so*

Melany Sun-Min Park

> The thing Kim Jong-il hates most and what he fears are the balloons and the radio receivers.
> —Lee Min-bok in *Yodok Stories* (2008)

North Korea constitutes one of the world's most contested geographies. Accurate information surrounding the everyday lives of its citizens is closely guarded, which mirrors the regime's tight control of resident activities and speech. Individuals are censured and incarcerated there for disparaging the statecraft or public persona of ruling Kim patriarchs,[1] and for accessing foreign radio or television.[2] So when, in December 2002, satellite photographs of a North Korean *kwan-li-so* first appeared in the *Far Eastern Economic Review*, its readership received an

[1] The Kim patriarchs comprise Kim Il-sung (1912–1994) and Kim Jong-il (1941–2011).

[2] Kim Young-soon, *Testimony before the House Committee on Foreign Affairs Subcommittee on Africa, Global Health and Human Rights*, September 20, 2011.

Figure 1 (overleaf) Map of the 13 *kwan-li-so* scattered across six North Korean provinces, 1994. The diagram below the map depicts its fenced grounds. Source: *Chosun Ilbo*, August 2, 1994.

Figure 2 A "puppet state" flag adorning the prison facility, standing for the North Korean regime. Source: *Chosun Ilbo*, April 13, 1982.

3   Specifically, the satellite imagery featured in the *Review* (published in Hong Kong and now defunct) showed Camp 22 in North Hamgyong province. David Hawk, "The Hidden Gulag: The Lives and Voices of 'Those Who are Sent to the Mountains,'" *A Report by the Committee for Human Rights in North Korea*, 2nd ed. (Washington, DC: US Committee for Human Rights in North Korea, 2012), 44. Hawk's first edition (*Hidden Gulag: Exposing North Korea's Prison Camps* [Washington, DC: US Committee for Human Rights in North Korea, 2003]) is considered to be the first definitive document published on North Korea's various detention camps and their systems of operation. I have used the McCune–Reischauer Romanization system for Korean, except when citing Korean names or proper nouns (for example, Kim Jong-il or Pyongyang respectively) that follow another system in publication or in general use. Where appropriate, I have followed the phonetic Romanization system of Korean terms found in cited sources (for example, *kwan-li-so*). Unless specified otherwise, the Korean surname appears first, followed by the hyphenated given name.

4   An Hŭi-ch'ang, "Saranaol su ŏmnŭn kot...chugŭmi 'hŭimang'" ["Where one cannot come out alive ... death is 'hope,'"] *Chosun Ilbo*, August 2, 1994, 4.

unprecedented view onto the geography and spaces that structure its people's existence.[3] The *kwan-li-so* are political penal labor colonies or concentration camps—what South Korean newspaper *Chosun Ilbo* has described as "North Korea's version of Auschwitz."[4] Four years after the English-language news magazine published images of the camp, Google Earth began documenting the Korean Peninsula with ever-increasing precision, enlarging the visual record of its northern territory and disclosing its geographic and political contours to an even wider audience.

The aerial representations of this secretive country, originating some 500 miles above the earth's surface, are incapable of capturing the daily operations and lived experiences of camp inhabitants: portraits of these have instead emerged in recent years through different media. Balloons carrying messages extolling alternative, democratic ways of life have begun to permeate the border between North and South Korea, traversing the fortified two and a half mile wide Korean Demilitarized Zone (DMZ) that divides the Korean peninsula. Highly visible vehicles for North Korean defectors' political enactments, they feature prominently in a 2006 musical, *Yoduk Story*, and the documentary film it inspired, *Yodok Stories*. Jung Sung-san wrote and directed the musical, inspired by the testimonies of seven defectors now residing in South Korea and by his own intimate knowledge of Camp Yoduk (also known as Camp 15), from which he fled in 1994. Jung's play—and the balloon-based activism it reenacts—provide harrowing accounts of the life and space of imprisonment, with details that surpass those available from views above.

Figure 3 An airborne balloon carrying information leaflets over the border to North Korea. A scene from *Yodok Stories*. Source: Tore Vollan © Piraya Film AS, 2009.

In *Yodok Stories*, Christian missionary Lee Min-bok—a former agricultural scientist imprisoned at a *jip-kyul-so* (short term labor-detention facility) from 1990 to 1991—prepares to release 39-foot-long, tube-shaped balloons filled with hydrogen gas from a cemetery located in South Korea near the DMZ. Understanding that the success of the balloons' four-hour crossing into the North Korean capital of Pyongyang depends upon northerly winds, Lee routinely checks the weather forecast, looking for possible launch dates. Beneath what appears to be a relatively modest political performance lies a heavier agenda: attached to the balloons are leaflets carrying information about the world external to the authoritarian state. Through this didactic medium, the scientist-turned-evangelist claims, approximately 80 percent of North Korea's defectors (numbering 10,000 at the time of the interview) became aware of the idiosyncrasies and clandestine operations of former-leader Kim Jong-il's political regime.[5]

5 *Yodok Stories*, directed by Andrzej Fidyk (Norway: Piraya Film AS, 2008). Between 2010 and 2011, there were some 23,000 North Koreans residing in South Korea, a number that grew nearly eightfold after 2003. Hawk, "Hidden Gulag," vii.

Viewers of the documentary witness one of the few instances in which North Korean citizens—now residing south of the DMZ—freely perform their political subjectivity. Since March 26, 2010, when North Korea allegedly sank the South Korean naval ship *Cheonan*, taking the lives of 46 on board, the democratic government rarely stops propagandists like Lee from launching balloons from the tourist park, Imjingak, located 90 miles southeast of Pyongyang in the city of Paju.[6] The movement of the propaganda balloons from south to north inversely mimics the territorial transgression performed by political defectors from the northern state. Yet unlike the balloon's linear trajectory across the military demarcation line, North Korean escapees embark on a protracted journey that first takes them northward into neighboring China. Most commonly, in winter they cross the frozen Yalu River; in other seasons, they ford the shallow bends in the Tumen River on the frontier between North Korea and northeast China. From here, defectors trek some 4,000 to 5,000 miles throughout Southeast Asia, a months-long journey along what is misleadingly called an "underground railroad": a network of South Korean embassies located in Vietnam, Laos, Cambodia, and Thailand.

Not all defectors successfully reach their target destinations. Just as some of the balloons fall back into South Korean territory, many defectors are repatriated to North Korea by guards posted at the frontier villages near the Chinese side of the Sino-Korean border. In many of these

6 Mark McDonald, "Balloon-Borne Messages to North Korea Have Detractors on Both Sides of Border," *New York Times*, April 26, 2011, http://www.nytimes.com/2011/04/27/world/asia/27iht-korea.html?pagewanted=all&_r=0.

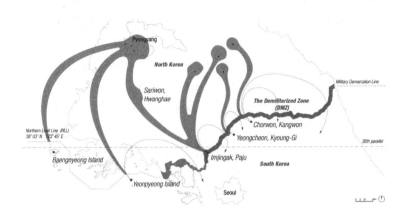

Figure 4 Balloon launch sites, their target regions, and the "reverse" movement of the balloons that fall back into South Korean territories. Source: Dongsei Kim.

villages, Chinese famers are known to deploy escapees as a labor force during the farming seasons.[7] So although North Korean escapees may successfully ingress into Chinese lands, they are at risk of being caught by Chinese police making door-to-door inspections. As a US Government Country Study on North Korea reported in 2008, "Beijing periodically has cracked down with arrests and the forced repatriation of some 200,000 to 300,000 of the North Korean refugees who had sought refuge in China since the mid 1990s."[8] The repatriations take place through five corridors connecting North Korean and Chinese geographies: Sinuiju and Hyesan corridors, which cross the Yalu River; and Musan, Hoeryong, and Onsong corridors, located on the Tumen River. A historically fraught site, the Tumen provided a route for Russian weaponry aid to North Korea during the Korean War (1950–1953) and for cargo exchange between the two nations up until the 1990s.[9] Upon arrival on the Korean side, the defectors are detained—

7   "North Korean Defectors' Escape Route and Their Fate upon Repatriation," *Daily*NK (2002), http://www.dailynk.com/english/keys/2002/9/03.php.

8   Robert L. Worden, ed., *North Korea: A Country Study*, 5th ed. (Washington, DC: US Government Printing Office, 2008), 102.

9   Other reported repatriation areas include Manpo, Rason, Saebyol, and Samjang. Hawk, "Hidden Gulag," 118.

sometimes for months—at *ku-ryu-jang* (interrogation facilities) run by two North Korean government agencies: the *Bo-wi-bu* (State Security Agency), which operates the *kwan-li-so* (political penal labor colonies); and the *An-jeon-bu* (Social Safety Agency), which administers the *kyo-hwa-so* (long-term prison-labor facilities).[10]

The interrogation processes reveal the arbitrary nature of North Korean authorities' decisions to send the repatriates to *kwan-li-so* rather than to other short-term penitentiary facilities.[11] Similarly, the wanton process that moves citizens residing in North Korean cities to labor camps confirms that North Korea does not support a Habeas corpus equivalent, either in its legal constitutions or on practical grounds: "The presumed offender is simply picked up, taken to an interrogation facility and frequently tortured to 'confess' before being deported to the political penal-labor colony."[12] Such repatriation practices reflect the lack of freedom with which North Koreans are able to exercise their mobility in and across various territorial scales. Its citizens generally cannot move between houses and places of work at their own will, nor travel outside the *do* (province) of their residence without a government-issued travel pass. It goes without mention that any politico-spatial practices of mutiny are debarred *in toto*.[13]

One North Korean defector's foreboding comment speaks to the authoritarian regime that depoliticizes the immobile body: "the average person dies where you were born."[14] Considered in this light, it is rather paradoxical

10 Ibid., 120. The formal and colloquial usages of the Korean words vary. As of 1998, *In-min-bo-an-seong*, which literally translates as "People's Safety Agency," replaced the regular police, or *An-jeon-bu*. Yet Hawk notes that many interviewed defectors continue to use the pre-1998 term. See ibid., 23. Some of the *kwan-li-so* such as Camp 18 are run by North Korean police rather than the State Security Agency. Yoon Yeo-sang et al., *Survey Report on the Political Prisoners' Camps (PPC) in North Korea*, trans. Kim Sang-hun (Seoul: National Human Rights Commission of Korea, 2009), 36.

11 Hawk, "Hidden Gulag," 121.

12 Ibid., 29. Also see Worden, ed., *North Korea: A Country Study*, 275.

13 See Yi Ki-ch'un et al., *T'ongil e apsŏ ponŭn Pukhan ŭi kajŏng saenghwal munhwa* (Seoul: Seoul Taehakkyo Ch'ulp'anbu, 2001), 226; and "North Korean Defectors' Escape Route."

14 Yi et al., *T'ongil e apsŏ ponŭn Pukhan ŭi kajŏng saenghwal munhwa*, 227.

that security personnel policing these penal colonies refer to the incarcerated subjects either as *e-ju-min* (migrant) or *ju-min* (resident)—terms which not only do not match their citizenship-lacking status but also wrongly proffer that they had once been granted liberty to decide on their places of dwelling. Such nomenclatures are used in lieu of identification as "political prisoner," a term which North Korea declared to the United Nations Human Rights Council in 2009 is "not in the DPRK's [Democratic People's Republic of Korea] vocabulary."[15] North Korea's statement contradicts the US State Department's Human Rights Country Report of 2003, which estimates that there were between 150,000 and 200,000 political prisoners incarcerated across North Korea.[16]

The indeterminate number of prisoners could be said to correlate with the changing location and size of the *kwan-li-so*. During the first half of the 1990s, the existence of 12 camps were confirmed; by 1999, 10 facilities; and by 2011, only 6—Yoduk (Camp 15) being one of them.[17] According to an anonymous defector who was interviewed in Seoul on January 19, 2005, "since the international community began using satellite photos to focus on Yoduk Concentration Camp, North Korea has begun to move the detainees at Yoduk to Dukchon Concentration Camp in South Hamgyong province."[18] Reasons for the closing of the *kwan-li-so* and for their merger with other, similar facilities therefore included the potential discovery of their location by international

15 Hawk, "Hidden Gulag," vii. North Korea's Penal Code was enacted in 1950 and amended six times; most recently, on April 29, 2004, when torture was prohibited. Yet the "issue of punishment is not expressly stated in the constitution or the criminal code." Worden, ed., *North Korea: A Country Study*, 201, 274.

16 Lee Keum-soon et al., *White Paper on Human Rights in North Korea 2009* (Seoul: Korea Institute for National Unification, 2009), 126.

17 Yoon Yeo-sang et al., *Pukhan chŏngch'ibŏm suyongso ŭi unyŏng ch'egye wa inkwŏn silt'ae* (Seoul: Pukhan Inkwŏn Chŏngbo Sent'ŏ pusŏl Pukhan Inkwŏn Kirok Pojonso, 2011), 79.

18 Quoted in Lee et al., *White Paper*, 126.

19 Yoon et al., *Survey Report*, 40.

20 Lee et al., *White Paper*, 131.

21 See Hawk, "Hidden Gulag," vii.

22 Worden, ed., *North Korea: A Country Study*, 274.

23 Lee et al., *White Paper*, 118.

observers.[19] The closure of some of these spaces could also be posited as a means to ensure the immobilization of prisoners: camps 12 and 13 in North Hamgyong province were closed in May 1987 and December 1990 (respectively) because they were considered too close to the Chinese border; Camp 26 in Seungho District was closed in January 1991 in light of its proximity to the South Korean border.[20] These closures thwarted attempts at defection by escapees because it rendered it difficult for prisoners to accurately testify to the existence and location of these spaces. Paradoxically, it was against a backdrop formed by such evidentiary testimony that North Korea claimed that the "so-called political prisoner camps [did] not exist."[21] In denying the facilities' existence, officials contradicted the country's own penal code, which supports "lifetime confinement to hard labor."[22]

The retributive motive with which these camps operate slightly differs from the nationalistic impulse that spurred their construction in the first place. Kim Jong-il initially conceived the *kwan-li-so* around 1947 (two years after Japan's 35-year colonial rule over Korea ended) to incarcerate factions of the pro-Japanese along with former landowners and religious personnel, who were considered enemies of the new communist state.[23] The operation of the *kwan-li-so* as fully-fledged political prisoner camps in the late 1950s thus reflected ongoing anti-Japanese feelings that had been present at the regime's founding. Many of the 13 *kwan-li-so* scattered throughout six North Korean provinces served to punish escapees to South Korea. This spatial segregation—played out at the scale of the nation and the camp—was central to both provoking and prompting a heighted sense of citizenship and belonging in the North Korean state.

The state-sponsored agenda of collective identification, tied to a sense of national belonging, called upon North Korean citizens to practice "mutual scrutiny" (to betray the behavior of others) in their everyday lives.[24] Suffice it to say, regulating the behavior of the general population in the form of a collective inquiry constituted a top-down approach. The State Security Department in charge of running the *kwan-li-so* also oversees North Korea's Surveillance Bureau. The latter is "a pervasive network of agents and informants from national to village levels" within which "each agent surreptitiously employs some 50 quasi-agents who, in turn, each retain about 20 base-level informants."[25] This national culture and system of incessant surveillance is continually reinforced in regime rhetoric, for every North Korean compatriot is expected to address his or her fellow citizens, regardless of their position in society, as *dongmu* (comrade), a Korean word traditionally associated with congeniality and friendship.[26]

24 Jiyoung Song, *Human Rights Discourse in North Korea: Post-Colonial, Marxist and Confucian Perspectives* (London: Routledge, 2011), 61.

25 Worden, ed., *North Korea: A Country Study*, 278.

26 The term *dongmu* is stigmatized in South Korea for its communist connotations and is no longer found in common usage there.

A COLLECTIVE BODY AT WORK

Kang Chul-hwan, an ex-prisoner at the Ipsok-ni compound of Yoduk describes the typical work routine enforced at the camps, making clear the kinds of overseeing that take place:

> Roll call is held at 5:30 every morning. Reporting late three times is considered equal to one day's absence from work and the prisoner is deprived of one full day of meals…. There is a study session at the end of every workday and an ideology lecture twice a week. The study sessions and ideology lectures are essential elements of education for personal reform and promoting the spirit of the revolution.[27]

27 Yoon et al., *Survey Report*, 91.

Kang's testimony vividly recalls the very motivation underlying the state's decision to construct Yoduk. This particular concentration camp, located 70 miles northeast of Pyongyang in the mountainous region of Yoduk-gun, South Hamgyong province, began construction in July 1969, following Kim Il-sung's speech calling for a "need to 'revolutionize' the Korean Workers' Party."[28] In other words, the late dictator's decision to build Yoduk had, in idea, conjoined two disparate collective bodies—the political party and its ruled subjects—believed to make manifest an ideological revolution. It is unsurprising then that the penal subjects were expected to carry forth the national ideology of *juche* (spirit of self-reliance) mandated ever since Kim trumpeted its need before his Korean Workers' Party on December 28, 1955.[29] In line with this, the prisoners at the *kwan-li-so* are left responsible to scavenge for their own food, resulting in unaccountable number of deaths and malnourishment at the

28 Hawk, "Hidden Gulag," 53.

29 It was only in 1963, when Soviet economic and military assistance to the North came to a halt, that Kim Il-sung officially installed the ideologies of self-sustenance and self-defense.

Imprisoned Bodies

camps, a hands-to-mouth existence with less than 4 ounces of corn supplied to each, as the 1994 *Chosun Ilbo* reported. In this case, the body bears witness to the failure of such "self-sufficient" measures.[30] As Kim Young-soon, one of the choreographers of *Yoduk Story* and a former dance teacher in North Korea, testified in front of the House Committee on Foreign Affairs Subcommittee on Africa, Global Health and Human Rights on September 20, 2011, "My three sons, one daughter, father and mother died from starvation; there were no coffins so their bodies were rolled in a straw mat and buried."[31]

Accordingly, the arrested subject is made responsible for the spaces that she or he would inhabit. It is common for prisoners to construct their own houses out of stones and quicklime. Much like "a temporary roof on a pig-pen," as Kang Chul-hwan described it, Yoduk housing is marked by poor construction and leaks in inclement weather.[32] Oh Myong-oh described the dwelling spaces at Camp 18 by saying, "houses they built were adequate for the North Korean standard of living."[33] Oh also recollected that the penal subjects in Camp 18 were expected to dig for coal to heat their houses in winter. Both observations speak to an equivalence between housing construction quality and typical living conditions inside and outside the *kwan-li-so*. The latter in particular is consistent with regime policy that imposes self-dependent modes of living, regardless of one's residential locale.[34]

What Oh's testimony invoked is how the ideology of "self-reliance" could be easily translated into (and

30   Kim, *Testimony*, 2011.

31   Ibid.

32   Yoon et al., *Survey Report*, 120, 130.

33   Ibid., 131.

34   Ibid.

executed through) a collective order, if the unit of the individual is expanded. To manage its labor activities and spaces most efficiently and to maximal effect, each individual in the *kwan-li-so* is incorporated into a traditional collective form: the familial unit. In fact, it is common practice for families of the convicted individual to be imprisoned as well. This reflects Kim Il-sung's desire to eradicate the bloodline of criminals so as to "destroy the seed of three generations."[35] In accordance with the North Korean policy of *yeon-jwa-je* (guilt by association), Kim Young-soon was arrested on August 1, 1970, and imprisoned a few months later on October 1 at Yoduk, together with her six immediate family members.[36] Once immobilized at the *kwan-li-so*, the productive penal subject is again tied to a collective comprised of actual family members and other prisoners. A "guidance officer" from the Security Agency is assigned to manage several of these family-based "work units" that form the "basic units for conducting daily routines."[37]

The availability of land on which the camp compounds were constructed catered to its wide-ranging workplaces: coalmines; construction sites; and food, clothing, paper, utensils, and cement factories; as well as farms.[38] As of the 1990s, the *kwan-li-so* ranged in size from 23 square miles at Dongshin (7,000 prisoners), to 146 square miles (50,000 prisoners) at Yoduk.[39] The first official *kwan-li-so*, Dukjang (Camp 18), was constructed in a coal mining region in Pukchang, South Pyongan province, in 1958.[40] The specificity of land and its

35   *Yodok Stories.*

36   Kim, *Testimony,* 2011.

37   Lee et al., *White Paper,* 133.

38   Ibid.

39   An, "Saranaol su ŏmnŭn kot," 4.

40   "Hwang Jang-yop Speaks: Testimonies of North Korean Defectors," http://www.fas.org/irp/world/rok/nis-docs/hwang5.htm. Evidently, the mapping of these geographies—visual, numerical, or otherwise—should not be taken at face value. The testimony of a person imprisoned at Camp 18 from 1975 to 2000—"all prisoners are pushed into an underground tunnel that turns out to be a mine"—reminds us that certain shapes of the land are not yet accounted for, and will remain this way. Yoon et al., *Survey Report,* 91.

Imprisoned Bodies

resources created the conditions of the camp and the type of prisoner work performed there.

Labor structured the siting and organization of the *kwan-li-so*, extending beyond the workplace to influence housing typology and the conduct of prisoner-laborers, who were expected to operate as collective units even when not working. Labor forces were made up of family units, which proved to be an expedient spatial arrangement of the *kwan-li-so*, for the family units were agglomerated together to be literally housed "under one roof," while single prisoners were domiciled in boarding houses. Shin Dong-hyuk, the only known detainee to have been born in a *kwan-li-so*, recalls of the Number 8 Work Unit at Camp 14: "about 40 families were living together as a work unit. There were one-level "row houses," and each housing unit had four one-rooms with small kitchens attached to each room. Since each family was assigned one room/kitchen, four families were living under one roof (one unit)."[41] Upon initial reflection, that families were "allowed" to live together surfaces as somewhat of an appeasing move on the part of the authorities. Yet what can also be gained from Shin's testimony is that the camps' dependency on such strictly enforced cohabitation strategically elides work and living situations.

Shin's description of the so-called row houses (or "harmonica flats," as prisoners referred to them) resemble the extant housing typology commonly found in North Korean cities and farming villages.[42] This model of collective living was typical of the North Korean context: only

41 Lee et al., *White Paper*, 133.

42 Yoon et al., *Survey Report*, 120.

43   Yi et al., *T'ongil e apsŏ*, 210.

44   Ibid., 209–10.

45   For harmonica apartments, see U Chŏng, *Pukhan sahoe kusŏngnon* (Seoul: Chinsol Buksŭ, 2000), 311–12. For a description of the same typology applied to standalone houses, see Yi et al., *T'ongil e apsŏ*, 211–12.

46   Yi et al., *T'ongil e apsŏ*, 210.

government officials were assigned to live in single-family dwellings.[43] In fact, 21.1 percent of the 158 North Korean defectors interviewed between December 1997 and February 1998 had, prior to their internment, lived in "harmonica houses"—a housing typology first constructed throughout North Korea in the 1950s.[44] The moniker referred directly to the formal arrangement of living spaces inside apartments or landed dwellings that took on the shape of a harmonica. In the case of the apartment model, a corridor linked each adjoining unit arrayed in a line on every floor. For more common, landed counterparts, each of the 49- to 66-foot-long blocks held about five to seven adjoining housing units. A single unit measured approximately 10 feet by 20 feet and contained a single room (10 feet by 13 feet) through which the family has direct access to a kitchen located at the rear (10 feet by 7 feet).[45] These harmonica houses are private spaces made inconspicuous to the public eye: high-rise apartments facing the highways in Pyongyang conceal spates of harmonica housing that lie behind them.[46] Thus in recollecting the type of housing in the city that cannot be seen or accessed easily, Shin's testimony of the harmonica flats at the *kwan-li-so* provides a view into the spaces of the status quo, where North Korean families are made to dwell as collective units.

It would be no exaggeration to adduce that enforcing collective labor at the *kwan-li-so* ran in tandem with enforcing collective modes of dwelling. This is a situation where "prisoners are not imprisoned in closed cells and prison buildings, like prisons in South Korea."[47] Yet this did not preclude the prisoners from being made aware—again, in spatial terms—that by occupying the internment facilities they carried individual responsibility for the collective. Single punishment cells could be found at the *kwan-li-so*; spaces where its prisoners were subjected to degrees of torture that were proleptic of their deaths that were to follow. Shin Dong-hyuk's memoir *Coming Out to the World* depicts his imprisonment in one of these cells following a 1996 incident, when his mother and brother failed to escape from Camp 14. Elsewhere he described his cell as "a concrete floor," a "simple toilet," and "about five feet square" of maneuvering space.[48] Its limited size prevented him from reclining comfortably with his legs outstretched, reinforcing torturous restraints on his movements:

> There were fetters on the shelf inside the cell, and the agents would fix the fetters on Shin's ankles and pull the ropes from outside, which caused him to hang upside down. This was one method of torture, but there was a separate torture chamber, where he had to undergo "water-boarding" tortures.[49]

47 Yoon et al., *Survey Report*, 120.

48 Lee et al., *White Paper*,

49 Shin Dong-hyuk, *Coming Out to the World* (Seoul: North Korean Human Rights Protection Center, 2007), 162–85, cited in Lee et al., *White Paper*, 134.

Ahn Myong-chol, a former prison guard, has also testified to restrictive and repressive conditions at camps 11, 13, and 26 from 1987 until 1994. From the perspective of an authority, he recalls the circumstances under which the individual body is made to cooperate, and how failure to do so sent the penal subject to a punishment chamber:

> Whenever a prisoner encounters a guard or SSA [State Security Agency] officer in the camp, the prisoner must stop his/her work and acknowledge the authority by dropping to his knees with eyes downcast, or by giving a deep bow in which the back is in 90 degrees to stiffened legs. Prisoners are mercilessly beaten or taken to a punishment chamber for violating this rule.[50]

50   Yoon et al., *Survey Report*, 89–90.

Given the state of affairs, the "training" of the bodies at the camps is analogous to the compliant bodies of North Korean civilians that, on occasion, have to negotiate with, and compensate for, space. For example, when there is insufficient housing in North Korea's capital city of Pyongyang (or more accurately, projected to be the case by the government), bodies are fixed to their residences. It is typical for recently married couples to have to live apart for more than one year before their workplaces qua state authority assign them dwellings fit for a conjugal relationship.[51]

51   Testimony of Song Kyong-ho, in Kang Kwang-sik, *Pukhan ŭi silt'ae: Punya pyŏl kyŏnghŏm charyo mit yebijŏk koch'al* (Kyŏnggi-do Sŏngnam-si: Han'guk Chŏngsin Munhwa Yŏn'guwŏn, 1987), 82.

In other instances, such as the Mass Games—the national spectacle par excellence that commemorates holidays and state achievements—the body is made to perform relentlessly in Pyongyang Indoor Gymnasium.

Officially dated as September 10, the performances at the 2003 Games were repeated twice daily for twenty days straight in a conspicuous effort to accommodate as many viewers as possible.[52] In an antagonistic situation where space lacks human presence, the body of the citizen enacts agency, albeit not of one's own volition. At Kijong-dong, a 1950s Potemkin village located within the DMZ between North and South Korea, selected civilians from the North were told to walk across the site to deceive its South Korean neighbors that the village functioned as an active settlement.[53] Space, when considered in isolation from the body, pales in comparison to this mechanism of power, because it is the body—a "marker" within and of space—that is trained to adjust accordingly.

It is not irrelevant here that the authoritarian regime equated the physical training of its citizens to the formulation of a communist body. Kim Jong-il had remarked, "Developing Mass Games is important in training schoolchildren to be fully developed communist people."[54] In other words, power expounds on its role as a force allied with the space in which it is enacted or where the body is placed; it is exerted onto the latter, contriving what Michel Foucault identifies as a docile body—"the body that is manipulated, shaped, trained, which obeys, responds, becomes skillful and increases its forces."[55] This body, when translated to the context of the *kwan-li-so*, could be "trained" in a space whose definition slides, although not unproblematically, into what Foucault categorizes as "heterotopias of deviation." For Foucault,

[52]   The entire city of 2 million people was mobilized on September 9, a day prior to the 2003 Mass Games celebrations, to commemorate the 55th anniversary of the founding of DPRK. A military parade was followed by a people's parade; at night there was dancing on Kim Il-sung Square and a Youth Torchlight Parade. *A State of Mind*, directed by Daniel Gordon (New York: Kino on Video, 2006), DVD.

[53]   Jessica Bridger, "Kijong Dong—Potemkin Landscape," *International Review of Landscape Architecture and Urban Design*, http://www.toposmagazine.com/blog/kijong-dong-potemkin-landscape.html.

[54]   *A State of Mind*, directed by Daniel Gordon.

[55]   Michel Foucault, "Docile Bodies," in *Discipline and Punish: The Birth of the Prison*, trans. Alan Sheridan, 2nd ed. (New York: Vintage Books, 1995), 136.

56   Michel Foucault, "Of Other Spaces," trans. Jay Miskowiec, *Diacritics* 16, no. 1 (Spring 1986): 25.

society's "other" spaces, such as rest homes, psychiatric hospitals, and prisons, contain individuals whose deviant behaviors contest societal norms.[56] The North Korean state, however, does not disclose to its citizens the classifications of deviant behavior that might be cast in opposition to the "normal." As Kim Young-soon points out, the reasons for isolating its citizens away from society are ex post facto explained, some of which include "the crime of defaming the authority and prestige of Kim Il Sung and Kim Jong-il; the crime of knowledge about the private life of Kim Jong-il and leaking information about it to the general public, thus defaming the prestige of the Great Leader."[57] It must be remembered, however, that a testimonial like Kim's stands as an exception within a larger practice.

57   Kim, *Testimony*, 2011.

Yoduk and Camp 18 offer unique examples, in that they each host a "revolutionizing process zone" where freeing prisoners is notionally feasible (the other *kwan-li-so* only operate as "full control zones"). From this designated space of opportunity, there have been no confirmed accounts of prisoner releases from Yoduk between 2009 and 2012, however.[58] It is at this juncture that the *kwan-li-so* as a model of heterotopic space can be contested. Though putatively confining, Foucauldian heterotopias make an allusion to the eventual release of bodies from these "other" spaces, following their disciplinary reformation. Therefore, the body of the prisoner at a *kwan-li-so* may be argued to be asymptomatic of the body disciplined in Foucauldian heterotopias of deviation,

58   Hawk, "Hidden Gulag," 15.

insofar as it cannot be freed from the space of captivity and "reform." This captures the authoritarian regime's attempt to curtail—and increase its clout over—the bodily mobility of its citizens, a mobilization that would otherwise confirm the effects of its power now displaced onto the body.

Figure 5 Individual punishment cells, dispersed among guards and prisoners witnessing a torture spectacle. A scene from *Yoduk Stories*. Source: Tore Vollan © Piraya Film AS, 2009.

YODUK STORY/IES

The trope of heterotopia need not be abandoned fully, particularly when considering how *Yoduk Story* recreates defectors' experiences in the space of theater. For Foucault, heterotopias are not just about distinct spaces of deviation: they are also about the connections that can be drawn across them. In the essay "Of Other Spaces," Foucault cautions against dismissing the various indices—of which humans could be said to be one—that carve out the relation *between* spaces:

> This problem of the human site or living space is not simply that of knowing whether there will be enough space for men in the world ... but also that of knowing what relations of propinquity, what

59   Foucault, "Of Other Spaces," 23.

type of storage, circulation, marking, and classifi-
cation of human elements should be adopted in a
given situation in order to achieve a given end. Our
epoch is one in which space takes for us the form
of relations among sites.[59]

Viewed in this light, bodies take on primacy in hinting at
the relations between the disparate locations—concentration camps, Mass Games, Kijong-dong, or theater—the
common denominator being that the bodies are disciplined from rebelling against the respective "work" at
hand (physical labor, performance).

While the very functional utility of similar stages
offers an obvious pretext for choreographing the body
that occupies it, it more interestingly couples the labored
body and the performed body. During a rehearsal of
Yoduk Story, Ahn Myong-chol, the former prison guard,
provides instruction regarding the beating process to
director Jung Sung-san and to the cast members who are
made to follow his directions:

Jung   "If a prisoner gives you trouble, are there punishment cells?"

Ahn   "Yes, there are special cells at the camp. Let's
call them physical punishment chambers. If
you're sent there, they beat you.
Where is the pole?
They put the pole behind your knees and order
you to kneel.
If the prisoner moves due to the pain, the
guard comes up and presses here with his foot

[demonstrates on the pole and on the cast member].

Later the prisoner is unable to walk. His flesh begins to rot here" [points to calf muscle].

...

Jung "Can you beat however you like?"

Ahn "You can beat so as not to kill. If someone dies during a beating, it doesn't really matter, but they reprimand you. They shout but don't punish you."

Jung "There are various kinds of public executions (at the camps). You know how it is done, so please show us."

Ahn "As far as shooting goes, you shoot in the head, chest or stomach, so he's tied here, here and here at the knees so he doesn't fall [gestures to the body of the cast member]."[60]

In perfecting a scene of punishment through regulated and repeated rehearsals, the musical conjures up bodily order as being central to the musical's enterprise. The "corrective" demonstration of this scene falls in line with Foucault's description that one of the roles of heterotopia is "to create a space that is other, another real space, as perfect, as meticulous, as well arranged as ours is messy, ill constructed, and jumbled."[61] It further shows how the body does not necessarily testify to violent exercises of power, but channels its non-violent (instructional and observational) forms. Paraphrasing Foucault's 1973 lecture "Le pouvoir psychiatrique," philosopher Arnold

60 *Yodok Stories.*

61 Foucault, "Of Other Spaces," 27.

Davidson revisits a similar idea, noting that power "need not be violent, in the sense of being unleashed, passionate, even though its point of application is the body.... [Foucault] emphasizes that this exercise of power on the body remains rationally organized and calculated even while being the physical exercise of a force."[62]

Moreover, given that it is a South Korean cast which is told how to perform, the musical rehearsals constitute an alternative site of surveillance for the performers enacting the tragic experiences of North Korean defectors. Correspondingly, the premiere of *Yoduk Story* may be viewed as a new site of political activism, a performance that is doubly displaced: on the stage and in the new geographical context of South Korea. To add to this, only a few months after its debut in Seoul in March 2006, *Yoduk Story* toured the United States. It showed at the Strathmore Music Center in Maryland on October 4, 2006, to an audience mostly comprised of Korean-American Christians and US government officials that American nongovernmental organizations (NGOs) such as the US Committee for Human Rights in North Korea and the National Endowment for Democracy had invited.[63]

In restaging the unimaginable realities of the *kwan-li-so* within the controlled environment of the theater stage, the heterotopic space of the musical set allows its audience, members of the public charged with a political agenda, to imagine the body politics of a regime otherwise inaccessible to them. It is common knowledge that

62   Arnold I. Davidson, introduction to *Abnormal: Lectures at the Collège de France, 1974–1975* (New York: Picador, 2003), xx.

63   US government officials invited for the premiere included Jay Lewkowicz, a special envoy for North Korean human rights. See Suk-young Kim, "Gulag, the Musical: Performing Trauma in North Korea through Yoduk Story," TDR: *The Drama Review* 52, no. 1 (Spring 2008): 120 fnt. 7.

South Koreans (the first audiences to watch the musical) are typically denied entry into North Korea, not to mention the spaces of incarceration. Under these restrictive circumstances, the authenticity of *Yoduk Story* is attached to the personal experiences of the play's writer-director Jung Sung-san and one of its choreographers, Kim Young-soon, who "openly claimed that the musical was a documentation of their own suffering in North Korea." In fact, they publicly noted their own incarceration "endowed the musical with the authority of an authentic confessional."[64] That is, the audience's conception of the actual spaces of the camps hinges on the accounts of Kim, who comments while surveying the stage props, "Why are these (prison) cells constructed so low? In reality, they were higher and abutted each other in a linear fashion."[65] To take such subjective accounts as evidence is to follow art historian Henry Saye, for whom the referent (the original space of the punishment cells at the *kwan-li-so*, in this instance) "anticipates, even authorizes, its many occurrences and somehow contains their variety."[66] Blaine Harden, the author of Shin Dong-hyuk's 2012 biography *Escape from Camp 14: One Man's Remarkable Odyssey from North Korea to Freedom in the West*, also credits the potency of a subjective "story" that is somatically and orally delivered:

> Talking to Shin in person, his story sounds believable. It's because of the intensity and precision of his memory. His body, too, is a map of what he endured, with burns on his back and legs, and his

64   Kim Suk-young, *Illusive Utopia: Theater, Film, and Everyday Performance in North Korea* (Ann Arbor: University of Michigan Press, 2010), 293.

65   *Yodok Stories.*

66   Henry Sayre, "Performance," in *Critical Terms for Literary Study*, ed. Frank Lentricchia and Thomas McLaughlin, 2nd ed. (Chicago: University of Chicago Press, 1995), 91.

67   Blaine Harden, quoted in Christian DuChateau, "'Escape from Camp 14,' A True North Korea Survival Story," CNN Living, April 3, 2012, http://www.cnn.com/2012/03/30/living/escape-camp-14-book-story/index.html.

68   Ibid.

69   Janet Maslin, "The Casual Horrors of Life in a North Korean Hell: 'Escape from Camp 14,' by Blaine Harden," New York Times, April 11, 2012, http://www.nytimes.com/2012/04/12/books/escape-from-camp-14-by-blaine-harden.html?_r=0.

70   Richard Spencer, "The Death Camps of N Korea Inspire a Musical," The Telegraph, March 16, 2006, http://www.telegraph.co.uk/news/worldnews/asia/southkorea/1513176/The-death-camps-of-N-Korea-inspire-a-musical.html.

partially severed finger. His arms are bowed from childhood labor. Confirming the details of his story is impossible, if you mean going to Camp 14 and asking questions of his captors and torturers.[67]

What Harden identifies as a "singular perspective" of life at the *kwan-li-so*, as portrayed by Shin and others, remains critical to the documentation of prisoners' experiences, so long as North Korea keeps unwanted visitors, including the International Committee of the Red Cross, out of the *kwan-li-so*.[68] This is notwithstanding Harden's discovery that Shin had lied about being uninvolved in the death of his mother and brother: he had told the camp security guards about his family's plans to leave, fully aware that the consequences of attempted escape was the death penalty.[69]

In this context, it was inevitable that the staging of such *prima facie* accounts as undertaken by *Yoduk Story* would stir up various political reactions. When interviewed in 2006, Jung Sung-san claimed to have been "pressurised by South Korean officials to tone down his play and backers withdrew funding. He pledged a kidney as collateral for a loan before a Norwegian human rights organization stepped in to help."[70] In a literal sense, Jung's reaction—to give up his body part—illuminates that while it might be the space of the stage that tries to recreate life at the camps, it is the currency of the mobilized and liberated bodies that ultimately stand as metonyms for these political spaces. Thus, if one of the initial functions of the *kwan-li-so* was to incarcerate critics of Kim

Il-sung and his regime, it is rather ironic that the oral accounts of former prisoners—arguably the least impartial fount of evidence yoked to the body—would testify to a national culture of internment that traversed the spatial scales of the country and the labor camps. Lodging rhetorical disdain against the North Korean regime had come full circle, albeit to new locations (South Korea, among others) that authorized a limited sense of political refuge and activism. As such, it would be the mobilization of individual as well as collective bodies that would reveal the operations of *kwan-li-so*—political spaces that enacted the everyday citizenship of North Koreans as much as they eradicated it.

"The truth is the entire country is one big concentration camp," preaches Lee Min Bok to an audience of churchgoers in South Korea near the finale of *Yodok Stories*.[71] Serendipitously, this sentiment was shared by *Chosun Ilbo*'s 1982 caricature illustrating the North Korean state as a single internment facility crowded with nondescript figures. The satire, together with Lee's pithy critique, pointedly captures the way in which the *kwan-li-so* camp functions as a spatial metonym for domestic governance. In other words, exceptional moments are not idiosyncratic episodes: they may well give better insight to the reality of living under an authoritarian regime. The problems that affect the camps are not all that different from those that impact the general population, as the UN Commission of Inquiry on Human Rights in the Democratic People's Republic of Korea (DPRK) evinced

71 *Yodok Stories.*

72 "Introduction," United Nations Human Rights Office of the High Commissioner for Human Rights, http://www.ohchr.org/EN/HRBodies/HRC/COIDPRK/Pages/AboutCoI.aspx.

73 Ambassador Oh Joon, permanent representative of the Republic of Korea to the United Nations, speech, delivered at Harvard Law School, March 13, 2015.

in its 2013 investigatory mandate, which addressed DPRK's general lack of "freedom of expression" and "freedom of movement," as well as human rights violations pertaining to the "prison camps," among other offenses.[72] Perhaps no other episode is more telling of the way in which corporal and geopolitical security concerns are entangled than the UN Security Council's decision to take up the human rights issues of North Korea, a situation that has hitherto pertained to only two other countries: Myanmar and Zimbabwe.[73] The UN Commission's observation highlighted the extent to which the *kwan-li-so* lay central to the politics of mobility (defection) and the politics of immobility (imprisonment), issues that remain firmly tethered to the politics of information circulation. The *kwan-li-so* thereby demonstrate how spatial control is critical to safeguarding state information and the bodies associated with it, and plays a vital role in obfuscating their accessibility and comprehensibility.

In contrast, one must remember that any physical geography is only susceptible of being politicized once the public can, at the very least, glimpse its existence. When images of these locked-up bodies do not appear en masse, a new kind of citizen is produced: a research dilettante who is eager to find out more about the camps and plays detective in their deciphering. Interested members of the public including ex-attorney Joshua Stanton and volunteer Daniel Bielefeld have created the website *One Free Korea* to piece together the locations of the camps. Using satellite images to plot the latitudinal and longitudinal coordinates of camps on Google Earth, they have unpacked a deluge of disparate data on their sites and boundaries, demarcated by guard towers and fences.[74] As links to web pages providing information on the camps are put up and some expeditiously taken down, findings grow increasingly prevalent albeit less coherent. What results is that information obtained from scholars, the public, the media, governmental organizations, NGOs, and private institutions coalesce to form a loose constellation, rather than a synthesized coordination, of public knowledge. Epistemological production and consumption can no longer be differentiated. The vulnerability as well as the enfranchisement of citizens— as consumers and producers of knowledge—surface at the intersection of the digital with the physical in the 21st century. And, as such, North Korea is only one instance where the virtual and physical manifestation of citizenship—the local-global shifting of information and cross-border mobilizing of bodies—is rendered mutually constitutive. That the former prisoners were asked—, and most likely able—to verify "with confidence" from the satellite photographs the "landmarks" of the camp sites to which they were exiled (housing, barracks, worksites, execution sites) underscores this claim.[75]

An analogue set of events provides an enticing medium with which to reflect on the musical. In recent coverage of new balloon launches on June 5, 2014, *Bloomberg Businessweek* sensationalized the incident as a "no-tech tactic"[76] Yet allied with the fetishization of the

74 Joshua Stanton worked alongside the US House of Representatives Committee on Foreign Affairs on issues related to North Korea, including those on human rights. "Mass Escape at N. Korean Concentration Camp; 120 Escape," http://freekorea.us/2007/02/06/mass-escape-at-n-korean-concentration-camp-120-vescape/.

75 Although the satellite photographs commercially sourced from Digital Globe and Space Imaging Corporation for Hawk's first edition of *Hidden Gulag* (2003) were of much lower resolution than those from Google Earth used in the second edition (2012), ex-prisoners were able to identify prison facilities in camp compounds. Hawk, "Hidden Gulag," 11–12.

76 Adam Higginbotham, "The No-Tech Tactics of North Korea's Most Wanted Defector," *Bloomberg Businessweek*, June 5, 2014, http://mobile.businessweek.com/articles/2014-06-05/the-no-tech-tactics-of-north-koreas-target-zero-park-sang-hak.

analogue is the embodied reality of constrained citizenship in the North Korean context, for which—as of today—only its defectors can verbally account (and then, only problematically). So long as the escapees continue to be implicated in the arc of knowledge circulation that unfolds, with their propagandist lobbies as well as their real bodily flights, the regime has no option but to continue to consider the whistleblowers a more-than-real threat to its clandestine biopolitics—operations that would otherwise remain buried.

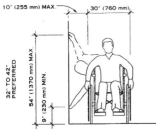

HIGH AND LOW SIDE REACH LIMITS

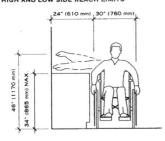

MAX. SIDE REACH OVER OBSTRUCTION

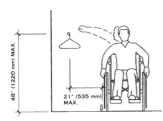

CLOSET

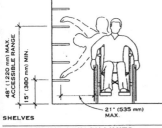

SHELVES

PARALLEL/SIDE REACH LIMITS

REACH RANGE

ANSI A117.1-1998 reduced the maximum reach range from 54 in. to 48 in. for unobstructed side reach and made the height limit the same as that for unobstructed forward reach, with the following exceptions:

1. A117.1 provides exception for existing elements located 54 in. maximum above the floor or ground.
2. A117.1 provides exception for elevator car controls, allowing buttons at 54 in. maximum, where the elevator serves more than 16 openings. This exception may be revisited in future editions, when the elevator industry has had an opportunity to develop alternate control configurations.

Lawrence G. Perry, AIA; Silver Spring, Maryland

UNOBSTRUCTED FORWARD REACH

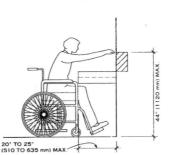

OBSTRUCTED HIGH FORWARD REACH

REACH RANGES

3. A117.1 does not apply the 48 in. restriction to tactile signs. Tactile signs must be installed so the tactile characters are between 48 and 60 in. above the floor. Below this height, tactile characters are difficult to read by standing persons, as the hand must be bent awkwardly or turned over (similar to reading upside down) to read the message.

FHAG requires controls and operating mechanisms in covered dwelling units to be installed at a maximum height of 48 in., with the following exceptions:

1. FHAG allows inaccessible controls in covered dwelling units if "comparable" accessible controls are provided.
2. Floor outlets are permitted if an adequate number of accessible wall outlets is provided.
3. Electric outlets above kitchen counters can be located in corners, provided additional outlets are located within reach.

Accessible controls and operating mechanisms should be operable with one hand and not require tight grasping, pinching, or twisting of the wrist, with the following exception: FHAG does not regulate the operating force or type of operation required for controls and operating mechanisms in dwelling units.

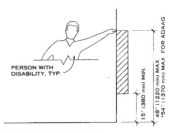

UNOBSTRUCTED SIDE REACH

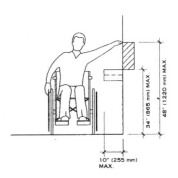

OBSTRUCTED SIDE REACH

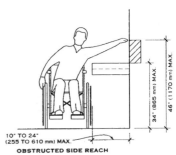

CHILDREN'S REACH RANGES FROM A WHEELCHAIR (IN., MM)

FORWARD OR SIDE REACH	AGES 3 AND 4	AGES 5–8	AGES 9–12
High (maximum)	36 (915)	40 (1015)	44 (1120)
Low (minimum)	20 (510)	18 (455)	16 (405)

SPECIFICATIONS FOR WATER CLOSETS SERVING CHILDREN (IN., MM)

DIMENSION	PRE-K, K (AGES 3 AND 4)	1ST–3RD (AGES 5–8)	4TH–7TH (AGES 9–12)
Water closet centerline	12 (305)	12–15 (305–380)	15–18 (380–455)
Toilet seat height	11–12 (280–305)	12–15 (305–380)	15–17 (380–430)
Grab bar height	18–20 (455–510)	20–25 (510–635)	25–27 (635–685)
Dispenser height	14 (355)	14–17 (355–430)	17–19 (430–485)

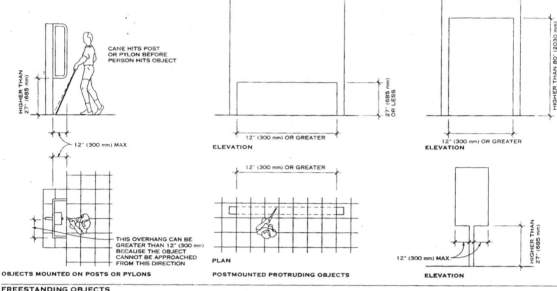

CANE HITS POST OR PYLON BEFORE PERSON HITS OBJECT

HIGHER THAN 27" (685 mm)

12" (300 mm) MAX.

THIS OVERHANG CAN BE GREATER THAN 12" (300 mm) BECAUSE THE OBJECT CANNOT BE APPROACHED FROM THIS DIRECTION

OBJECTS MOUNTED ON POSTS OR PYLONS

12" (300 mm) OR GREATER

27" (685 mm) OR LESS

ELEVATION

12" (300 mm) OR GREATER

PLAN

POSTMOUNTED PROTRUDING OBJECTS

HIGHER THAN 80" (2030 mm)

12" (300 mm) OR GREATER

ELEVATION

12" (300 mm) MAX.

HIGHER THAN 27" (685 mm)

ELEVATION

FREESTANDING OBJECTS

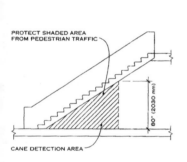

PROTECT SHADED AREA FROM PEDESTRIAN TRAFFIC

80" (2030 mm)

CANE DETECTION AREA

OVERHEAD HAZARDS—EXAMPLE

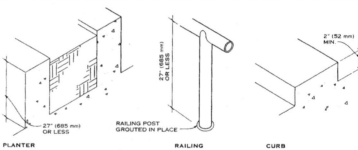

27" (685 mm) OR LESS

PLANTER

27" (685 mm) OR LESS

RAILING POST GROUTED IN PLACE

RAILING

2" (52 mm) MIN.

CURB

NOTES

1. Protection from overhead hazards can be provided by permanent, built-in elements or by movable elements such as furniture and potted plants.

2. Thoughtful, informed design can reduce or eliminate most overhead hazards (e.g., low headroom hazards can be avoided by enclosing areas under stairs and escalators).

OVERHEAD HAZARD PROTECTION—EXAMPLES

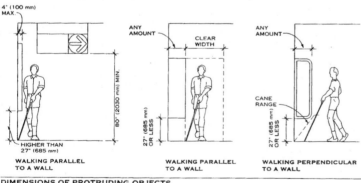

4" (100 mm) MAX.

80" (2030 mm) MIN.

HIGHER THAN 27" (685 mm)

WALKING PARALLEL TO A WALL

ANY AMOUNT

CLEAR WIDTH

27" (685 mm) OR LESS

WALKING PARALLEL TO A WALL

ANY AMOUNT

CANE RANGE

27" (685 mm) OR LESS

WALKING PERPENDICULAR TO A WALL

NOTES

1. Wall sconces, fire alarm appliances, environmental controls, door hardware, signs, and suspended lighting fixtures are examples of protruding objects.

2. Some standards specify the extent to which doorstops and door closers may protrude into the 80 in. (2030 mm) vertical clearance, generally allowing a 2 in. maximum projection.

3. Protruding objects are not permitted to reduce the required width of an accessible route (36 in., except 32 in. width permitted for a 24 in. length).

DIMENSIONS OF PROTRUDING OBJECTS

Lawrence G. Perry, AIA; Silver Spring, Maryland

The Right to Live in the World: Architecture, Inclusion, and the Americans with Disabilities Act

Wanda Katja Liebermann

On March 12, 1990, lawmakers and tourists were startled by the sight of dozens of disabled people who had cast off wheelchairs, canes, and crutches at the foot of the United States Capitol Building to crawl on hands and knees up its 83 stone steps. "What do we want? ADA!" they shouted, demanding a vote on the Americans with Disabilities Act, which had been stalled for months in the House of Representatives.[1] The "Capitol Crawl," organized by Americans Disabled for Accessible Public Transit, viscerally displayed the everyday barriers that the built environment poses for people with disabilities. Sprawling and straining, the protestors' bodies exposed their embodiment of a world designed to exclude them.

1   Zim, "'Capitol Crawl' – Americans with Disabilities Act of 1990," September 9, 2013, http://www.historyby zim.com/2013/09/capitol-crawl-americans-with-disabilities-act-of-1990/. See also William J. Eaton, "Disabled Persons Rally, Crawl Up Capitol Steps," *Los Angeles Times*, March 13, 1990, http://articles.latimes. com/1990-03-13/news/ mn-211_1_capitol-steps.

Figure 1   Accessibility design guidelines as illustrated in *Architectural Graphic Standards*. Source: Drawings by Lawrence G. Perry, AIA for Charles George Ramsey, Harold Reeve Sleeper, and John Ray Hoke, eds., *Architectural Graphic Standards*, 10th ed. (New York: Wiley, 2000), 957–58.

Figure 2 "Capitol Steps Crawl," protest in support of the Americans with Disabilities Act (ADA) organized by Americans Disabled for Accessible Public Transit (ADAPT), March 12, 1990. Source: Tom Olin.

The event sped the passage of the ADA, groundbreaking legislation that President George H. W. Bush signed into law on July 26, 1990, before 2,000 invited guests on the White House lawn. Coming after decades of disability rights activism, the ADA's goals focused on equal opportunity, full participation, independent living, and economic self-sufficiency. The first major legislation since the Civil Rights Act of 1964, it grants "civil rights protections to individuals with disabilities similar to those prohibiting discrimination on the basis of race, color, sex, national origin, age, and religion."[2] It expanded the scope of previous legislation, such as the Architectural Barriers Act of 1968 and the Rehabilitation Act of 1973, by further opening up opportunities for the disabled in education,

2   Margaret C. Jasper, *Americans with Disabilities Act* (New York: Oceana, 2008), xi.

The Right to Live in the World

employment, communication, and public spaces. As I. King Jordan, the first deaf president of Gallaudet University, declared at the protest, "We're not asking for any favors. We're simply asking for the same rights and equality any other American has."[3]

Whereas the first four decades of US disability policy focused on the vocational rehabilitation of people with disabilities, the ADA reconceptualized the relationship between disability and society. Initial legislative approaches, like the Smith-Fess Act of 1920, aimed, through medical approaches, to "transform people with disabilities rather than to transform society."[4] Although disabled veterans of World War II and the wars in Korea and Vietnam legitimized calls for integration into mainstream society, civil rights ideology and rhetoric of the 1960s greatly influenced the moral and legal argument for inclusion of the disabled. In particular, it informed an unnoticed provision of the 1973 Rehabilitation Act. As sociologist Richard Scotch writes, "Section 504 transformed federal disability policy by conceptualizing access for disabled people as a right rather than as a welfare benefit."[5] Through protests and publicity in support of Section 504 and many other mobilizations, disability groups throughout the United States developed a minority group identity, grounded in a common history of discrimination based on cultural and legal definitions of disability.[6]

Formalizing disability rights held up the subjectivity of people with disabilities to critical inquiry, disclosing a

3   I. King Jordan, cited in Zim, http://www.history-byzim.com/2013/09/capitol-crawl-americans-with-disabilities-act-of-1990/.

4   Susan Gluck Mezey, *Disabling Interpretations: The Americans with Disabilities Act in Federal Court* (Pittsburgh, PA: University of Pittsburgh Press, 2005), 10.

5   Richard K. Scotch, *From Good Will to Civil Rights: Transforming Federal Disability Policy* (Philadelphia, PA: Temple University Press, 1984), 156.

6   For more on the rich topic of disability rights, see Joseph P. Shapiro's classic book on the subject, *No Pity: People with Disabilities Forging a New Civil Rights Movement* (New York: Three Rivers Press, 1994).

seeming distinction from other identities. Like gender and racial identities such as "woman" and "black," "disabled" was historically and socially constructed according to a medical model of limitation. However, the hurdle to overcome the "thought of the disabled as being naturally limited rather than as being artificially limited by arbitrary and prejudiced social practice" faced a unique challenge: medical science cast people with disabilities as dependents who require help to overcome outside barriers encountered by their deficient bodies.[7] Lawmakers that recognized the hegemony and paternalism of the medical model and who underwrote opportunities for self-reliance in the law had a significant impact on "whether the physically disabled are allowed to move about and be in public places."[8] For legal scholars such as Jacobus tenBroek, however, physical and social barriers produced by law, science, and society still limit a disabled person's access to education, employment, and public life—in short, the "right to live in the world."[9]

Title III, Public Accommodations and Commercial Facilities, a groundbreaking provision of the ADA, provides remedies for discrimination against the disabled embedded in the built environment. Unlike the 1968 Architectural Barriers Act and the 1973 Rehabilitation Act, which applied only to government owned and funded buildings, Title III requires that any facility "generally open to the public"—that is, any privately owned business, such as a store, bank, school, theater, gas station, or doctor's office—be accessible to people with dis-

7   Leslie Francis and Anita Silvers, *Americans with Disabilities: Exploring Implications of the Law for Individuals and Institutions* (New York: Routledge, 2000), xv–xvi.

8   Jacobus tenBroek, "The Right to Live in the World: The Disabled in the Law of Torts," *California Law Review* 54, no. 2 (May 1966): 842. This groundbreaking essay informs the title of this piece.

9   Ibid.

abilities.[10] Recognizing people with disabilities among those who make up "the public," this section of the law addresses the importance of accessible public space to the social inclusion of the disabled. Unlike traditional civil rights legislation, which calls for "equality and a level playing field," "accommodation" requires material and practical remedies to support people with disabilities.[11] Consequently, the ADA has the unique distinction of a graphic corollary, the Accessibility Guidelines (ADAAG), to specify architectural accommodations. As public interest lawyer Frank Laski puts it, for disability, you "can't simply end discrimination by treating a disabled person like everybody else."[12] The ADA thus underwrites affirmative acts of inclusion to enable formal equality.

The provisions of the law and the design guidelines that govern its implementation necessarily define "disabled" and spatialize equality of opportunity for people with disabilities through legal, architectural, and building practices. And while passage of ADA has undoubtedly improved physical access for many, it has also produced unintended consequences. By examining the building regulations and their interpretation by the architects, government officials, and courts tasked with enforcing them, a portrait of access in the United States emerges. This portrait reveals how and to whom the implementation of the ADA and its consequent design procedures affords social, economic, and political opportunities today.

10   Americans with Disabilities Act of 1990. Public Law 101-336. §§ 3. 108th Congress, 2nd session (July 26, 1990), http://www.ada.gov/ada_title_III.htm.

11   Mezey, *Disabling Interpretations*, 37.

12   Frank Laski, quoted in ibid.

Even the noblest law comes to ground in implementation. What constitutes "disability" and "disabled" under the law is crucial to its application. Defining disability— in essence, "setting parameters of disability under law"— has involved political, economic, moral, and medical principles.[13] Rather than enumerate forms of disability, the ADA defines as disabled any person "who has a physical or mental impairment that substantially limits one or more major life activities, a person who has a history or record of such impairment, or a person who is perceived by others as having such impairment."[14] Lawmakers left it to the courts to determine what constitutes a "major life activity" but implied walking, working, and breathing counted. As social theory scholar Fiona Kumari Campbell noted, "What this means for niche activities not practiced or considered to be important by a majority of the population will remain to be seen."[15]

The ADA's public accommodations component requires that both government and private entities make physical and organizational changes to support disabled people participating in society. Rebuilding the physical environment is expensive, setting up contests between differing interests. Because this provision imposes financial costs, the courts have sought to limit the definition of who qualifies for such accommodations. Whereas most critics say that the spirit of the ADA argues for a broad interpretation of disability, in lawsuits charging ADA

13   Fiona Kumari Campbell, "Legislating Disability," in *Foucault and the Government of Disability*, ed. Shelley Tremain (Ann Arbor: University of Michigan Press, 2005), 122.

14   ADA, preamble, http://www.ada.gov/cguide.htm.

15   Campbell, "Legislating Disability," 125.

violations courts have repeatedly interpreted the meaning narrowly in order to avoid "opening the floodgate" to unworthy claims.[16] In fact, most cases brought under the ADA before the courts have been rejected because plaintiffs failed to show standing on the point of qualifying disability.[17]

In this process of adjudicating disability, the state relies on medical experts to determine the degree of a claimant's abilities in a variety of circumstances and settings. For example, in *Sutton v. United Airlines, Inc.*, the Supreme Court ruled that the plaintiffs were sufficiently impaired (they had poor vision) that the company could fire them, but because they could use corrective aids (contact lenses) to mitigate the impairment they did not qualify as disabled under the ADA and therefore did not have standing to press their claim in court.[18] The ADA is the only civil rights law in which a plaintiff needs to meet a physiological threshold of identity.[19]

The wheelchair user, who represents a small fraction of the disabled population, dominates legal and architectural representations, as well as the popular imagination of disability.[20] This quintessential image of a disabled person is rooted in two different projects of the disability rights movement: the Independent Living and minority group models.[21] The Independent Living movement promotes social integration of the disabled through services developed by the disabled themselves. Its spirit informed a version of negative rights which is expressed in the concept of the autonomous individual needing protection

16 Patricia Illingworth and Wendy E. Parmet, "Positively Disabled: The Relationship between the Definition of Disability and Rights under the ADA," in Jasper, *Americans with Disabilities Act*, 13.

17 Mezey, *Disabling Interpretations*, 136.

18 *Sutton v. United Airlines, Inc.*, 527 US 41 (1999).

19 Mezey, *Disabling Interpretations*, 165–67.

20 Out of an estimated 54 million people with a disability, only 3.3 million people over the age of 15 use a wheelchair. See https://www.census.gov/newsroom/releases/archives/facts_for_features_special_editions/cb10-ff13.html. Liat Ben-Moshe and Justin J.W. Powell, "Sign of Our Times? Revis(It)Ing the International Symbol of Access," *Disability & Society* 22, no. 5 (2007): 489–505.

21 Samuel Bagenstos, *Law and the Contradictions of the Disability Rights Movement* (New Haven, CT: Yale University Press, 2009), chapter 2.

from interference in the exercise of his freedoms. In the context of the ADA, the beneficiary of negative rights is an idealized subject (based on the experience of young, healthy male veterans who have lost the use of their legs), capable of competing in mainstream social and commercial arenas.[22] This strand aligns with the ADA's objective of moving people with disabilities from welfare to work, which garnered the support of Congressional conservatives.

Supporters of the minority group model of disability considered the ADA as the next step in a liberal democratic trajectory, linking it to the African American struggle for justice. Making accommodations often requires affirmative measures to "restore a just distribution" of rights and benefits, beyond the so-called level playing field.[23] Resolving the political tension between these two ways of thinking about disability has hinged on funneling the ADA's entitlements to those who meet the definition of "truly disabled, but genuinely capable."[24]

The ADAAG, the instrument that promulgates the spatial dimension of public accommodations, reinforces a beneficiary synthesized from both disability rights projects.[25] The guidelines and their building code interpretation consist of verbal and graphic instructions for designers. Of particular importance are the numerous dimensioned diagrams of disabled figures performing various tasks in space. Although some include female wheelchair users, most depict a well-groomed white male, neatly dressed in a crewneck sweater over a button-down

22   Jon Sanford and Sheila J. Bosch, "An Investigation of Non-Compliant Toilet Room Designs for Assisted Toileting," *Health Environment Research and Design* 6 (Winter 2013): 44.

23   Bagenstos, *Law*, 65.

24   Ibid., 38.

25   The standards can be found at http://www.ada.gov/2010ADAstandards_index.htm.

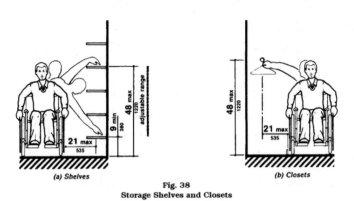

Figure 3 The wheelchair user, as depicted in the ADA Design Guidelines. Source: Americans with Disabilities Act, Accessibility Guidelines for Buildings and Facilities.

(a) Shelves

(b) Closets

Fig. 38
Storage Shelves and Closets

shirt and slacks. Shown reaching up to shelves and bending over water fountains, the figure demonstrates his unhampered range of upper body motion, strength, and dexterity. The inclusion of only manual wheelchairs (not electric wheelchairs used by people with more significant disabilities) further signals the user's physical strength and self-reliance. Other than the fact that he is in a wheelchair, this subject appears much like a "normal"—or rather, normalized—body in motion.[26]

Both "truly disabled" and "genuinely capable," this image of disability symbolically reconciles conflicting concepts of rights within the ADA. With his obvious mobility impairment reduced to being unable to walk, the figure clearly qualifies as disabled. Just as clearly, he can benefit from the removal of barriers, thereby becoming an autonomous and productive member of society— without government handouts. As critical disability studies scholar Kelly Fritsch observes, speaking about the design of the disability symbol, "The disabled person … doesn't need the welfare state to push [his] wheelchair.

26   On the normalization of architectural users, see Beatriz Colomina, ed., *Sexuality & Space* (New York: Princeton Architectural Press, 1992); Craig Wilkins, *The Aesthetics of Equity: Notes on Race, Space, Architecture and Music* (Minneapolis: University of Minnesota Press, 2007).

27   Kelly Fritsch, "Beyond the Wheelchair: Rethinking the Politics of Disability and Accessibility," *briarpatch magazine*, March 10, 2014. http://briarpatchmagazine. com/articles/view/beyond-the-wheelchair. I have replaced the author's feminine pronouns with the masculine given that the wheelchair figure of the ADAAG code is most often depicted as male.

Instead, this upwardly mobile subject wheels [him]self wherever neoliberalism will take [him]."[27] This ideal of disability suggests that these bodies are made whole or "normal" through the prescribed material accommodations. For the majority of people with disabilities, however, a wheelchair ramp alone does not address the entrenched problems they typically face, which include unemployment, poverty, and social isolation.

CODIFYING INCLUSION

Under the ADA, the social inclusion of people with disabilities is promulgated through technical amendments to state building codes, which afford public access to safety and health. Today's design guidelines evolved from the American Standard Specifications for Making Buildings and Facilities Accessible to, and Usable by, the Physically Handicapped, which was developed by a government task force led by Tim Nugent, the director of a student program for World War II veterans at the University of Illinois Champaign-Urbana.[28]

28   This is also known as the ASA A117.1-1961. The American Standards Association is the forbearer of today's American National Standards Institute (ANSI). Selwyn Goldsmith, *Designing for the Disabled: The New Paradigm* (Oxford: Architectural Press, 1997), 8.

Greatly expanding this precedent, the ADAAG redresses disabling built environments and distributes the cost of remedies to the public and private sector, which participated in the law's development. Because inaccessibility is so pervasive, the ADA allows business owners to phase renovations required to meet the code and permits exemptions in cases where owners can prove that executing the work would constitute an "undue hardship."

Through negotiations with the National Federation of Independent Businesses and the Building Owners and Managers Association, terms like "reasonable accommodations" and "readily achievable" were inserted into the law to provide leeway for owners managing the cost to their business.[29] As Stan Eichner notes, the ADA "is the only civil rights law in which rights are balanced against costs."[30] The compromises resulted in design guidelines that are a "hybrid, hodge-podge" of measures rather than a full reflection of the needs of disabled participants.[31]

The ADAAG has been adopted into the US model building code as well as almost all state and municipal codes. It has also been adopted into the 2010 ADA Standards for Accessible Design, the principal enforceable document of the Department of Justice (DOJ) for addressing the design of spaces and fixtures, from site work to plumbing. The DOJ certifies state and local codes that meet or exceed ADA requirements.[32] Several codes may govern a project, depending upon the type and location of the project and its funding source.

The code determines the most critical sites of disabled access. In order of importance, they include the entrance, the path of travel (the route from the entrance to the areas of primary function), restrooms, public telephones, and water fountains. The law does not require that all areas of the building be made accessible. For example, for building alterations, areas of "primary function" include "the customer services lobby of a bank, the dining area of a cafeteria, [and] the meeting rooms in a

29 Doris Zames Fleischer and Frieda Zames, *The Disability Rights Movement: From Charity to Confrontation* (Philadelphia, PA: Temple University Press, 2001), 88.

30 Stan Eichner, quoted in Mezey, *Disabling Interpretations*, 37.

31 Mary Lou Breslin, interview by author, Berkeley, California, November 15, 2011.

32 It is important to note that not all state and local codes have completed the certification procedure.

33   2010 ADA Standards. Section 36.403 "Alterations: Path of Travel."

conference center" but not "boiler rooms, supply storage rooms, employee lounges or locker rooms."[33] In defining areas of "primary function" and by prioritizing certain areas for accessibility over others, the ADA prescribes a realm of access for the disabled that enables some social and economic activities while precluding others.

The ADA has created new "disabled standards" for building, which transmutes the fluidity and heterogeneity of disability into three spatial codes for impairment, dividing the body into parts.[34] Following what sociologist Steven Epstein would call "niche standards," the ADA does not eliminate standardized thinking as much as it proliferates types of embodiment into differentiated standards within naturalized and reductive categories.[35] The legal-spatial implications of these "disability types" vary dramatically. The code contains few provisions for visual and auditory disabilities. The primary accommodations for the visually impaired include contrast markings at changes in elevation, detectable warnings like truncated domes at crosswalks, and Braille signage. For the hearing impaired, the only significant code change is the added requirement for strobe light emergency alarms. These provisions generally take up little space, are relatively inexpensive to implement in both new and retrofit construction, and have little impact on architectural form. By contrast, accommodating the wheelchair user (the only mobility impairment usually considered) has a large impact on design and consequently receives the most attention from architects and code administrators.

34   Martin Sullivan, "Subjected Bodies: Paraplegia, Rehabilitation, and the Politics of Movement," in Tremain, ed., Foucault and the Government of Disability, 36.

35   Steven Epstein, "Beyond the Standard Human," Standards and Their Stories: How Quantifying, Classifying, and Formalizing Practices Shape Everyday Life, eds. Martha Lampland and Susan Leigh Star (Ithaca, NY: Cornell University Press, 2009), 36.

The code for public restrooms best illustrates how design guidelines based on this disabled standard delimit disability. Access to toilets is critical to participating in the public sphere. Indeed, the public toilet has been important to civil rights movements throughout the 19th and 20th centuries, constituting a site where women, blacks, the disabled, and most recently, transgender people have struggled for accommodation and dignity.[36] For people with disabilities, a common problem with the restroom access standard involves the grab bars used to transfer between wheelchair and toilet.[37] The code mandates that toilets be located with their centerline 18 inches from the adjacent wall outfitted with grab bars. Depending on their position, toilets facilitate a person moving from either the left or right side. Typical design and construction practices mirror single or multiple occupancy toilet rooms on either side of a plumbing wall, with one accessible toilet provided for each sex. Consequently, it is not uncommon to find that an accessible toilet in the men's room allows users to transfer from one side, while the accessible toilet in the women's room allows transfer from the opposite side. Because

36   Kathryn H. Anthony and Meghan Dufresne, "Potty Parity in Perspective: Gender and Family Issues in Planning and Designing Public Restrooms," *Journal of Planning Literature* 21, no. 3 (2007): 267–94; Sheila L. Cavanagh, *Queering Bathrooms: Gender, Sexuality, and the Hygienic Imagination* (Toronto: University of Toronto Press, 2010); and Harvey Molotch and Laura Noren, eds., *Toilet: Public Restrooms and the Politics of Sharing* (New York: New York University Press, 2010).

37   Inaccessible, noncompliant toilets pose a far greater problem, but that topic lies outside the focus of this essay.

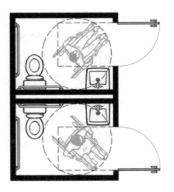

Figure 4   Typical plan of back-to-back men's and women's accessible toilet rooms. Source: http://www.ada.gov/regs2010/title111_2010/reg3_2010_appendix_b.htm.

Figure 5   Toilet with fold-down grab bars, popular in Europe and assisted living facilities in North America. Source: Wanda Katja Liebermann.

impairments are often asymmetrical (for example, in people who have suffered a stroke), the code creates a mismatch between architectural accommodations and the bodies they are designed to serve.

Some criticism goes deeper. Critical disability scholars contend that current design guidelines reiterate the disdain that able-bodied culture has for "any kind of mutually supportive activity."[38] A case in point is a recent study conducted at Georgia Institute of Technology that compared the functionality of an ADA-compliant toilet design with a non-ADA-compliant yet accessible design commonly used in Europe.[39] Most study participants preferred the non-ADA compliant design because it offered better flexibility and safety for both the person with disabilities and their caregiver. The design in the study, which specified a toilet centered on a wall with fold-down grab bars on both sides, is found in the United States mostly in hospitals and nursing homes. Because its design emerged from consideration of a disabled person accompanied by an attendant, it repudiates the idea of "independent living" as linked to "fully functioning" that legitimizes the inclusion of people with disabilities into mainstream society.[40] Critics present this as an example of the ADA's "privileging of independence," concluding that it "may underestimate the social and ethical values that accompany dependence: reciprocity, caring, and cooperation."[41] Through restroom design guidelines, the law affirms the identity of the autonomous disabled person, while overlooking a wider spectrum of disabled people.

38   David Serlin, "Pissing without Pity: Disability, Gender, and the Public Toilet," in Molotch and Noren, eds., *Toilet*, 174.

39   Ibid., 176; Sanford and Bosch, "An Investigation."

40   Serlin, "Pissing Without Pity," 176.

41   Ibid., 179, referring to Eva Feder Kittay, *Love's Labor: Essays on Women, Equality, and Dependency* (New York: Routledge, 1999).

Architectural Graphic Standards, the "architect's bible" since 1932, presents thousands of templates and diagrams that provide shortcuts for designing spaces for specific tasks.[42] Until recently, *Graphic Standards* did not include female bodies, much less bodies with impairments.[43] More generally, architectural historians and critics interested in gender and racial inequality contend that architectural culture and practices are rooted in white, masculine values.[44] One elaboration of this idea comes from architect Joel Sanders, who describes a design culture that tends to identify structural integrity with masculinity.[45] A similar sensibility permeates architectural education and design studio internships, where grueling tests of physical and mental endurance shape the personal identity and professional expectations of the architect as a strong male body. For these and other reasons, architects rarely view themselves as the object of ADA accommodations, creating empathic distance between the architect and the disabled end user.

To realize the objectives of ADA, federal codes govern architectural practice, in effect making architects instruments of civil rights. Through their interpretation of building codes, architects distribute spatial justice to the public, including disempowered groups. How architects incorporate the ADA design guidelines and standards into design practice depends on legal, institutional, and popular representations of disability, as well as bureaucratic

42   Like the Physician's Desk Reference, these dense volumes are standard references for practicing architects. Professional offices often hold multiple editions, each containing many drawings that depict anthropometric standards of building use and access at the time of publication. The latest editions reflect a century of labor optimization studies as well as new accessibility standards. For the most widely used edition published since the American Disabilities Act passed in 1990, see Andy Pressman and the American Institute of Architects, *Architectural Graphic Standards* (Hoboken, NJ: John Wiley & Sons, 2007).

43   Lance Hosey, "Hidden Lines: Gender, Race, and the Body in 'Graphic Standards,'" *Journal of Architectural Education* 55, no. 2 (2001): 101–12.

44   On the spatialization of racialized and gendered bodies, see Jane Rendell, Barbara Penner, and Iain Borden, *Gender Space Architecture: An Interdisciplinary Introduction* (New York: E & FN Spon, 1999); On the spatialization of race, see Craig L. Wilkins, *The Aesthetics of Equity*; Diane Harris, "Race, Space, and the Destabilization of Practice," *Landscape Journal* 26, no. 1 (2007): 1–9; and Craig Evan, *Sites of Memory: Perspectives on Architecture and Race* (New York: Princeton Architectural Press, 2001.

45   See Joel Sanders. *Stud: Architectures of Masculinity*, 1st ed. (New York: Princeton Architectural Press, 1996), 11, for a discussion of the male protagonist Howard Rourk in Ayn Rand's *The Fountainhead*. See also Anthony Vidler, "The Building in Pain: The Body and Architecture in Post-Modern Culture," *AA Files* 19 (Spring 1990): 3–10.

enforcement of the design regulations. Guidelines consist of written and graphic instructions for scope and compliance requirements. Covered spaces must conform to highly prescriptive diagrams detailing the configuration, material, shape, and size of architectural components. Using the restroom again as an example, codes determine the location, type, and height of the toilet; distance of the toilet from the wall; the configuration of knee clearances under the lavatory; and the mounting height of mirrors and dispensers; as well as specifications regarding the (previously discussed) grab bars, including their location, height, length, circumference, and material. The disabled figure is reduced to an envelope of space of standard arm reach and wheelchair turnaround: the human user, essentially elided with the spatial and kinetic requirements of the wheelchair. Because in most instances the guidelines require the designer to replicate code prescriptions exactly, creative interpretation of accessible features and consideration of how they are used rarely occurs. The dilemma of accessible architecture is that, in making it broadly operational, the law and bureaucratic processes differentiate designing for disability from "regular" ways of designing.

The design review system exacerbates the discourse of compliance, liability, and safety that has come to dominate the provision of access. Architectural drawings are typically submitted to municipal building departments. There, plan checkers evaluate designs for structural conformity, fire and life safety, energy code compliance, and so forth. Accessibility, however, often comes under the jurisdiction of multiple agencies, including the buildings department and the department of public works, which oversees a city's infrastructure. In addition, new agencies created in response to the enactment of the ADA (such as San Francisco's Mayor's Office on Disability) make sure that access compliance is integrated across all municipal endeavors. While these agencies ostensibly advocate for access, their role is also to protect the city from lawsuits under the ADA. Their agenda is to enforce, not the code per se, but the civil rights statute, which they often interpret broadly in order to minimize the city's legal liability. This frequently amplifies bureaucratic inflexibility in responding to nonstandard design solutions, especially in the case of building renovations. In integrating new construction within existing spatial and technical parameters, architects often fall back on the "readily achievable" to negotiate hybrid solutions to "reasonable accommodation."[46] These compromises increase the risk of differences in interpretation between agencies and architects.

Given all of this, it is not surprising that architects perceive the code as constraining their professional expertise—a "design police," with plan checkers and building inspectors serving as its inflexible, inconsistent, and narrowly focused agents.[47] Many architects are frustrated by the dominance of accessibility over other urgent issues. This resentment surfaces in many places, including an online tutorial discussing access regulations architects are required to know in order to pass the exam

46   Daniel Adams, former Director of Program Development, San Francisco Mayor's Office of Housing, interview with author, Oakland, California, June 4, 2014.

47   See Sarah Sherman and Jean Sherman, "Design Professionals and the Built Environment: Encountering Boundaries Twenty Years after the Americans with Disabilities Act," *Disability & Society* 27, no. 1 (2012): 51–64.

48   AIACC Accessibility
Course #aeck-A103: "Dis-
abilities Access for Dwellings," presented by Kerwin
Lee, Senior Consulting
Architect, Rolf Jensen &
Associates, Inc. Lee's comments occur in chapter 5,
"FHA Compliance."
Throughout the course,
implicit and explicit conflicts
arise between providing
access and minimally com-
plying with regulations.
Recently, licensing bodies in
many states have begun
focusing compulsory con-
tinuing education exclusively
on disabled access.

49   Samuel R. Bagenstos,
"Perversity of Limited Civil
Rights Remedies: The Case
of 'Abusive' ADA Litigation,"
UCLA Law Review 54, no. 1
(October 2006): 23.

50   Sanjoy Mazumdar and
Gilbert Geis, "Achieving
Accessibility through the
Americans with Disabilities
Act: An Examination of
Court Decisions," Journal of
Architectural & Planning
Research 27, no. 4 (2010):
304.

51   Mita Chatterjee,
"Access Denied and Not
Designed: The Ninth Circuit
Drafts a Narrow Escape for
Architect Liability under the
Americans with Disabilities
Act in Lonberg v. Sanborn
Theaters, Inc.," Villanova
Sports & Entertainment Law
Journal 9, no. 2 (2002): 294.
Litigation remains the pri-
mary tool for ADA enforce-
ment and compliance nearly
25 years after the law's pas-
sage. See Bagenstos, "Per-
versity of Limited Civil
Rights Remedies," 1, 22;
Mezey, Disabling Interpreta-
tions, 7; and Fleischer and
Zames, The Disability Rights
Movement, 106–7. For an
example of alarmist media
treatment, see John Stossel,
"No Good Deed Goes
Unpunished?," FoxNews.
com, 2010, http://www.
foxnews.com/opin-
ion/2010/09/02/john-stossel-
americans-disabilities-act-
ada-irs-rules-
labordepartment-exxon/

required for relicensing in California. In addition to
outlining various accommodations, the tutorial presents
various "way[s] to get around" providing them.[48] The
imposition of ADA legislation on architectural practice—
in the form of licensure renewal requirements and com-
plicatedplanreviewstoensurecompliancewithregulations—
has incited legal scholars such as civil rights law expert
Samuel Bagenstos to contend that these "mind-numb-
ingly boring" remedies reiterate disability's difference.[49]

Licensure, it should be noted, makes architects custo-
dians of public health, safety, and welfare. As instruments
of justice under the ADA, architects who produce designs
that do not comply with the law are not merely guilty of
breaches of professional conduct but also of discrimination. In fact, according to legal scholars Sanjoy
Mazumdar and Gilbert Geis, Title III has "created more
conflicts in implementation than any other aspects of the
ADA."[50] Although the courts are split on the issue of architectural liability under the ADA, there is anxiety among
architects that they can be sued for design infractions.
This fear is stoked by alarmist news stories of wheelchair
users suing businesses over inaccessible facilities.[51] A
landmark legal case established the profession's official
position on this issue. In 1996, the Paralyzed Veterans of
America sued Ellerbe Beckett Architects and Engineers
over inadequate and unequal seating in the MCI Center
Sports Arena in Washington, DC.[52] In an unsolicited
amicus curiae, the American Institute of Architects (AIA),
the national professional organization, supported Ellerbe

52   See Sanjoy Mazumdar
and Gilbert Geis, "Acces-
sible Buildings, Architects,
and the ADA Law: The MCI
Center Sports Arena Case,"
Journal of Architectural &
Planning Research 19, no. 3
(2002): 195–217; and Sanjoy
Mazumdar and Gilbert Geis,
"Architects, the Law, and
Accessibility: Architects'

Approaches to the ADA in
Arenas," Journal of Architectural & Planning Research 20,
no. 3 (2003): 199–220.

The Right to Live in the World

Becket's argument that it was not at fault because it merely carried out its paying client's wishes. The AIA's position, as paraphrased by Mazumdar and Geis, maintained, "We are merely innocent subservient agents of all-powerful employers."[53] Its argument reflects a professional disregard for accessibility, even as—ironically—the architects' loss of this suit demonstrates the risks of maintaining this stance.

53 Mazumdar and Geis, "Accessible Buildings," 205.

A major problem stems from the incompatibility of legal and design knowledge. As Mazumdar and Geis write, "The quest for judges is certainty, and their rulings reflect their desire to specify solutions rather than to focus on innovative or better design solutions.... Laws are not very good for producing internal drive, long-term proactive actions, passion, creativity, or innovation."[54] The vast majority of architects simply look accessible requirements up in the codebook rather than tackle access as a creative problem. Indeed, "in stretching the envelope, thinking outside the box, and incorporating innovations, designers might fall afoul of the law."[55] The epistemological chasm between law and architecture is partly responsible for the unanimated, formulaic accessible designs that reaffirm disability as outside of architecture's ambit.

54 Mazumdar and Geis, "Achieving Accessibility," 317.

55 Ibid., 318.

Where accommodations are provided, their design and development takes place at a distance from users. Design for disability has become the purview of engineers and occupational therapists, and the design of objects for the disabled rarely incorporates the exploration, celebration, and play that design culture fosters. Designers often treat their task largely as a technical and functional problem rather than an opportunity to produce positive experiences and aesthetic spaces for users.[56] Apart from end-of-the line adjustments, the closed world of disability aids' development and provision takes place in clinics and rehabilitation offices, immune to the forces of the consumer market. Consequently, ubiquitous accessible designs—ramps clumsily tacked onto building entrances, large toilet stalls with metal grab bars, and low elevator control buttons—take on a "technologized" appearance through factory fabricated components, controls, sensors, and safety features, finished in metal or "beige melamine."[57] Such bad design reveals not only the exclusion of the disabled from commodity capitalism but also the low social status accorded the beneficiaries of these accommodations.

56   Graham Pullin, *Design Meets Disability* (Cambridge, MA: MIT Press, 2009), 121. See also Nigel Thrift, *Non-Representational Theory: Space, Politics, Affect* (New York: Routledge, 2008).

57   Ju Gosling, quoted in Pullin, *Design Meets Disability*, 121.

DISABLED SPACES

It is difficult to comprehensively map the ways in which disability has been spatialized by a quarter century of designing, building, and living under the ADA. It is possible, however, to make some general observations about what bodies and practices the ADA includes and excludes from the contemporary American social landscape. The ADA has undoubtedly made public space—including privately owned commercial space—more physically accessible to the disabled. The provision of curb ramps,

The Right to Live in the World

elevators, building entrances, restrooms, Braille signage, handicap parking spaces, and the like offers new levels of mobility to millions of people. At the same time, both by inclusion and omission, the ADA has produced spatial and symbolic divisions that extend the dichotomy between able and disabled. The limits of the ADA's architectural scope, the code's narrow construction of the disabled subject, and lax enforcement of the law combine to produce uneven, partial, and discontinuous levels of inclusion.

One of the most significant realms of spatial exclusions under the ADA is private single-family residences—the largest sector of the US housing market. Although both the 1988 Fair Housing Act and Section 504 of the 1973 Rehabilitation Act establish quotas for accessible units in multi-unit and federally subsidized housing, neither they nor the ADA extend this requirement to the "typical American home."[58] Given that this is where the majority of the disabled live, the regulations undermine one of the key objectives of the ADA: mainstream inclusion.[59] The vast majority of private single-family homes are inaccessible to wheelchair users and those with visual, hearing, and other ambulatory disabilities. The ramifications—apart from renting and owning—are that people with limited mobility can't visit friends and relatives. Many disabled people consider the inaccessibility of single-family homes to be one of the biggest obstacles to taking part in a normal life because it makes it nearly impossible to have social contact outside the fraction of residences covered by law.[60]

58 Hope VI and federally funded single-family detached housing provide two exceptions, which, however, represent only a tiny fraction of single-family housing. Stanley K. Smith et al., "Population Aging, Disability and Housing Accessibility: Implications for Sub-National Areas in the United States," *Housing Studies* 27, no. 2 (2012): 253. Also, the Fair Housing Act, did not include provisions concerning the discrimination against people on the basis of disability when it was first passed in 1968.

59 Nicholas Farber et al., "Aging in Place: A State Survey of Livability Policies and Practices," report, AARP Public Policy Institute and the National Conference of State Legislatures, 2011, 46.

60 Ralf Hotchkiss, interview by author, Berkeley, CA, June 13, 2011. Hotchkiss is a pioneering inventor of "low-cost, high-science" wheelchairs; see http://www.sfgate.com/news/article/Mr-Mobility-Wheelchair-pioneer-assembles-2935591.php.

The omission of private, single-family homes from the ADA attests to the near-inviolability of private property rights in American law and culture; it also encourages the erroneous view that people with disabilities are not like "typical" US homeowners and live instead in government subsidized housing. Failure to regulate access in this sector may reflect the ADA's antecedents in government-provided vocational rehabilitation services, which focused on restoring disabled people's productivity and thus overlooked domestic spaces. Given this history, however, the current exclusion of the disabled from workplaces and places of business is more troubling. Implicit in the ADAAG specifications for employee support areas is the belief that the disabled—if they frequent places of business at all—do so as customers rather than as employees.[61] The guidelines reify the historically low employment rates among the disabled, and insidiously converge, practically and symbolically, with juridical rulings in favor of a narrow definition of what "functioning" means for people with disabilities.[62] Ultimately, ADAAG directives formalize provisional and partial—rather than secure and universal—access to space.

Furthermore, who deserves to use these amenities, once provided, is formally prescribed and informally policed through visual culture. Handicap parking tags signal qualification for accommodations to the general public while proving eligibility to legal and governmental bodies. Placards displayed on vehicles and ID badges worn on the disabled person's body distinguish disabled

61   Tanya Titchkosky, *The Question of Access: Disability, Space, Meaning* (Toronto: University of Toronto Press, 2011), 81.

62   Ani B. Satz, "Fragmented Lives: Disability Discrimination and the Role of 'Environment-Framing,'" *Washington & Lee Law Review* 68, no. 1 (2011): 190.

spaces and bodies from those of "able" consumers and "normal" citizens. Access signage, entrances, curbs, parking spots, and transit seats in a new disciplinary chroma—blue—enable "people with impairments [to be] simultaneously accommodated ... [and] separated or segregated."[63]

63   Ben-Moshe and Powell, "Sign of our Times?," 494.

Aided by these spatial markers, non-disabled citizens often take on the responsibility of ensuring that undeserving people do not exploit the advantages provided for the disabled. They translate the meanings of the handicap signs and develop tacit rules around who is allowed to use accessible amenities. Such unofficial citizen policing practices as well as official programs (such as police recruiting volunteers to assist with enforcing "handicap parking" laws)[64] presume that anyone can determine whether a person is disabled just by looking at him or her. A person must appear to be disabled to use special parking spaces or seats on buses or else face social opprobrium. An anthropologist whose disability is not apparent unless she is walking writes that when she sits in a reserved seat on the bus, people sometimes comment about her lack of manners. "This misinterpretation is resolved," she notes, upon standing, "when my moving body communicates clearly that I am entitled after all to use facilities for disabled people."[65] Attesting to a similar experience, another writer who has difficulty walking but does not always use a wheelchair describes how her body contests the normative image of disability. Although she could not climb the stairs of a bus, the driver denied her

64   Edward T. Jennings, "Using Volunteers in Handicap Parking Law Enforcement: Report for the Kentucky Council on Developmental Disabilities," Martin School of Public Policy and Administration, June 30, 2004, http://chfs.ky.gov/NR/rdonlyres/0B29A6DB-200B-450B-8D06-97BA247452C1/150156/UsingVolunteersin HandicappedParkingLaw Enforcement0.pdf.

65   Karen Morgendorff, "Doing Frogs and Elephants: Or How Atypical Moving Bodies Affect and Are Affected by Predominantly Able-Bodies," *Medische Antropologie* 22, no. 2 (2010): 330–31.

request to use the bus lift, as regulations require its users to be seated in a wheelchair secured to the lift by the bus driver. She writes, "in that moment, as I stared at the ISA [International Symbol of Access] sign, I realized that I was both disabled and not disabled enough—or not disabled in the right way to access this accessible bus."[66]

66   Fritsch, "Beyond the Wheelchair," n.p. This incident occurred in Canada, yet it nevertheless exposes how the continual reiteration of legally and symbolically sanctioned categories of disability shape narrow understandings of disability and access.

INCLUSION/EXCLUSION

With the 1990 passage of the ADA, the state recognized the disabled and granted these bodies new rights to move. Liberals and conservatives alike hailed the legislation as the next step in democracy's march toward greater social inclusion and equality. The ADA is seen as a victory, the 25th anniversary of which the disability community celebrates this year. However, although the ADA has brought about greater social and physical mobility for many disabled people, at the same time most disability advocates and legal scholars judge its implementation to be a great disappointment. In many ways the bureaucratic and legalistic ramifications of the law itself have stymied its egalitarian spirit. Critics view its juridical unfolding, in particular, as a perversion of its progressive politics.

The law emerged from disabled people living in mainstream society demanding their right to occupy public and private spaces. Turning to the state to guarantee and adjudicate accommodation depends on a "discourse of rights and freedoms," which geographer Felix Driver notes, "has the function of effacing relations of domination in order to present them as legitimate."[67] The assumption, political scientist Wendy Brown adds, is that the state itself is, at worst, benign and that its mechanisms do not reproduce and promulgate relations of power.[68] In this case, the ADA and its attendant design documents stabilize a concept of the disabled as the opposite of able, weaving into the fabric of legal rights and built environments the very powerlessness, subjection, and alienation that claimants have suffered.

An important dimension of this is that the ADA, like other civil rights law, codifies classes of impairment based on a historical "state of injury"[69]—that is, exclusion or subordination based on negative stereotypes. Whereas legal rights built upon historic wrongs have provided the primary pathway to recognition and justice for marginalized groups, these laws and their regulatory networks also enshrine a fixed and unitary identity for their members. However, because the ADA does not specifically spell out which disabilities are included, the very mutability of disability has meant that juridical discourse, regulatory implements, administrative processes, and design standards define disability.

A fixed concept of the disabled, coupled with weak state support for the law (seen in its narrow interpretation, for example, and the lack of resources dedicated to its enforcement), paradoxically recognizes disability yet designates it as exceptional to "regular" society. Disability studies scholar Tanya Titchkosky calls this

67 Felix Driver, "Power, Space, and the Body: A Critical Assessment of Foucault's *Discipline and Punish*," *Environment and Planning D: Society & Space* 3 (1985): 436.

68 Wendy Brown. *States of Injury: Power and Freedom in Late Modernity* (Princeton, NJ: Princeton University Press, 1995), ix.

69 Ibid.

70 Titchkosky, *Question of Access*, 78.

71 Breslin, interview.

72 Tremain, ed., "Foucault, Governmentality, and Critical Disability Theory: An Introduction," in *Foucault and the Government of Disability*, 21.

constructing the disabled as the "justifiably-excludable type" of citizen, which lawmakers, lawyers, and lay people reinforce through a mesh of practices, discourse, and spaces engendered by the ADA.[70] Nearly a quarter century after ADA's passage, routine practices for many disabled people are formally excluded from the public domain and informally inhibited in the private domain. Code and enforcement gaps require that people with disabilities discipline themselves by developing navigational techniques for an able-bodied world (such as making mental maps, and other forms of "making-do").[71] A trenchant insight into inclusion as assimilation is that it "invariably requires work on the self."[72] Temporal-spatial reconnoitering and countless other adjustment practices shift one's relationship to and knowledge of the urban environment in ways that underline the "specialness" of the accommodations needed to include certain bodies in public life.

Both the abstraction and minutiae of disability identity ramify through the ADA's spatial accommodations. Architectural provisions for the wheelchair user have been the most public and visible, enlisting many members of society both officially and informally to play a part in supervising the use of these accommodations. The interplay between representation, practices, and built form plays a critical role, simultaneously enabling new levels of access and regulating its terms. This has gradually shifted from a process of "simple" exclusion due to inaccessible spaces to sorting classes of subject through perceptible new forms and spatial practices. In this way architecture distends the ADA's juridical effects: "The law's continual reiteration of 'defective corporeality,' through the designation of legal categories of 'disability' and 'disabled person,' disallows the 'disabled' subject any escape from the normalizing practices of compensation and mitigation."[73] The ADA's mode of regulating architecture produces a reciprocal antagonism between access objectives and designers' creative freedom that reinforces the exceptionality of the disabled subject of architecture. This exception is often realized in forms that are read as prosthetics to "real" architecture, distinguishing the disabled as needing compensations to restore them to "normalcy."

Spaces and amenities which signal that they are for the use of people with disabilities not only emphasize categorical divisions but also underscore the idea that only those thought of as "the disabled" need accessible architecture; or in other words, only these particular bodies need objects and spaces to be adjusted to them. This makes access—design, in fact—something that matters, in terms of accommodation, only for atypical or "different" bodies. The interplay between disabled bodies and spaces designed without their needs in mind produces that difference. Built environments distribute competency to the bodies for which they were designed. In that sense the world is an omnipresent prosthesis for so-called normal bodies. Conversely, standards produce an outside to architectural norms, defining which bodies are

73 Campbell, "Legislating Disability," 126.

complete through their smooth fit with the environment, and which bodies need architectural and other types of "accommodations" in order to fit in. This discloses a central paradox of access, namely that "accommodations," as they are often currently designed, foreground disability as abnormal.

Politics of Expertise

To address the question of who governs and shapes cities, studies on the "politics of expertise" explore the knowledge base and practices of professionals, officials, and citizens. These groups' conflicting interests and claims to authority politicize city formation. A diverse literature on the topic focuses on political institutions that lead these processes, public–private partnerships, citizen empowerment in planning practices, global actors influencing urbanization, and social and material networks that coproduce civic space and direct its future development. To contribute to this discourse, the following three essays emphasize the importance of spatial knowledge in urban politics. They attempt to demarcate more fluid boundaries of expertise among government and civic agents, corporate entities, design professionals, and the lay public.

Orly Linovski (p. 307) examines negotiations between city officials and design consultants in the development of a major park in downtown Los Angeles, identifying the risks involved in entrusting the "public good" to private hands.

Michael Mendez (p. 337) explores environmental justice advocacy in Oakland, where community groups, planners, and climate change experts fought to include local needs and knowledge in global mitigation strategies.

H. Fernando Burga (p. 367) revisits 50 years of growth in Miami-Dade County to examine the political strategies of minority communities and their incorporation within planning processes, leadership structures, and urban branding.

In each case, the definition of expertise is expanded, suggesting that the location of knowledge—who has it, where it comes from, and how it is codified around public decision-making processes—is paramount to how cities are made.

ON POLITICAL INSTITUTIONS, PUBLIC–PRIVATE PARTNERSHIPS,
AND PROFESSIONAL EXPERTISE

Dahl, Robert A. *Who Governs? Democracy and Power in an American City.* New Haven, CT: Yale University Press, 2005.

Fainstein, Susan S. *The City Builders.* 2nd ed. Lawrence: University Press of Kansas, 2001.

Friedmann, John. *Planning in the Public Domain: From Knowledge to Action.* Princeton, NJ: Princeton University Press, 1987.

Harvey, David. "From Managerialism to Entrepreneurialism: The Transformation in Urban Governance in Late Capitalism." *Geografiska Annaler,* Series B, *Human Geography* 71 (1989): 3–17.

Larson, Magali Sarfatti. *The Rise of Professionalism: A Sociological Analysis.* Berkeley: University of California Press, 1977.

Thomas, June Manning. *Redevelopment and Race: Planning a Finer City in Postwar Detroit.* Baltimore, MD: Johns Hopkins University Press, 1997.

ON SCALES AND DIRECTIONS OF KNOWLEDGE, FROM GLOBAL TO LOCAL AND
GRASSROOTS SOURCES

Fischer, Frank. *Citizens, Experts, and the Environment.* Durham, NC: Duke University Press, 2000.

Friedmann, John, and Goetz Wolff. "World City Formation: An Agenda for Research and Action." *International Journal of Urban and Regional Research* 6, no. 3 (September 1982): 309–44.

Fung, Archon. *Empowered Participation: Reinventing Urban Democracy.* Princeton, NJ: Princeton University Press, 2004.

Jasanoff, Sheila. *Designs on Nature: Science and Democracy in Europe and United States.* Princeton, NJ: Princeton University Press, 2005.

Mukhija, Vinit. *Squatters as Developers? Slum Redevelopment in Mumbai.* Aldershot: Ashgate, 2003.

ON THE INFLUENCE OF ACTOR–NETWORK THEORY ON URBAN STUDIES

Amin, Ash, and Nigel Thrift. *Cities: Reimagining the Urban.* Cambridge: Polity Press, 2002.

Graham, Stephen, and Simon Marvin. *Splintering Urbanism: Networked Infrastructures, Technological Mobilities and the Urban Condition.* London: Routledge, 2001.

Latour, Bruno. *Reassembling the Social: An Introduction to Actor-Network Theory.* Oxford: Oxford University Press, 2007.

Epistemologies of
Public and Private
Urban Design Expertise

Orly Linovski

At the civic dedication of Grand Park in downtown Los
Angeles, one of the initiators of the project, a noted philanthropist and private developer, announced to the
assembled political officials and news media, "This park
was built without any taxpayer money. Let me repeat
that, this park was built without any taxpayer money."
Although the dignitaries standing behind him clapped
enthusiastically, his implication that this was a private
project was misleading. Grand Park received private
funding as part of a complex redevelopment project, but
the new civic space was built on public land. The money
that changed hands between the private funders and the
County was for the right to develop the publicly owned
property, and the funds arguably could have been used

Figure 1   View of downtown Los Angeles from the Hall of
Administration, 1966. The close proximity of the Civic
Center Mall to the County Courthouse (1), Music Center
(2), and Department of Water and Power (3) is evident from
the 8th floor window. Source: Los Angeles Public Library,
HE box-226.

for any public project. The blurring of the boundaries between the public and private realms is apparent not only in the funding of civic projects but also in how professional urban design practices operate. As the development of Grand Park shows, contestations over public space are negotiated and mediated through networks of professional expertise, and often can hinge on the ability of professionals to construct their expertise and their practices.

Contemporary urban design resides at the juncture of public policy and private development, with practitioners operating within both of these spheres.[1] Attention to the nature of this relationship can provide an important perspective on how private and public actors shape built form policies, as well as the structural and idiosyncratic factors that determine the influence of private sector actors. Early conceptions of the role of consultants saw their work limited to areas that had few redistributive implications or were not marked by competing political interests.[2] However, since the 1970s, there has been a turn toward entrepreneurialism in urban government, marked by characteristics "once distinctive to the private sector [such as] risk-taking, inventiveness, promotion and profit motivation."[3] The division between public and private actors is shifting in many sectors, with traditionally public functions provided either through the private market or through public-private partnerships.[4] Examining the planning profession in recent decades, Eugene J. McCann remarks on its changing nature, such that there

1   Urban design as public policy is one of the primary, though not the only, way of understanding contemporary urban design practices.

2   Dorothy Nelkin, "The Political Impact of Technical Expertise," *Social Studies of Science* 5, no. 1 (1975): 35–54.

3   David Harvey, "From Managerialism to Entrepreneurialism: The Transformation in Urban Governance in Late Capitalism," *Geografiska Annaler. Series B. Human Geography* 71 (1989): 3–17; Phil Hubbard, "Urban Design and City Regeneration: Social Representations of Entrepreneurial Landscapes," *Urban Studies* 33, no. 8 (1996): 1441.

4   Øystein Blymke, "Government Agencies and Consultancy—A Norwegian Perspective," in *Ethics and Consultancy: European Perspectives*, ed. H. Von Weltzien Hoivik and A. Føllesdal (Dordrecht: Kluwer Academic Publishers, 1995); Denis Saint-Martin, "The New Managerialism and the Policy Influence of Consultants in Government: An Historical-Institutionalist Analysis of Britain, Canada and France," *Governance* 11, no. 3 (1998): 319–56; and Denis Saint-Martin, *Building the New Managerialist State: Consultants and the Politics of Public Sector Reform in Comparative Perspective* (Oxford: Oxford University Press, 2000).

is "an increasing permeability in the institutional boundaries of urban planning, characterized by an ongoing privatization of planning services and outsourcing of its functions to private consultants."[5]

This can be seen in part in the employment of urban design consultants, who represent a significant, though under-studied, group of professionals who actively negotiate between public and private spheres of influence. In the field of urban design, consultants may undertake work formerly seen as the domain of government, such as writing policy, regulating development, and managing civic projects, while still engaging with—and employed by—the private sector. The slippages in the roles between public and private sector practitioners raise questions as to the power of urban design professionals to advance political goals, the nature of public-private interaction in regulating the built environment, and the implications of these in the design of urban form. The confluence of political actors, public land, and design professionals from both sectors makes sites such as Grand Park in Los Angeles an ideal place to investigate the evolving politics of professional practice.

5   Eugene J. McCann, "Collaborative Visioning, or Urban Planning as Therapy? The Politics of Public-Private Policy Making," *Professional Geographer* 53, no. 2 (2001): 209.

EPISTEMIC CULTURES OF URBAN DESIGN PROFESSIONALS

Designing urban public space involves negotiating and mediating complex networks of professional design knowledge and expertise. The epistemic culture of urban designers—that is, the ways in which these professionals create, codify, and deploy their disciplinary knowledge—has gone largely unexamined with respect to the differences between public and private sector professionals. In this sense, design professionals can be understood as an epistemic community, actively involved in shaping policy and influencing decision makers.[6] The concept of epistemic communities emphasizes the role of professional expertise, defining these groups as "networks of experts who persuade others of their shared causal beliefs and policy goals by virtue of their professional knowledge.... Their reliance on expert knowledge, which they validate within their group, is what differentiates them from other actors that seek to influence policy."[7] An epistemology of urban design practice accounts for the implicit knowledge inherent in the practice-based professions, as well as how this knowledge is constructed and used for political purposes. However, despite the clear relationship between expertise and political power, little is known about differing epistemic cultures of public and private sector urban design professionals.

Urban design scholarship rarely addresses issues of expertise in professional practice. In the instances where it does, the interaction among professionals, the political realm, and the production of knowledge often remain in the background.[8] The understanding of professional practice in urban design has often vacillated between "black box" and "glass box" conceptualizations—that is, between the notion of urban design as an artistic and

6   While the notion of epistemic communities has traditionally been applied to studies of international relations and diplomacy, the focus on professional expertise and its relationship to policy and decision-making make it an apt concept for understanding design practices.

7   Mai'a K. Davis Cross, "Rethinking Epistemic Communities Twenty Years Later," *Review of International Studies* 39, no. 1 (2013): 142.

8   Notable exceptions include Donald Schön, "Some of What a Planner Knows: A Case Study of Knowing-in-Practice," *Journal of the American Planning Association* 48, no. 3 (1982): 351–64; Donald Schön, *The Reflective Practitioner: How Professionals Think in Action* (New York: Basic Books, 1983); and Dana Cuff, *Architecture: The Story of Practice* (Cambridge, MA: MIT Press, 1991).

creative moment and as a rational process where actions follow logical steps. [9] Much research on urban design practices tends to focus on how the public sector shapes the urban environment as a matter of public policy.[10] However, we know little about the nature of the relationship between public and private design professionals in developing epistemic cultures, as well as the conflicting goals and priorities that may exist between them and how these play out in the built form.[11]

By focusing attention on the epistemic community of urban design experts and the application of their professional knowledge in the creation of a public, civic space such as Grand Park in Los Angeles, we can bring their interactions with other actors seeking to influence policy into sharper focus. We can begin to account not only for how this knowledge is constructed but also how it is used for political purposes, how it is actively deployed in shaping policy and how it is influencing decision makers. From there, we can reflect on how urban form is created and manipulated, the city shaped and reshaped.

This essay focuses on the interactions and negotiations that private sector urban design consultants engage in to shape the built environment. How do urban design consultants establish their role in shaping the built form for public projects? Through an examination of the development of Grand Park in Los Angeles—a city with limited public sector urban design capacity—this essay explores the relative power of private sector professionals to influence built form and shift priorities related to

9   Ian Bentley, *Urban Transformations: Power, People and Urban Design* (London: Taylor & Francis, 1999); and Tridib Banerjee and Anastasia Loukaitou-Sideris, eds., *Companion to Urban Design* (New York: Routledge, 2011), 276.

10   Jonathan Barnett, *Urban Design as Public Policy: Practical Methods for Improving Cities* (New York: Architectural Record Books, 1974); and John Punter, "Urban Design as Public Policy: Evaluating the Design Dimension of Vancouver's Planning System," *International Planning Studies* 7, no. 4 (2002): 265–82.

11   Further complicating our understanding of urban design practice is the ambiguous role played by the public sector as the client of professional services. The relationship between client and professional is widely acknowledged as a source of tension within the urban design process; Koicha Mera's description of the strain between "nominal" and "substantive" clients touches upon this issue: see "Consumer Sovereignty in Urban Design," *Town Planning Review* 37, no. 4 (1967): 305–12.

12 The work draws on interviews conducted in 2012 and 2013 with 22 actors involved in urban design practices in Los Angeles. This included public and private sector urban designers and planners, political actors, and real estate professionals. Interviewees are refereed to here by their role and by a reference code assigned by the author.

development and design.[12] Examining the development of this civic space brings to the forefront the ways through which professional expertise is created and deployed, as well as the implications for our understanding of how urban space is formed.

SITUATING DESIGN PRACTICES

13 Grand Avenue Committee, *Reimagining Grand Avenue: Creating a Center for Los Angeles* Los Angeles, 2003; and Loss Angeles Grand Avenue Committee, *Request for Proposals (RFP): Reimagining Grand Avenue*, Los Angeles, 2004.

14 Early redevelopment documents refer to the space as Civic Park.

The Grand Park project is located in the Civic Center area of downtown Los Angeles, a district historically associated with government activities. The park was initiated as part of a larger development scheme on Grand Avenue that included residential, commercial, and cultural uses on four underutilized parcels of land owned by public authorities. Largely attributed to the vision and direction of noted Los Angeles developer and philanthropist Eli Broad, the plan sought to create a cultural corridor linking major institutions along Grand Avenue as well as to enhance the civic district.[13] Grand Park was created in response to the plan's provision for a redeveloped civic space on county land.[14]

Figure 2 Grand Park, mapped among redevelopment parcels in downtown Los Angeles. Source: Orly Linovski.

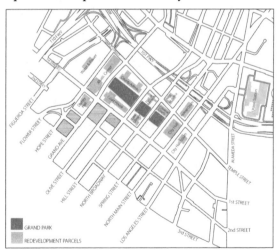

The park exists in a public space formerly known as the Civic Center Mall. Flanked on both sides by government buildings, interrupted by public streets, and marked by a steep topographical grade, the site was long considered a difficult space to encourage public use. Additional constraints were posed by ramps that led to underground parking and created a barrier between the civic space and the street. In redeveloping the space, the ramps along Grand Avenue were removed and a sloping lawn, water features, distinctive furniture, and a small stage were included.

Figure 3 Grand Park, looking south along its axial walkway. This elevated perspective on the park affords a view of few buildings besides City Hall. Source: Orly Linovski.

The development of Grand Park was structured through a leaseback agreement, where the chosen developer leased the county-owned property and was responsible for the design and implementation of the park: once the park was completed, ownership and management of the park was returned to the County. The funding of the park in advance, with the funds held by a joint powers authority, meant that the civic space development proceeded despite the residential and commercial redevelopment projects' stalling. As part of this agreement, the developer, along with the Grand Avenue Committee, was heavily involved in the design and implementation of the park, including the hiring and supervising of urban design consultants.

Consultants participated during multiple stages of the project's development, from initiation to design to implementation. They developed guidelines, lead public consultation processes, and created the design for the public space, among other tasks, interacting with public sector staff and political actors on different levels.

SHIFTING PRIORITIES

In discussing the political implications of technical expertise, it has been argued that, "the planner may not be the first to identify 'problems' of an urban area, but he puts them on the agenda and plays a large part in defining the terms in which the problem will be thought about—and those terms in effect play a large part in determining the solution."[15] This agenda setting—as negotiated through constructions of professional expertise—can be influential in structuring urban design outcomes. Thus, asking how an agenda is set in discussions about urban design policies is a highly pertinent question. In the development of Grand Park, the structuring of priorities often came from the private sector, which

15   Nelkin, "The Political Impact," 39.

was able to exert significant control over professional practices.

Examining the development of Grand Park within the context of its planning and design history clarifies how priorities for the project shifted. The Civic Center district was originally conceived as the site of centralized government services—a vision that persisted largely unchanged from the 1920s onward. As late as the 1990s, plans argued for residential and commercial intensification in other areas downtown but maintained the Civic Center almost exclusively for government use. The replacement of these goals with others largely directed toward spurring private development signals the growing influence of private sector visions in shaping the city's urban design projects. Despite years of consistent recommendations and guidelines for the area, the plans shifted substantially to allow for the development of Grand Park. The change in plan came in response to private-sector initiatives and pressure, and the results stand in stark contrast to the historical vision for the area. The evolution of these design documents offers a perspective onto the way professional practices shape built form and design.

While contemplated as early as 1910, the idea of an area of concentrated government services was formalized in the interwar period. During the 1920s the Los Angeles Planning Commission included plans for a civic administrative center in connection with the new City Hall. A joint resolution by the Los Angeles City Council and Los

Angeles Board of Supervisors reinforced the area as a site for government services:

> WHEREAS, it is the desire of the City Council of the City of Los Angeles, as well as of the Board of Supervisors of Los Angeles County, to conveniently locate all of the public buildings in which will be housed the offices of the several governmental departments of the City, County and State in a given area, to the end that an administrative center may be created in such a manner as to give the greatest possible opportunity for harmonious treatment in the design of the public buildings to be erected as well as the public grounds and streets surrounding the same.[16]

16   City of Los Angeles Council and Los Angeles Board of Supervisors, 1927.

Dating from a time when City Hall and other key government buildings were recently built or still under construction, these early plans emphasized that the area should be exclusively for government uses and that the land should be acquired through public means and for public purposes. The civic orientation of this era of plans is explicit, not only in the function and use of buildings but also in the design of spaces for public uses.

A series of planning and design exercises accompanied the construction of City Hall and Union Station between 1927 and 1939. These exercises and subsequent plans maintained government services as the focus for the area. One substantial plan—the "Civic Center Development Plan" of 1969—was created by the Civic Center Authority in conjunction with the advisory board

Epistemologies of Public and Private Urban Design Expertise

that directed the General Plan of Los Angeles.[17] This plan is centered on maintaining current government services and allowing for additional government offices to locate in the area in the future. The objectives of the plan include:

> To provide central locations for major governmental offices, grouped by jurisdiction, in order to promote efficient administration of government affairs, increase the convenience of citizens' transactions with government, and facilitate intergovernmental communication.
> To provide sufficient flexibility to accommodate future change in the functions and administration of government.[18]

Government services maintain a dominant role in later plans as well. A 1972 plan depicted the future development of the area in 1990 as a "government nerve center of Southern California," with "expansion of government uses southward and between Grand and Hill Streets, north of Temple."[19] Although many of the elements sketched out by the 1972 plan failed to materialize, parts of the Civic Center plan were reiterated in later plans. The Downtown Strategic Plan, undertaken by the Community Redevelopment Agency (CRA/LA) in the 1990s, continued to envision the Civic Center area as focused primarily on government services: "The Downtown Strategic Plan proposes that government uses continue to be concentrated Downtown. The Plan supports the continued development of the Civic Center as a regional

17   Civic Center Authority, "Civic Center Development Plan: An Element of the General Plan of Los Angeles," City of Los Angeles, Department of City Planning, 1969.

18   Ibid.

19   Committee for Central City Planning, "Central City Los Angeles 1972/1990: Preliminary General Development Plan" City of Los Angeles, 1972.

20   Downtown Strategic
Plan Advisory Committee,
"Downtown Strategic Plan
Los Angeles," Los Angeles
Community Redevelopment
Agency, 1992, 5.

center for Los Angeles City, County, State and Federal government activity."[20] While other downtown districts detailed in the Strategic Plan are shown as undergoing substantial change, the Civic Center is seen as an area of relative stability throughout the generations of plans. This historical vision of the area, which shows little deviation from the 1910 vision of a government center up to the late 1990s, is distinct from the contemporary positioning of Grand Park as a tool for catalytic change.

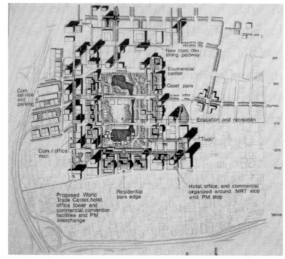

Figure 4   Preliminary General Development Plan, rendering, 1972. The plan makes little intervention in the form or experience of the Civic Center area. Source: Committee for Central City Planning (1972); Central City Los Angeles 1972/1990: Preliiminary Development Plan. Los Angeles.

Figure 5   Populated, not crowded, on a clear day in Los Angeles, a section of Grand Park looking onto a fountain. Source: Orly Linovski.

In contrast to the long history of the Civic Center as a "government nerve center," the anticipated real estate potential of four key parcels adjacent to Grand Avenue and Grand Park are associated with a rapid shift not only in the vision for the area but in its actual transformation as well. In the early 2000s, the Los Angeles Grand Avenue Authority began the process of redeveloping publically owned development parcels and the adjacent County Mall. A new plan for the area began to emerge through a series of documents issued by the Authority, including a Request for Qualifications (RFQ) and Request for Proposals (RFP).[21] While the RFQ and RFP were issued with the goal of finding developers for the four under-utilized parcels,[22] the redevelopment of the civic mall was included as a possible part of the project, to be developed either simultaneously or in a future phase.

The key change in thinking about the district is its re-visioning as a "vital urban destination," with activity re-oriented toward Grand Avenue and a redeveloped Civic Park. In describing the development goals for the area, the park is portrayed as transforming into a city-wide attraction as well as a space for local residents and workers:

> The Authority is also seeking a development that is coordinated with the nearby Civic Park and extension of the existing County Mall north of First Street. The new park will be a central

21 Los Angeles Grand Avenue Committee, *Request for Qualifications* (RFQ): *Reimagining Grand Avenue*, Los Angeles, 2003; and Los Angeles Grand Avenue Committee, RFP.

22 Two of the parcels were owned by the county and two were owned by the redevelopment agency (CRA/LA), and at the time all of the parcels were being used for parking.

23   Los Angeles Grand
Avenue Committee, RFQ, 4.

gathering place for all Angelenos and the setting of civic events, outdoor performances, and casual daily interaction of neighboring residents and workers.[23]

The emphasis on Grand Avenue as the central corridor for activity in the area represents a marked departure from earlier plans for the Civic Center. While there are significant differences between previous plans for the area and the *Reimagining Grand Avenue* documents, prepared in anticipation of the redevelopment project, the new plan attempts to portray a sense of continuity. One Grand Avenue Committee document states that despite there being many plans for the Civic Center area over the decades, "what remains consistent is the agreement that this area is a focal point in the downtown."[24] While interest in the Civic Center area has indeed been consistent, the new, now-realized project shifts the focus away from the historic, civic, activity around City Hall and Union Station and onto the development potential of vacant parcels.

24   Ibid., 70.

The importance of policy documents in shaping urban design is notable, as the urban redevelopment strategies of the 1950s and 1960s began to lose favor. After years of mass clearances in the name of urban "renewal," a sense that urban design plans should have identifiable public goals emerged.[25] As one former public sector urban designer stated:

25   More broadly, the movement toward urban design as public policy also typifies this. See Barnett, *Urban Design as Public Policy*; Punter, "Urban Design as Public Policy"; and Orly Linovski and Anastasia Loukaitou-Sideris, "Evolution of Urban Design Plans in the United States and Canada: What Do the Plans Tell Us about Urban Design Practice?," *Journal of Planning Education and Research* 33, no. 1 (2013): 66–82.

> Most redevelopment project plans were somewhat template documents that met the standards of

state law for those documents, which is that they had a finding of blight in them, and then they laid out basic authorities and powers. But as redevelopment evolved, in order to get us support of property owners and others who were, I think, suspicious of what had happened [in other redevelopment areas] ... the documents became more and more policy-oriented and they also had more and more planning bells and whistles attached to them in order to ensure that higher levels of planning goals and objectives would be met.[26]

26   The respondent is referring to Bunker Hill in downtown Los Angeles, the site of a major slum clearance and redevelopment program in the 1950s. Interview, private sector staff (LA1).

Increasingly, a case had to be made for urban design projects and plans: these policy documents offer a way of understanding both the motivation for projects and the rhetoric that was used to justify them. In the case of Grand Park, the documents reveal that the goal was not only to create a civic space but also to increase development and to shift the perception of the area.

Under the Grand Park plan, the park is largely seen as a tool for catalyzing change, with important real estate implications. This considerable difference from earlier plans demonstrates a shift in how public spaces are conceived and developed, and importantly, their role in encouraging development. One way of understanding this model is by examining the professional and epistemic practices involved in the reorientation of the public priorities and decision making that shaped Grand Park.

Many issues clearly came into play in creating a new vision for the Civic Center: not only had there been major demographic and political shifts in the city but the relative importance of the downtown core had also changed.[27] The redevelopment proposal documents discuss the new Civic Park as an important public space for all residents of the city. They provided a vague framework for its creation, but the development of the park's design and many aspects of its implementation were left to the competing development firms. The negotiations around professional expertise—and importantly, its relative independence and neutrality—were key to the design process. These negotiations established private sector knowledge as both distinct from and more valuable than the knowledge held by public actors. Furthermore, because of the supposed neutrality of professional expertise, the development sector was allowed to have a substantial—and largely unchallenged—role in shaping the space, through their control of the design consultants. The role of these various professional cultures in shaping built form moves beyond the policy framework into the realm of the physical through the epistemic practices involved in the creation of design expertise.

In the creation of an epistemic community—one that is able to influence policy decisions—the role of independent professional expertise is paramount. By establishing professional expertise as neutral it can be used to assert

27 See Anastasia Loukaitou-Sideris and Tridib Banerjee, *Urban Design Downtown: Poetics and Politics of Form* (Berkeley: University of California Press, 1998).

power for certain groups of professionals.[28] However, analyses of professional expertise as a source of power rarely assume a comparative model to distinguish between the relative expertise of different groups *within* a profession. In the Grand Park case, the construction of private sector professional expertise as both neutral and superior can be seen as a tool that allowed for that sector's control over urban design and policy processes. While both public and private sector professional actors have political identities, the ability of consultants to portray their expertise as largely free from political concerns allocates them substantial power over the form-making processes.

In the development of Grand Park, the segregation of professional knowledge between public and private sector actors was explicit. Rather than a unified epistemic community based on professional knowledge, perception of the types of expertise held by designers working in the public or private sectors was divided. One private sector professional explained, "I think in Los Angeles an urban designer who works within the municipal realm is there to administer and manage design goals and objectives, and an urban designer who works in the private realm is really there to formulate design options and implement projects."[29] The knowledge of public sector designers is characterized as largely administrative and bureaucratic, whereas that of the private consultant is described as creative and design oriented. The consultant explained further:

28　Nelkin, "The Political Impact"; Magali Sarfatti Larson, *The Rise of Professionalism: A Sociological Analysis* (Berkeley: University of California Press, 1977); and Magali Sarfatti Larson, "Professions as Disciplinary Cultures," in *The Blackwell Companion to the Sociology of Culture*, eds. Mark D. Jacobs and Nancy Weiss Hanrahan (Oxford: Blackwell, 2005).

29　Interview, private sector staff (LA1).

What you are going to need in cities is highly trained, incredibly smart individuals who are capable of managing their private consultants for the public good, but they are not going to be producing the plans, they're going to be basically managing the policies, and re-managing the policies.[30]

30   Ibid.

While few of the practitioners in Los Angeles that were interviewed for this research could point to explicit reasons why public designers are conceived as limited to administrative roles, the division between public and private sector knowledge was reiterated by many.[31] One private sector designer conceptualized it as such:

31   The public and private sector urban designers surveyed for this research had few differences in their academic and professional training. The majority of both municipal staff and consultants had professional degrees in architecture or landscape architecture.

It seems like that [the use of outside consultants by cities] reduces the people who are in those project positions in the City to a kind of managerial role that strips ... well, either strips them of any opportunity for creativity or more likely, attracts to it those people who really want to make sure that the numbers all line up and everything is in order and don't really have the passion for implementing it.[32]

32   Interview, private sector staff (LA10).

The distinctions between these constructions of professional knowledge limit the realm of action for public sector actors. Private sector consultants have an advantage in portraying their expertise as not only different but also more valuable than that of public employees. While this is not surprising given the fee-based structure of private firms, it has largely gone unchallenged by public actors. Public employees did not actively contest the view that consultants were "more expert" in providing design and creative services or that private designers could have competing goals related to their work for both public and private organizations. While consultants presumably experience conflicts in negotiating between public and private sector work, these have largely been subsumed under the cloak of professional neutrality, and accepted (perhaps surprisingly) by both private and public actors.

The professional expertise of private sector firms was used as an argument for their independence in developing Grand Park. Although it would be expected, given the public nature of the project, that there would be significant interaction between consultants and public staff, interaction was often limited. Public sector actors were to have oversight over the process, however their description of conflicts that arose during the process reveals that the public sector had largely removed itself from the process: "It was all wonderful, you know ... I think there was sort of universal approval of the design approach.... [F]rom an urban design point of view, it was just so welcome to have this project happening.... [T]here weren't too many issues, really."[33] The lack of conflict between public and private sector goals reflects the supposed neutrality of professional expertise. This is equally evident in the way in which public designers spoke of the independence of private designers: one public sector designer tellingly stated, "The design firm showed us the designs early on and I just had some suggestions, but ... you know, with such a good design firm, I knew that they would do a good job."[34] The argument described here for the lack of

33 Interview, public sector staff (LA5).

34 Interview, public sector staff (LA35).

public sector intervention is not related to traditional reasons for outsourcing public functions, such as a necessary reduction in costs. Rather, professional expertise is the key factor: the firm is able to provide "good" design advice, so public oversight or contestation is not required. The work of private consultants is embedded as neutral and independent, a conceptualization largely unquestioned by public actors.

By establishing professional knowledge as neutral and as free of competing political and economic interests, the power of private sector expertise can be allowed to proceed unchecked. With actors working on public policy and private development projects simultaneously—and often with conflicting goals—the potential for bias is certainly present. Despite this, professional expertise, deployed as independent and neutral, is used as an effective guise to minimize the conflicts inherent in blurring the lines between public and private.

CONTROLLING PROFESSIONAL PRACTICES

With the neutrality of private sector professional expertise established and largely accepted by public actors, questions arise as to which groups were able to exercise power in shaping design and implementation processes. Sociologist Judith Blau addresses how the range of decision-making opportunities factors into understanding power: "power is measured by influence in major decision areas; they are major in that they involve the productive work of the firm, and they are largely professional rather than administrative in nature."[35] The development of Grand Park, built on publicly owned land and intended as a civic space, must be examined with respect to those who had substantive influence over the work of the design consultants. In addition to some public sector involvement, it was the developer selected for the redevelopment project who had substantial engagement in the day-to-day negotiations around design and form, actively shaping the work of consultants. Combined with the assumed neutrality of professional expertise, this allowed control over the substantive work of design and implementation to be held by the private developer rather than the public sector.

The role of the developer in managing the process was one of active engagement and direction. Those involved in the process as representatives of the private-sector funder saw themselves as shaping the project and negotiating with both the design consultants and the public sector actors. The developer asserted that they were involved with all aspects of the project, from project design to community outreach: "So we, the developer, coordinated the design, we hired [the design consultants] and the structural, civil, plumbing, electrical designers, did a big community outreach effort and put together a plan to improve and expand the park."[36] Others involved in the design and implementation processes reiterated the position of the developer. One political actor affirmed:

35   Judith R. Blau, "Expertise and Power in Professional Organizations," *Work and Occupations* 6, no. 1 (1979): 104.

36   Interview, private sector staff (LA27).

Yeah, [the developer] ... actually had one of their construction project managers who was on our team, and he oversaw the construction. You know they were paid for it, of course, but they were intimately involved in the whole process. They had a guy who was at every meeting, and he was equally accountable for managing the construction, as was the County. [37]

While the public sector representatives maintained a position in the process, they acknowledged the role of the developer, stating that the public actors "worked hand-in-hand" with the developer in directing the consultants.[38] However, because the developer was given significant oversight with respect to managing the process, they were able to present options that benefitted them. A representative of the developer explained:

I worked with [the consultants] every day, talked to [them] almost every day on the design portion. [It was] ... to strategize on the best way to spend the money ... how to present that to the public entities to get their buy-in, and really important, was I did a construction budget based on the schematic drawings and came up with a bunch of price options so when we presented it we gave the County and the JPA [joint powers authority] options on how they wanted to spend the money, and we kind of, you know, spun it the way we thought the money should be spent.[39]

37   Interview, public sector staff (LA29). Other participants questioned whether the development company was paid for their involvement in managing the project. Regardless, the conflict in having the developer involved in actively managing the development of public space was not considered.

38   Interview, public sector staff (LA5).

39   Interview, private sector staff (LA27).

Epistemologies of Public and Private Urban Design Expertise

The relationship described here is one of collaboration between the developer and the consultant, with options then being "spun" to the public sector. The differing goals of the developer, who had significant interest in increasing both the value of surrounding properties and their marketability for residential development, were not identified as problematic in their managing of the design and implementation phases. It is difficult to understand this urban design process as one of the public sector managing private consultants to achieve municipal or civic goals. Rather, it is one largely directed and managed by development interests, despite the public orientation and purported goals of the project.

The consultants working on the Grand Park project were cognizant of the role of the developer and viewed them—in addition to the public sector—as a client. In describing to whom the consultants were responsible, they acknowledged that control of the project had largely been ceded to the private sector:

> We also had another client, which was the developer, who was brought in to oversee and manage the whole process. When [the County] had to give up the $50 million dollars to do their development, they also had to give up their time beyond that to kind of oversee the whole process through design.... And they were sort of ... it was kind of said that the County had given up control to them to do this process and then we'd get control back.[40]

40   Interview, private sector staff (LA15).

Despite the public nature of the project, a large proportion of the design negotiations occurred between the consultant and the developer, rather than with the public sector. In discussing conflicts that occurred during the design and implementation of the project, the developer described not only how closely it worked with the consultant but also how their goals were very much aligned:

> [The consultants] understood there was a limited budget. I gave them options, we strategized together on what we thought was the best way to spend the money, and then together we came up with a strategy on how to present it and you know, even how to put together renderings, how to describe the alternates. So no, there was never really much disagreement with [the consultant]. I mean, I did have to go to them and say, "we just can't afford this," and they understood.... I don't think we ever had much of a disconnect on what to build, and their work product.[41]

41   Interview, private sector staff (LA27).

The role of the development sector in managing consultants for a public project—and their relative power in shaping that process—represents a type of urban design not traditionally associated with public projects. Rather than a process that is actively engaged in or contested by the public sector, the Grand Park project's urban design practices were dominated by private sector interests, able to capitalize on the portrayal of professional expertise as neutral and unbiased.

When professional practices are accepted as fundamentally neutral, there are implications for the design of cities, especially in the context of diminishing support for the public sector. It is impossible to understand Grand Park, and the epistemic practices that enabled it, without also examining the shifting purposes of urban design. Whereas early plans for the area focused on the civic value of urban design—whether through the provisioning of public space, access, and transparency of government services or through ensuring the quality of the built environment—one of the primary concerns in creating Grand Park was the area's development potential. While this is not surprising in the context of the neoliberal turn, how these development processes intersect with the epistemic practices of professionals raises concerns.

Reflecting back on the creation of Grand Park through the use of development money, a public sector official stated:

> Well, in a sense it is [private money] because, it was given by a private firm but the fact is it's public money. [It was] paid to the County for the use of the County's lands, so it is a public project. The County *could* have, I suppose, done anything it wanted with the money. It could have built hospitals, it could have built parole camps, it could have improved our jails, there's many things the County does that need attention.[42]

42 Interview, Public sector staff (LA37).

Indeed, the funding could have been used for any public purpose but as the creation of Grand Park demonstrates, increasingly urban design is used as a tool for stimulating development. Professional practices are wrapped up in this. Firstly, the lack of a public form of urban design, created and engaged in by a strong public sector, ensures that there are no serious challenges to privately initiated and controlled projects. Secondly, the creation of an epistemic community of private-sector urban design practitioners that is premised on the neutrality and independence of professional expertise furthers these goals. Private-sector consultants were able to successfully represent their expertise as free from the considerations and biases that accompany professional practices. Despite the conflicts inherent in the private sector fee-based business model, there was little challenge to the independence of outside consultants. The pervasiveness of consultant involvement is shown to be not only in the design of civic spaces but also in the shaping of government policy. The combination of these two factors allowed for the creation of an ostensibly public project that was largely shaped by private development goals.

If, as Alan Kreditor argues, "theories of urban design can be revealed through professional behavior," understanding contemporary urban design is considerably more complicated than public sector regulation of private development.[43] Given the complexity of public and private involvement in developing projects at the urban design scale, examining the nature of professional

43 Alan Kreditor, "The Neglect of Urban Design in the American Academic Succession," *Journal of Planning Education and Research* 9, no. 3 (1990): 161.

knowledge and epistemic cultures *across* sectors is critical to understanding the production of urban form. Epistemic communities of professional practitioners are able to negotiate their expertise in ways that diminish their competing political and economic goals. In the context of a broader restructuring of both public sector institutions and the purposes of urban design, reevaluating the role that these epistemic practices have in shaping our cities is crucial.

It's Not just abo[ut]

CLIMATE JUSTICE

s also about

YOU(th)!.

and the future of OAKLAND!

ntact:
nanda Wake, Youth Organizer at Asian Communities for

ut Polar Bears

YOUTH
TEACH-IN

on the *Oaklan*
Climate Action RALL
(March 30th 4:30 @ Frank Ogaw

Sponsored by ACR
SAFIRE Youth Progra

Mon. March 29th 201

4:30-6:00p

@ ACRJ's Offic

1440 Broadway, Suite 9

near Downtown Oaklan
BART & B

Learn Up on what o
are doing in Oakland
fight for climate just
and how youth c

roductive Justice

From the Street: Civic Epistemologies of Urban Climate Change

Michael Mendez

Climate change is commonly thought of as a global issue—an abstract, scientific phenomenon that melts ice caps and robs the polar bear of its natural habitat. However true, such representations have little relevance for how climate change impacts the lived experience of individuals within local communities. In recent decades, spatial ways of knowing climate change and assessing its impact have shifted from a global scale to the scale of the city. Recognizing that municipal governments are uniquely positioned to reduce global greenhouse gas (GHG) emissions in light of their ability to influence local patterns of urban development, economic activity, transportation infrastructure, and energy use, cities around the world have begun to develop their own climate action plans (CAPs).[1]

Figure 1 "It's not just about polar bears!" Flier for the Oakland Climate Action Coalition (OCAC) Rally, 2012. Source: OCAC.

1 Isabelle Anguelovskik and JoAnn Carmin, "Something Borrowed, Everything New: Innovation and Institutionalization in Urban Climate Governance," *Current Opinion in Environmental Sustainability* 3 (2011): 169–75; and Cynthia Rosenzweig et al., "Cities Lead the Way in Climate-Change Action," *Nature* 467 (2010): 909–11.

2   Adam Millard-Ball, "The Limits to Planning: Causal Impacts of City Climate Action Plans," *Journal of Planning Education and Research* 20, no. 10 (2012): 1–15; and Angela Park, "Everybody's Movement: Environmental Justice and Climate Change," report, Environmental Support Center, 2009.

3   Sara Hughes, "Justice in Urban Climate Change Adaptation: Criteria and Application to Delhi," *Ecology and Society* 18, no. 4 (2013): 48.

4   Ibid.; Harriet Bulkeley et al., "Climate Justice and Global Cities: Mapping the Emerging Discourses," *Global Environmental Change* 23 (2013): 914–25; Ellen M. Douglas et al., "Coastal Flooding, Climate Change, and Environmental Justice: Identifying Obstacles and Incentives for Adaptation in Two Metropolitan Boston, Massachusetts Communities," *Mitigation and Adaptation Strategies for Global Change* 17 (2012): 537–62; and Donovan Finn and Lynn McCormick, "Urban Climate Change Plans: How Holistic?," *Local Environment* 16, no. 4 (2011): 397–416.

5   Seth Shonkoff et al., "Environmental Health and Equity Impacts from Climate Change and Mitigation Policies in California: A review of the Literature" (Sacramento: California Air Resources Board, 2009).

6   Saffron O'Neill and Sophie Nicholson-Cole, "Fear Won't Do It: Promoting Positive Engagement with Climate Change through Imagery and Icons," *Science Communication* 30 (2009): 355–79.

7   For the purposes of this study, "co-benefit" is used to signal an ancillary benefit of a GHG mitigation or adaptation policy that is produced in addition to the benefit targeted by the policy. See Karen Pittel and Dirk Rubbelke, "Climate Policy and Ancillary Benefits: A Survey and Investigation into the Modeling of International Negotiations on Climate Change," *Ecological Economics* 68 (2008): 210–22.

Local climate action planning has emerged as an expert-driven process that emphasizes reductions in GHG emissions through economic and technological fixes.[2] These plans have significant benefits and consequences for urban populations as they reconfigure urban infrastructures, services, and decision-making processes.[3] There is growing evidence to suggest, however, that local climate planning is neglecting issues of equity and human health.[4] Municipal CAPs rarely analyze or consider the disproportionate impact that climate change will have on low-income communities and communities of color with regard to heat waves, air pollution, public health, and environmental justice.[5] The disconnect between public health and climate change can leave these communities disengaged from the policymaking process and under-represented in mitigation and adaptation plans.[6]

Incorporating public health and equity into climate action plans is challenging for several reasons. First, the structural conditions that created environmental health inequities are often concealed by universal scientific variables such as GHG emission reductions, mean temperature, and regulatory technologies. These are regional or global variables that do not account for the inequitable distribution of health co-benefits in local communities that are disproportionately affected by environmental impacts.[7] Secondly, there is a disconnect between climate planning and public health because greenhouse gases are considered to have "no direct public health impacts" since they are global pollutants that mix uniformly in the atmosphere.[8] They do not have localized health effects like particulate matter (PM) and ground-level ozone (O_3)—the key ingredients of smog.[9] Studies further suggest that since GHG emissions are invisible and because we breathe them without getting sick, many policymakers and laypersons have a difficult time making the links between GHG emissions, local air quality, and public health.[10]

Public health and equity might be better served by local climate planning that follows a relational approach—that is, one that acknowledges how climate change is connected to other types of knowledge about the local environment and that allows different ways of knowing to play a part in framing a culture of climate change and its corresponding policy responses.[11] Close examination of the Energy and Climate Action Plan (ECAP) of the City of Oakland, California, reveals how environmental justice groups in that city are approaching climate change in this manner. They employ a localized approach by analyzing climate change through people's lived experience, relationship to community, and local knowledge rather than solely through universal metrics developed by experts.[12] These new forms of local knowledge and governance can be understood as an articulation of civic epistemology: "the institutionalized practices by which members of a given society test and deploy knowledge claims used as a basis for making collective choices."[13] Examining the ECAP through the concept of

8   Exposure to GHG emissions has human health impacts in concentrated form, such as their use in the workplace. Wisconsin Department of Health Services, "Chemical Fact Sheet," 2013, http://www.dhs.wisconsin.gov/eh/ChemFS/fs/CarbonDioxide.htm. However, outdoor exposure levels are considered to be trivial; GHG emissions dilute as they mix uniformly in the atmosphere. California Air Resources Board, "AB 32 Scoping Plan," 2008, http://arb.ca.gov/cc/scopingplan/scopingplan.htm.

9   California Air Resources Board, "AB 32 Scoping Plan,"

10   Susanne Moser and Lisa Dilling, *Creating a Climate for Change: Communicating Climate Change and Facilitating Social Change* (Cambridge: Cambridge University Press, 2007).

11   Catharine Brace and Hilary Geoghegan, "Human Geographies of Climate Change: Landscape, Temporality, and Lay Knowledges," *Progress in Human Geography* 35, no. 5 (2010): 284–302.

12   Local knowledge is defined by international development literature as: (a) information linked to a specific place, culture or identify group; (b) dynamic and evolving knowledge; (c) know-how belonging to groups of people who are intimate with the natural and human system within which they live; and, (d) knowledge that has some qualities that distinguishes it from formal scientific knowledge. Jason Corburn, "Bringing Local Knowledge in Environmental Decision-Making: Improving Urban Planning for Communities at Risk," *Journal of Planning Education and Research* 22 (2003): 420; Park, "Everybody's Movement"; and Rachel Morello-Frosch et al., *Facing the Climate Gap: How Environmental Justice Communities Are Leading the Way to a More Sustainable and*

Equitable California (Berkeley: University of California, 2012).

13   Sheila Jasanoff, *Designs on Nature: Science and Democracy in Europe and the United States* (Princeton, NJ: Princeton University Press, 2005), 255.

14   Ibid., 9.

15   Robin Grove-White, "Review Symposium: Controlling Biotechnology: Science, Democracy and 'Civic Epistemology,'" *Metascience* 17, no. 2 (2008): 177–98; Alistair Illes, "Identifying Environmental Health Risks in Consumer Products: Non-Governmental Organizations and Civic Epistemologies," *Public Understanding of Science* 16 (2007): 371–91; and Clark Miller, "New Civic Epistemologies of Quantification: Making Sense of Indicators of Local and Global Sustainability," *Science Technology Human Values* 30, no. 3 (2005): 403–32. Civic epistemology includes a range of knowledge production processes, including scientific peer review, public participation mechanisms, methods of reasoning, government statistics, standards of evidence, and norms of expertise that typify public debates and political institutions. Illes, "Identifying Environmental Health Risks," 371–91.

civic epistemology, this case study demonstrates how environmental justice groups are transforming a priori policy approaches to produce place-specific conceptualizations of climate change that underscore population health and community well-being.

In this case of climate action planning, the concept of civic epistemology may productively be used to examine geographically specific and sociocultural ways of knowledge production at the subnational level. Originally conceived by science and society scholar Shelia Jasanoff, civic epistemology was developed as an analytical tool to understand the practices, methods, and institutions by which a society identifies new policy issues, generates knowledge relevant to their resolution, and puts that knowledge to use in policymaking. Through this concept and cases of biotechnology and climate change, she explains the different ways in which citizens in Germany, Britain, and the United States "come to know things in common and to apply their knowledge to the conduct of politics."[14] Other scholars working on nation-state civic epistemologies also find national contingencies, such as administrative and legal codes and styles as well as culturally specific conceptions of risk, vulnerability, and impact, shape scientific definitions and policy responses to climate change.[15] Thus, scientific studies deemed reliable and legitimate in one country may be dismissed as inadequate for policy guidance in another, even when similar social, political, and economic variables influence regulators in both countries.

From the Street

A focus on "urban" civic epistemologies reveals that local relationships with the science of climate change are quite different from those that occur at the national level. Civic ways of knowing urbanity assist in the construction of global climate change because of, rather than in spite of, their roots in local knowledge, culture, and history. Embeddedness and rootedness are not explicitly acknowledged in Jasanoff's concept of civic epistemology. Her nation-state approach privileges knowledge production by elite global actors without acknowledging that local and community-based actors develop and implement significant scientific and regulatory processes. Nor does the nation-state approach analyze how race, gender, class, or power differentiate and shape civic epistemologies. By attending to spatial ways of knowing civic action, diverse publics—not just scientists, planners, and policymakers—define, measure, and govern environmental health and climate change.

CONFIGURING OAKLAND'S CLIMATE(S)

With a population of nearly 400,000, of whom almost two-thirds are people of color, Oakland has a long and rich history of civil rights and environmental activism. This activism is partly in response to a legacy of inequitable development practices that continue to cause environmental degradation in local communities. Toxic facility sitings, low socioeconomic status, economic activity from one of the state's largest ports, and lack of a

16   California Energy Commission, *Community-Based Climate Adaptation Planning: Case Study of Oakland, California*, white paper, Pacific Institute and Oakland Climate Action Coalition, 2012; and Meredith Minkler et al., "Community-Based Participatory Research and Policy Advocacy to Reduce Diesel Exposure in West Oakland, California," *American Journal of Public Health* 101, no. S1 (2011): S166–75.

17   CalEnviroScreen uses existing environmental, health, and socioeconomic data to create a "cumulative impacts" score for communities across the state. The tool compares areas of the state against other areas, creating a relative ranking. An area with a high score would be expected to experience greater cumulative impacts, as compared to areas with low scores. Cal EPA, "Draft California Communities Environmental Health Screening Tool (CalEnviroScreen)," policy report, State of California, 2014.

18   Ibid. The working definition of cumulative impacts adopted by the Cal EPA in 2005 reads: "Cumulative impacts means exposures, public health or environmental effects from the combined emissions and discharges, in a geographic area, including environmental pollution from all sources, whether single or multi-media, routinely, accidentally, or otherwise released. Impacts will take into account sensitive populations and socioeconomic factors, where applicable and to the extent data are available." "Emissions" in the definition include the co-pollutants of climate change.

fair distribution of environmental goods has created a built environment in many Oakland neighborhoods that leads to increased pollution and public health risks, such as asthma, heart disease, cancer, premature death, birth defects, and neonatal problems.[16]

Local pollution sources located within the city also contribute to an international environmental health threat: the greenhouse gas emissions that fuel global climate change. The Environmental Health Screening Tool (CalEnviroScreen) developed by the California Environmental Protection Agency (Cal EPA) recently highlighted Oakland's role in global-local environmental health degradation.[17] It noted that more than 50,000 residents in Oakland live in census tracts that rank in the top 20 percent of tracts for cumulative environmental impact across the state.[18] Neighborhoods in these high-scoring census tracts sit next to a busy shipping container facility port, airport, rail yard, or freeway. Residents living there are exposed daily to higher levels of air pollution from vehicle exhaust and commercial operations than people living in other census tracks.

Motivated by these disproportionate environmental burdens, the City of Oakland and local environmental justice groups sought ways to explicitly link urban planning, public health, and climate change. They developed an urban civic epistemology that partially displaced the types of expert-driven processes that characterize climate action plans across the United States. Previous research has shown that local governments generally develop climate action plans by establishing task forces with scientists and experts from universities, research centers, and technical organizations that rarely address issues of public health and equity.[19] Conversely, after a three-year collaboration with the Oakland Climate Action Coalition (OCAC), in December 2012 Oakland adopted one of California's highest city-scale GHG emissions reduction targets.[20] In this process, environmental justice groups configured a holistic concept of the environment that identified geographically and socially uneven impacts of climate change and promoted health equity.[21]

In applying the framework of civic epistemology at the urban scale, one discovers that environmental justice actors are also influencing environmental policy by learning how to "become" city planners and health practitioners when they interact with highly specialized knowledge and practices. Research by Tom Angotti and Julie Sze shows that social justice activists in San Francisco and New York City have used the concept of environmental justice as an analytic framework to understand community health and environmental problems and to advocate for solutions through community organizing and policy development.[22] In these two cities and in Oakland, disparate health and environmental effects are what triggered community organizing. Environmental justice advocates consistently defined health as more than disease rates. They developed strategies that reimagined urban development and advanced public health policies in local and holistic terms. When global,

19 Bulkeley et al., "Climate Justice"; Douglas et al., "Coastal Flooding"; Joyce Rosenthal and Dana Breechwald, "Climate Adaptive Planning for Preventing Heat-Related Health Impacts in New York City," in Climate Change Governance: Climate Change Management, eds. Jörg Knieling and Walter Leal Filho (Berlin: Springer Verlag, 2013), 205–25; Cynthia Rosenzweig and William Solecki, "Introduction to Climate Change Adaptation in New York City: Building a Risk Management Response," Annals of the New York Academy of Sciences 1196 (2010): 13–17; and Jason Corburn, "Cities, Climate Change and Urban Heat Island Mitigation: Localising Global Environmental Science," Urban Studies 46, no. 2 (2009): 413–27.

20 The Draft ECAP was approved by the City Council in March 2011. However, final adoption was taken in December 2012, after the state required Environmental Impact Report was completed.

21 Health equity is achieved when every person has the opportunity to "attain his or her full health potential" and no one is "disadvantaged from achieving this potential because of social position or other socially determined circumstances." Paula A. Braveman, "Monitoring Equity in Health and Healthcare: A Conceptual Framework," Journal of Health, Population, and Nutrition 21, no. 3 (2003): 181.

22 Tom Angotti and Julie Sze, "Environmental Justice Praxis: Lessons for the Theory and Practice of Interdisciplinary Urban Health," in Urban Health and Society: Interdisciplinary Approaches to Research and Practice, ed. Nicholas Freudenberg et al. (San Francisco: Jossey-Bass, 2009), 19–41.

scientific knowledge of climate policy is downscaled to different geographies and sociopolitical contexts, the democratic procedures of regulatory practices, public participation, and legitimating science differ greatly. Accordingly, urban civic epistemologies offer a particular way and scale of knowing, reasoning, and organizing the politics of climate change.

COMMUNITY-BASED CLIMATE PLANNING IN OAKLAND

The Oakland Climate Action Coalition was first conceived in the small cinder-block basement of the Ella Baker Center for Human Rights in early 2009. This was shortly after the city announced that it would develop an ECAP, and the Center identified this as a strategic moment. It organized more than 50 people from 30 community-based organizations to brainstorm how to produce a comprehensive local climate action plan to address the needs of Oakland residents most impacted by pollution and poverty.

The Center began the strategic planning meeting by asking, "What would a People's Energy and Climate Action Plan look like in Oakland?" After several hours of facilitated discussion, participants covered the small basement walls with neon pink, green, and yellow Post-it® notes detailing their suggestions and ideas for Oakland's climate action plan. Some of these suggestions included demands for locally produced renewable energy projects in disadvantaged communities, affordable housing as a GHG emissions reduction strategy, and increased public transit options to reduce co-pollutants and improve local air quality. Through this grassroots meeting, the OCAC was created. The Ella Baker Center for Human Rights went on to be the convener of the cross-sector coalition's 50 organizations as it expanded to include environmental and social justice groups, labor unions, green businesses, and advocates for sustainable development. The Ella Baker Center provided staff to coordinate the coalition, led the drafting of the coalition's mission statement and goals, and facilitated Steering Committee and Coalition meetings to ensure compliance with OCAC benchmarks.

OCAC's strength and success are largely due to the diversity of its coalition members. The organization recruited members from Oakland's many disparate neighborhoods. Together, they provided multi-sector expertise on a host of issues, including transportation and housing, energy, urban agriculture, adaptation planning, and community engagement. According to Emily Kirsch, founding OCAC Coordinator and Green Jobs Organizer for the Ella Baker Center:

> Having a diverse coalition with strong expertise is important in these types of policy initiatives. So we knew we were not experts on climate change. When you talk about climate change, its food, water, transportation, housing, energy, health equity, and everything you possibly can think of. So we went around to our friends and allies to find out what sort of climate-related projects they were working on and the type of expertise they could bring to the coalition. Then we strategized how we could get these projects included in the ECAP and on the books as part of the city's plans.[23]

Ultimately, the coalition's range of expertise allowed it to work jointly with the city to move the ECAP beyond abstract technical metrics to a community-based plan.

In developing the framework for the ECAP, the city initially followed conventional methods. It identified GHG emissions reduction targets, environmental priority areas, and strategies to address GHG targets by consulting with experts at nongovernmental organizations like ICLEI-Local Governments for Sustainability and the private consulting firm Circlepoint, Inc.[24] The city organized public workshops with 200 people representing the OCAC, government agencies, utilities, interest groups, businesses, and individual residents. Early in the process,

23 Emily Kirsch, lead organizer for the Oakland Climate Action Coalition, Ella Baker Center for Human Rights, personal communication, October 26, 2011.

24 Most cities typically participate in the Cities and Climate Protection Program developed by the ICLEI-Local Governments for Sustainability (founded in 1990 as the International Council for Local Environmental Initiatives). The program helps cities establish targets for carbon emissions reductions by developing GHG emissions inventories and mitigation strategies, including provisions for monitoring and evaluation. Gotelind Alber and Kristine Kern, "Governing Climate Change in Cities: Modes of Urban Climate Governance in Multi-Level Systems," policy report, OECD Conference on Competitive Cities and Climate Change, 2008, 9–10.

OCAC approached the City of Oakland to be more directly involved in the city's ECAP development. OCAC asked the city not to establish a formal expert taskforce and to instead allow a community-based approach. The coalition included politically influential and long-established members of Oakland's community, so the OCAC was able to persuade the city council to allow them to facilitate and fund their own, parallel community advisory process. As OCAC's representative recall:

> The city did host their own workshops but they are pretty boring and held at 2 pm in the afternoon. We attended and gave our input. That is because we get paid to attend. But we wanted to hold workshops that were more accessible to the public and were fun and engaging.... So we hosted a series of workshops in the flatlands of East and West Oakland, knowing that communities most impacted by climate change are often least represented in terms of decision making. So we hosted workshops with coalition members that already had relationships in those communities.[25]

25 Kirsch, personal communication.

Through their collaboration, Oakland passed the one of the highest municipal greenhouse gas reduction targets in California: 36 percent reduction from 2005 levels by 2020 and 85 percent reduction by 2050. While other cities across the state have also set goals to reduce GHG emissions, Oakland's target levels are the first to comply with the reductions recommended by the Intergovernmental Panel on Climate Change.[26] These reductions

26 California Air Resources Board, "AB 32 Scoping Plan."

surpass California's statewide requirement for achieving 1990 levels by 2020 and are more than double the California Air Resources Board's recommendation that local governments reduce GHG emissions 15 percent below today's levels by 2020.[27]

27   Ibid.

The OCAC strategically pushed for higher GHG reduction targets as leverage for additional measures to represent their social equity-based definition of urban climate change. As a result, Oakland is one of the first cities to explicitly develop evaluative criteria to incorporate co-benefits for traditionally disadvantaged communities. In addition, the ECAP considered whether the benefits of the plan outweighed the burdens imposed on disadvantaged communities. This included ensuring that GHG emissions reduction measures like transit-oriented development (TOD) would not displace low-income residents by preserving affordable housing options in TOD projects. The OCAC argued that although constructing TOD projects in existing high-density neighborhoods is an effective GHG mitigation measure, it can also displace low-income people, seniors, and renters and undercut GHG mitigation strategies. As older housing stock is replaced with new market-rate units, lower-income residents would be forced to move out to cheaper suburban locales with even fewer transit options. Many individuals may be forced to buy a car to commute to work and access community services, thereby increasing not only the region's vehicle miles traveled (VMT) but also its GHG emissions. Oakland was the first city in the country to explicitly link climate change policy with affordable housing. The OCAC also fought for the inclusion of neighborhood-scale adaptation planning in the ECAP to address the most harmful impacts to socially vulnerable communities in the near term. This is in contrast to conventional adaptation studies, such as regional sea-level rise models, which typically only focus on protecting hard assets like vital city infrastructure or ecological systems from the impacts of climate change.

In addition to its role in incorporating community-based climate policies into the ECAP, the OCAC was key in moving an innovative climate action plan forward. Garrett Fitzgerald, sustainability coordinator for the City of Oakland, praised their efforts: "The OCAC made my job a lot easier by providing smart, specific recommendations for the plan and doing a lot of work to bring more of Oakland's voices into the process. It's rare to find community partners as dedicated and willing to collaborate with city staff as the OCAC."[28] Even before city staff released their first draft of the ECAP, the OCAC had already developed and presented their own comprehensive ECAP to city officials based on the community workshops they hosted in Oakland's low-income and immigrant neighborhoods. City staff incorporated the majority of the proposed ECAP policies into the final plan, which was adopted by the city council. The OCAC illustrated that by working together, across sectors and organizations, they could effectively focus climate action planning on measures that not only reduce GHG emissions but

28   Garrett Fitzgerald, sustainability manger, City of Oakland, personal communication, November 16, 2011.

29 After the city released its first and second drafts, the OCAC submitted edits via Track Changes, which allowed the city to simply copy and paste their suggestions into the updated and final drafts. Kirsch, personal communication; Aaron Lehmer, campaigns director, Bay Localize, personal communication, November 4, 2011.

30 Fitzgerald, personal communication.

31 Catalina Garzon, director, Pacific Institute's Community Strategies for Sustainability and Justice Program, personal communication, June, 13, 2013.

32 Ibid.; Kirsch, personal communication. Coalition members also participated in monthly General Coalition meetings. The OCAC Steering Committee was made up of cochairs of the OCAC's policy committees.

also provide local communities with direct benefits.[29]

The OCAC's parallel policy development process enabled the coalition to produce 50 of the 150 GHG reduction measures and goals in the ECAP.[30] This was primarily achieved through community-based policy committees, which studied and provided justification via research and local community knowledge for certain GHG reduction measures and targets.[31] Policy committees included Transportation & Land Use; Building & Energy Use; Consumption & Solid Waste; Food, Water & Urban Agriculture/Forestry; Adaptation & Resilience; and Community Engagement. Two cochairs—one from a policy-based organization and the other from a grassroots group—led each committee to ensure that there was a balance of expertise in policy development and on-the-ground experience. The committees convened several times a month to conduct research and develop policy.[32]

The committees were further guided in their efforts by a number of key OCAC principles:

1 Climate Justice and Equity
2 Clean Up Air Pollution and Create Healthy Communities
3 Create Local Green-Collar Jobs
4 Community Local Knowledge
5 Climate Adaptation and Community Resilience
6 Polluters Pay

Typically, municipalities represent public participation in formulating climate change risks and strategies as a normative goal. They claim they are unable to garner significant public interest because the science is complex and because climate change is a long-term and uncertain process.[33] As a result, many cities opt instead to establish an expert taskforce and hire environmental consultants to compensate for a lack of public participation. Compared to most municipal climate policy planning, then, Oakland represents a unique case (see Table 1).[34]

The Oakland ECAP differs in six key ways: (1) it included local knowledge in the development of climate policy; (2) public participation was embedded in the regulatory science and policy processes; (3) climate impacts focused on the human-scale; (4) CAP measures were chosen for their potential health co-benefits; (5) adaptation plans focused on socially vulnerable communities; and (6) the CAP includes explicit references to social equity and environmental justice.

33   Few, Brown, and Tompkins, "Public Participation."

34   The results included in Table 1 are derived from the author's survey of 41 California CAPs in cities with census tracts ranked in the 20th percentile under Cal EPA's CalEnviron Screen Tool, and a review of the literature on the development of CAPs, including Bullkeley et al., "Climate Justice"; Millard-Ball, *The Limits to Planning*; Anguelovski and Carmin, "Something Borrowed"; California Energy Commission, *Community-Based Climate Adaptation Planning*; and Roger Few, Katrina Brown, and Emma Tompkins, "Public Participation and Climate Change Adaptation: Avoiding the Illusion of Inclusion," *Climate Policy* 7 (2007): 46–59.

	Conventional CAP	Oakland ECAP
Regulatory Science & Policy Processes	Climate policy, protocols, models, methods and strategies primarily established via expert commissions, consultants, and university partnerships. Expert/Professional knowledge emphasized	Climate policy, protocols, models, methods, and strategies developed through a community-based process (local knowledge). Lay-expert knowledge engaged
Public Participation	Normative goals achieved during mandatory public comment periods or workshops, and after the regulatory science & policy protocols have been established	Occurred concurrently with the regulatory science & policy processes and public comment periods and workshops
Focus of Climate Impacts	Ecological systems and citywide infrastructure	Human-scale, socially vulnerable neighborhoods/ populations, ecological systems, and citywide infrastructure
Co-Benefits of CAP	Cost-savings, efficiency, economic development	Public health, cost-savings, efficiency, local green jobs and energy
Focus of Adaptation	Normative goals typically only focused on citywide infrastructure and ecological systems. No comprehensive neighborhood-scale studies or risk models	Focus on human health, socially vulnerable neighborhoods/populations and citywide infrastructure. Comprehensive neighborhood-scale studies and risk models undertaken
Explicit References to Social Equity or Environmental Justice	Rarely cited in documents	Cited as a guiding principle

Table 1   Climate Action Plan (CAP) metrics in California.

The OCAC climate policy development process represents a rupture in conventional practice in local climate action planning by deemphasizing the primacy of scientific advisors and validating the coalition and communities' local knowledge. Oakland's ECAP is an exceptional case, moreover, because the OCAC is officially listed on the ECAP as a major contributor to the plan's development. Rarely are social and environmental justice organizations listed on such government documents as official knowledge producers of climate policy. As a long-serving member of the Oakland City Council notes, their collaboration with the OCAC produced an ECAP that stands in sharp contrast to previous environmental documents produced by the city: "I've been a Council member for 16 years and I've seen a lot of environmental plans. Oakland's Energy and Climate Action Plan is unique because it lifts the voices of low-income communities and communities of color."[35]

35   Nancy Nadel, Oakland City Council member, Oakland Climate Action Coalition (OCAC) and Ella Baker Center for Human Rights, "A Toolkit to Create Climate Action in Your Community," 2012, http://ellabakercenter.org/sites/default/files/downloads/OCAC-Toolkit.pdf.

The work of the OCAC to develop, pass, and implement the city's ECAP makes Oakland a model for what urban communities across the country can do to localize urban climate change solutions. The direct engagement of OCAC in the development of the Oakland ECAP represents a transformation in how urban climate governance is established and defined. First, the ECAP focused on socially vulnerable communities that have the most to lose from the impact of climate change and suggested not only mitigation measures but also adaptation plans for these areas. Second, the coalition helped create a sustainable development model based on GHG reductions, health co-benefits, local renewable energy, anti-housing displacement from transit-oriented developments, community-based planning, and local green jobs development. And third, it brought together a diverse group of community interests that created a transformative space to contest techno-scientific power and expertise at the local level.

LOCALIZING CLIMATE CHANGE FOR COMMUNITY ACTION

The OCAC effectively localized climate knowledge by changing its conceptualization from an abstract to an urban and local phenomenon. It did so through community engagement, organizing, political mobilization, and education. The coalition's work with community residents—low-income families and communities of color— was highly popular and inclusive. This was a key factor in the adoption of the coalition's recommendations and local expertise in the final plan.[36]

To transform how climate change was perceived in Oakland, the OCAC convened and funded 14 urban climate change workshops throughout the city. These workshops were mainly held in Oakland's low-income and immigrant neighborhoods and engaged more than 1,500 residents to develop local solutions to urban climate change. Several of the workshops were conducted in multiple languages. For example, the nonprofits Movement

36 Kirsch, personal communication; Lehmer, personal communication; Fitzgerald, personal communication.

Generation and Asian Pacific Environmental Network (APEN) facilitated Spanish- and Chinese-language workshops that included many immigrant residents. The inclusive process led to widespread support and engagement for the plan by Oakland residents most impacted by pollution and poverty. These OCAC events are a significant accomplishment in community engagement in their attendance numbers alone: as previously noted, only 200 individuals attended the city-sponsored workshops.

The OCAC further localized climate knowledge through youth engagement programs. For example, the OCAC hosted a solar-powered concert featuring legendary hip-hop artists Pete Rock and C. L. Smooth to promote a Climate Adaptation Work Day at Laney Community College. More than 350 Oakland residents, many of them youth, helped install a garden and rainwater catchment system at the college. OCAC member Forward Together organized 80 high school students in East Oakland in role-playing activities on what climate solutions look like in their homes, schools, and neighborhoods. A Community Convergence for Climate Action Day was also held that included a theatrical performance on climate change by high school girls, live hip-hop concerts, and a report from Oakland community residents who attended OCAC's climate workshops in East and West Oakland. The Community Convergence event intended to demonstrate the high level of interest by local residents in the development of the ECAP and to create a space for residents to participate in climate solutions that went beyond the conventional abstract GHG emission reduction strategies.

Additionally, the OCAC facilitated workshops on disaster preparedness for low-income communities that focused on the impact of climate change through interactive games and learning initiatives. These included the *Are You a Climate Change Survivor?* activity workbook, board games like the Climate Justice Human Bingo and Community Resilience Lifeboat, and fact sheets that provided engaging activities to raise awareness about climate change impacts in Oakland neighborhoods. Through such collaborative projects, Oakland set the trend for a holistic approach to climate action planning. The interactive activities were developed to focus on creating spaces where diverse people and organizations could imagine and implement solutions that protect Oakland residents from the threat of local impacts of climate change, such as heat waves, floods, wildfires, poor air quality, and rising utility costs. Brian Beveridge, co-executive director of the West Oakland Environmental Indicators Project and OCAC member, reports:

> We have developed climate action education tool kits and a series of fact sheets that grew out of our previous work on air quality, health, and transportation. We held several community trainings to explore how to engage community residents on these issues. We started by bringing people together and talking about assets and vulnerability; talking about things they want to protect. It

starts as a mapping exercise, we look at all the places we are strong before we look at our vulnerabilities.... At the community level it is not technocratic. You can't just say there is some technological fix for people because we are really not protecting hard assets; we are talking about people surviving as a community during a disaster.[37]

37   Brian Beveridge, personal communication, June 3, 2013.

In addition to community engagement events, the OCAC turned to electoral politics—specifically, the 2010 mayoral and city council races. On March 30, 2010, the OCAC organized a 200-person rally at City Hall, where Oakland City Council members and candidates listened to labor and green business leaders' recommendations on how the ECAP should be developed and adopted. Andreas Cluver, secretary-treasurer for the Alameda County Building Trades Council, described a relationship between climate change, local politics, and community interests: "I spoke at the [city hall] rally to show that labor leaders and community leaders are united for job-creating climate solutions. By passing a strong ECAP, we can get our members off the bench and into jobs."[38] The OCAC also hosted a larger formal event, the Green Mayoral Forum, on September 14, 2010, where more than 200 local residents—a majority of them people of color—convened to listen to the candidates' responses on how they would advocate for the implementation and adoption of the ECAP. Hosting the Green Mayoral Forum and the rally at City Hall set a strong precedent that elected officials in the city needed to have an explicit

38   Andreas Cluver, quoted in OCAC and Ella Baker Center, "A Toolkit," 3.

policy agenda that linked climate change with job creation and environmental health equity.[39]

39 Garzon, personal communication; Beveridge, personal communication; and Kirsch, personal communication.

URBAN CIVIC EPISTEMOLOGIES AND OAKLAND'S TRANSFORMATIVE CLIMATE

Through the framework of urban civic epistemologies, the ECAP has become a site of innovation in both the production of knowledge and the ordering of political activity (see Table 2). The ECAP is more than just a technical development in how a locality measures and tracks climate change: it represents new experiments in environmental governance. Such experiments, according to environmental policy scholar Clark Miller, "are important features of new emerging civic epistemologies in local, regional, and global settings.... [T]hey are technologies through which people are co-producing new ways of knowing and ordering the world at these scales."[40] The construction of urban climate change in Oakland is the result of extensive experimentation with public participation in expert advisory processes at various scales. These processes create new local civic epistemologies that developed a new conceptual model of 'nature' for defining and measuring urban climate change.

40 Miller, "New Civic Epistemologies," 405.

The concept of civic epistemology highlights the contested roles and rights of residents in regard to the production of public knowledge. The government's role as producer and consumer of knowledge holds an important space in the development of civic epistemologies.

Governments often define environmental issues and the terms in which residents are included in relevant policy decisions and debates. This process influences which knowledge claims are more likely to be considered valid and used in environmental governance processes.[41]

41 Illes, "Identifying Environmental Health Risks."

42 Miller, "New Civic Epistemologies," 406.

Table 2 Transformative urban climate change in the Oakland ECAP.

Transformative ECAP Action Measures	Outcomes
One of the Highest GHG Reduction Goals in the State	A higher GHG reduction target allowed the coalition to demand local measures that represented their definition of urban climate change
Community Knowledge and Expertise shaped the ECAP	Through the framework of environmental justice, the ECAP is an innovation in both the production of knowledge and political activity
Social Equity in Urban Climate Action Plan	Strengthened the diversity and stability of neighborhoods by preventing tenant displacement and preserving affordable housing. Required local adaptation plans in the most vulnerable communities. Defined "urban climate change as the greatest public health challenge." Built community resilience by growing food on idle, underutilized, and vacant lots
Energy Democracy	Provided locally produced renewable energy options within the city. Provided alternatives to service provided by the investor owned utility, Pacific Gas & Electric. Established a Community Choice Aggregation district to pool electric utility users to form a co-op
Holistic Approach to Urban Climate Action Planning and Community Engagement	ECAP represents a new conceptual model of nature and society and new relationships among experts, residents, and the public for defining and addressing urban climate change

Governments also use quantitative statistics as an instrument of statecraft, "to imagine society, the economy, and the nation and to lend to the exercise of public policy a semblance of rationality, control, and accountability."[42] The concept of downscaled climate change has gained relevance in policy settings partly through methods to quantify and measure global GHG emissions reductions and to use the results to guide public decisions. Therefore, use of local knowledge and the consideration of community benefits in the development of Oakland's ECAP measures provide examples of how this occurrence took place against the use of quantitative knowledge in environmental governance.

The contestation of quantitative knowledge in local climate action planning, or what some may call "carbon fundamentalism," was evident in the early stages of the Oakland ECAP. In the case of the urban climate change in Oakland, the ECAP helped environmental justice communities transform the environment into an object that is comprehended, managed, and governed locally. According to Aaron Lehmer, one of OCAC's Steering Committee members:

> The ECAP was seen as an environmental justice and local green economic development strategy for the community and coalition. From the city's standpoint initially it was a bit of struggle to frame it in this manner. At first they held a carbon fundamentalism that often comes with climate work, where people get focused just on the GHG emissions and they lose sight of the broader community benefits.... But working closely with talented city staff, we were able to reframe it to the city council as a plan that could address GHG emissions and also public health and equity.[43]

Defining both local and global climate change depends on how knowledge is produced and on relationships of power between heterogeneous actors in society.

43   Lehmer, personal communication, 2011.

44 Marybeth Long Martello, "A Paradox of Virtue?: 'Other' Knowledges and Environment-Development Politics," *Global Environmental Politics* 1, no. 3 (2001): 114–41.

45 Sheila Jasanoff and Marybeth Long Martello, eds., "Globalization and Environmental Governance," introduction to *Earthly Politics: Local and Global in Environmental Governance* (Cambridge, MA: MIT Press, 2004), 5.

By focusing on the urban civic epistemologies of climate change (see Table 3), we can see how local knowledge forms as an alternative to techno-scientific instruments and overcomes problems of introducing universal science and policy into "local" contexts.[44] In this process we understand that "global solutions to environmental governance cannot realistically be contemplated without at the same time finding opportunities for local self-expression."[45]

Table 3 Source: Adapted from Clark Miller, "New Civic Epistemologies of Quantification: Making Sense of Indicators of Local and Global Sustainability," *Science Technology Human Values* 30, no. 3 (2005): 414.

Civic Epistemologies of Oakland's Climate Change

Spatial Frame	Multiscalar: Local/Regional/Global
Form of Knowledge	Professional expertise and local knowledge
Institutional Organizations	Community-based organizations, government agencies, businesses
Policy Relevance	Local Land-Use Planning, State & Regional Climate Action Plans, Population Health Goals
Regime of Trust	Community Participation, expert-lay engagement
Definition of Climate Change	Urban environment, equity, public health, green economic development, co-pollutants, GHG emissions, community resilience

The way in which residents and government have addressed climate change in Oakland has created a distinct social order that is changing epistemic cultures and democratic societies. This process is forcing professional experts and policymakers to give up some control over how climate change is defined as well as how research is formulated and conducted. In Oakland climate change policies are entwined with attempts to reimagine what the city stands for and how environmental citizenship is produced. The environmental citizen that emerges in response to global climate change can have decidedly local roots. Through the use of local knowledge and practice, the environmental citizen can earn some degree of voice, representation, and agency.[46] As shown in Oakland, environmental justice communities feature centrally in the city's urban climate change interventions. They have earned valuable recognition for what they know about the socio-ecological dynamics of their environments and how they put that knowledge to use in the policymaking process to benefit their communities.

A theoretical analysis of civic epistemologies is emerging that focuses on the interaction between the regulatory science of climate change and environmental justice groups to develop strategies that integrate climate change interventions with population health at the local level. The case of urban climate change in Oakland illustrates how various actors gather, evaluate, and use scientific and public health knowledge in different ways when determining which climate change risks require policy intervention. Expert commissions typically limit the data that they will consider in their deliberation and may be less open to resident input: in this instance, environmental justice groups demanded that definitions of climate change risk include human health impacts in addition to threats to city infrastructure and ecological systems.

46   Marybeth Long Martello, "Arctic Indigenous Peoples as Representations and Representatives of Climate Change," *Social Studies of Science* 38, no. 3 (2008): 351–76.

This case study of climate change governance in Oakland demonstrates how environmental and social justice groups created new forms of knowledge to inform public policy decisions. Oakland's ECAP represents power and scalar shifts in environmental governance: from global, techno-scientific practice to local, environmental justice praxis. This process is also changing the location of authority, as community advocates have displaced government experts from having exclusive control over the definition and production of technical knowledge. It is important to note that these types of local strategies have limitations and are not easily replicable. Climate planning and science can only be influenced by lay publics that expend a significant amount of social capital to organize local coalitions, develop knowledge frameworks, and mobilize political strategies to change climate policy. For disorganized communities, the opportunities to integrate GHG reduction measures, public health, and social equity into a city's climate action plan are not likely to materialize.

As an emerging analytical and policy domain, urban climate change policy represents a series of challenges for scientists, city planners, lay publics, and policymakers. The combination of uncertain science, local relevance, and heterogeneous policy contexts requires new mechanisms for environmental governance that acknowledge the difficulty of localizing global climate change while maintaining technical legitimacy and social authority.[47] Environmental knowledge production and governance

47 Corburn, "Cities, Climate Change and Urban Heat Island Mitigation."

are linked to human self-understanding and social relations: to discover and address new knowledge about nature, institutionalized practices need to be revised in innovative ways. Urban climate change initiatives in Oakland highlights a novel approach in environmental governance that values and reflects historical experience, culture, social practices, and lay understanding, which are quite different from knowledge produced through lab experiments or disciplined empirical observations.

Oakland's climate change action plan, in essence, is a representation of the natural world that gained validity through a local, mutually sustaining interaction between the *is* and the *ought*: of how things are and how they should be.[48] Conventional climate policies are problematic because they separate the epistemic from the normative, divorcing *is* from *ought*. Sheila Jasanoff elaborates, noting that "conventional policies detach global fact from local value, projecting a new totalizing image of the world as it is, without regard for the layered investments that societies have made in worlds as they wish them to be. It therefore destabilizes knowledge at the same time as it seeks to stabilize it."[49] By contrast, as Oakland demonstrates, the epistemic claims of environmental science are trusted more when techno-scientific practices, cultural values, and democratic politics are more closely integrated.

The conceptual construction of climate change in Oakland exemplifies the emergence of local knowledge as a resource for achieving GHG reductions, health co-

48   Sheila Jasanoff, "A New Climate for Society," *Theory, Culture & Society* 27, nos. 2–3 (2010): 233–53.

49   Ibid., 236.

benefits, and community well-being. Through the framework of urban civic epistemology, the definition of "expert" is transformed and expanded to include lay publics in developing conceptions and strategies about climate change. Environmental justice groups are generating new data inputs for the localization of climate change that go beyond universal approaches to climate policy. In so doing, they have called critical attention to the cultural and experiential dimension of knowledge production and local practice.

Immigrant Spatial Politics in Metropolitan Miami, 1957–2005

H. Fernando Burga

Planning literature has documented the presence of
immigrants in American cities as stakeholder groups in
need of advocacy but has underemphasized the agency
and capacity of immigrants to shape planning practice
through alternative political claims. The planning history
of Metropolitan Miami demonstrates that planning data,
knowledge, and techniques are subject to mobilization
not only by urban planners in their traditional roles but
also by particular groups seeking political control.
Emergent political actors—including new immigrant,
ethnic, and local communities—take part in planning
processes and make their own political claims on the city.
These groups, exemplified by Cuban Americans in the
case of Miami, employed public policy, planning data,

Figure 1 Mariel Boatlift Encampments, Orange Bowl
stadium parking lot, 1980. Source: *Miami Herald* via the
South Florida Historical Museum.

urban development, the remapping of political territories, and novel governance mechanisms to claim collective agency and influence the new social order according to their own agendas.

I call the practices carried out by immigrant groups claiming political power through urban space "immigrant spatial politics." From the perspective of planning practitioners, immigrant spatial politics is descriptive of a politics of consensus, multiculturalism, and public interest. But it also manifests a contentious politics based on ethnic affiliation, racial disenfranchisement, the experience of exile, and entitlement rights. Immigrant spatial politics defines conflicts between diverse communities claiming recognition, political agency, and territory in milieus redefined by the arrival of new populations. Metropolitan Miami has developed from these tensions and has been shaped by the work of planning professionals, the practices of immigrant communities, and the claims of competing communities.

The urbanism that characterizes metropolitan Miami developed through a combination of boom-and-bust real estate cycles and the arrival of transplanted populations.[1] Bounded by the Atlantic Ocean to the east and the Everglades to the west, the city acquired much of its present land area by the mid-20th century. Its frontier mentality, supported by a tropical climate, affordable property values, and proximity to the Caribbean and Latin America, attracted real estate developers, speculators, and northern industrialists, as well as a diverse

1   Melanie Shell-Weiss, *Coming to Miami: A Social History* (Gainesville: University of Florida Press, 2009). I use "metropolitan Miami" (Metro) and Dade County interchangeably to refer to the same region, and I distinguish "metropolitan Miami" (the larger county area) from the municipal area, which I call Miami or the City of Miami. According to the 2010 US Census, Miami is home to 399,457 people. It is the largest of 34 municipalities and unincorporated areas located in Dade County, which has a total population of 2,496,435.

group of migrants and immigrants seeking economic opportunity there. In the early 1950s, Dade County's population reached one million. Metropolitan Miami's rapid geographic, economic, and population growth strained the area's natural resources and the city's infrastructure.[2] A vast conglomeration of segregated municipalities and unmanaged, unincorporated settlements, metropolitan Miami found itself in need of basic services, local decision-making mechanisms, and updated public policies.[3] Similarly, the region's promise as a strategic hemispheric hub linking investments between the United States, the Caribbean, and Latin America called for comprehensive planning to intervene.

Recognizing these needs, local political leaders and business elites introduced the Dade County Home Rule Charter in 1956.[4] The charter sought to establish a centralized form of regional government (hereafter called Metro) directed by a nine-member commission, to be elected countywide. The commissioners would not only lead Metro's newly established government and represent the people of Dade County, they would also exercise authority over regional planning matters and the creation of new municipalities.

Once passed, the Home Rule Charter put in place a comprehensive framework for urban policy that had three main consequences.[5] First, it created the Dade County Department of Planning and Zoning (DP&Z), in charge of metropolitan planning policies, services, and provisions. Second, it established a first (or upper) "county"

2 Dade County Development Department, "Economic Survey of Metropolitan Miami," report, Dade County Developmental Department, Miami, FL, 1963.

3 Ibid.

4 G. Serino, "Miami's Metropolitan Experiment," *Civic Information* 28 (Gainesville: Administration Clearing Service of the University of Florida, 1958).

5 Dade County Development Department, "Economic Survey."

tier of governance, concerned with regional public services, and a second (or lower) "municipal" tier, responsible for the needs of local municipalities. According to this scheme, the county commission would represent the regional tier, and municipal mayors and their city commissioners would manage local affairs.[6] Third, the charter designated a county commission to manage Dade County's remaining unincorporated areas, making Metro directly accountable in the future development of these areas to the citizens of the entire region.

The Home Rule Charter was highly contentious, as it opposed the progressive ideals of good governance against the traditional interests of speculative development. Metro's federated system dramatically influenced the pattern of uncontrolled development that had previously prevailed in the Miami area. Inspired by the progressive urban reform movement of the 1940s and 1950s, the home rule charter transformed the political dynamics of urban development by forging a new unit of governance —the county commission—and granting it legal power to balance the interests of developers and municipal leaders against regional public interests. Metropolitan planning emerged at this juncture: at the dusk of a local political culture driven by speculative development and the dawn of a new political system emphasizing technocratic management, centralization, and reformist governance.[7]

Beginning in the early 1960s, the county commission mandated a series of planning studies to address the lack of coordinated management within Dade County's

6   The county tier, under the supervision of Metro, was charged with the management of the airport, seaport, crime labs, regional parks department, metropolitan planning department, and environmental regulation. The municipal tier was responsible for the operation of local parks, public works, police, municipal planning and zoning, public libraries, and fire and rescue departments.

7   Edward Sofen, "The Miami Metropolitan Experiment," *Metropolitan Action Studies* 2 (Bloomington: Indiana University Press, 1961).

burgeoning suburbs. This included comprehensive programs to control zoning, land use, traffic, and transportation; spending priorities for regional infrastructure and repair; and the implementation of building-permit mechanisms, property taxation, and processes to ensure that residents in unincorporated areas had political representation. During the 1960s and 1970s, several comprehensive plans were enacted to address these issues. Each plan represented an increasing degree of sophistication, technological innovation, precision, and knowledge about how metropolitan Miami was changing.

The first of these efforts was the Dade County Preliminary Land Use Plan of 1960. In this comprehensive study, metropolitan planners envisioned the rapid, continuing pace of suburban expansion into the Everglades and southwest Dade County. They established basic parameters for proposed urban densities based on Euclidean zoning and the locations of key regional infrastructure. This plan was quickly followed by the Existing Land Use Plan of the same year. This plan mapped the city's built-out areas, providing planners, politicians, and the public with a first view of the extent of Miami's physical growth. It assigned specific land use categories to existing census tracts and located existing street networks, green areas, and major regional infrastructure, such as the airport, seaport, and canals. Through in-depth analysis of existing urban morphology, this plan began to show how existing land uses—or their absence—affect urban development.

Figure 2 Existing Land Use in Dade Country, as mapped by county planners, 1960. This Planning Department document follows professional conventions and reveals limited local knowledge of how Miami's diverse population used its many different spaces. Source: Metropolitan Dade County Planning Department.

These early plans provided the foundation for the 1965 General Land Use Master Plan (GLUMP), a refinement of all previous planning efforts. The GLUMP was the first document of its kind in South Florida, prescribing a detailed future land use footprint for metropolitan Miami. It specified more precise land use designations. It also extended the suburban grid to the edge of the Everglades, imagining a suburban metropolis with densities of less than twelve dwelling units per acre over 80 percent of its territory. Recognizing the planning

challenges posed by such a pattern of sprawl, it also recommended guidelines for regulating and halting urban
development in the city's southwestern and western
areas. However, county commissioners approved it by
resolution rather than by ordinance, rendering its recommendations non-legally binding. During the next decade,
the GLUMP would remain a reference document rather
than an actual instrument of public policy.[8]

By the early 1970s, a new attitude emerged regarding
the value of comprehensive planning. The change in
public opinion was led by activists who called for a new,
comprehensive land use plan to confront the degradation
of natural ecologies across the region.[9] These local efforts
occurred in the context of a national environmental
movement. In 1975, the State of Florida passed the
Local Government Comprehensive Planning Act,
which instructed every city and county in Florida to
adopt a planning blueprint with specific provisions for
the future.[10] Thereafter, Metro adopted its first
Comprehensive Development Metropolitan Plan (CDMP)
by ordinance. By doing so, the core objective of Metro's
official planning policy was to protect South Florida's
natural ecology. The first CDMP emphasized the creation
of an urban growth boundary to prevent future development in the newly designated Everglades National Park
and a balanced distribution of land uses to protect other
ecological preserves. Planners achieved this balance by
creating a series of population distribution maps, which
incorporated statistical calculations of future population

8   Harvey Ruvin, speech delivered to Dade County Commission, Miami, Florida, 1990.

9   Luther J. Carter, *The Florida Experience: Land and Water Policy in a Growth State* (Baltimore, MD: Johns Hopkins University Press, 1974).

10   See Metropolitan Dade County Planning Depart-ment Comprehensive Planning Act of 1975, ss. 163.3161-163.32211 F.S.

Figure 3 The 1985 Metropolitan Development Pattern for Dade County, as proposed in 1975. Source: Metropolitan Dade County Planning Department.

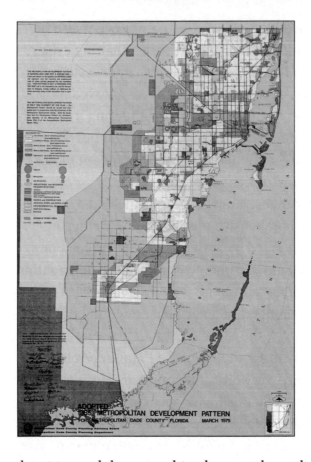

11 Ibid.

densities and demographic changes through 1985.[11] Armed with these projections, they planned facilities such as roadways, mass transit infrastructure, and water and sewer lines accordingly.

THE UNPLANNED POLITICS OF CENTRALIZATION

The two-tier system led to a mode of metropolitan planning focused on the public interest and regional governance. But it also set the stage for new tensions between the power of a centralized Metro government and the lack of political decision-making capacity among residents of the county's unincorporated areas. This tension derived from two main conditions and became a force for ethnic political empowerment within the city of Miami and the region.

One condition was the unfulfilled promise of local governance. When Metro government was conceived in the 1960s, planners envisioned a rational pattern of growth based on the gradual absorption of unincorporated areas. Their expectations were never realized, however, due to an absence in political will and of coordination among county commissioners, leadership problems within existing municipalities, and a lack of organization among suburban and rural residents. The problem of managing local issues in unincorporated areas persisted and, after basic services and provisions had been neglected for decades, eventually turned into an urgent call for action. Residents in unincorporated areas believed that Metro commissioners were detached from the everyday realities that they governed: the public interests that Metro was supposed to serve were left unattended, except during election season.

As this dynamic unfolded, a second condition arose: the demographic transformation of Metropolitan Miami. This process involved the expansion of immigrant populations who had defined Miami's early urbanism in gateway enclaves (such as Little Havana in Miami) and suburban areas. As the number and ethnic composition of these new populations grew and expanded, Metro's management budget, reach, and scope became overburdened. Metro government was slow to develop a system of local representation. New residents in unincorporated areas started to demand access to land use decision making and raised zoning and local governance issues. Meanwhile, wealthy residents in unincorporated areas expressed concern that their taxes were being used to support the financial burden of service provision to new immigrant residents.

Tensions rose between "recipient communities"— poorer, usually immigrant residents of unincorporated areas—and "donor communities," more affluent residents of unincorporated areas and incorporated municipalities. Over time the imbalances between Miami's old and new communities led to political polarization. Different service demands and political constituencies appeared across locations in Dade County in a new social patchwork, composed of existing communities—usually white and African American—and new immigrant communities of Cuban and Hispanic origin.

The changing composition of new immigrants had a deep effect on Metro governance and planning practices and transformed urban politics at both municipal and county levels. Immigrants of Caribbean and Latin-American descent—notably Bahamians, Puerto Ricans, and Cubans—had been coming to South Florida since the first part of the 20th century to join the local tourism

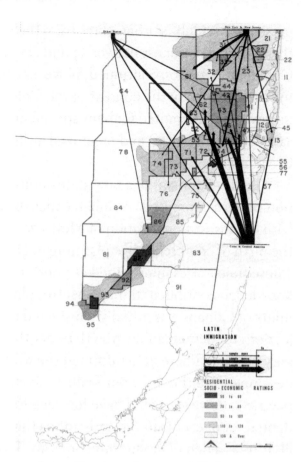

Figure 4   Latino immigration and migration to metropolitan Miami, both of which
concentrated in the eastern
half of Dade County during
the late 1960s. Source:
Metropolitan Dade County
Planning Department.

industry's labor markets. During the 1960s Cubans
started to become a visible minority in Dade County.[12]
Population flows between Miami and Havana had been
commonplace during the 1940s and 1950s for a number
of reasons: among them were Miami's proximity to
Cuba, American political hegemony in the Caribbean,
and US support for the Batista regime. The Cuban
Revolution of 1959 drastically changed this, causing
large waves of Cuban emigration. Fleeing political

12   According to a 2003
demographic profile of Dade
County, "In 1960, only about
five percent of the population was Hispanic and 80
percent was non-Hispanic
White. By 1970 Hispanics
were still less than a quarter
of the population, but in
1980 they were more than a
third." Planning Research
Division, Department of
Planning and Zoning,
"Demographic Profile:
Miami Dade County, Flor-
ida, 1960–2000," Dade
County Planning Research
Division Florida, September
2003, 9.

persecution, Cuba's urban elites were the first to transfer their families, business networks, and capital to Miami. Cuban immigration continued, however, throughout the 1960s and 1970s in the context of the Cold War, as the US government granted Cubans special provisions (such as refugee entry visas) and organized airlifts from Havana to Miami.[13]

13   Alejandro Portes and Alex Stepick, *City on the Edge: The Transformation of Miami* (Berkeley: University of California Press, 1993).

The development of a new state-sponsored immigration pattern composed of Cuban exiles thus coincided with the institutionalization of Metro government and the birth of comprehensive planning in Dade County. These trajectories intertwined as politics and planning knowledge continued to shape Metropolitan Miami. The influx of Cubans was initially considered in planning projections for demographic growth under the broad category "Latin." These data informed the work that planners developed. Neither they nor Dade County's leaders and planners, however, could have foreseen the unprecedented set of events in the early 1980s that would turn "Latin" as a demographic category into "Hispanic" as a political force. The transformation from population flow to political machine would ultimately reshape their plans, usurp urban politics, and reconfigure the political geography of Dade County.

CUBAN-AMERICAN SPATIAL POLITICS

The presence of Cuban exiles in Miami gave the city a distinctive multicultural identity in the 1970s. Cuban

Americans were embraced by locals as model citizens: hardworking, entrepreneurial, and most importantly for the US government, fiercely anticommunist. Following a decade of turmoil in American cities, characterized in part by identity politics and the civil rights movement, Miami's Cuban-American community exemplified an expedient ideological counterpoint to other groups seeking political representation and citizenship. The mostly white leadership of metropolitan Miami embraced the steady influx of Cubans and the increasing internationalization of the city. They celebrated the economic and cultural capital of Latin America as a unique urban brand.

In 1980 a series of events initiated a 12-year period of intense social change that would redefine the city's political structure and unravel the previous work of metropolitan planning. In one year, Miamians experienced urban riots resulting from the acquittal of white police officers in the beating of Arthur McDuffie, the arrival of 125,000 Cuban and 40,000 Haitian refugees, and a violent drug-trafficking crime wave.[14] In the ensuing decade, Cuban Americans went from being a model minority to a grassroots social movement that elected Cuban-American municipal and county leaders and radically reconfigured the city's political status quo. As this process developed metropolitan planners sought to address the ongoing Latin-Americanization of the city. This time, the objectives of their public mandate consisted of assessing Miami's immigrants to identify their impact on future planning projects, community budgets, and the alloca-

14　According to Portes and Stepick, the Mariel Boatlift, the Haitian exodus to Miami, and the racial tensions provoked by the McDuffie beating created the perception that Miami had become a "Third World" city. Marvin Dunn notes that the McDuffie beating led to the most "violent racial spasm in the history of the city." Marvin Dunn, *Black Miami in the Twentieth Century* (Gainesville: Florida University Press, 1997), 267.

tion of local resources. Their planning activities—the collection, recording, and interpretation of demographic data, and the demarcation of census tracts to regulate, manage, and plan the urban territory—were used to mobilize Cuban Americans and their allies. These political-planning engagements can be characterized broadly under five interlinked categories: performative, community-development, discursive, electoral, and coalition-building. The resulting spatial politics of Miami's immigrant population emerged in three distinct phases: crisis, community development, and ethnic empowerment.

CRISIS

The Mariel Boatlift brought an influx of Cuban political refugees in need of immediate emergency aid, protection, shelter, and support to Miami. Following the occupation of the Peruvian Embassy in Havana and the opening of the Mariel port in April 1980, scenes of Cuban Americans chartering boats from Miami and Key West to collect Cuban refugees dominated television screens over the span of six months. From May to September 1980, as a geopolitical tug of war between the United States and Cuba played out from the Florida straits to Miami's streets, the crisis devolved into a local urban calamity. The US government, county and municipal leaders, Cuban Americans, and metropolitan planners all became involved in the largest immigrant humanitarian crisis to ever hit a major US city.

Figure 5   Mariel Processing Center, Key West Air Force Base Hangar, 1980, housing Cuban refugees. Source: *Miami Herald* via the South Florida Historical Museum.

Figure 6   A Mariel encampment, constructed underneath Interstate 95, 1980. Encampments such as these handled overflow from Miami's processing center for Cuban refugees. Source: *Miami Herald* via the South Florida Historical Museum.

Former City employee Cesar Odio—a Cuban immigrant who arrived to Miami in the 1960s and worked as assistant city manager during the time of the crisis— recalled how he dealt with the unexpected volume of refugees at the request of federal immigration officials.[15] Circumventing the city's decision-making hierarchy,

15   Elaine Del Valle "Mariel: New Leaders Were Forged in the Heat of Mariel Crisis," *Miami Herald*, April 04 2005, http://www. cubanet.org/CNews/y05/ apro5/05e2.htm.

Odio worked with a local network of Cuban-American not-for-profit leaders to set up the first impromptu arrival centers in Little Havana. Odio's strategy took care of the initial waves of refugees, but the continuing volume of arrivals soon overwhelmed Little Havana, forcing him and city staff to improvise additional locations amid continuing municipal, county, and federal paralysis. At the height of the crisis, Marielitos were processed at the Key West Naval Air Station and then placed on buses and driven up Interstate 95 to new arrival centers across metropolitan Dade County.[16] These locations included tent cities in some of Miami's most familiar spaces: underneath the I-95 expressway, in the Orange Bowl, at Tamiami Park, and on the Opa-Locka Air Force Base.

As many as 1,500 Cuban Americans volunteered at these sites as part of a mass relief effort. They fulfilled critical functions; facilitating interactions between local, state, and federal agencies and the Cuban refugees, for example, and working as translators, fingerprint assistants, record keepers, interviewers, and handlers.[17] During a particularly intense period of activity, the center at Tamiami Park processed more than 1,500 refugees in eighteen days. Registered, housed, and monitored in these locations, Marielitos were welcomed by their fellow Cuban brothers and sisters and then released to family members or transferred to encampments in other states.

The immediate reaction of Cuban Americans like Cesar Odio and hundreds of others define the *performative* practice of immigrant spatial politics, the first of five

16 "Marielitos" is the term given to Cuban arrivals from the port of El Mariel.

17 Silvia M. Unzueta, "The Mariel Exodus: A Year in Retrospect" (Miami: Metropolitan Dade County Government Office of the County Manager, 1981).

practices that can be said to characterize immigrant spatial politics. Performative practices involve the transformation of individual actions into a collective political identity through the use of urban space. In this case, Cuban Americans established cross-border solidarity through common ethnic ties, shared political experience, and humanitarian ideals. The scale of the urban spaces where these practices took place mattered. The human scale of the street and its reconfigured spaces—the tent city, the plaza, and sidewalk—became incubators for individual performances of spontaneous solidarity that problematized the dichotomous essentialisms of national origin and citizenship. Within the improvised spaces of the tent cities, the processing centers, and their waiting zones, face-to-face interactions, humanitarian bricolage, and self-actualized agency assembled a new political awareness that signaled a nascent urban citizenship.

Cuban Americans' emotional and visceral encounters with their Cuban brothers and sisters forced difficult evaluations of the arrivals' inclusion as noncitizens and residents' status as a model immigrant community. Cuban Americans came out not only to help their fellow countrymen and women but also to assist their community and, in the process, to represent the city which had incorporated them and had become ethnically more Cuban. For many other residents in Miami, however, the Mariel Boatlift denoted how the city's Latin-Americanization was turning it into a dystopia rather than a paradigm of multiculturalism. Six months after the

Mariel Boatlift, the city continued to overflow with refugees, and discontent with Miami's Cuban community began to appear.

COMMUNITY DEVELOPMENT

Like Cuban Americans, metropolitan planners were called to immediate action in response to the boat crisis. The sudden increase in population caused by the Marielitos rendered recent national census data obsolete.[18] This development complicated metropolitan planning, which depended upon demographic data to develop statistical estimates for public services. Neighborhood agencies ranging from community development corporations to municipal planning departments used this data to help design anti-poverty measures, program workforce trainings and educational initiatives, determine the need for public housing and rental housing vouchers, and distribute community development block grants to organizations in need. Without an accurate count and assessment, the equitable allocation of public funds was impossible. The influx of refugees placed urban management in jeopardy.

Metropolitan planners were aware that the Marielitos' arrival would strongly impact area demographics. After decades of advocacy by Latino groups (including Cuban Americans) at the federal level, the 1980 census unveiled the term "Hispanic" as a statistical category.[19] For the first time in American history, Spanish-origin and

18   Census data was collected until April 1980, a month before the crisis. Peter O'Donnell [pseudo], former head of the Dade County Planning Department, Research Division, interview with author, Miami, Florida, October 12, 2008.

19   G. Christina Mora, *Making Hispanics: How Activists, Bureaucrats and Media Constructed a New American* (Chicago: University of Chicago Press, 2014).

Spanish-speaking groups—Chicanos, Mexican Americans, Texanos, Puerto Ricans, and Cubans—would be counted. Thus, a community that had remained geographically and ideologically divided across the United States became a national minority and gained representation at the urban scale. In December 1980, four months after the end of the boatlift, an executive order by President Carter authorized metropolitan planners to collaborate with the National Census Bureau to gather new demographic statistics.[20] With this directive in hand, Metro planners began to track the habitat trajectories and transitory flows of new arrivals. They aimed to determine the living patterns of new arrivals based on demographic concentrations. The technocratic imperative of counting the new arrivals encouraged immediate coordination between different scales of government—from the city to the county, from the state to the federal government. By mid-1981 the effort began to provide new statistical profiles. The picture that emerged offered compelling evidence of the social service repercussions of the Mariel crisis.[21]

In the immediate years after the Mariel crisis, a not-for-profit community development system grew in metropolitan Miami under the leadership of a network of Cuban-American activists to help provide services to new arrivals and poor Cuban Americans. This apparatus was largely set up by the Cuban National Council (CNC) and its local community development subsidiary, the Corporacion de Desarrollo Comunitario (CODEC). Both

20 White House Executive Order 12256, Census Statistics on Legal Immigrants, 15 December 1980, http://www.presidency.ucsb.edu/ws/?pid=44410.

21 Planning Research Division, "Demographic Profile," 6.

the CNC and CODEC provided wide-ranging services, supported by a network of rising Cuban-American political leaders, executives, and scholars who engaged in public policy debates concerning poverty and immigration issues. This system represented Cuban-American political interests by developing a coherent discourse from community members' contributions and embarking upon an ambitious urban development agenda centered on affordable housing.[22]

The CNC policy discourse emphasized Cuban-American voting practices, economic activities, and cultural life as positive signs of assimilation that challenged refugee stereotypes lingering from the Mariel crisis.[23] The CNC produced reports disclaiming that Miami was politically divided or fragmented due to the presence of Cuban Americans, and it called for tolerance among its different ethnic communities. This policy discourse also aligned with the economic agendas of local Cuban-American businesses and interest groups[24] and focused on the basic needs of Marielitos and poor segments within Miami's Cuban-American community.[25] The CNC confronted the general perception that Cuban Americans were ideologically driven and reactionary by reframing their political positions and economic interests as moderate, tolerant, and most importantly, deeply patriotic according to American ideals.

The CNC's urban development projects focused particularly on the funding, design, construction, and management of public and affordable housing. Before 1980

22   C. Verdecia, "Help Hispanics Adapt," *Miami Herald*, January 13, 1988, 2F.

23   Guarione M. Diaz, *Ethnic Block before Voting and Polarization in Miami* (Miami, FL: Cuban American National Council, 1991); and Guarione M. Diaz, *Laws and Politics in Florida's Redistricting* (Miami: Cuban American National Council, 1992).

24   Miguell Del Campillo and Guarione M. Diaz, "Miami's Latin Businesses," report, Cuban American National Council, Miami, 1988; Strategy Research Corporation, "The South Florida Latin Market," report, Strategy Research Corporation, Miami, 1988; Thomas D. Boswell, "The Cubanization and Hispanization of Metropolitan Miami," report, Cuban American National Council with the Cuban American Policy Center and Department of Geography, University of Miami, Florida, 1995.

25   Guarione M. Diaz, "Evaluation and Identification of Policy Issues in the Cuban Community," report, Cuban American National Council, Miami, 1981; Guarione M. Diaz, "The Challenge of Education: No Time to Waste, No Room for Failure," report, Cuban American National Council, Miami, 1990; Guarione M. Diaz, "Housing Needs of the Hispanic Elderly in Greater Miami," report, Cuban American National Council, Miami, 1992; B. Gutierrez, "More Hispanic Elderly Face Poverty," *Miami Herald*, October 14, 1984, 1G.

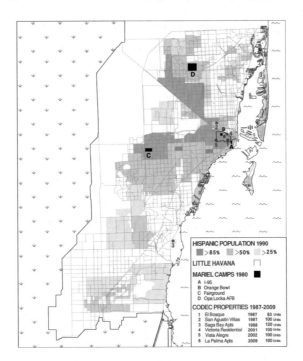

Figure 7 The Hispanic population in Dade County, 1990. Those living in Mariel encampments and CODEC properties are depicted in black and red, respectively. Source: H. Fernando Burga.

metropolitan Miami did not have an institution dedicated to the housing needs of Hispanics.[26] The CNC initiated CODEC in 1981 as a nonprofit branch dedicated to securing low-income housing for Hispanics. During the first half of the 1980s, CODEC bought and developed prime real estate to build affordable apartment units throughout Miami's Little Havana. The funds for these projects came from Dade County taxpayers and were channeled into new construction and the provision of mortgage subsidies for low-income Hispanics across the metropolitan region.[27] In 1985 CODEC enlarged its urban development scope by incorporating two for-profit

26   C. Boyd, "Firm Complements Public Housing," *Miami Herald*, December 28, 1986, 7H.

27   Metropolitan Dade County Planning Department, "What the Surtax Does," *Miami Herald*, October 21, 1987, 1B.

agencies that assisted in building management, housing acquisition, and loan management for poor Hispanics living in Dade County. Over the course of 30 years, CODEC built a total of 1,900 housing units across the United States, including 150 condominiums for working families in Florida.[28] Units built in Miami were located primarily in Little Havana, where the need for public housing was evident in the recalibrated 1981 census and where historically there has been a concentration of Cuban immigrants and poor Hispanics.[29]

28 CNC, "Elderly," http://cnc.org/elderly/.

29 A. Figueroa, "200 Apartments to House Elderly, Disabled," *Miami Herald*, October 22, 1987, 7.

The realization of a community development apparatus on behalf of Cuban-American interests illustrates another key practice of immigrant spatial politics: the use of planning data, techniques, and knowledge to facilitate the political agenda of an immigrant community. In this case the community development system employed discursive practices and electoral practices. The discursive practices introduced an alternative political order by emphasizing the benefits of Cuban-American immigration in Miami. These benefits included social, political, and economic contributions: multicultural diversity, the celebration of assimilation and democracy, and Miami's transformation into an international hub of business.

This strategic rhetoric also enabled a platform that would stimulate political action in the form of electoral practices. The locations of CODEC's projects emphasized the spatial relationship between affordable housing built by the Cuban-American community development system and the settlement patterns of Cuban immigrants in

Little Havana. This co-location would not have been possible without the demographic data developed by metropolitan planners during the 1980s to justify the need for social service provision within specific immigrant neighborhoods. This concentration of residents, which led to the construction of new housing, spurred additional residential concentrations that would create powerful new Cuban-American voting blocs. These would in turn bring Cuban Americans to power in the city of Miami in the mid-1980s, and on the Dade County Commission in the 1990s.

ETHNIC EMPOWERMENT

During the second half of the 1980s, Cuban-American empowerment entailed another practice that defines immigrant spatial politics: coalition building. Such a practice involves the formation of political alliances to redistribute political power in an urban space. Cuban-American machine politics developed in tandem with a Cuban-American community development system.

In late 1980 the overwhelming presence of Marielitos in Miami's streets and the pressure they brought to municipal and county budgets provoked a xenophobic backlash in the form of an English-only referendum. The measure challenged the use of public funds for bilingual education and English-language training programs aimed at refugees and Cuban-American residents. Supported by mostly white (and some African American)

30 Guillermo J. Grenier, "The Politics of Language in Miami" in *Miami Now! Immigration, Ethnicity, and Social Change*, ed. Guillermo J. Grenier and Alex Stepick (Gainesville: University of Florida Press, 1992), 119.

English-speaking residents in metropolitan Miami, the measure passed with unanimous support.[30] As a result, Cuban Americans felt tarnished by the stigma of the Mariel crisis. By helping Marielitos, they went from being held as a model minority to being marginalized in a city they had called home for two decades.

In response, Cuban Americans organized over the next four years to consolidate their political base. They mobilized a political machine that brought the city of Miami—and eventually Metro—under their control. The political awakening of Cuban Americans was achieved with the support of the Cuban-American community development apparatus. It involved the deployment and reproduction of rhetorical frames that exalted the local contributions of Cuban Americans in print (with a campaign aimed at the *Miami Herald*) and over the airwaves (through its courtship of Little Havana's radio stations). It also involved "Votatones," voting registration and publicity campaigns initiated by organizations such as the Spanish-American League Against Discrimination (SALAD). The main goal was to build Cuban support and enhance awareness about social issues affecting Cuban Americans in Miami. As Cuban-American leaders and not-for-profit agencies coalesced around a common identity and the political imperative of representation, SALAD, the CNC, and others aligned the political future of Cuban Americans with the well-being of Marielitos.

The fruits of these efforts came in 1985 when Xavier Suarez became Miami's first Cuban-American mayor.[31]

31 D. Sewell, "Miami Elects First Cuban Born Mayor," *Daily Reporter*, November 13, 1985, 3A.

Immigrant Spatial Politics in Metropolitan Miami, 1957–2005

Suarez's rise to power marked the beginning of a wave of electoral victories that brought more Hispanics (mainly Cuban Americans) to municipal power across Dade County.[32] Cuban-American political leaders then aimed their efforts at Metro government. The initial challenge was to change both the composition of Metro's county commission and its voting system, in order to establish the necessary concentration of voters to elect new leaders.

In 1986 the *Meek v. Metropolitan Dade County* lawsuit set in motion a series of verdicts and appeals to change Metro's governance structure to reflect the electoral power of Black and Hispanic residents. A coalition of African American and Hispanic activists, which included Mayor Suarez, represented the plaintiffs in the suit. They claimed that Metro was in violation of Section Two of the Federal Voting Rights Act of 1965 and that the county's new demographic composition required a revised framework of political representation.[33] Their legal argument was based on demographic data supplied by metropolitan planners in the 1980s. The plaintiffs argued that although Metro was founded in 1957 on the equal representation of all of Dade County, the number and composition of county commission seats had not evolved to represent the increase in ethnic minorities in the city. Instead, the homogenous composition of Metro's leadership and representation structure diluted the underrepresented majority of ethnic votes.

In 1991 the Meek coalition won the lawsuit, which meant that all district boundaries would be redrawn to

32 Following Suarez's victory, Cuban-American leaders galvanized around a discourse of successful assimilation, stating that Miami had become an important hub of tourism, business, and finance as a result of Cuban-American economic and cultural contributions. Portes and Stepick, *City on the Edge.*

33 See *Meek v. Metropolitan Dade County*, Fla 805 F. Supp 967, No. 86-1820-CIV, 11 September 1992, Miami, Florida. By 1992 Hispanics and Blacks made up 70 percent of the county population but had inadequate representation in county governance.

reflect the demographic reality of Dade County. The plaintiffs, together with staff from the Dade County elections department and metropolitan planning officials, established an ad hoc committee to determine how the legal decision could be implemented: their work changed the Dade County voting system from a nine-member commission elected from the population at large to a thirteen-member commission elected from specific districts. Together with redistricting, this established a new structure of representation for the 1992 election as well as a new blueprint for Metro's political future.

Metropolitan planners' data and expertise determined the size and configuration of the new voting precincts. In this process, metropolitan planners assessed the potential socioeconomic repercussions of shifting boundaries according to the new demographic concentrations. They sought to provide accurate information in various scenarios where ethnic concentrations could be balanced among different areas to prevent extreme socioeconomic, racial, and ethnic divisions in the metropolitan Miami. Despite their efforts, the political strategies of committee members undermined their recommendations. Peter O'Donnell, former head of the Dade County Planning Department, Research Division, explained:

> The working group would touch base with us [metropolitan planners]: What about this alignment? What about that alignment? What would it mean in terms of the shift of population percentages, etc. The committee would send us a draft

alignment. We would give them the recommendation. Our work was turned into "ifs": What if I did
this x percent more Hispanic in that neighborhood? What if that group was not included in the
Black commissioners' new district? But the decisions were made by them and by the judge. It was
like a school desegregation issue. In many cases it
was an ad hoc decision of the players who were
involved from those areas, their municipalities,
their representatives, and their consultants.[34]

34   O'Donnell, interview.

According to O'Donnell, the plaintiffs strategically
identified the placement of new district boundaries.
They wanted these areas to be defined according to
zones where their constituencies were politically active
and where the named plaintiffs carried political clout. In
this way decisions over district boundaries were not only
determined on a block-by-block basis in light of their ethnic composition and numbers, they were also based on
the imperative of concentrating African American and
Hispanic votes to ensure specific candidates would win
the elections.

The *Meek v. Metropolitan Dade County* lawsuit produced a new political geography for metropolitan Miami.
It dramatically redistributed power according to a strategic alliance between African American and Hispanic
groups seeking to end the political dominance of white
communities. This coalition took the political concerns
of Cuban-American and African American enclaves and
brought them to the regional scale, where a common

democratizing force could be forged on legal grounds. At the beginning of the 1990s, metropolitan planning practice would once again be reshaped by immigrant spatial politics. The legacy of disenfranchisement in the city's unincorporated areas, however, would continue to foster a new political force to challenge the core ideals that underlined their various practices.

COUNTERING IMMIGRANT SPATIAL POLITICS

Metro confronted a new social landscape, and a complicated future, after the 1980s. The rise of ethnic power in the county commission and its perceived historic inefficiency led to a series of secessionist mobilizations that challenged its legitimacy and central authority. In the early 1990s, "communities of interest"—mostly white and affluent residential groups that self-identified as donor communities—mobilized against Metro's failure to establish services in unincorporated areas and provide appropriate local representation.[35] Their discourse was framed by the need for police protection, governmental accountability, and access to local government and zoning control.

Two historical tensions had intersected in the early 1990s to create this result. The first was Metro's institutional failure to establish an effective local government presence in unincorporated areas as the population of metropolitan Miami grew. The second was the empowerment of Miami's ethnic (mainly Cuban-American) communities—a development that was not anticipated by

35   The term "communities of interest" was first used to describe smaller areas in unincorporated Dade County that perceived the county commission was unresponsive. Citizen's Advisory Committee, "Metro Dade County Citizen's Advisory Committee on County-Wide Incorporation, Final Report, February, Dade County Charter Sec. 5.05" (Miami, FL: Metropolitan Dade County, 1992), 4.

Metro's leaders and planners. The new political geography established in 1991 by the *Meek* decision intensified the perception that county leadership had fallen into the hands of ethnic minorities. The subsequent 1992 Dade County election led to new leadership on the commission based on a majority of minorities. Under these circumstances the political influence of "communities of interest" weakened, and municipal incorporation came to be seen as the best tool to both achieve representation and counteract the loss of power.

Municipal rebellions began in Miami's intercoastal communities and moved westward into unincorporated areas. In 1991 the village of Key Biscayne became independent from Dade County, marking the first time in the 30-year history of Metro that residents of an area had voted for self-determination.[36] The island's revolt caught the attention of other groups with similar concerns, who mobilized to achieve similar results. Neighbors, activists, and rising political figures drove get-out-the-vote campaigns, organized petitions and demonstrations, and guided the work of Dade County officials and planners. Residential communities claimed political control over their neighborhoods by forming autonomous political territories under mandates of self-determination.

Between 1995 and 2005, eight new municipalities were formed. These rebellions took place in two waves. In the first wave—from 1995 to 1997—"communities of interest" revolted while metropolitan planners improvised urban policy recommendations and county leaders

36 A. Faiola, "Key Biscayne: Dade's 1st New City in 30 Years," *Miami Herald,* June 16, 1991, 1B.

voted on measures to slow the pace of incorporation. Three cities gained independence before the establishment of a moratorium on incorporation: Aventura, Pinecrest, and Sunny Isles. The second wave of incorporation took place from 2000 to 2005, after the first moratorium was lifted due to impending lawsuits and rising discontent among residents in unincorporated areas. Metro allowed additional "communities of interest" to incorporate if they accepted budgetary restrictions to address the problem of fiscal disparity. The new municipalities that formed during this time were Miami Lakes, Palmetto Bay, Miami Gardens, and Cutler Bay. Thereafter, a second moratorium on incorporation was instituted in 2005.

In the context of both immigrant spatial politics and municipal rebellions, metropolitan planning became a contested field where the spatial dimensions of social transformation were manifested. Planners' labor, expertise, and knowledge were just as entangled in the rebellions of municipal incorporation as they were intertwined with the practices that defined Cuban-American empowerment. Among other activities, metropolitan planners had to invent new planning mechanisms to deal with the incorporation movements, and as the rebellions became imminent, they had to adopt formal steps to manage incorporation requests, evaluate petitions, develop area studies analyzing boundaries, assess tax bases, and provide demographic information needed to evaluate the financial sustainability of proposed new municipalities.

The incorporations confirmed metropolitan planners' worst fear: the socioeconomic disintegration of Dade County. At the core of secessionism lay the problem of fiscal solvency for both Metro and the communities seeking incorporation. On the one hand, the rapid series of secessions threatened the fiscal base of Dade County, as rich donor communities took expensive property tax inventories into newly incorporated territories. Poorer communities seeking incorporation also endangered the economic solvency of potential new cities of concentrated poverty. On the other hand, the more recent effects of the 2008 foreclosure crisis on county government budgets, operations, and municipal management energized the concepts of self-determination, decentralization, and smaller government. Some of the communities that incorporated during the 1990s and early 2000s are today among the most financially stable cities in Dade County. Their success provides lessons, tactics, and strategies for those hoping to form new municipalities in the future.

Although the municipal rebellions eroded Metro government, they also represented a form of counter-spatial politics at multiple scales. By adopting many of the practices of immigrant spatial politics to produce counter-claims, they symbolized the continuation of a complex process of urban democratization that began with Cuban-American empowerment in the 1980s. The rebellions expanded the theater of spatial politics from immigrant empowerment to the realm of hyper-local secessionism.

I have traced the key episodes in the history of metropolitan planning in Dade County to examine the relationship between immigrant incorporation, planning, and urban politics. By focusing on the case of Cuban-American empowerment, I have attempted to develop the concept of immigrant spatial politics, which defines the practices that immigrant groups may use to gain political control through the use of urban space. I have defined this concept to involve performative, community-development, discursive, electoral, and coalition-building practices.

The concept of immigrant spatial politics considers not only how urban space is shaped by the urban politics of immigrant empowerment but also how urban politics is reformulated by the way immigrants use urban space to self-empower. Additionally, immigrant spatial politics recognizes that political practices carried out by immigrants have physical and scalar qualities. Its practices and outcomes range from the scale of the street in individual performances bound by collective interests, to the scale of the neighborhood in the intervention of community-development toolkits. It includes the scale of the region in the legal mandates that dictate planning documents, and multi-scalar activities in the municipal incorporation efforts carried out by communities of interest.

The methods for determining immigrant spatial politics do not constitute a determined or linear approach.

Immigrant spatial politics represents a moving field where multiple historical trajectories, discourses, and concrete actions overlap over a long period of time to establish associations between planned, unplanned, and counter-planned outcomes. The history of immigrant spatial politics is not linear, heroic, or monumental; it is a history based on the cumulative results of discreet actions defined by the negotiation, contestation, and consensus of groups who have power and those who claim it in a city transformed by immigration.

Planning history in United States cities requires the formulation of concepts articulating how immigrants claim both individual and political agency by using urban space to reshape not only their social milieu but also planning practice. The concept of immigrant spatial politics offers a framework derived from the combination of data gathered from interviews, historical archives, and spatial analysis to identify the practices employed by immigrant groups to achieve political control. In doing so it advances understanding of the relationship between immigrant incorporation, planning, and urban politics.

Afterword: A Conversation with Toni L. Griffin

Fallon Samuels Aidoo

In an interview conducted in August 2015, Toni L. Griffin discussed how, as an urban planner, social advocate, and director of the J. Max Bond Center on Design for the Just City (JMBC), she addresses injustice in American cities.[1] The conversation covered both planned and spontaneous interventions, ranging from strategic planning and public-private partnerships to crowd-sourced design and grassroots organizing. What became clear is that there is no clear path toward a just city. That being said, individuals who collectively advocate for justice—not just equity but also ownership, inclusivity, and connectivity—have made a way for political empowerment and equality, especially in "legacy cities," the nation's older, depopulated urban areas. The spatial politics of such collective action provides the focus of this excerpt, and hopefully, future research and reflection.

Fallon Samuels Aidoo (FSA)   How does the JMBC engender justice in places where injustice remains unaddressed or repressed?

Toni L. Griffin (TLG)   If we are to learn more about social and spatial justice and put more learning into practice, JMBC must be a place that helps critically assess, review, and put back out into the world some critique, analysis, and understanding of what's working and what's not, what's missing and how to fill the gap. Hopefully our latest project—a methodology for measuring design's impact on justice in the built environment—will enable communities of any size or type to assign themselves "just city" values, assess deficiencies, and benchmark where they are in the process of realizing their goals. With metrics that help us know justice and injustice when we see them, we can motivate new interventions and investments that achieve a greater presence of justice.

1   Housed within the Spitzer School of Architecture on the City College of New York (CCNY) Harlem campus, the design center offers coursework, hosts a Vimeo channel, and collaborates on the revitalization of America's "legacy cities." Griffin, one of the first female African Americans licensed to practice architecture in Illinois, is the center's founding director.

FSA   To what extent are scalar epistemologies of politics critical to conceptualizing a just city?

TLG   It depends on what scale you're working at when figuring out which partnership models work best. For example, *Detroit Future City* began as a mayoral initiative ("Detroit Works Project") to address real-time urgencies while also thinking strategically about long-term outcomes. However, it became clear that the city's effort to comprehensively address Detroit's challenges through strategic intervention citywide instead required cross-sector stewardship, inclusive of government, civic, community, philanthropic, and business leaders. A steering committee composed of these leaders led the effort, together with over 160,000 local participants, to incorporate different scales of information and types of informants— neighborhood-focused and citywide, statistical and experiential— into a data-driven and inclusive planning process. For instance, grassroots community groups that inventoried property conditions in their census tracts bridged Detroit's one-time "windshield survey"[2] of residential property conditions and a stagnant Vacant Properties database.... Being able—and willing—to adopt cross-sectoral leadership for a range of different issues engenders broader civic participation, which then engenders more trust in the process and allows us to integrate and prioritize a broad range of issues that impact how cities move forward.

FSA   What kinds of transformative partnerships do you envision making a difference?

TLG   Quite frankly, and maybe controversially, I think we're at a time, particularly in cities that are so polarized … when the table [needs] to be set for everyone. We can no longer rely solely on top-down or bottom-up approaches to urban transformation; instead we must build partnerships that include the grassroots and the grass-

---

2   Neither extensive nor experiential, windshield surveys are a vehicle-based form of spatial and social observation that identifies community needs and assets worthy of further inquiry or intervention.

tops.... People and organizations, whether formal or informal, begin to understand the power of their agency when they align with others who share common thinking and work together in pursuit of their interconnected agendas. At the moment, many advocates of tactical urbanism contend, "We don't have to create elaborate structures or processes that include government to get things done. That's just going to slow us down. There's a need to be met, and we can problem-solve how to do it by ourselves. Let's find some resources and just do it." Tactical interventions at smaller scales have yielded some extraordinary impacts in communities across the country, but in some instances they raise questions about inclusivity—who initiates action?, who is engaged?, and who owns assets?—the same questions we ask ourselves at larger planning scales.

FSA   In your experience, what is the value of thinking spatially about justice?

TLG   I want to believe that the work I do as a designer has a meaningful impact on social injustice, but there really isn't any body of work that systematically and critically assesses what those impacts are. How does the way I design a public park, a streetscape, or an affordable housing project really affect equity, and for whom? Is spatial justice a quest for "Black Lives Matter" or for "All Lives Matter"? ... Perhaps the roles I've played throughout my career—architect, urban designer, public planning official—speak to a personal journey to find where my design agency would be most impactful. I have been fortunate to find rewarding opportunities to promote public good and affect good design even when I wasn't the designer with the pen in hand. Working to redevelop Harlem, New York, Chicago's "Black Metropolis" (Bronzeville), Newark, Detroit, and Washington, DC, I've come to understand the connection between social justice and design, particularly the importance of establishing public trust as a part of regulating design and reinvestment. Ultimately [laughter], I think I've managed to get something done. And by "get something done" I mean to actually change the civic engagements, physical landscapes, and development processes that folks are trying to stabilize, improve, and transform.

Contributor Biographies

DELIA DUONG BA WENDEL

is an architectural historian and cultural geographer who studies
how communities rebuild and recover from conflict and disaster.
Her current research focuses primarily on Central Africa and draws
significantly from anthropology, cultural theory, and peace and
development studies. She is completing her PhD in the History and
Theory of Architecture and Urban Planning at Harvard University
with a finishing grant from the American Council of Learned
Societies and fellowships from the Social Science Research Council
and the Edmond J. Safra Center for Ethics. Her teaching experience includes appointments as a Visiting Lecturer at Harvard and as
a tenure-track Lecturer at the University of Edinburgh, where she
taught courses in architectural and urban history, theory, and
design, and in social studies, informed by cross-disciplinary peda-
gogy. Wendel's work has been published in the *Journal of Urban
Design, New Orleans and the Design Moment*, and the *Handbook of
Architectural Theory*. She is coeditor of *Spatializing Politics*.

FALLON SAMUELS AIDOO

is a historian of urban industrialization and postindustrial urbanism
in the Americas. She teaches architectural and urban history from
comparative and constructivist perspectives, currently at
Northeastern University and previously at Harvard, where she is
completing a PhD in Urban Planning. She holds master's degrees in
Architectural and Planning History from MIT and Harvard, where
she studied the production and preservation of metropolitan infrastructure. Supported by the Tobin Project, Hagley Library, and
Volvo Foundation, her research broadly concerns the role of non-
governmental bodies—corporations, consultants, and communities—in sustaining transport sites and services. She is curating a
multi-media digital archive of historical records, artifacts, and plans
that facilitates scholarly and popular engagement with railway conservation. Her previous works of public history informed
Smithsonian and National Building Museum exhibitions. Aidoo's
writing on sustainable transit will be published in the *Encyclopedia
of Greater Philadelphia*. She is coeditor of *Spatializing Politics*.

H. FERNANDO BURGA

is an Assistant Professor in the Planning Department at the University of Minnesota's Humphrey School of Public Affairs. He received his PhD in 2013 from the Department of City and Regional Planning at the University of California, Berkeley and holds master's degrees in Architecture and Urban Design from the University of Miami. Burga's research explores equity and the politics of identity, race, and citizenship in urban design and planning policy. He combines ethnographic fieldwork, the study of planning history, and the analysis of urban policy to investigate the methods urban designers and planners use to address the needs of Latino immigrants and to assert their collective agency and build political capacity. His current project applies participatory action research and community design techniques to plan with undocumented Latino immigrants in San Jose, California.

KERRY RYAN CHANCE

is a political and legal anthropologist with a specialization in African Studies and Urban Studies. She is a Lecturer on Social Studies and an Oppenheimer Fellow at Harvard University. She joined the Anthropology Department as a College Fellow and American Council of Learned Societies Fellow in 2011 after receiving a PhD in Socio-Cultural Anthropology from the University of Chicago. She has published scholarly articles in *Cultural Anthropology, Anthropological Quarterly, Social Analysis*, and *Transition*, among many others. She is currently completing a book entitled *Living Politics* that examines governance and political mobilization in three South African cities from the mid-1980s to the present. Chance's research has been supported by grants from the Fulbright Foundation, the Social Science Research Council, the Wenner Gren Foundation, and the National Endowment for the Humanities.

RYNE CLOS

is a cultural historian of Latin America and a peace scholar interested in issues of mobilization, peacebuilding, and social justice.

His chief area of interest and expertise lies in 20th-century Central America; in particular, Nicaragua during the Cold War years. He is currently a doctoral candidate at the University of Notre Dame in History and in Peace Studies. His publications include the article "In the Name of the God Who Will Be: Mobilization of Radical Christians in the Sandinista Revolution," *Journal for the Study of Radicalism* (2012).

SUSAN S. FAINSTEIN

is a professor and scholar of urban planning, theory, redevelopment, and comparative urban policy in the United States, Europe, and East Asia. Her authored works include *The Just City*, which received the Association of American Schools of Planning Davidoff Book Award; *The City Builders: Property, Politics, and Planning in London and New York*; *Restructuring the City*; and *Urban Political Movements*. In addition, she has published countless edited volumes, book chapters, and journal articles grounded in empirical study, planning theory, and issues of gender and social equity, among others. Fainstein has served as Professor of Planning at the Harvard Graduate School of Design, Columbia University, and Rutgers University, and was named Distinguished Educator by the ACSP for a lifetime of career achievements. Her emphases on progressive planning, meaningful reform, equity, diversity, participation, and material well-being for all city residents have guided robust engagements across urban policy, theory, research, and continents.

TONI L. GRIFFIN

is Professor of Architecture and the founding Director of the J. Max Bond Center on Design for the Just City at the City College of New York. An educator, social advocate, urban designer, and planner, her work has had broad impact on community and economic development in cities across the United States. Recent research, design, and policy projects include the Legacy City Design Initiative, which explores innovative design solutions for cities with shrinking populations, and the *Detroit Future City* plan, a comprehensive framework for urban transformation and resident inclusion. Griffin maintains a private practice in New York—Urban Planning for the American City—and was previously the Director of Community Development for the City of Newark, New Jersey; the Deputy Director for Revitalization and Neighborhood Planning in Washington, DC; and the Vice President for Planning and Tourism Development for the Upper Manhattan Empowerment Zone Development Corporation in New York City.

JOY KNOBLAUCH

is a historian, theorist, and educator focusing on architecture's intersection with the social and medical sciences. She is an Assistant Professor of Architecture at the University of Michigan as well a Fulbright Scholar in Philosophy and Public Health. She holds a PhD in the History and Theory of Architecture from the Princeton University School of Architecture and has worked as an architect in Ithaca, New York and San Francisco. Supported by the National Science Foundation, the Canadian Centre for Architecture, and the Fellowship of Woodrow Wilson Scholars, Knoblauch's research has appeared in the essay collection *In Search of the Public* and in the journals *Manifest*, *Architecture Theory Review*, and *Pidgin*. Her forthcoming book, *Going Soft*, interprets institutional architecture as a symptom of larger political changes taking place in the United States during the 1960s and 1970s.

WANDA KATJA LIEBERMANN

is an architect and scholar. She received a Doctorate of Design from the Harvard Graduate School of Design in 2013. Between 1996 and 2007, she taught design at University of California, Berkeley, where she is currently a Visiting Scholar in the Department of Architecture. Her research focuses on theories and practices of architecture and urbanism in the United States and the European Union. It critically analyzes the relationship between architecture and embodiment across a range of spatial practices, from urban design to material conservation, connecting it to discourses of self-hood, agency, and citizenship. One such engagement is a project titled "critical non-compliance," where Liebermann translates her theoretical work on space and embodiment into design.

ORLY LINOVSKI

is currently an Assistant Professor in the Department of City Planning at the University of Manitoba, where she teaches studios and seminar courses on urban design and transportation. Her research, teaching, and public engagement are motivated by a concern for the social and political production of built form. Her work focuses on the nature of contemporary urban design practices, issues of equity in planning and design, and urban design theory. Linovski obtained her doctorate in Urban Planning from the University of California, Los Angeles and holds a Master of Science in Planning from the University of Toronto. Her work has been published in the *Journal of Planning Education and Research*, *Journal of Urban Design*, and *Built Environment*. She also served as Editor of *Critical Planning*.

MICHAEL MENDEZ

studies how the built environment, policymaking process, and social movements influence sustainability and population health in low-income neighborhoods and communities of color. His research is informed by urban planning, public health, and science and technology studies. He currently serves as the inaugural Provost Postdoctoral Fellow at the University of San Francisco, with an appointment in the Environmental Studies Department. His academic work is informed by his experience in the public and private sectors, including consultancy and leadership roles within the California State Legislature's Assembly Select Committee on Environmental Justice and Sacramento's Planning Commission. In these positions, he conducted applied research and actively engaged in policymaking processes. Mendez holds a PhD in Environmental Planning and Community Economic Development from University of California, Berkeley and a master's in City Planning from MIT.

ANH-THU NGO

earned her PhD in Social Anthropology, with a secondary focus on Film and Visual Studies, at Harvard University. Her dissertation explores emergent artistic expressions in the context of political repression and transforming market socialism in Ho Chi Minh City, Vietnam. Ngo's research and teaching focus on art, aesthetics, and media, experimental ethnography, gender, memory, phenomenology, political economy, and urbanism. Her scholarly production and art practice intersect through work in video, poetry, performance, and curation. Her background is in nonprofit administration in the arts and education sectors.

MELANY SUN-MIN PARK

is a PhD student in the History and Theory of Architecture at Harvard University. Her research focuses on 20th-century Korean architecture and, in particular, its relationship to professional organizations and institutions that emerged in the postwar period. Her current work examines the corporate history of modern architecture in South Korea and its intersection with political economy in the Park Chung-hee era. She holds a Master of Design Studies with Distinction from the Harvard Graduate School of Design and has received fellowships from Harvard's Korea Institute and the Society of Architectural Historians. Her essay on Singapore's avant-garde art collective, the Artists Village, was published in the volume *Home + Bound: Narratives of Domesticity in Singapore and Beyond*, which she co-edited, and her interview with Chi Soon, South Korea's first registered female architect, will become part of Mokchon Architecture Archive's oral history project.

MARGO SHEA

is an Assistant Professor of Public History at Salem State University. She teaches undergraduate and graduate courses in public, local, and urban history and heritage, and museum studies. Trained in cultural geography, public history, and the study of memory at the University of Massachusetts, Amherst, her recent work has focused primarily on Northern Ireland. Her expertise extends to community economic development, service learning, and campus-community partnerships. Shea is currently a Mellon Fellow and resident scholar at the Collaborative for Southern Appalachian and Place-Based Studies at Sewanee: The University of the South, where she explores how collaborative engagements of place and memory can aid community development and public health initiatives.

Index

An *n* in an entry denotes a footnote reference;
an *f* denotes a figure caption.

access: regulation of, 273–300; public, 21, 170,
    201, 331; pedestrian, 29, 174; vehicular, 29,
    35; to housing, 54, 56, 60–61, 69–71, 74; to
    employment opportunities, 71, 181–82; to
    community centers and resources, 32, 39–41,
    44, 348; to decision-making, 346–48, 376,
    394, 402–3; to healthcare, 71; to
    information, 243, 268; to public utilities,
    see infrastructure; 256, 264, 267–68;
    restrictions, 190–95, for disabled persons,
    213, 273–300
accessibility. *See* access
activism, xi, 7, 15–23, 29, 41–45, 52–53, 57, 64–65,
    71–72, 76–81, 85–89, 96–97, 100–101, 103–
    10, 244–47, 250, 260, 263–65, 267, 273–74,
    341, 344–53, 368, 380, 382–83, 385–89,
    389–92, 394–97, 401–3
actor network theory, 304
agonism, 10n13, 15–16, 88
anthropology, xi, 11, 55–56, 87–88, 91, 100,
    99–101, 103, 120n1, 122, 125, 136–48, 295
antipolitics, 195n10
apartheid, 54, 59–61, 62–63, 64, 68, 69n31
architectural history, xi, 12
architecture: accessibility of, 273–76, 292–300;
    architectural theory, 3n3, 4n5, 214;
    architectural imaginaries, 9–10, 109n35; as
    infrastructure, 55–59, 153–55, 157–58, 161–
    64, 195–99; bureaucracies of, 8n8; design
    standards in, 273f1, 276, 282–80, 291–92;
    discipline of, xi, 2, 4n5, 11; of racial
    integration, 59–76: of racial and gender
    differentiation, 116, 285n36, 287n44; of
    security, 24–25; 26–28, 33n27; landscape
    architecture, discipline of, 154n3, 259n53;
    political history and theory of, 7, 12, 16;
    profession of, 7, 289–91, 310n8, 324n31,
    401n1; programming of, 220–24, 221n5; of
    imprisonment, 248–50, 253–56; of mental
    healthcare, 217–24, 226–28, 230n31, 232, 235,
    236–40; representational role of, 133; 195–202
art, 11, 86–88, 89f3, 103–4, 106–7, 109, 229

back-to-the-city movements, 155, 160, 161,
    161n22, 176
belonging, 9, 64, 72, 76, 132, 192, 250–51
biopolitics, viii, 12, 213–300
branding, of urban areas, 86, 95, 108, 303, 379

Cape Town, South Africa, 51, 53–55, 58n21,
    60–61, 62–65, 65f2, 66, 71, 78, 122n5
case study method, use of, 2n1, 13f1, 157, 310n8,
    340, 342n16, 362, of micro-history, 157

catchment area, 222, 233, 234n26, 234f8
charrette, 222, 235
Chestnut Hill, Philadelphia, Pennsylvania,
    153–81
citizenship, 55, 59, 64–65, 79–81, 116, 188–89,
    205, 249–51, 267–70, 361, 379, 383
civic epistemology, 339–64
civil rights. *See* rights: civil
civil society, 60n15. *See also* community-based
    organizations; neighborhood associations;
    nonprofit associations; philanthropy
civil unrest, 15–19, 21, 23, 34, 36, 46
civil war, 21, 190
class, analysis of, 7, 26, 51, 54, 59, 61, 62n18, 66,
    68, 69n30, 81, 93, 124, 153–82, 195, 228, 262,
    341
climate change, 303; policy, planning and
    politics of, 337–64
coalition building, 181, 191, 195, 208, 337f1,
    337–64, 380, 389, 391, 393, 398
coexistence, challenges of, 120–21, 134–40,
    147–50
collectivity, xi, 9n11, 39, 53, 56, 76, 80, 86,
    91–95, 109, 115, 141, 154, 157, 166, 173,
    176n54, 178, 180, 230, 251–55, 256–57, 267,
    359, 368, 383, 398, 401
commonality, xii, 11, 91, 115, 124–25, 128, 154, 157,
    171, 179–80, 253, 254–55, 275, 337, 340, 383,
    390, 393–94, 403
communities: of color, 176, 228, 274, 338, 341,
    352–56; health of, 231, 280, 350; immigrant,
    224, 349, 353–54; low-income, 228, 338,
    348–49, 352–53, 387; minority, 91n7, 237n28,
    275, 279–80, 303, 377–79, 385, 390; rural, 11,
    63, 115, 119–20, 128, 131n9, 136, 219, 222, 234,
    374; suburban, 115, 153–81; urban, 14–18,
    19–50, 51–84, 85–112, 153–81, 217, 302–89,
    401–3; development, 156, 181, 380, 384–85,
    388–90, 398
community-based organizations, 155–82, 344–
    56, 360
compliance, as a political strategy, 289, 290, 345
concentration camps, 11, 244–70
concession, acts of, 155n7, 156–57, 159, 161,
    160n20, 167, 169, 173, 178–82, 192, 195n11
conflict, analysis of, viii, 12. *See also* contentious
    politics
consensus, analysis of, viii, 12, 114–18, 119–52,
    153–84, 185–210
conservation, 154–81
conservatism, 176, 180, 180n60, 280, 296
contentious politics, analysis of, 14–18, 19–50,
    51–84, 85–112, 158, 368–70
cooperative ownership, 127, 153, 155–57, 159–61,
    174–75, 178–79, 313–14, 401

decentralization, 29, 132, 213, 397. *See also*
    suburbanization

decision making, 310n6, 321, 326, 338, 339, 369, 375–76, 381
defensible space, 27–29
democracy, 4n3, 67, 192, 197, 240, 264, 296, 304, 340n13, 340n15, 358, 388
Democratic People's Republic of Korea (North Korea), 249, 267, 268n73
demolition, 23–24, 39, 43, 45–46, 63, 63–87, 103
detention facilities, 190, 199–202, 224, 239, 244n3, 245. See also architecture of imprisonment
disability, 273–300
displacement, 52–53, 55n5, 63, 101n30, 120–21, 120, 125–26, 134, 136, 143–46, 162, 261, 264, 342, 348, 352, 358, 362

economic development, 163, 351, 359, 360
egalitarianism, 166, 297
emplacement, 120–21, 126–27, 136, 140, 148
empowerment, 8, 100–101, 107, 112, 373, 380, 389, 394, 396–97, 398, 401
Environmental Climate Action Plan (ECAP), 338–39, 343–44, 346, 349–50, 352–56
environmental design, 13, 27–28
environmental justice, 303, 339, 338, 340–43, 350, 359, 361, 364
epistemic cultures, 309–11, 332, 360
epistemology. See civic epistemology, spatial epistemology
equity, 167, 175, 281n26, 287n44, 338–39, 342–43, 346, 351, 357–58, 360, 362, 401, 403
everyday life, 5, 9n9, 11, 92, 100, 109, 120, 146, 224, 284n35
everyday urbanism, 110–12
eviction, 51–55, 60–65, 73–80, 96, 99, 101n20, 104
exclusion, 7, 7n6, 9, 15, 24, 61, 292–94, 297–98
expertise: politics of, 12, 57, 111, 178, 217, 220, 222, 224, 288, 303, 308–9, 310, 312, 314, 322; professional, 10, 322–26, 350; lay (see also public knowledge), 339n11, 351, 353–58, 360–64; local, 176, 339, 341, 350–52, 359–61, 364; technical, 107n31, 282, 289, 308n2, 307–64

facilities management, 155, 157
fascism, 197, 203, 204n15
forgiveness, 143–45, 147
Foucault, Michel, 3n3, 12, 55–56, 213–14, 230–31, 259, 260n56, 261, 262n59, 263–64, 284n55, 297n67, 298n72
freedom: of expression, 268; of movement, 268

gender, analysis of, 7, 230, 276, 285n36, 286n38, 287, 298, 341
genocide, 131, 133n20, 139, 141, 149
gentrification, 16, 158n13, 161n21, 348
geography, discipline of, 12, 26n24, 31, 395

governance: authoritarian, 23–36, 87, 90–95, 110, 115, 187, 190–200, 243–70; communist, 25, 89, 90–95, 101, 108, 110, 191–92, 210n18, 250–51, 259, 379; democratic (see also democracy), 52, 64, 66, 220, 244, 246, 280, 344, 360, 364; distributed, 15, 130, 159–60, 167, 172, 178–81, 213, 393; entrepreneurial, 7, 155, 173, 304, 308–9; global, 67, 249, 268n72, 268n73, 337–40; local, 153–83, 337–66, 375–76
governmentality, 55, 56n5, 96–97, 186–90, 202, 213–300
Grand Park (Los Angeles, California), 40n39, 77n41, 111, 180n60, 238, 303, 307–33
grassroots organizing, 16, 20–23, 34, 122n5, 166–82, 243–45. See also activism
grasstops, 402. See also activism

hegemony, 3n1, 89, 98, 198, 276, 377
heterotopia, 214, 258–63
Ho Chi Minh City (HCMC), Vietnam, 85–112
home rule, 369–70
hospitals, 52, 124, 158, 217–40, 260, 286, 331
housing, 219, 240, 253, 255–56, 258, 269, 289, 293–94, 346, 353, 381f5; affordable, 345, 348–49, 358, 403; public, 384, 387–89
Houston, Texas, 221

identity: formation, 81, 116; group, 139, 275, 298, 383, 390; individual, 4, 9, 15, 81, 132, 141, 287; national, 185, 188n3, 208, 386; of cities, 378; political demonstration of, 273–74, 379
ideology: analysis of, 11, 115, 149; communist, 93–95, 252–53; liberal, 186–90; regime, 116, 185–89, 193–95, 199–200, 204n15, 209, 210n18, 230n22, 253, 259, 261, 264, 267, 270, 360
immigrants, 224, 349, 353–54, 367–99
imprisonment, 107, 137, 139n17, 193, 199, 213
incorporation: minority, 303, 347–52, 402–3; municipal, 394–99, 402–3
inequality, 4–7, 15–16, 51–83, 123, 131n9, 276–86, 293–96
inclusion: accommodations for, 277, 280–85, 351n34; advocacy for, 6, 110, 273–75, 349, 383, 401–3. See also incorporation
informality, vii, 51–81, 97, 101n27, 294, 298, 402
infrastructure: built forms of, viii, 4n4, 11, 25, 49–50, 53–54, 64, 69, 153, 238, 289, 337, 338, 351, 362, 369, 375; critical infrastructure protection, 157n9, 161n21, 176n4, 177, 180, 349; disinvestment, 7, 157–61; expropriation, 76–77, 161, 170–73, 179–81; governance of, 153–57, 166–69; housing as, 51–52, 72–73; infrastructural politics of the poor, 57, 76–81; of artistic practice, 87, 106; maintenance and repair of, 5, 95, 156–57,

163–66, 371; redevelopment of, 33, 37, 160–61; social theory of, 55–59, 81, 304
interpellation, 186, 188–90, 203, 205, 208

Korean Demilitarized Zone (DMZ), 244–46, 259

labor: camps, 243–70; cheap, 63; collective, 164–67, 174–75, 177–79, 182, 257; contract, 165, 169, 179; domestic, 70, 286n41; informal, 70; "of love," 157, 178; markets, 356, 377; optimization, 87; penal, 244–45, 247–50, 255; physical, 167–69, 262, 266; professional, 154, 157, 165–67, 396; unionized, 156–57, 164–65, 345, 356
land reform, 92–94
land tenure, 65, 93, 131
landscape architecture, discipline of, xi, 154n3, 359n33
landscape: cultural, 26, 101, 137, 143, 175, 178–79; preservation, 156, 179–81
Lefebvre, Henri, vii, 3n2, 9n9, 16, 58, 89, 98, 109
liberalism, 60n13, 193, 199, 204, 214, 282
liberation, 22n3, 54, 62, 66, 68, 76–77, 89, 93, 108, 114, 193f3, 231, 361
London/Derry (also Londonderry; Derry), Northern Ireland, 19–48

Marxism, 93, 109–10, 210n18, 251n24,
Managua, Nicaragua, 185–209
Mariel Boatlift, 367–90
mental health, 11, 217–40
metonymy, 120, 127–29, 145
Miami, Florida, 302, 367–99
mobilization, 6, 8, 15–16, 55, 69, 157, 158n13, 177, 180, 261, 267, 275, 352, 367, 394
monuments, 14, 42, 45, 115, 185, 190, 196–97, 199–202, 204–5, 206, 210, 224, 299
Musekeweya (radio program), 119–50

narrative: of space, 40n39, 91–92, 96–97, 120–22, 123–29, 132–35, 138–40, 146–49
negotiation, as a political strategy, 7, 80, 90, 101, 177n37, 283, 303, 311, 322, 326–27, 330, 338n7, 399
neighborliness, 6, 9, 21, 31, 36, 41, 46–47, 70–71, 137, 144–46, 154, 175, 177, 192, 197–98, 200, 204, 251, 259, 320; and the Good Neighbor Policy, 197, 251; and neighborhood associations, 6, 154, 156n8, 175–76
nonprofit organizations,160n20, 161, 166, 169, 178, 353–54, 387

Oakland, California, 289n46, 303, 337–64
occupation: of housing, 73–76; of land, 53–57, 66, 77–78, 130
open space: production of, 27, 29–32; protection of, 130, 169, 170–76; redevelopment of, 158–62, 168–69

parks: absence of, 32, 38; design and development of, 204, 206, 303, 311–23, 327–33, 403; as sites of protest, 11, 246; municipal, 303, 307–9, 382; national, 185f1, 202–4, 206, 373; neighborhood, 6–8; parkways, 171, 181; reclamation of, 161–62; regional, 370n6; vernacular forms and uses of, 6–8, 31, 101n29, 163n19. See also open space
parking, 153, 295, 367f1; producers of, 159–64, 168–72, 175, 293, 294–95
participation, civic, 20, 66, 100n27, 107, 110, 175, 274, 304, 344, 350, 351n34, 360, 403; in planning and governance, 343–56; in research, 342n16; tools and techniques of, 119–22, 106, 222, 225, 353–57, 340
peacebuilding, 19, 115, 119–22, 124–26, 134–35, 140–42, 145, 147, 148–50
penal colonies. See labor, penal
performance art. See art
philanthropy, 165, 173, 219, 307, 313, 402
place making, vii, 35, 39, 48, 59–67, 80, 142, 156, 174, 181, 203, 259, 393. See also emplacement
place naming, 19n1, 91, 100, 190, 199, 204–6
planning: discipline of, 12, 16, 159n17, 158n15, 367, 397; metropolitan, 359, 370–94, 396, 398; participatory (see participation)
police state, 186–89
political encounter, theory and analysis of, 3n2, 4, 9–12, 13f1, 15, 115
political prisoners, 193, 199, 248n10, 249–50. See also imprisonment
privatization, 70, 180, 309
progressivism, 63, 154n3, 173, 296, 370
propaganda, 98, 124, 219, 238, 246
protest, 15, 27n18, 29, 33–35, 46, 53, 60, 65f2, 67, 71–72, 76, 78, 80f4, 80, 88, 89f3, 96, 99, 101, 104, 240, 273–75, 274f2
psychiatry, architecture of, 217–18, 219n4, 220–22, 220f2, 221f3, 223n10, 225, 227, 228–30, 229f6, 235–37, 260, 263
psychology, 219–20, 224–25, 228, 225n13, 228n16, 230n30, 232, 234n26, 239
public accommodations, 38, 74, 276–300
public health, 66, 218–22, 224n12, 290, 338–42, 351, 358, 360–62
public restrooms, 11, 282, 285, 286, 288, 293
public utility commissions, 154, 160, 174, 176, 179–80
public-private development, 79, 309
public-private partnership, 164, 173, 179, 303, 304, 308, 401

race, analysis of, 7, 16, 51–81, 116, 169, 175, 180, 228–29, 230n20, 274, 276, 287n44, 281n26, 287n43, 287n44, 304, 341, 367–99, 379n14, 392, 393, 394, 401–3. See also communities, of color

rebellion, 20, 199, 210, 231, 395–97
reconciliation, 115, 122n5, 147–48
redistricting, 138, 386, 392
refugees, 247, 378–86, 381f5, 381f6, 389
regime ideology. *See* ideology; regime
regulatory science, 351, 361
repatriation, 63, 247, 248
repression, 60, 230–32, 258, 401
research and development (R&D), 155, 162
right to the city, viii, 16, 58–72, 170–81
right to work, 115, 157–82
rightsizing, 158–59, 402
rights: civil, 20–21, 22f2, 24, 27n18, 40, 47, 240,
        274–75, 277, 279, 283–85, 287, 290, 287, 341,
        379; of disabled people, 274–75, 279–80,
        283n29, 290n51; human, 124n7, 207n17, 243,
        244n3, 248n30, 249n26, 249, 251n24, 253,
        257n49, 264, 266–67, 269n74; property,
        155n7, 156, 167–69, 172–73, 178–82, 294; of
        residential renters and commercial lessees,
        68, 73, 95, 130–31, 153, 159–60, 169, 174–75,
        181, 348 (*see also* occupation); of way, 153–81
riots, 19–21, 29, 35, 57n26, 228, 251, 379, 374, 386
ritualized space, 121, 135–37, 146, 149–50
Rwanda, 115, 119–50

Saigon, Vietnam. *See* Ho Chi Minh City
San Francisco, California, 221, 227f5, 289, 343
science and technology studies, 12, 304;
        methodologies of, 340–41, 360, 363
security, 15, 22, 26–35, 51, 70, 76–77, 156, 157n9,
        165, 213–14, 230n22, 248–51, 254, 266–68
segregation, 6, 8n6, 63, 77, 142, 251, 295, 323,
        369, 393
self-reliance, 252–53, 276, 281
slums: as infrastructure, 55–59; "shantytowns,"
        11, 15; criminalization of, 59–67
Situationist International, 108–9
social capital, 154n4, 165, 176n54, 362
South Korea, 244–46, 247f4, 250–51, 257, 259,
        264–67
sovereignty, 55, 76, 213, 230–32, 311n11
spatial epistemology, 2–12, 122, 190, 199
standardization, 222, 232, 284
statecraft, 186–89, 204, 243, 358
stewardship, 28, 153–81, 402

storytelling, 44n51, 57, 61, 73, 77–79
subjectivity, 3n3, 4, 9, 10–12, 109, 119, 127, 140–
        41, 144, 146, 148, 150, 188, 200, 204, 213,
        246, 265, 275, 297
suburbanization, 154n4, 175, 180n60; history of,
        180
Surrealists, 108–9
surveillance, 26, 29, 31–32, 35, 47, 55n4, 79, 175,
        187, 208, 213, 251, 264
sustainability, 5, 61, 155, 337, 339n12, 340n15,
        345–46, 349, 350n31, 353, 360f46, 396

tactical urbanism, 159, 403
therapy, 239, 309n5
third-sector organizations, theory of, 157n11
torture, 193, 199, 207n17, 248, 249n15, 257, 261f5
train stations, 115, 153–81
transit camps, 51f1, 53–57, 63, 67, 68f3, 69,
        71–74, 79–81
transit-oriented development, 348, 353
Troubles, The (in Northern Ireland), 19–23, 26,
        31, 34, 36, 40, 42, 46–47, 136
typology, of buildings, 89n3, 217, 220n2, 222,
        235–36, 238, 240, 255, 256

urban design, discipline of, 33, 47, 240, 259n53,
        307–33, 403
urban development: agency and authority for,
        317, 319–22, 327; projects of, 23, 59, 307,
        312n14, 312f2, 314; reversal of, 93, 214, 303–4;
        uneven, 8n8, 15, 89n3, 130, 343
urban renewal, 15, 19, 23–36, 39, 40n39, 46–47,
        176, 219, 239n31
utopia, 4, 27, 62, 81, 94, 265n64

vacant property, 5, 32, 35, 41, 45, 163, 164, 320,
        358, 402
violence, viii, 9n10, 12, 15, 19–22, 34–35, 46–47,
        52, 66, 75, 80, 119, 124–28, 133–34, 139–42,
        146, 149, 198n11, 240, 263–64, 379
vulnerability: of cities, 340, 355–56;
        of communities, 269, 349, 351, 352, 355, 356,
        358

Washington, DC, 290, 403
world–class city 51, 54, 61, 62n18, 68

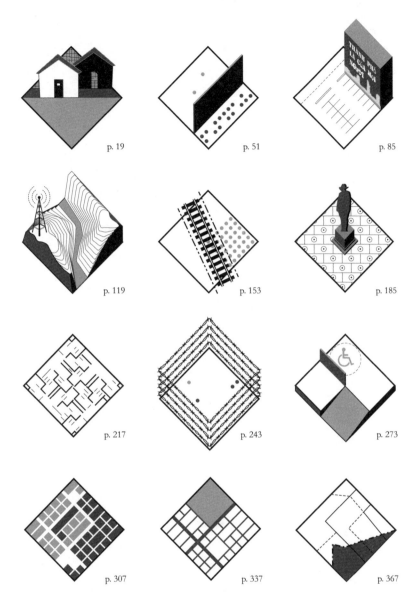

p. 19

p. 51

p. 85

p. 119

p. 153

p. 185

p. 217

p. 243

p. 273

p. 307

p. 337

p. 367

Visual index of the 12 essays in *Spatializing Politics*. Source: Delia Duong Ba Wendel, 2015.

Spatializing Politics: Essays on Power and Place
Delia Duong Ba Wendel, Fallon Samuels Aidoo (eds.)

Project Editor
  Nancy Eklund Later
Designer
  Sam de Groot
Typeface Customization
  Dinamo.us
Printer
  Die Keure, Belgium
Distributor
  Harvard University Press

Harvard Design Studies is published by the Harvard University Graduate School of Design

Dean and Alexander and Victoria Wiley Professor
  Mohsen Mostafavi
Assistant Dean for Communications
  Benjamin Prosky
Editor in Chief
  Jennifer Sigler
Senior Editor
  Melissa Vaughn
Associate Editor
  Leah Whitman-Salkin
Publications Coordinator
  Meghan Sandberg
Cover Illustration
  Commemoration march in Kigali, Rwanda, for the first anniversary of the genocide. Source:
  photographer unknown, 1995. Retrieved by Delia Duong Ba Wendel from "130301-1-9655"
  Personal Papers, Rwanda

Sponsored by the Graham Foundation for Advanced Studies in the Fine Arts

ISBN 978-1-934510-46-9

All chapter introduction texts were written by Delia Duong Ba Wendel.

Harvard University
Graduate School of Design
48 Quincy Street
Cambridge, MA 02138
gsd.harvard.edu

Library of Congress Cataloging-in-Publication Data
Wendel, Delia Duong Ba, editor. Aidoo, Fallon Samuels, editor.
    Spatializing politics: essays on power and place / Delia Duong Ba Wendel,
        Fallon Samuels Aidoo (eds.).
    Cambridge: Harvard University Graduate School of Design, 2015.
    Series: Harvard design studies
    Includes bibliographical references and index.
    LCCN 2015041536
    ISBN 9781934510469
    1. Space—Social aspects. 2. Space—Political aspects. 3. Landscapes—Social aspects.
        4. Landscapes—Political aspects. 5. Power. (Social sciences)
    LCC HM654 .S67 2015
    DDC 303.3—dc23